# Microeconomics

# Microeconomics

Vikash Kumar

RANDOM PUBLICATIONS
NEW DELHI (INDIA)

**Microeconomics**

---

ISBN 978-93-5111-637-0


Published in 2015 in India by

**RANDOM PUBLICATIONS**

4376-A/4B, Gali Murari Lal, Ansari Road
New Delhi-110 002
Phone : +9111-43580356, 011-23289044, 011-43142548
e-mail: sales@randompublications.com,
info@randompublications.com, randomexports@gmail.com

Reprint 2022

*Type Setting by* : Friends Media, Delhi-110089
*Digitally Printed at* : Replika Press Pvt. Ltd.

# Preface

Microeconomics is the study of decisions that people and businesses make regarding the allocation of resources and prices of goods and services. This means also taking into account taxes and regulations created by governments. Microeconomics focuses on supply and demand and other forces that determine the price levels seen in the economy.

Microeconomics is considered the starting point of Macroeconomics, and deals with individual and small business economic decisions. These individual decisions, in aggregate, affect the demand and supply of goods and services throughout the entire economy. One of the most commonly analyzed topics in microeconomics is the model of supply, demand and equilibrium. Under this model, the producers and consumers of a good determine how its price and quantity is traded between them. In a free market, the price of goods will vary until it hits an equilibrium point, which is defined as the point at which the total quantity of goods demanded equals the quantity of goods supplied.

Microeconomics looks at the behavior of individual people and companies within the economy. It is based on the idea of a market economy, in which consumer demand is the driving force behind the prices and production levels of goods and services. Microeconomics is interested in how specific parties choose to use the limited resources that are available to them. It focuses on what drives them to make their decisions, as well as the ways in which their decisions affect the supply and demand of particular goods and services. In turn, these choices influence the price levels of various commodities.

Microeconomics also examines how the decisions of individuals impact specific industries. For example, economists studying at the micro level might be interested in discovering how current consumer demand is affecting the well-being of the oil industry. Another basic principle of microeconomics is the "theory of the firm." This studies the actions of businesses as they strive to increase their profits. It looks at which resources they choose to utilize as inputs, how much they produce, and what they charge for their goods or services. In summary, microeconomics concerns itself with the human beings whose purchasing and production-related decisions come together to form the backbone of a given economy. Even when it involves companies, the focus of microeconomics is always at the personal level.

Microeconomics focuses on supply and demand and other forces that determine the price levels seen in the economy.

I would like to thank my team for standing beside me throughout my career and writing this book. My special thanks go to "Random Publications" who have published the book.

*– Vikash Kumar*

# Contents

# 1

# Microeconomics: An Introduction

As early as the 18th century, economists were studying the decision-making processes of consumers, a principal concern of microeconomics. Swiss mathematician Nicholas Bernoulli (1695-1726) proposed an extensive theory of how consumers make their buying choices in what was perhaps the first written explanation of how this often mysterious and always complex process works.

According to Bernoulli's theory, consumers make buying decisions based on the expected results of their purchases. Consumers are assumed to be rational thinkers who are able to forecast with reasonable accuracy the hopefully satisfactory consequences of what they buy. They select to purchase, among the choices available, the product or service they believe will provide maximum satisfaction or well-being.

For some 200 years beginning in the mid-1700s, the dominant economic theory was Adam's Smith'slaissez-faire (French for "leave alone" or "let do") approach to the economy, which advocated a government hands-off policy regarding free markets and the machinery of capitalism.

The laissez-fairetheory argues that an economy functions best when the "invisible hand" of self-interest is allowed to operate freely, without government intervention.

## SMITH AND MARSHALL

Scottish-born Smith (1723-1790) wrote in his book, "Wealth of Nations," that if the government does not tamper with the economy, a nation's resources will be most efficiently used, free-market problems will correct themselves and a country's welfare and best interests will be served. Smith's views on the economy prevailed through two centuries, but in the late 19th and early 20th century, the ideas of Alfred Marshall (1842-1924), a London-born economist, had a major impact on economic thought.

In Marshall's book, "Principles of Economics, Vol. 1." published in 1890, he proposed, as Bernoulli had three centuries earlier, the study of consumer decision making. Marshall proposed a new idea as well - the study of specific, individual markets and firms, as a means of understanding the dynamics of economics. Marshall also formulated the concepts of consumer utility, price elasticity of demand and the demand curve, all of which will be discussed in the following chapter.

**KEYNES**

At the time of Marshall's death, John Maynard Keynes (1883-1946), who would become the most influential economist of the 20th century starting in the 1930s, was already at work on his revolutionary ideas about government management of the economy. Born in Cambridge, England, Keynes' contributions to economic theory have guided the thinking and policy-making of central bankers and government economists for decades, both globally and in the U.S.So much of U.S., monetary policy, the setting of key interest rates, government spending to stimulate the economy, support of private enterprise through various measures, tax policy and government borrowing through the issuance of Treasury bonds, bills and notes, have been influenced by the revolutionary ideas of Keynes, which he introduced in his books and essays.What all these concepts had in common was their advocacy of government management of the economy. Keynes advocated government intervention into free markets and into the general economy when market crises warranted, an unprecedented idea when proposed during the Great Depression.

Government spending to stimulate an economy, a Keynesian idea, was used during the Depression to put unemployed people to work, thus providing cash to millions of consumers to buy the country's products and services. Most of Keynes' views were the exact opposites of Adam Smith's. An economy, for optimum functioning, must be managed by government, Keynes wrote.Thus was born the modern science of macroeconomics – the big picture view of the economy – evolving in large part from what came to be called Keynesian economic theory. These are among the tools of microeconomics, and their principles, along with others, are still employed today by economists who specialise in this area. Keynes' policies, to varying degrees, have been, and continue to be, employed with generally successful results worldwide in almost all modern capitalist economies. If and when economic problems occur, many economists often attribute them to some misapplication or non-application of a Keynesian principle.

## MICROECONOMIC REVITALISATION

While Keynesian economic theory was being applied in most of the world's major economies, the new concept of microeconomics, pioneered by Marshall, was also taking hold in economic circles. The study of smaller, more focused aspects of the economy, which previously were not given major importance, was fast becoming an integral part of the entire economic picture. Microeconomics had practical appeal to economists because it sought to understand the most basic machinery of an economic system: consumer decision-making and spending patterns, and the decision-making processes of individual businesses.The study of consumer decision-making reveals how the price of products and services affects demand, how consumer satisfaction – although not precisely measurable – works in the decision-making process, and provides useful information to businesses selling products and services to these consumers. The decision-making processes of a business would include how much to make of a certain product and how to price these products to compete in the marketplace against other similar products.

The same decision-making dynamic is true of any business that sells services rather than products.Although economics is a broad continuum of all the factors - both large and small - that make up an economy, microeconomics does not take into direct account what macroeconomics considers.

Macroeconomics is concerned principally with government spending, personal income taxes, corporate taxes, capital gains taxes and other taxes; the key interest rates set by the Federal Reserve, the banking system and other economic factors such as consumer confidence, unemployment or gross national product, which may influence the entire economy. Economics, like all sciences, is continually evolving, with new ideas being introduced regularly, and old ideas being refined, revised, and rethought.

### Utility Theory

Some 200 years after Bernoulli's theory was first introduced, it was expanded upon by Hungarian John von Neumann (1903-1957), and Austrian Oskar Morgenstern (1920-1976). A more detailed and nuanced theory than Bernoulli's and Marshall's emerged from their collaboration, which they called utility theory.

The theory was elaborated in their book, "Theory of Games and Economic Behaviour," published in 1944. In the 1950s, Herbert A. Simon (1916-2001), a 1978 Nobel Memorial Prize-winner in economics, introduced a simpler theory of consumer behaviour called "satisficing". The satisficing theory contends that when consumers find what they want, they then abandon the quest and decision-making processes, and buy the product or service which seems to them as "good enough." (For more on the Nobel Memorial Prize, read Nobel Winners Are Economic Prizes.)

## ASSUMPTIONS AND UTILITY

### DEFINITION OF UTILITY ASSUMPTIONS

To study utility we make three assumptions about consumer behaviour that is reasonable and is intended to describe the basis of what we mean when we say consumers make choices in rational ways.

### Completeness

Completeness means that when a consumer is faced with two options of goods, A or B, the consumer is able to state which good he or she prefers. Most reasonable people would be able to choose whether or not they prefer product A to product B and would not be paralysed by indecision. Transitivity - We assume that individuals can state which product they prefer completely and clearly. We would not expect a reasonable consumer to contradict their complete statement of which product they prefer. If a consumer states that he prefer A to B and prefers B to C, then we would assume that he prefers A to C. If he stated otherwise, his statements would be inconsistent and he would be very confused.

### Decision Making Process

The decision-making process of the individual consumer is critically important in the study of microeconomics because consumer spending accounts for about 70 per cent of the economy. Consumers also save money, invest it, stash it away for the future in banks, stocks, bonds, money market or mutual funds, or other forms of savings. Microeconomics also studies the decision-making processes that determine how much a household may save, where it is saved, for how long and why. But because consumer spending is the engine that drives the economy, businesses continually pursue knowledge of how the consumer decision-making process works to better serve their markets with the most desired of products and services at usually, but not always, competitive prices.

### Microeconomic Assumptions

A basic assumption of microeconomics is that because a consumer does not have an unlimitedbudget, his or her available cash for spending must be judiciously allocated for maximum benefit. Microeconomics also supposes that individual consumers make their buying decisions in an effort to obtain the most happiness at the least cost - in other words, maximizing happiness or benefit.Happiness, of course, cannot be quantified. But there are methods and assumptions in the microeconomics tool box for calculating a reasonable approximation of this elusive concept. In microeconomics, happiness is measured by a concept called utility. The standard unit of measurement that microeconomics uses to measure utility is called the util.

### Utils and Utility

The util has no concrete numerical value like an inch or a centimeter. It is merely an arbitrary, subjective and convenient way to assign value to consumer choices and to measure the consumer utility or utils of one choice against another choice.

As an example, a consumer may go to the supermarket with $100 to spend, along with a phantom 100 utils representing 100 per cent of the happiness the consumer expects to garner from all the purchases he makes. Two-thirds of that dollar amount is spent on necessities - meat, bread, milk, produce and other food staples. Although 67 per cent of the money budgeted for purchases is spent on food stuffs, the number of utils assigned to those purchases - arbitrarily and subjectively - may only be 40. The remaining one-third of the money is spent on chocolate bars, ice cream, frozen pizza, soda pop and other unnecessary goodies. But the utils assigned to these purchases total 60.

So a rough numerical measure of consumer satisfaction is derived - what microeconomics callscardinal utility, which refers to the cardinal numbers, starting with 1, 2, 3 and so on.There's a problem, however, with this concept, convenient though it may be: consumers don't as a rule calculate the numerical utility value of their purchases; only microeconomists do.

Ordinal utility, another term widely used in microeconomics, may be a more useful way of determining consumer satisfaction because it simply denotes consumer preferences without assigning them numerical values.

**Further Considerations**

A consumer, for example, may prefer hot dogs to hamburgers; or he may purchase a coat at Targetrather than Wal-Mart. These are consumer preferences - their rankings of one product or brand against another. These preferences may be influenced by pricing, quality, convenience and other measurable factors along with the subjective, which is unquantifiable.

Why are such arbitrary and seemingly inexact measurements used in microeconomics? They provide at least some insight into the complexities of consumer decision-making. Both the numerical data - cardinal utility and the preferences data, ordinal utility - are extremely useful to businesses. Using this information, businesses can decide how much of a product or service to offer in the marketplace, and determine their optimum price for maximum sales.

Another term for consumer utility - cardinal utility, in this case - is consumer benefit. In any situation where a consumer buys more than one item of a product, the utility value may start to diminish as the consumer purchases or consumes more the product. For instance, a single ice cream cone at a certain price may have a 75 per cent utility value for the consumer. A consumer with two children who also want ice cream cones may assign a utility value of 100 per cent, if price discounts are given for the purchase of additional ice cream cones.

Additional ice cream cones at additional price reductions, however, would have a declining utility value. Why? It is because there are only three consumers of the theoretical ice cream cones. Furthermore, the consumer is disinclined to buy the additional ice cream cones at a discounted price because by the time he or she gets them home, they'll have melted away. Further, the consumer does not want his or her children to consume more than one cone a day. Therefore, the utility value goes up along a certain trajectory that can be plotted on a chart, and declines along a descending trajectory at a certain point on the chart. The term for this decline is diminishing marginal utility.

In their quest for happiness - or utility - resulting from their purchases, consumers choose what to buy from a huge array of products and services offered in the marketplace, based on a variety of factors which contribute to their perception of utility.Economists have pointed out a major flaw in the utility theory, however, which somewhat compromises its validity: Consumers do not always, or consistently, act in a logical, rational manner. Other elements may influence their decision-making, some of which they may be aware of, and others of that may be subconscious.

Nobel Memorial Prize winner in economics, Herbert A. Simon, postulated his theory of "satisficing" to address this apparent flaw.

### Satisficing

Let's say that a consumer wants to buy a used car. Utility theory holds that consumers would evaluate an indeterminate number of used cars, calculate the value of their variables and then buy the car with the highest number derived from that formula. Simon's satisficing theory suggests that consumers may just evaluate a limited number of used cars in a used car lot conveniently nearby. The consumer then makes a buying choice he or she considers "good enough." This theory seems reasonable, and eliminates some of the flaws inherent in the utility theory.

## MICROECONOMICS IN ACTION

In order to best understand how microeconomics applies to the real world, we'll go over the case of a car maker, General Motors (OTCBB:GMGMQ). Once, General Motors was among America's most profitable companies and a colossus of the automobile industry.

### MICROECONOMIC BREAKDOWN

By 2008, GM had fallen on hard times, the victim of a slumping U.S., and global economy and a series of microeconomic decisions that turned out to be wrong. Trouble at the microeconomic level began for General Motors several years before its problems worsened in late 2008. As Japanese automaker Toyota (NYSE:TM) began steadily eating into GM's market share, GM did not meet its competition head-on.

Toyota made a cheaper car with better gas mileage that was of better overall quality, and was engineered for greater durability than its chief competitor, GM. Consumers naturally gravitated away from GM to Toyota and demand for the once-popular GM automobiles declined slowly and continually as Toyota and other Japanese cars won an ever-increasing share of the automobile market.

**Dreadful Decision-Making**

Although the general economy may also be responsible to some degree for GM's fall, which eventually led to its bankruptcy in 2009, several GM management decisions at the microeconomic level contributed to the problem.

First, prior to its bankruptcy, GM was selling eight different brands of cars – Buick, Cadillac, Chevrolet, GMC, Hummer, Pontiac, Saab and Saturn. The number of units manufactured for each of these brands represented too much output, a situation in which the marginal revenue is less than the marginal costs.

Second, as gasoline prices rose, spurred by rising oil prices, GM continued to build gas-guzzling SUVs and pick-up trucks, and failed to produce cars that kept pace with the high mileage-per-gallon vehicles produced by Toyota and other Japanese manufacturers. Despite the obvious decline in demand for automobiles that were not fuel-efficient, GM persisted in marketing them, reflecting a microeconomic decision of management that seemed to disregard data on consumer preferences.Finally, in response to high consumer demand for fuel-efficient or alternative-energy vehicles, GM began developing hybrid vehicles, but only long after its competitors had brought them to the market.

GM's problems staggering debt and the costs of honouring contracts to provide pensions to its retirees and handsome health benefits and other costly benefits to its union-represented employees only contributed to its decline. Too many microeconomic decisions at GM have apparently proved unsuccessful. The result was abankruptcy filing for a firm that once made huge profits and reigned supreme over its industry.

**Microeconomic Achievement**

On the success side of the microeconomic ledger are many companies whose top management made the right decisions as start-ups, or in their restructuring efforts in the face of changing market conditions.One typical success story is FedEx (NYSE:FDX). Founded in 1971, the service firm is now the world's largest express transportation company. Initially, FedEx had a simple but powerfully effective business strategy that was summed up in its early advertising slogan: "When it absolutely, positively has to be there overnight."Frederick W. Smith, who founded FedEx, was aware of the growing consumer demand for prompt, dependable overnight delivery of packages and documents. Smith's microeconomic research in advance of starting his firm provided the data necessary to confirm an idea he first developed when he was studying economics at Yale.

**Understanding Demand and Adaptation**

In the early 1970s, the U.S. Postal Service was not as reliable as it would later become, and postal rates were increasing. Smith's unknown start-up firm would provide the service that the post office could not, at a reasonable price, and demand for Fed Ex service grew exponentially through the years. As the firm matured, several new and critical price and technological challenges arose, which threatened FedEx's market share. These included the entry into the express carrier business of the U.S. Postal Service, Emory Airborne Freight and United Parcel Service of America (UPS), among others.

On the technological side, fax transmissions and e-mails could now deliver almost instantaneously what previously could only be delivered overnight. In response to this challenge, FedEx concentrated on items that could not be dispatched via phone lines or electronically and expanded into foreign markets. With its own fleet of aircraft, FedEx was an effective competitor against most of the other carriers, which used commercial flights for delivery.

These moves reflect simple microeconomic decisions - when demand declined for overnight deliveries of materials which could be sent via e-mail or fax, the firm focused on other services, vigourously advertising what the market demanded at a competitive price. In the slumping economy of late 2008, with consumer budgets and disposable income shrinking through job loss, the declining value of their investments, and a lack of consumer confidence, consumer decision-making took a new direction.

**Customer Spending During a Downturn**

Consumer spending during the period of economic downturn that began in 2008 still expressed the microeconomic concepts of opportunity costs, cardinal utility and ordinal utility, which are used in decision-making in good economic times. Opportunity costs, as discussed in a previous chapter, are the tradeoff concept. With a limited budget, a consumer may be able to afford two items he or she desires, but cannot buy both. Buying one rather than the other is the opportunity cost.Suppose a consumer wants an expensive chocolate cake, a loaf of bread and a pound of sliced ham to make sandwiches for her school children. In a down economy the consumer on an abbreviated budget would likely chose the more practical purchases, the bread and ham. The cost for this decision - the opportunity cost - is the chocolate cake. (To learn more see, Economics Basics.) The cardinal utility - in microeconomics, the numerical value of satisfaction to the consumer - may not be measurable. But the ordinal value, which only denotes consumer preference, without assigning actual numbers, is obvious. In hard times, consumers prefer the necessities. This consumer preference for necessities and competitive pricing during a recessionary period was also demonstrated in a reported increase in brand switching and the use of discount coupons at supermarkets and other retailers. A consumer may prefer one brand of toothpaste at a certain price, but if a coupon for a different brand of toothpaste is offered at a significant discount, consumers may decide to buy the cheaper brand.

**Micro Meets Macro**

At this point, the principles of macroeconomics - the big-picture economy - came into play in the 2007-2009 recession. The Federal Reserve lowered the key interest rate to encourage borrowing. The federal government embarked on a costly but necessary rescue plan for the financial industry, and a plan to help home owners either facing default, or in default of their mortgages.

The government also rescued certain mortgage firms and investment banks with infusions of cash, principally Fannie Mae and Freddie Mac, and JPMorgan Chase to purchase failing investment firm Bear Sterns.

Additionally, through a legislative act called The Troubled Assets Relief Programme (commonly called "the bailout"), the federal government appropriated some $750 billion to buy toxic debt (non-performing or questionable debt) and to lend money to banks and other institutions to get the economy moving again.

## MACROECONOMIC BALANCE IN THE SHORT-RUN AND IN THE MEDIUM-RUN

The model tells us that both buyers and producers of goods and services in the aggregate determine how much output (y) the economy produces and the inflation rate (INFL). Formally, output and the inflation rate move towards their equilibrium levels. Because the behaviour of producers is different in the short-run and medium-run, short-run equilibrium can differ from medium-run equilibrium.

In the medium-run, since production occurs at the natural level of output, all three curves cross at the natural level of output (yf). This is illustrated below at point EMR, where medium-run equilibrium occurs at output level yf and inflation rate INFL1.

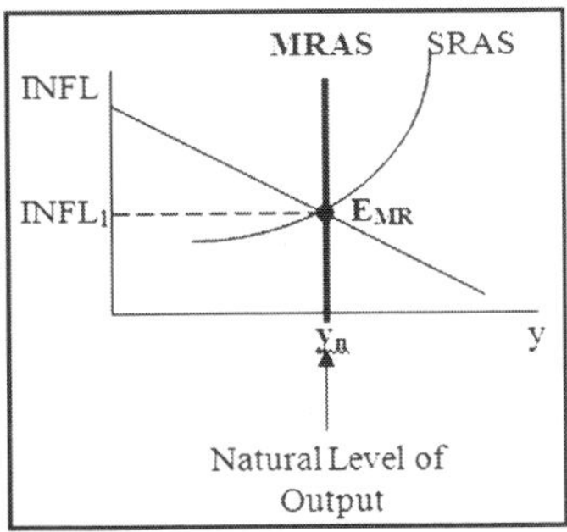


In the short-run, *i.e.*, temporarily, output can differ from the natural level (yf). Thus, short-run equilibrium can occur at a level of output that differs from the natural level. Graphically short-run equilibrium occurs where the aggregate demand curve crosses the short-run aggregate supply curve. The left panel of the diagram below shows a short-run equilibrium in which output exceeds the natural level and the right panel shows a short-run equilibrium where output is less than the natural level.

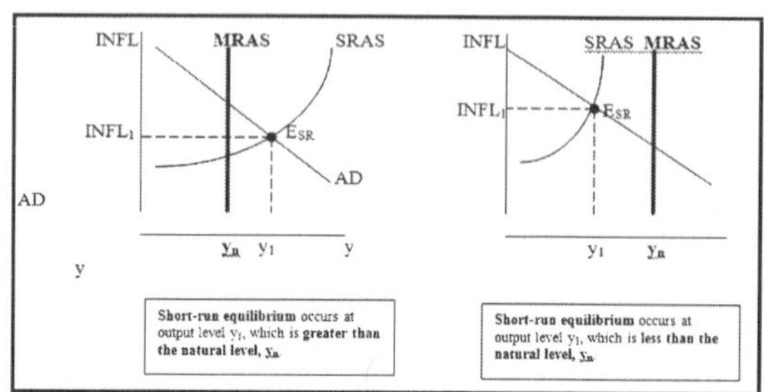


Output can only differ from the natural level temporarily. In the medium-run, macroeconomic forces push production towards the natural level. Graphically, in the medium-run the short-run aggregate supply curve shifts so that it intersects the aggregate demand curve at the natural level of output (yn).

Specifically, if output exceeds the natural level in the short-run, production costs, like wages and the prices of raw materials will increase, shifting the SRAS curve to the left. Likewise, if output is less than the natural level in the short-run, production costs will decrease, shifting the SRAS curve to the right.

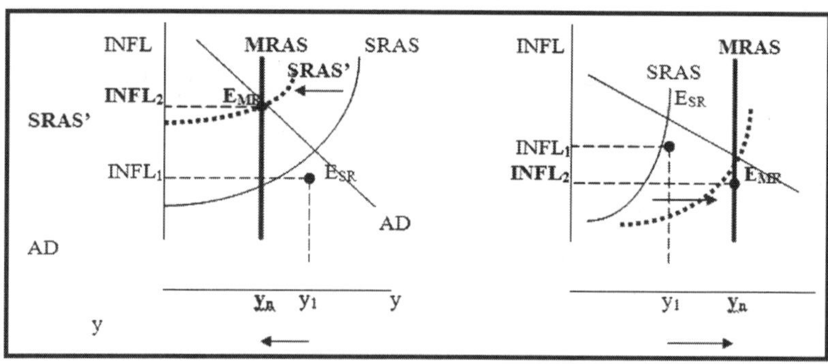


## THE CONSEQUENCE OF CHANGES IN AGGREGATE DEMAND IN THE SHORT-RUN

The aggregate demand – aggregate supply model allows us to see what factors influence prices and real output in the short-run, or as the economy proceeds through the business cycle.

### Changes in Aggregate Demand can "Move" the Economy through the Business Cycle

a. A decrease in aggregate demand moves the economy into recession with a rise in cyclical unemployment.

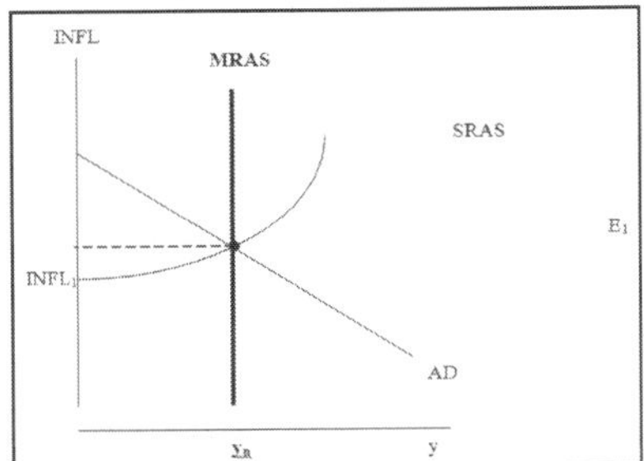


b. An increase in aggregate demand causes a recovery that returns production to natural levels and reduces cyclical unemployment.

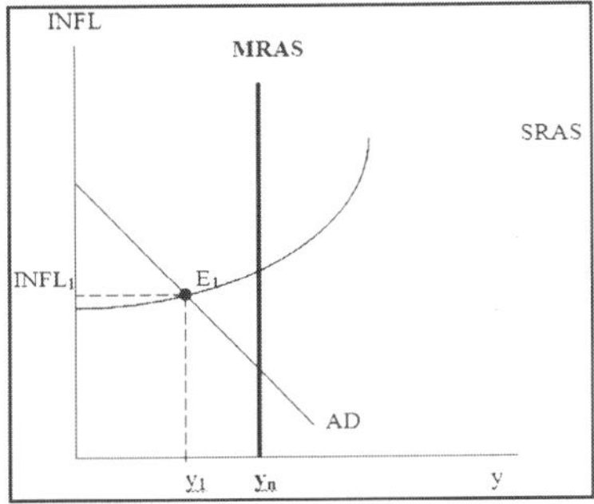


c. An increase in aggregate demand, especially when the economy is at the natural level of output, increases the inflation rate with very little change in real output.

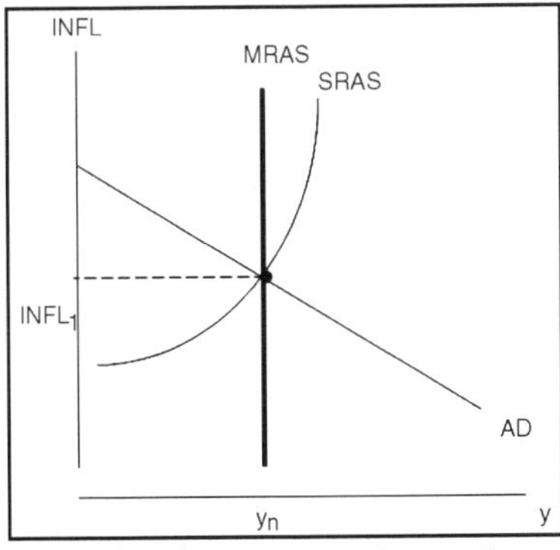


Even though production increases above the natural level, the increase is limited because resources are virtually "fully-employed." Firms can convince some workers to work overtime or can entice some people who are not normally part of the labour force, like housewives and retired people, to work, but such efforts will not yield much. Further any increases in production are temporary because costs will begin to rise and push production back towards the natural level in the medium-run. Because this inflation is due to increases in aggregate demand, it is called demand-pull inflation.

Discretionary or countercyclical fiscal and monetary policy, implemented by the government, can help the macroeconomy achieve the natural level of output with low inflation in the short-run.

**Discretionary or Counter Cyclical Fiscal Policy**

Deliberate changes in federal government spending or taxes to control production and employment or demand-pull inflation. Changes in spending and taxes at the federal level require that Congress pass legislation and that the president sign it. The actual spending plans and taxation are carried out by the US Department of the Treasury.

- *Problem:* Demand-Pull Inflation because aggregate demand has increased too much or too quickly, as illustrated in the following diagram.

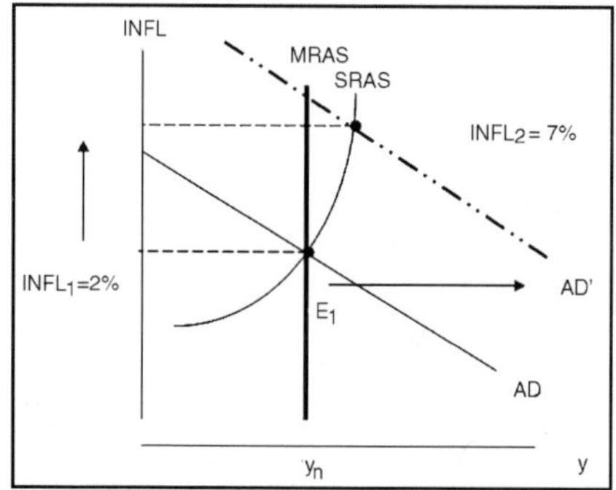


- *Policy Goal*: Reduce aggregate demand. Policy action: Contractionary Fiscal Policy
- *Problem:* Recession because aggregate demand is decreasing or is too low resulting in production falling below the natural level, as illustrated in the following diagram.

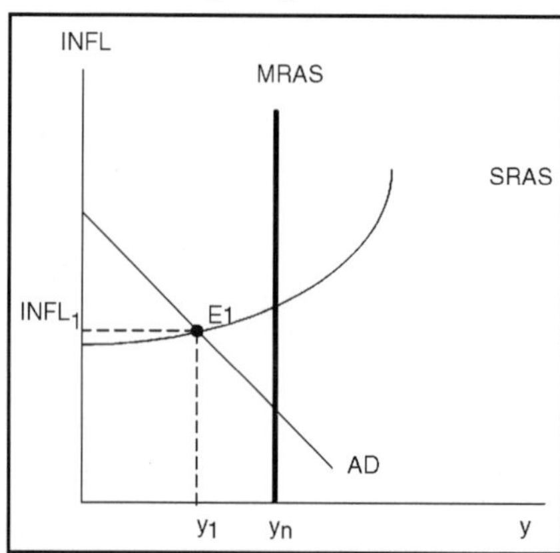


- *Policy Goal*: Increase aggregate demand. Policy action: Expansionary Fiscal Policy ("stimulus".

While fiscal policy is an option that the government can use to control inflation and unemployment, it only occasionally uses it for this purpose. The legislative process is slow and cumbersome, and therefore it is difficult to get fiscal policy changes in place in a timely fashion. However, economists had information fairly early on that the last recession (2008-2009) was likely to be very severe and long-lasting. As a result, Congress passed two packages of expansionary fiscal policy measures ("stimulus") in 2008 and 2009.

**Discretionary or Countercyclical Monetary Policy**

Deliberate changes in the money supply (the amount of money circulating), and therefore in short-term interest rates, to control production and unemployment or demand-pull inflation. Monetary policy is determined and carried out by the U.S., central bank known as the Federal Reserve System ("Fed").

- *Problem:* Demand-Pull Inflation because aggregate demand is increasing too fast.
- *Policy Goal:* Reduce aggregate demand. Policy action: Contractionary Monetary Policy
- *Problem*: Recession because aggregate demand is decreasing or is too low.
- *Policy Goal*: Increase aggregate demand. Policy action: Expansionary Monetary Policy

Monetary policy is the major means by which the authorities attempt to regulate inflation, output, and unemployment in the short-run.

## THE CONSEQUENCE OF CHANGES IN AGGREGATE SUPPLY IN THE SHORT-RUN

Changes in the rate of change in input prices/costs (due to changes in the wage rate of labour, the price of energy, and the price of raw materials) shift the short-run aggregate supply curve (SRAS). For example, during the 1970's "oil" or "energy" crises, the price of oil and therefore of energy in general began to rise more rapidly. This resulted in recession and "cost-push" inflation.

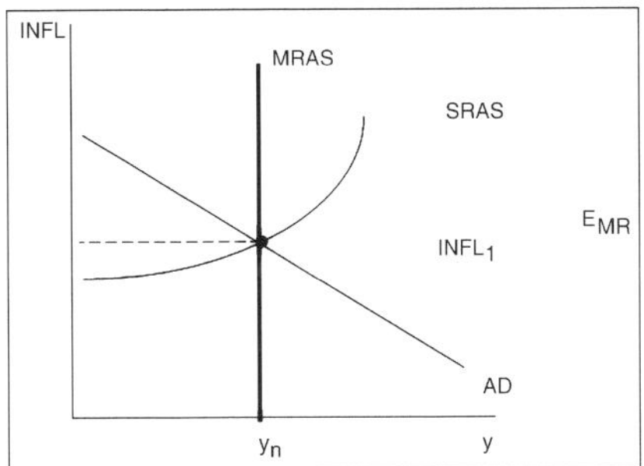


## THE MACROECONOMY IN THE LONG-RUN

In the medium-run, according to the model, the economy produces at its natural level of output. So far, we have been assuming that the natural level of output is fixed. In fact, over periods of 20 years or more (the long-run), the amount of goods and services the economy can produce noticeably changes. Thus it seems reasonable that most economies experience an increase in the natural level of output over very long periods of time. The amount of output the economy can produce when the unemployment rate is at the natural rate can change if there is a change in the size of the labour force or in the productivity of labour.

*The major factors that change the productivity of labour are:*

- Changes in the amount of capital,
- Changes in the skills and education of the labour force, and
- Changes in technology.

Graphically, these factors shift the medium-run aggregate supply curve (MRAS). For example, if there is technological change, the amount of output the economy can produce when unemployment is the natural rate increases (from yn1 to yn2 in the diagram below).

We draw a new MRAS at yn2. Eventually (in the long-run), equilibrium will occur at the higher natural level of output as illustrated in the diagram below. We say that the economy has experienced long-run economic growth.

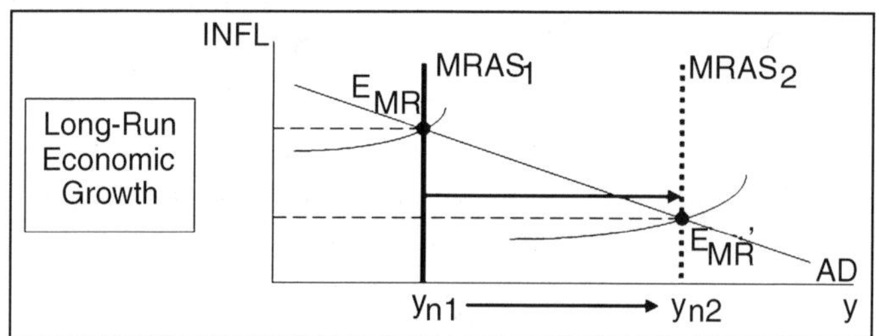


## MODERN ECONOMICS AND ECONOMIC THEORY

### WHAT IS ECONOMICS ABOUT?

*Economics* is a social science that studies individuals' economic behaviour, economic phenomena, as well as how individual agents, such as consumers, firms, and government agencies, make trade-off choices that allocate limited resources among competing uses.

People's desires are unlimited, but resources are limited, therefore individuals must make trade-offs. We need economics to study this fundamental conflict and how these trade-offs are best made.

### Four Basic Questions must be Answered by any Economic Institution

1. What goods and services should be produced and in what quantity?
2. How should the product be produced?

3. For whom should it be produced and how should it be distributed?
4. Who makes the decision?

The answers depend on the use of economic institutions.

*There are two basic economic institutions that have been so far used in the real world:*

1. *Market Economic Institution:* Most decisions on economic activities are made by individuals. This primarily decentralized decision system is the most important economic institution discovered for reaching cooperation amongst individuals and solving the conflicts that occur between them. The market economy has been proven to be only economic institution, so far, that can keep sustainable development and growth within an economy.
2. *Planed Economic Institution*: Most decisions on economic activities are made by governments, which are mainly centralized decision systems.

**What is Modern Economics?**

*Modern economics,* mainly developed in last sixty years, systematically studies individuals' economic behaviour and economic phenomena by a scientific studying method—observation → theory → observation—and through the use of various analytical approaches.

**What is Economic Theory?**

An *economic theory*, which can be considered an axiomatic approach, consists of a set of assumptions and conditions, an analytical framework, and conclusions that are derived from the assumptions and the analytical framework. Like any science, economics is concerned with the explanation of observed phenomena and also makes economic predictions and assessments based on economic theories. Economic theories are developed to explain the observed phenomena in terms of a set of basic assumptions and rules.

**Microeconomic Theory**

Microeconomic theory aims to model economic activities as the interaction of individual economic agents pursuing their private interests.

## KEY ASSUMPTIONS AND DESIRED PROPERTIES COMMONLY USED ECONOMICS

*Economists usually make all or some of the following key assumptions and conditions when they study economic problems*:

- *Individuals are Rational*: Self-interested behaviour assumption;
- *Scarcity of Resources:* Individuals confront scarce resources;
- *Economic Freedom:* Voluntary cooperation and voluntary exchange;

- *Decentralized Decision Makings:* One prefers to use the way of decentralized decision making. Why? This is because most economic information is incomplete or asymmetric to a decision marker;
- *Incentive Compatibility of Parties:* The system or economic mechanism should solve the problem of interest conflicts among individuals or economic units;
- Well-defined property rights;
- Equity in opportunity;
- Allocative efficiency of resources;

Relaxing any of these assumptions may result in different conclusions.

## THE BASIC ANALYTICAL FRAMEWORK OF MODERN ECONOMICS

*The basic analytical framework for an economic theory consists of five aspects or steps*:

1. Specification of economic environments,
2. Imposition of behavioural assumptions,
3. Adoption of economic institutional arrangements,
4. Determination of equilibria, and
5. Evaluation of outcomes resulting from a undertaken institution. The framework is a framework that uses to deal with daily activities and is used to study particular economic issues and questions that economists are interested in. Almost of all theoretical economics papers adopt this framework. As such, to have a solid training in economics and doing research, it is very important to master this basic analytical framework, specifically.

   *It can helpful at least in the following three aspects*:

   1. Help to understand economic theories and their arguments relatively easily.
   2. Help to find research topics.
   3. How to write standard scientific economics papers.

Understanding this basic analytical framework can help people classify possible misunderstandings about modern economics, and can also help them use the basic economic principles or develop new economic theories to solve economic problems in various economic environments, with different human behaviour and institutional arrangements.

### Specification of Economic Environments

The first step for studying an economic issue is to specify the economic environment.

*The specification on economic environment can be divided into two levels:*

1. Description of the economic environment, and
2. Characterization of the economic environment.

To perform these well, the description is a job of science, and the characterization is a job of art. The more clear and accurate the description of the economic environment is, the higher the possibility is of the correctness of the theoretical conclusions. The more refined the characterization of the economic environment is, the simpler and easier the arguments and conclusions will obtain.

Modern economics provides various perspectives or angles to look at real world economic issues. An economic phenomenon or issue may be very complicated and be affected by many factors. The approach of characterizing the economic environment can grasp the most essential factors of the issue and take our attention to the most key and core characteristics of an issue so that we can avoid unimportant details.

*An economic environment usually consists of:*

- A number of individuals,
- The individuals' characteristics, such as preferences, technologies, endowments, etc.
- Informational structures, and
- Institutional economic environments that include fundamental rules for establishing the basis for production, exchange, and distribution.

**Imposition of Behaviour Assumptions**

The second step for studying an economic issue is to make assumptions on individuals' behaviour. Making appropriate assumptions is of fundamental importance for obtaining a valuable economic theory or assessment. A key assumption modern economics makes about an individual's behaviour is that an individual is self-interested. This is a main difference between individuals and other subjects. The self-interested behaviour assumption is not only reasonable and realistic, but also have a minimum risk. Even this assumption is not suitable to an economic environment, it does not cause a big trouble to the economy even if it is applied to the economy. A rule of a game designed for self-interested individuals is likely also suitable for altruists, but the reverse is likely not true.

**Adoption of Economic Institutional Arrangement**

The third step for studying an economic issue is to adopt the economic institutional arrangements, which are also called economic mechanisms, which can be regarded as the rules of the game. Depending on the problem under consideration, an economic institutional arrangement could be exogenously given or endogenously determined. For instance, when studying individuals' decisions in the theories of consumers and producers, one implicitly assumes that the undertaken mechanism is a competitive market mechanism takes it as given. However, when considering the choice of economic institutions and arguing the optimality of the market mechanism, the market institution is endogenously determined. The alternative mechanisms that are designed to solve the problem of market failure are also endogenously determined. Economic arrangements should be designed differently for different economic environments and behaviour assumptions.

### Determination of Equilibria

The fourth step for studying an economic issue is to make trade-off choices and determine the "best" one. Once given an economic environment, institutional arrangement, and other constraints, such as technical, resource, and budget constraints, individuals will react, based on their incentives and own behaviour, and choose an outcome from among the available or feasible outcomes. Such a state is called *equilibrium* and the outcome an *equilibrium outcome*. This is the most general definition an economic "equilibrium".

### Evaluations

The fifth step in studying an economic issue is to evaluate outcomes resulting from the undertaken institutional arrangement and to make value judgments of the chosen equilibrium outcome and economic mechanism based on certain criterion. The most important criterion adopted in modern economics is the notion of efficiency or the "first best". If an outcome is not efficient, there is room for improvement. The other criterions include equity, fairness, incentive-compatibility, informational efficiency, and operation costs for running an economic mechanism.

In summary, in studying an economic issue, one should start by specifying economic environments and then study how individuals interact under the self-interested motion of the individuals within an exogenously given or endogenously determined mechanism. Economists usually use "equilibrium," "efficiency", "information", and "incentive-compatibility" as focal points, and investigate the effects of various economic mechanisms on the behaviour of agents and economic units, show how individuals reach equilibria, and evaluate the status at equilibrium. Analysing an economic problem using such a basic analytical framework has not only consistence in methodology, but also in getting surprising conclusions.

## METHODOLOGIES FOR STUDYING MODERN ECONOMICS

Any economic theory usually consists of five aspects. Discussions on these five steps will naturally amplify into how to combine these five aspects organically. To do so, economists usually integrate various studying methods into their analysis. Two methods used in modern economics are providing various levels and aspects studying platforms and establishing reference/ benchmark systems.

**Studying Platform**

A studying platform in modern economics consists of some basic economic theories or principles. It provides a basis for extending the existing theories and analysing more deep economic issues.

*Examples of studying platforms are:*

- Consumer and producer theories provide a bedrock platform for studying individuals' independent decision choices.
- The general equilibrium theory is based on the theories of consumers and producers and is a higher level platform. It provides a basis for studying interactions of individuals within a market institution and how the market equilibrium is reached in each market.
- The mechanism design theory provides an even higher level of studying platform and can be used to study or design an economic institution. It can be used to compare various economic institutions or mechanisms, as well as to identify which one may be an "optima".

**Reference Systems/Benchmark**

Modern economics provides various reference/benchmark systems for comparison and to see how far a real world is from an ideal status. A reference system is a standard economic model/theory that results in desired or ideal results, such as efficiency/the "first best".

The importance of a reference system does not rely on whether or not it describes the real world correctly or precisely, but instead gives a criterion for understanding the real world. It is a mirror that lets us see the distance between various theoretical models/realistic economic mechanisms and the one given by the reference system. For instance, the general equilibrium theory as suggested, study in the notes is such a reference system. With this reference system, we can study and compare equilibrium outcomes under various market structures with the ideal case of the perfectly competitive mechanism. The first-best results in a complete information economic environment in information economics. Other examples include the Coase Theorem in property rights theory and economic law, and the Modigliani-Miller Theorem in corporate finance theory.

Although those economic theories or economic models as reference systems may impose some unrealistic assumptions, they are still very useful, and can be used to make further analysis. They establish criterions to evaluate various theoretical models or economic mechanisms used in the real world. A reference system is not required, in most cases it is actually not needed, to predicate the real world well, but it is used to provide a benchmark to see how far a reality is from the ideal status given by a reference system.

The value of a reference system is not that it can directly explain the world, but that it provides a benchmark for developing new theories to explain the world. In fact, the establishment of a reference system is very important for any scientific subject, including modern economics. Anyone can talk about an economic issue but the main difference is that a person with systematic training in modern economics has a few reference systems in her mind while a person without training in modern economics does not so he cannot grasp essential parts of the issue and cannot provide deep analysis and insights.

### Analytical Tools

Modern economics also provides various powerful analytical tools that are usually given by geometrical or mathematical models. Advantages of such tools can help us to analyse complicated economic behaviour and phenomena through a simple diagram or mathematical structure in a model.

*Examples include:*

- The demand-supply curve model,
- Samuelson's overlapping generation model,
- The principal-agent model, and
- The game theoretical model.

## ROLES, GENERALITY, AND LIMITATION OF ECONOMIC THEORY

### Roles of Economic Theory

*An economic theory has three possible roles*:

1. It can be used to explain economic behaviour and economic phenomena in the real world.
2. It can make scientific predictions or deductions about possible outcomes and consequences of adopted economic mechanisms when economic environments and individuals' behaviour are appropriately described.
3. It can be used to refute faulty goals or projects before they are actually undertaken. If a conclusion is not possible in theory, then it is not possible in a real world setting, as long as the assumptions were approximated realistically.

### Generality of Economic Theory

An economic theory is based on assumptions imposed on economic environments, individuals' behaviour, and economic institutions. The more general these assumptions are, the more powerful, useful, or meaningful the theory that comes from them is. The general equilibrium theory is considered such a theory.

### Limitation of Economic Theory

When examining the generality of an economic theory, one should realise any theory or assumption has a boundary, limitation, and applicable range of economic theory. Thus, two common misunderstandings in economic theory should be avoided.One misunderstanding is to over-evaluate the role of an economic theory. Every theory is based on some imposed assumptions. Therefore, it is important to keep in mind that every theory is not universal, cannot explain everything, but has its limitation and boundary of suitability.

When applying a theory to make an economic conclusion and discuss an economic problem, it is important to notice the boundary, limitation, and applicable range of the theory. It cannot be applied arbitrarily, or a wrong conclusion will be the result.

The other misunderstanding is to under-evaluate the role of an economic theory. Some people consider an economic theory useless because they think assumptions imposed in the theory are unrealistic. In fact, no theory, whether in economics, physics, or any other science, is perfectly correct. The validity of a theory depends on whether or not it succeeds in explaining and predicting the set of phenomena that it is intended to explain and predict. Theories, therefore, are continually tested against observations. As a result of this testing, they are often modified, refined, and even discarded.

The process of testing and refining theories is central to the development of modern economics as a science. One example is the assumption of perfect competition. In reality, no competition is perfect. Real world markets seldom achieve this ideal status. The question is then not whether any particular market is perfectly competitive, almost no one is.

The appropriate question is to what degree models of perfect competition can generate insights about real-world markets. We think this assumption is approximately correct in certain situations. Just like frictionless models in physics, such as in free falling body movement, ideal gas, and ideal fluids, frictionless models of perfect competition generate useful insights in the economic world.It is often heard that someone is claiming they have toppled an existing theory or conclusion, or that it has been overthrown, when some condition or assumption behind it is criticized.

This is usually needless claim, because any formal rigorous theory can be criticized at anytime because no assumption can coincide fully with reality or cover everything. So, as long as there are no logic errors or inconsistency in a theory, we cannot say that the theory is wrong. We can only criticize it for being too limited or unrealistic.

What economists should do is to weaken or relax the assumptions, and obtain new theories based on old theories. We cannot say though that the new theory topples the old one, but instead that the new theory extends the old theory to cover more general situations and different economic environments.

## ROLES OF MATHEMATICS IN MODERN ECONOMICS

Mathematics has become an important tool in modern economics. Almost every field in modern economics uses mathematics and statistics. The mathematical approach to economic analysis is used when economists make use of mathematical symbols in the statement of a problem and also draw upon known mathematical theorems to aid in reasoning.

It is not difficult to understand why the mathematical approach has become a dominant approach since finding the boundary of a theory, developing an analytical framework of a theory, establishing reference systems, and providing analytical tools all need mathematics.

If we apply a theoretical result to real world without knowing the boundary of a theory, we may get a very bad consequence and hurt an economy seriously.

*Some of the advantages of using mathematics are that*:

- The "language" used and the descriptions of assumptions are clearer, more accurate, and more precise,
- The logical process of analysis is more rigorous and clearly sets the boundaries and limitations of a statement,
- It can give a new result that may not be easily obtained through observation alone, and
- It can reduce unnecessary debates and improve or extend existing results.

It should be remarked that, although mathematics is of critical importance in modern economics, economics is not mathematics. Economics uses mathematics as a tool in order to model and analyse various economic problems. Statistics and econometrics are used to test or measure the *accuracy* of our predication, and identify causalities among economic variables.

## CONSUMER CHOICE IN THE NEO-CLASSICAL MODEL FOR MICRO ECONOMICS

In economics, the standard textbook model of consumer is an outstanding example of the Neo-classical paradigm: a hyper-rational agent maximises something by choosing an *"optimal"* bundle of things. Here, the hyper-rational consumer maximises utility (i. e. an overall generic measure of well-being) by exhausting a given budget.

He has a pre-defined income to spend on - for simplicity's sake - two goods, called X and Y, respectively. He could spend his entire income buying only X, thus purchasing a quantity of X equal to income divided by the price of X.

Let's take a numerical example that you find here in the animated graph and that you can replicate with the software: when his income is 50 and the Y price is 10, the consumer can purchase 5 units of Y (higher red point on Y axis).

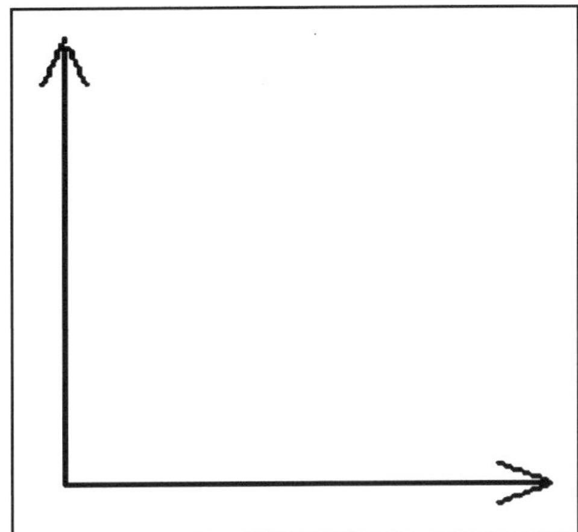

If the graph is not animated, just reload this page.

Or he could spend his entire income buying only X - the other good - thus purchasing a quantity of X equal to his income divided by the price of X. If X price is 6, the consumer can purchase at most 8.33 units of X (lower red point).

Or he can afford (at most) to buy any combination of quantities of X and Y that costs exactly as the income. These combinations give rise to the budget line you see between the two red points.How to choose? Well, by having a consistent set of judgements about how much utility the consumer will enjoy by consuming each possible bundle of goods.The typical well-behaved structure of utility of bundles is offered by indifference curves, *i.e.* all bundles giving the same level of utility to the consumer.Here below you can see two indifference curves: the higher indifference curve is characterised by a higher level of utility.

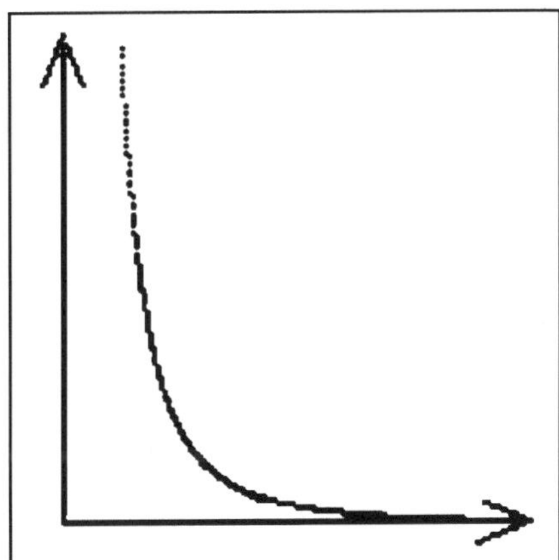

Simultaneously, now we should consider both the budget constraint (the budget line) and the utility structure (the indifference curves). The optimal bundle of goods belongs to the highest possible indifference curve crossing the budget line.

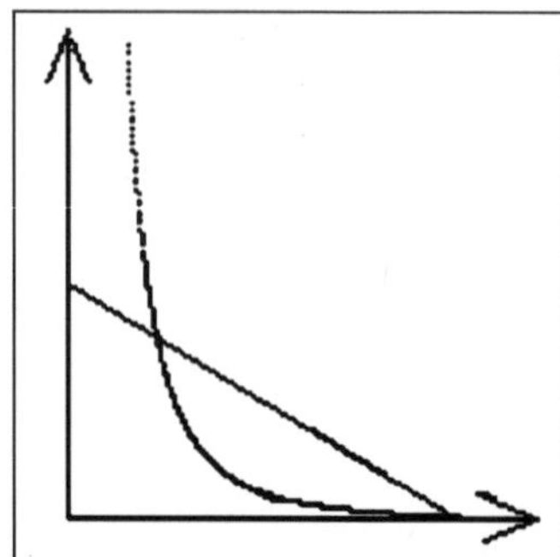

The red point is the rational consumer's choice (the chosen bundle), since it maximises utility, given the budget constraint.

Everything sounds very logical and convincing - within the unrealistic setting offered by this kind of mathematics. The deductive style of this microeconomics in consumer theory takes very little care of empirical analysis and of any reasonably open experimentation. Still, let's now see some numerical examples of what we said.

**How to use this Software**

Based on Hicksian approach to indifference curves and budget lines, this is free software to draw economic graphs, diagrams, demand curves, singling out individual choices of (hyper) rational consumers choosing the optimal bundle. The Progamme starts with a consumer having 50 as income and facing the price of some X good of 6 and the price of Y of 10.

The "*Draw*" button produce the graphical representation of the budget line, *i.e.* the quantities of X and Y that the consumer can afford exhausting his income. Push it a first time: you are drawing the budget line and computing the value of its slope, equal - in absolute value - to the relative price of X to Y.

Increase income and re-draw the graph. The quantities on the budget line are systematically higher. No surprise. Make more experiments varying income and prices. What happens when you increase the price of X? See it on the screen rotations and translations and ask yourself the reasons.

As we said, the Neo-classical approach uses "*indifference curves*" to represent the preferences of the consumer. By choosing an indifference curve type (instead of "*none*" - the default), you'll see - always with the button "Draw" - which combination of X and Y the consumer will optimally choose. For instance, by choosing the well-behaved Cobb-Douglas type you obtain (in the default position of income = 50, px = 6, py = 10) that the consumer buys 5.83 units of X and 1.5 units of Y. In this way he reaches a utility level (a general happiness) of 3.88.As it can see the effect of changes in income and prices on demanded quantities (so-called "*income elasticity*" and "*price elasticity*") and on utility by changing the input data. In particular, an increase of income will normally boost both quantities of X and Y [1] - as well as the utility enjoyed.However, the effect of price on demanded quantities shows that the increase of the price of X is a damage: utility falls and the quantity of X decreases as well. Try now some systematic experiment. Keeping income at the same level, gradually increase the price of X, as it would happen maybe due to rising business costs. How does the quantity bought of X change? By collecting your observations, you'll get the demand function, linking the quantity purchased of a good with its price.

Symmetrically, by keeping prices at the same level, changes in income give rise to the Engel curve, as can be seen from the graph in the screen activated by the line *"Engel's curve"* in the *"Issues"* Menu. The (indirect) link from income to utility - mediated by the optimally chosen bundle of goods - can be represented by the so-called *"indirect utility function"*. The indirect utility function is the maximum utility attained with given prices and income. It should first experiment in the basic screen by annotating the utility levels obtained at different levels of income, then draw more systematic curves in the new screen opened by the *"Effects of income and prices on utility"* line of the *"Issues"* Menu.

Now reflect: if an increase of income fosters utility whereas an increase of price depresses it - and everything is very precise - there should be the possibility of keeping the consumer exactly at the same level of utility by giving some additional amount of income to compensate for the price increase. This is exactly the idea of the so-called *"Hicksian compensation"*: the consumer is given sufficient income to reach his original utility level, the price increase notwithstanding.

## ECONOMICS OF UNCERTAINTY

Until now, we have been concerned with the behaviour of a consumer under conditions of certainty. However, many choices made by consumers take place under conditions of uncertainty. In this stage, we explore how the theory of consumer choice can be used to describe such behaviour.

The board outline of this stage parallels a standard presentation of microeconomic theory for deterministic situations.It first considers the problem of an individual con-sumer facing an uncertain environment. It shows how preference structures can be extended to uncertain situations and describes the nature of the consumer choice problem.We then processed to derive the expected utility theorem, a result of central importance. We discuss the concept of risk aversion, and extend the basic theory by allowing utility to depend on states of nature underlying the uncertainty as well as on the monetary payoffs. We also discuss the theory of subjective probability, which offers a way of modelling choice under uncertainty in which the probabilities of different risky alternatives are not given to the decision maker in any objective fashion.

### EXPECTED UTILITY

Under minor additional assumptions, the theorem concerning the existence of a utility function may be applied to show that there exists a continuous utility function $u$ which describes the consumer's preferences; that is,

$$p \circ x \oplus (1-p) \circ y \succ q \circ w \oplus (1-q) \circ z$$

if and only if,

$$u(p \circ x © (1-p) \circ y) > u(q \circ w \oplus (1-q) \circ z).$$

Of course, this utility function is not unique; any monotonic transform would do as well. Under some additional hypotheses, we can find a particular monotonic transformation of the utility function that has a very convenient property, the expected utility property:

$$u(p \circ x \oplus (1-p) \circ y) = pu(x) + (1-p)u(y).$$

The expected utility property says that the utility of a lottery is the expectation of the utility from its prizes and such an expected utility function is called von Neumann-Morgenstern utility function. To have a utility function with the convenient property, we need the additional axioms:

A4 (Continuity). $\{p$ in $[0, 1]: p \circ x \oplus (l-p) \circ y \succeq z\}$ and $\{p$ in $[0, 1]: z \succeq p \circ x \oplus (1-p) \circ y\}$ are closed sets for all $x$, $y$ and $z$ in $L$. Axiom 4 states that preferences are continuous with respect to probabilities.

A5 (Strong Independence). $x \sim y$ implies $p \circ x \oplus (1-p) \circ z \sim p \circ y \oplus (l-p) \circ z$. It says that lotteries with indifferent prizes are indifferent. In order to avoid some technical details as suggested, make two further assumptions.

A6 (Boundedness). There is some best lottery $b$ and some worst lottery $w$.

For any,

$$x \text{ in } \mathcal{L}, b \succeq x \succeq w.$$

A7 (Monotonicity). A lottery $p \circ b \oplus (1-p) \circ w$ is preferred to $q \circ b \oplus (1-q) \circ w$ if and only if $p > q$. Axiom A7 can be derived from the other axioms. It just says that if one lottery between the best prize and the worse prize is preferred to another it must be because it gives higher probability of getting the best prize. Under these assumptions we can state the main theorem.

*Theorem*: *If* $(L, \succeq)$ *satisfy Axioms 1-7, there is a* utility function u defined on L that satisfies the expected utility property:

$$u(p \circ x \oplus (1-p) \circ y = pu(x) + (1-p)u(y)$$

*Proof*: Define $u(b) = 1$ and $u(w) = 0$. To find the utility of an arbitrary lottery $z$, set $u(z) = pz$ where $pz$ is defined by

$$pz \circ b \oplus (1-pz) \circ w \sim z.$$

In this construction the consumer is indifferent between $z$ and a gamble between the best and the worst outcomes that gives probability $pz$ of the best outcome.

*To ensure that this is well defined, we have to check two things*:

1. Does $pz$ exist? The two sets $\{p$ in $[0, 1]: p \circ b \oplus (1-p) \circ w \succeq z\}$ and $\{p$ in $[0, 1]: z \succeq p \circ b \oplus (1-p) \circ w\}$ are closed and Non-empty by the continuity and boundedness axioms (A4 and A6), and every point in

[0, 1] is in one or the other of the two sets. Since the unit interval is connected, there must be some $p$ in both—but this will just be the desired $pz$.

2. Is $pz$ unique? Suppose $pz$ and $p'z$. are two distinct numbers and that each satisfies. Then one must be larger than the other. By the monotonicity axiom A7, the lottery that gives a bigger probability of getting the best prize cannot be indifferent to one that gives a smaller probability. Hence, $pz$ is unique and $u$ is well defined.

We next check that $u$ has the expected utility property. This follows from some simple substitutions:

$$p \circ x \oplus (1 ¡ p) \circ y$$
$$\sim_1 p \circ [px \circ b \oplus (1-px) \circ w] \oplus (1-p) \circ [py \circ b \oplus (1-py) \circ w]$$
$$\sim_2 [ppx + (1-p)py] \circ b \oplus [1-ppx-(1-p)py] \circ w$$
$$\sim_3 [pu(x) + (1-p)u(y)] \circ b \oplus (1-pu(x)-(1-p)u(y)] \circ w:$$

Substitution 1 uses the strong independence axiom (A5) and the definition of $pz$ and $py$: Substitution 2 uses the compounding axiom (A3), which says only the net probabilities of obtaining $b$ or $w$ matter. Substitution 3 uses the construction of the utility function.

It follows from the construction of the utility function that

$$u(p \circ x \oplus (1-p) \circ y) = pu(x) + (1-p)u(y).$$

Finally, we verify that $u$ is a utility function. Suppose that $x \succ y$.

Then,

$$u(x) = pz \text{ such that } x \sim px \circ b \oplus (1-px) \circ w$$
$$u(y) = py \text{ such that } y \sim py \circ b \oplus (1-py) \circ w$$

By the monotonicity axiom (A7), we must have $u(x) > u(y)$.

## UNIQUENESS OF THE EXPECTED UTILITY FUNCTION

We have shown that there exists an expected utility function $u$: $\mathcal{L}-R$. Of course, any monotonic transformation of $u$ will also be a utility function that describes the consumer's choice behaviour.But will such a monotonic transform preserve the expected utility properly?

Does the construction characterize expected utility functions in any way?

It is not hard to see that, if $u(.)$ is an expected utility function describing some consumer, then so is $v(.) = au(.)+c$ where $a > 0$; that is, any a±ne transformation of an expected utility function is also an expected utility function.

This is clear since,

$$\begin{aligned} v(p \circ x \oplus (1-p) \circ y) &= au(p \circ x \oplus (1-p) \circ y) + c \\ &= a[pu(x) + (1-p)u(y)] + c \\ &= pv(x) + (1-p)v(y). \end{aligned}$$

It is not much harder to see the converse: that any monotonic transform of $u$ that has the expected utility property must be an affine transform. Stated another way:

*Theorem*: *An expected utility function* is unique up to an affine transformation.

*Proof*: According to the remarks we only have to show that, if a monotonic transformation preserves the expected utility property, it must be an affine transformation.

*Let $f$: $R \rightarrow R$* be a monotonic transformation of $u$ that has the expected utility property.

Then

$$f(u(p \circ x \oplus (1-p) \circ y)) = pf(u(x)) + (1-p)f(u(y)),$$

or

$$f(pu(x) + (1-p)u(y)) = pf(u(x)) + (1-p)f(u(y)).$$

But this is equivalent to the definition of an affine transformation.

## OTHER NOTATIONS FOR EXPECTED UTILITY

We have proved the expected utility theorem for the case where there are two outcomes to the lotteries. As indicated earlier, it is straightforward to extend this proof to the case of a finite number of outcomes by using compound lotteries. If outcome $xi$ is received with probability $pi$ for $i = 1,....,n$, the expected utility of this lottery is simply,

$$\sum_{t=1}^{n} p_i u(x_i).$$

The expected utility theorem also holds for continuous probability distributions. If $p(x)$ is probability density function defined on outcomes $x$, then the expected utility of this gamble can be written as, $\int u(x)p(x)dx.$

We can subsume of these cases by using the expectation operator. Let $X$ be a random variable that takes on values denoted by $x$.

Then the utility function of $X$ is also a random variable, $u(X)$. The expectation of this random variable $Eu(X)$ is simply the expected utility associated with the lottery $X$. In the case of a discrete random variable.

## EXPECTED UTILITY THEORY

### Lotteries

The first task is to describe the set of choices facing the consumer. We shall imagine that the choices facing the consumer take the form of lotteries.

Suppose there are $S$ states. Associated with each state $s$ is a probability $p_s$ representing the probability that the state $s$ will occur and a commodity bundle

$x_s$ representing the prize or reward that will be won if the state $s$ occurs, where we have $p_s \geqq 0$ and

$$\sum_{s=1}^{S} Ps = 1.$$

The prizes may be money, bundles of goods, or even further lotteries. A lottery is denoted by,

$$p_1 \text{ o } x_1 \oplus p_2 \text{ o } x_2 \oplus ..... \oplus p_S \text{ o } x_S.$$

*For instance, for two states, a lottery is given $p$ o $x \oplus (1-p)$ o $y$ which means*: "The consumer receives prize $x$ with probability $p$ and prize $y$ with probability $(1-p)$."

Most situations involving behaviour under risk can be put into this lottery framework. Lotteries are often represented graphically by a fan of possibilities as in Figure.

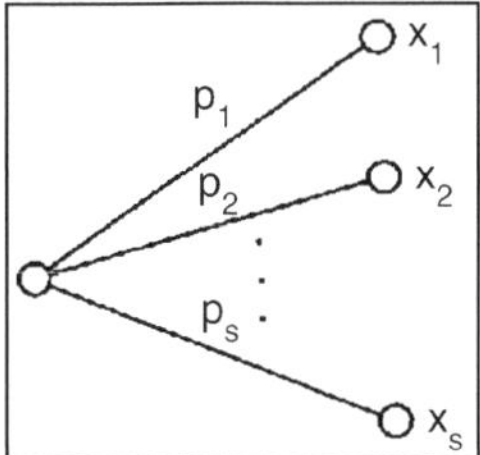


**Fig**: A Lottery.

A compound lottery is shown in Figure. This lottery is between two prizes: a lottery between $x$ and $y$, and a bundle $z$.

As suggested, make several axioms about the consumers perception of the lotteries open to him.

A1 (Certainty). 1 o $x \oplus (1-1)$ o $y \sim x$. Getting a prize with probability one is equivalent to that prize.

A2 (Independence of Order). $p$ o $x \oplus (1-p)$ o $y \sim (1-p)$ o $y \oplus p$ o $x$. The consumer doesn't care about the order in which the lottery is described–only the prizes and the probabilities of winning those prizes matter.

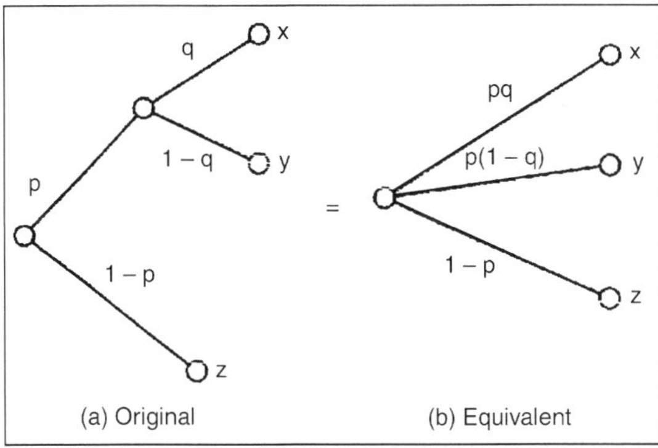


**Fig**: Compound Lottery.

A3 (Compounding). $q \circ (p \circ x \oplus (1-p) \circ y) \oplus (1-q) \circ y \sim (qp) \circ x \oplus (1-qp) \circ y$. It is only the net probabilities of receiving the a reward that matters. It is a fundamental axiom used to reduce compound lotteries—by determining the overall probabilities associated with its components. This axiom sometimes called "reduction of compound lotteries."

Under these assumptions we can define $\mathcal{L}$, the space of lotteries available to the consumer. The consumer is assumed to have preferences on this lottery space: given any two lotteries, he can choose between them. As usual as suggested, assume the preferences are complete, reflexive, and transitive so it is an ordering preference. The fact that lotteries have only two outcomes is not restrictive since we have allowed the outcomes to be further lotteries. This allows us to construct lotteries with arbitrary numbers of prizes by compounding two prize lotteries. For example, suppose we want to represent a situation with three prizes $x$, $y$ and $z$ where the probability of getting each prize is one third. By the reduction of compound lotteries, this lottery is equivalent to the lottery

$$\frac{2}{3} \circ \left[\frac{1}{2} \circ x \oplus \frac{1}{2} \circ y\right] \oplus \frac{1}{3} \circ z.$$

The consumer only cares about the net probabilities involved, so this is indeed equivalent to the original lottery.

# 2

# Demand Theory of Consumer Behaviour

The branch of economics devoted to the study of consumer behaviour, especially as it applies to decisions related to purchasing goods and services through markets. Consumer demand theory is largely centered on the study and analysis of the utility generated from the satisfaction of wants and needs. The key principle of consumer demand theory is the law of diminishing marginal utility, which offers an explanation for the law of demand and the negative slope of the demand curve.

Consumer demand theory provides insight into an understanding market demand and forms a cornerstone of modern microeconomics. In particular, this theory analyses consumer behaviour, especially market purchases, based on the satisfaction of wants and needs (that is, utility) generated from the consumption of a good. A basic version of this theory, primarily taught in introductory courses, involves the analysis of total and marginal utility, especially the role played by the law of diminishing marginal returns. A more sophisticated version of the theory, more commonly found at the intermediate course level and above, relies on the analysis of indifference curves and relative utility, with a key role play by decreasing marginal rate of substitution. Both versions provide insight into the law of demand and the negative slope of the demand curve.

## DOING DEMAND

Demand, the willingness and ability to purchase a range of quantities at a range of prices, is one half of the market. The law of demand, which gives rise to a negatively-sloped demand curve, is an essential principle underlying market analysis. Modern microeconomic theory, among other topics, is concerned with understanding and explaining the law of demand.

Insight into this law can be found with consumer demand theory. The explanation is relatively simple--on the surface. Consumers purchase goods that satisfy wants and needs, that is, generate utility. Those goods that generate more utility are more valuable to consumers and thus buyers are willing to pay a higher price. The key to the law of demand is that the utility generated declines as the quantity consumed increases. As such, the demand price that buyers are willing to pay decreases as the quantity demanded increases.The notion that market demand depends on the satisfaction of wants and needs has been an essential part of the economic analysis of markets since at least the time of Adam Smith. However, three scholars working in progression from the late 1700s to the late 1800s gave the development of consumer demand theory a large, formal boost.

- *Jeremy Bentham*: The first major advance in the development of consumer demand theory was provided by Jeremy Bentham in the late 1700s. Bentham coined the term "utility" in reference to the satisfaction of wants and needs. He also developed the notion that people are motivated by the desire to maximize utility. Bentham firmly believed that utility was a measurable, quantifiable characteristic of a person, much like height or weight.
- *John Stuart Mill*: The theoretical work developed by Bentham was extended and popularised by John Stuart Mill, whose father James Mill was a contemporary and close friend of Bentham. The elder Mill introduced the younger Mill to the thoughts and teachings of Bentham at an early age. John Stuart Mill expanded and promoted these consumer demand principles in a number of publications, including his book, Principles of Political Economic, which was the dominate economics textbook for several decades.
- *William Stanley Jevons*: A major improvement in consumer demand theory was provided by William Stanley Jevons with the notion of marginal utility. Jevons also developed the rule of consumer equilibrium, stating that consumers purchase goods such that the ratio of marginal utilities is equal to the ratio of prices. Along the way, Jevons helped to transform consumer demand theory (as well as microeconomics in general) into a rigourous mathematical science.

**Table. Utility Analysis.**

| Rides (util) | Total Utility (util) | Marginal Utility |
|---|---|---|
| 0 | 0 | |
| 1 | 11 | 11 |
| 2 | 20 | 9 |
| 3 | 27 | 7 |
| 4 | 32 | 5 |
| 5 | 35 | 3 |
| 6 | 36 | 1 |

| | | |
|---|---|---|
| 7 | 35 | –1 |
| 8 | 32 | –3 |

## BASIC FORMULATION OF CONSUMER DEMAND

A basic formulation of consumer demand theory involves an analysis of the total utility and marginal utility derived from the consumption of a good. The focal point of utility analysis is usually a table of the total and marginal utility generated by consuming different quantities of a good, such as the one displayed in the exhibit to the right.

This analysis is based on the presumption that the amount of utility generated from the consumption of a good can be explicitly measured. The standard measurement unit is "utils." This particular set of numbers illustrates the total and marginal utility generated by riding a roller coaster at the local amusement park.

*The key bits of information presented in this table are:*

- First, the far left column presents the number of rides on the roller coaster, which is the quantity of the good consumed. It increases from 0 hours to 8 rides.
- Second, the middle column indicates the total utility, or the cumulatively amount of utility, obtained from the rides. For example, taking 3 roller coaster rides generates 27 utils of total utility. Most notably, total utility generally increases with the number of rides. However, it does reach a maximum for the 6 rides, then declines.
- Third, the far right column shows marginal utility, or the amount of additional utility derived from each extra ride. For example, because 2 rides generates a total utility of 20 utils and 3 rides generates a total utility of 27 utils, the amount of extra utility generated by taking the third ride on the roller coaster is 7 utils.
- Fourth, marginal utility in the far right column declines with additional rides on the roller coaster. This reflects the law of diminishing marginal utility, the key economic principle underlying utility analysis.

## THE LAW OF DIMINISHING MARGINAL UTILITY

The law of diminishing marginal utility states that marginal utility, or the extra utility obtained from consuming a good, decreases as the quantity consumed increases. In essence, each additional good consumed is less satisfying than the previous one. This law is particularly important for insight into market demand and the law of demand. If each additional unit of a good is less satisfying, then a buyer is willing to pay less. As such, the demand price declines. This inverse law of demand relation between demand price and quantity demanded is a direct implication of the law of diminishing marginal utility.

**Unresponsiveness Curves**

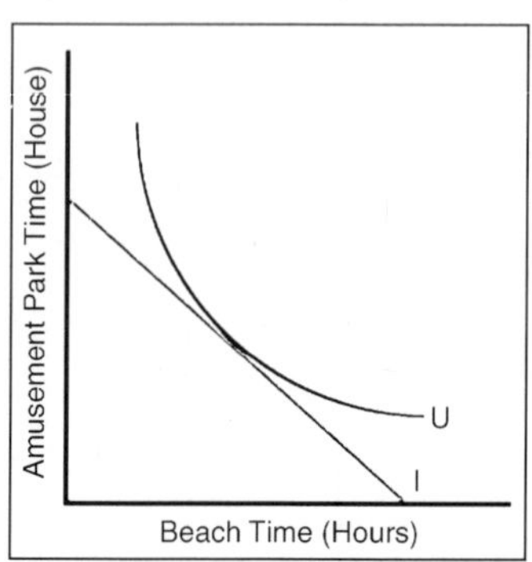


**Fig.** Unresponsiveness Curve Analysis.

A more advanced form of consumer demand theory involves the analysis of indifference curves. An indifference curve, such as the one labeled U in the exhibit to the right, presents all combinations of two goods that provide the same amount of utility. Hence a consumer is "indifferent" between consuming any combination of the two goods anywhere on the curve. Indifference curve analysis relies on a relative ranking of preferences between two goods rather than the absolute measurement of utility (utils) derived from the consumption of a particular good.

*Key bits of insight obtained from this diagram are*:

- First, the indifferent curve representing equal utility obtained from any consumption combination of the two goods (time at the beach and time at an amusement park) is represented by U.
- Second, the consumer is faced with an income or budget constraint,I, which shows the alternative combinations of the two goods that the buyer can purchase given a specific amount of income and existing prices.
- Third, the negative slope of the budget constraint reflects the tradeoff between the consumers ability to purchase the two goods. Purchasing more of one good necessarily means the consumer must purchase less of the other.
- Fourth, the negative slope and convex shape of the indifference curve reflects the tradeoff between the consumers willingness to purchase the two goods. In particular, the convex shape reflects the decreasing marginal rate of substitution between the two goods.

**Decreasing Marginal Rate of Replacement**

The decreasing marginal rate of substitution means that a consumer is willing to give up increasingly smaller quantities of one good in order to obtain more of another good. The reason is that as more of a good is consumed it becomes relatively less satisfying. A decreasing marginal rate of substitution generalises the law of diminishing marginal utility. However, rather than stating that the incremental satisfaction declines absolutely, it states that incremental satisfaction declines relative to that obtained from other goods.

Moreover, like the law of diminishing marginal utility, the decreasing marginal rate of substitution used in indifference curve analysis provides insight into market demand and the law of demand. If a good generates less relative satisfaction, then a buyer is wiling to pay a relatively lower price, which also explains the inverse law of demand relation between demand price and quantity demanded.

### Applying the Theory

Consumer demand theory is primarily directed towards an understanding of market demand and the law of demand. However, it provides a great deal of insight into all sorts of human behaviour and activities.

*A short list includes:*

- *Labour Supply*: Insight into the quantity of labour that workers are willing to supply at different wages can be obtained with consumer demand theory by analysing the tradeoff between labour and leisure activities.
- *Household Production*: In a similar manner, insight into the amount of work performed around the house, without explicit compensation, be analysed using consumer demand theory.
- *Crime*: The choice between committing a crime and not committing a crime can also be investigated using consumer demand theory, with the "price" paid for criminal activities based on the probability of being caught and punished.
- *Voting*: The amount of time and effort devoted to voting in elections has also been subjected to analysis using consumer demand theory.

A complete list of areas that have been or can be analysed and better understood using consumer demand theory is limited only by the choices people make and the types of activities they pursue. In essence, consumer demand theory can be applied to virtually any form of human behaviour that involves a tradeoff and a choice.

## CONSUMER BEHAVIOUR

The consumption set represents the set of all individually feasible alternatives or consumption plans and sometimes also called the choice set. An initial endowment represents the amount of various goods the consumer initially has and can consume or trade with other individuals. The preference relation specifies the consumer's tastes or satisfactions for the different objects of choice. The behaviour assumption expresses the guiding principle the consumer uses to make final choices and identifies the ultimate objects in choice. It is generally assumed that the consumer seeks to identify and select an available alternative that is most preferred in the light of his/her personal tasts/ interstes.

## DEFINING CONSUMER BEHAVIOUR

*Consumer Behaviour may be defined as "the interplay of forces that takes place during a consumption process, within a consumers' self and his environment:*

- This interaction takes place between three elements, *viz.*, knowledge, affect and behaviour;
- It continues through pre-purchase activity to the post purchase experience;
- It includes the stages of evaluating, acquiring, using and disposing of goods and services".

The "consumer" includes both personal consumers and business/industrial/ organisational consumers.Consumer behaviour explains the reasons and logic that underlie purchasing decisions and consumption patterns; it explains the processes through which buyers make decisions.The study includes within its purview, the interplay between cognition, affect and behaviour that goes on within a consumer during the consumption process: selecting, using and disposing off goods and services.

## NATURE OF CONSUMER BEHAVIOUR

- The subject deals with issues related to cognition, affect and behaviour in consumption behaviours, against the backdrop of individual and environmental determinants. The individual determinants pertain to an individual's internal self and include psychological components like personal motivation and involvement, perception, learning and memory, attitudes, self-concept and personality, and, decision making. The environmental determinants pertain to external influences surrounding an individual and include sociological, anthropological and economic components like the family, social groups, reference groups, social class, culture, sub-culture, cross-culture, and national and regional influences.
- The subject can be studied at micro or macro levels depending upon whether it is analysed at the individual level or at the group level.
- The subject is interdisciplinary. It has borrowed heavily from psychology (the study of the individual: individual determinants in buying behaviour), sociology (the study of groups: group dynamics in buying behaviour), social psychology (the study of how an individual operates in group/groups and its effects on buying behaviour), anthropology (the influence of society on the individual: cultural and cross-cultural issues in buying behaviour), and economics (income and purchasing power).

- Consumer behaviour is dynamic and interacting in nature. The three components of cognition, affect and behaviour of individuals alone or in groups keeps on changing; so does the environment. There is a continuous interplay or interaction between the three components themselves and with the environment. This impacts consumption pattern and behaviour and it keeps on evolving and it is highly dynamic.
- Consumer behaviour involves the process of exchange between the buyer and the seller, mutually beneficial for both.
- As a field of study it is descriptive and also analytical/ interpretive. It is descriptive as it explains consumer decision making and behaviour in the context of individual determinants and environmental influences. It is analytical/ interpretive, as against a backdrop of theories borrowed from psychology, sociology, social psychology, anthropology and economics, the study analyses consumption behaviour of individuals alone and in groups. It makes use of qualitative and quantitative tools and techniques for research and analysis, with the objective is to understand and predict consumption behaviour.
- It is a science as well as an art. It uses both, theories borrowed from social sciences to understand consumption behaviour, and quantitative and qualitative tools and techniques to predict consumer behaviour.

## RANGE OF CONSUMER BEHAVIOUR

The study of consumer behaviour deals with understanding consumption patterns and behaviour.

*It includes within its ambit the answers to the following:*

- 'What' the consumers buy: goods and services
- 'Why' they buy it: need and want
- 'When' do they buy it: time: day, week, month, year, occasions, etc.
- 'Where' they buy it: place
- 'How often they buy' it: time interval
- 'How often they use' it: frequency of use

The scope of consumer behaviour includes not only the actual buyer but also the various roles played by him/ different individuals.

## BASIC COMPONENTS

- *Decision Making (Cognitive and Affect):* This includes the stages of decision making: Need recognition, Information search, Evaluation of alternatives, Purchase activity, Post purchase behaviour.
- *Actual Purchase (Behaviour):* This includes the visible physical activity of buying of goods and/or service. It is the result of the interplay of many individual and environmental determinants which are invisible.

- *Individual Determinants and Environmental Influences:* The environmental factors affect the decision process indirectly, through way of affecting individual determinants.
- *Buying roles:* Actual Buyer vis a vis other users. There are five buying roles, *viz.*, Initiator, Influencer, Decider, User, Buyer. The initiator is the person who identifies that there exists a need or want; the influencer is the one who influences the purchase decision, the actual purchase activity and/or the use of the product or service; the decider is the one who decides whether to buy, what to buy, when to buy, from where to buy, and how to buy; the buyer is theone who makes the actual purchase; and, theuser is the person (s) who use the product or service. These five roles may be played by one person or by different persons. A person may assume one or more of these roles. This would depend on the product or service in question.
- *Buyers and Sellers:* They are the key elements in consumer behaviour. They have needs and wants and go through a complex buying process, so as to be able to satisfy the need through purchase of the good or service offering. They enter into an exchange process with the seller, which leaves both the parties (buyer and seller) better off than before. In fact the exchange process is value enhancing in nature, leading to satisfaction of both the parties.

## PROPERTIES OF CONSUMER DEMAND

As suggested, examine the comparative statics of consumer demand behaviour: how the consumer's demand changes as prices and income change.

### INCOME CHANGES AND CONSUMPTION CHOICE

It is of interest to look at how the consumer's demand changes as we hold prices fixed and allow income to vary; the resulting locus of utility-maximizing bundles is known as the income expansion path. From the income expansion path, we can derive a function that relates income to the demand for each commodity.

These functions are called Engel curves.

*There are two possibilities:*

1. As income increases, the optimal consumption of a good increases. Such a good is called a normal good.
2. As income increases, the optimal consumption of a good decreases. Such a good is called interior good.

For the two-good consumer maximization problem, when the income expansion path is upper-ward slopping, both goods are normal goods.

When the income expansion path could bend backwards, there is one and only one good that is inferior when the utility function is locally non-satiated; increase in income means the consumer actually wants to consume less of the good.

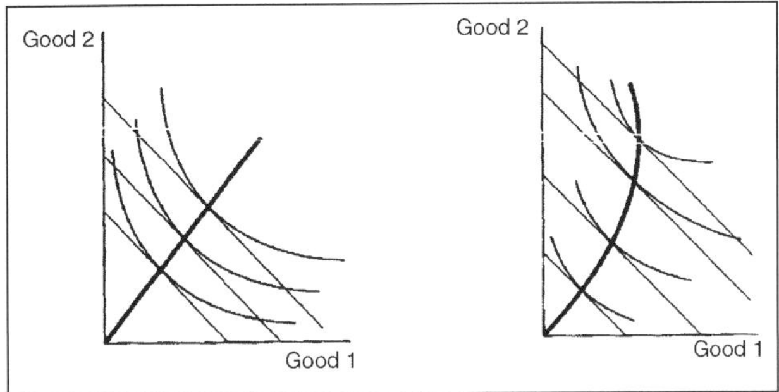


**Fig.** Income Expansion Paths with an Interior Good.

## PRICE CHANGES AND CONSUMPTION CHOICE

We can also hold income fixed and allow prices to vary. If we let $p_1$ vary and hold $p_2$ and $m$ fixed, the locus of tangencies will sweep out a curve known as the price offer curve.In the first case in Figure, we have the ordinary case where a lower price for good 1 leads to greater demand for the good so that the Law of Demand is satisfied; in the second case we have a situation where a decrease in the price of good 1 brings about a *decreased* demand for good 1. Such a good is called a Giffen good.

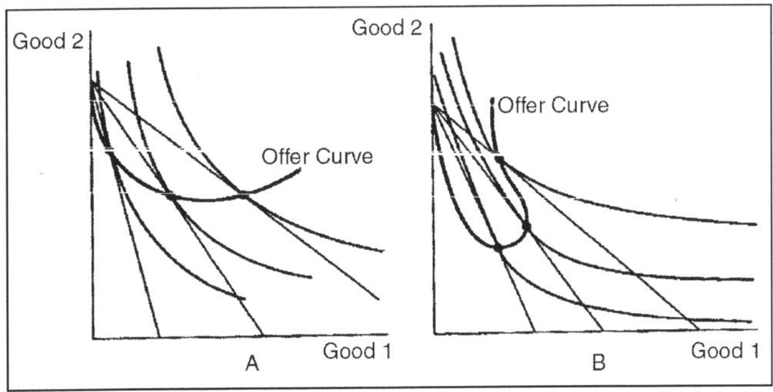


**Fig.** Offer Curves. In Panel A the Demand for good 1 Increases as the Price Decreases so it is an Ordinary Good. In Panel B the Demand for Good 1 Decreases as its Price Decreases, so it is a Giffen Good.

## INCOME-SUBSTITUTION EFFECT: THE SLUTSKY EQUATION

We see that a fall in the price of a good may have two sorts of effects: substitution effect—one commodity will become less expensive than another, and income effect—total "purchasing power" increases.

A fundamental result of the theory of the consumer, the Slutsky equation, relates these two effects. Even though the compensated demand function is not *directly* observable, the derivative of the Marshallian demand with respect to price and income. This relationship is known as the Slutsky equation.

$$\frac{\partial x_j(p,m)}{\partial p_i} = \frac{\partial h_j(p,v(p,m))}{\partial p_i} - \frac{\partial x_j(p,m)}{\partial m} x_i(p,m)$$

*Proof*: Let x* maximize utility at (p*,$m$) and let $u^* = u(\mathrm{x}^*)$. It is identically true that

$$h_j(\mathrm{p}^*, u^*) \equiv x_j(\mathrm{p}, e(\mathrm{p}, u^*)).$$

We can differentiate this with respect to $p_i$ and evaluate the derivative at p* to get

$$\frac{\partial h_j(p^*,u^*)}{\partial p_i} = \frac{\partial x_j(p^*,m^*)}{\partial p_i} + \frac{\partial x_j(p^*,m^*)}{\partial m}\frac{\partial e(p^*,u^*)}{\partial p_i}.$$

Note carefully the meaning of this expression. The left-hand side is how the compensated demand changes when $pi$ changes.

The right-hand side says that this change is equal to the change in demand holding expenditure fixed at $m^*$ *plus* the change in demand when income changes *times* how much income has to change to keep utility constant. But this last term, $\partial e(\mathrm{p}^*, u^*)/\partial p_i$, is just $x_i^*$; rearranging gives us,

$$\frac{\partial x_j(p^*,m^*)}{\partial p_i} = \frac{\partial h_j(p^*,u^*)}{\partial p_i} - \frac{\partial xj(p^*,m^*)}{\partial m} x_i^*$$

which is the Slutsky equation.There are other ways to derive Slutsky's equations that can be found in Varian.

The Slutsky equation decomposes the demand change induced by a price change $\Delta p_i$ into two separate effects: the substitution effect and the income effect:

$$\Delta x_j \approx \frac{\partial x_j(p,m)}{\partial p_i}\Delta p_i = \frac{\partial h_j(p,u)}{\partial p_i}\Delta p_i - \frac{\partial x_j(p,m)}{\partial m} x_i^* \Delta p_i$$

The restrictions all about the Hicksian demand functions are not directly observable. However, as indicated by the Slutsky equation, we can express the derivatives of h with respect to p as derivatives of x with respect to p and $m$, and these are observable. Also, Slutsky's equation and the negative sime-definite matrix on Hicksian demand functions given in Proposition give us the following result on the Marshallian demand functions:

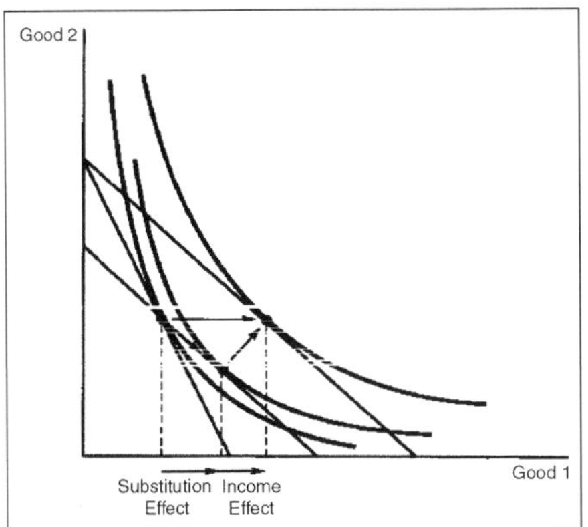


**Fig.** The Hicks Decomposition of a Demand Change into Two Effects: The Substitution Effect and the Income Effect.

*Proposition: The substitution matrix*

$$\left(\frac{\partial x_j(p,m)}{\partial p_i}+\frac{\partial x_j(p,u)}{\partial m}x_i\right)$$

is a symmetric, negative semi-definite matrix. *This is a rather Non-intuitive result*: a particular combination of price and income derivatives has to result in a negative semidefinite matrix.

*Example*: Let us check the Slutsky equation in the Cobb-Douglas case. In this case we have

$$\upsilon(p_1,p_2,m)=mp_1^{-\alpha}p_2^{\alpha-1}$$
$$e(p_1,p_2,u)=up_1^{\alpha}p_2^{1-\alpha}$$

$$x_1(p_1,p_2,m)=\frac{\alpha m}{p_1}$$
$$h_1(p_1,p_2,u)=\alpha p_1^{a-1}p_2^{1-\alpha}u.$$

Thus

$$\frac{\partial x_1(p,m)}{\partial p_1}=-\frac{\alpha m}{p_1^2}$$

$$\frac{\partial x_1(p,m)}{\partial m}=-\frac{\alpha}{p_1}$$

$$\frac{\partial h_1(p,u)}{\partial p_1}=\alpha(\alpha-1)p_1^{\alpha-2}p_2^{1-\alpha}u$$

$$\frac{\partial h_1(p, v(p,m))}{\partial p_1} = \alpha(\alpha-1)p_1^{\alpha-2}p_2^{1-\alpha}mp_1^{-\alpha}p_2^{\alpha-1}$$
$$= \alpha(\alpha-1)p_1^{-2}m.$$

Now plug into the Slutsky equation to find

$$\frac{\partial h_1}{\partial p_1} - \frac{\partial x_1}{\partial m}x_1 = \frac{\alpha(\alpha-1)m}{p_1^2} - \frac{\alpha}{p_1}\frac{\alpha m}{p_1}$$
$$= \frac{\left[\alpha(\alpha-1)-\alpha^2\right]m}{p_1^2}$$
$$= \frac{-\alpha m}{p_1^2} = \frac{\partial x_1}{\partial p_1}.$$

## CONTINUITY AND DIFFERENTIABILITY OF DEMAND FUNCTIONS

Up until now we have assumed that the demand functions are nicely behaved; that is, that they are continuous and even differentiable functions. Are these assumptions justifiable?

*Proposition*: *Suppose* $\succeq$ *is continuous and weakly convex, and* $(p,m) > 0$. *Then,* $x(p,m)$ *is a upper hemi-continuous convex-valued* correspondence. Furthermore, if the weak convexity is replaced by the strict convexity, $x(p,m)$ *is a continuous single-valued function.*

*Proof*: First note that, since $(p,m) > 0$, one can show that the budget constrained set $B(p,m)$ is a continuous correspondence with non-empty and compact values and $\succeq_i$ is continuous. Then, by the Maximum Theorem, we know the demand correspondence $x(p,m)$ is upper hemi-continuous. We now show $x(p,m)$ is convex. Suppose $x$ and $x'$ are two optimal consumption bundles. Let $x_t = t_x + (1-t)x'$ for $t \in [0; 1]$. Then, $x_t$ also satisfied the budget constraint, and by weak convexity of $\succeq$, we have $x_t = t_x + (1-t)x' \succeq x$. Because $x$ is an optimal consumption bundle, we must have $x_t \sim x$ and thus $x_t$ is also an optimal consumption bundle.

Now, when $\succ$ is strictly convex, $x(p,m)$ is then single-valued by proposition, and thus it is a continuous function since a upper hemi-continuous correspondence is a continuous function when it is single-valued.

A demand correspondence may not be continuous for non-convex preference ordering. Note that, in the case depicted in Figure, a small change in the price brings about a large change in the demanded bundles: the demand correspondence is discontinuous.

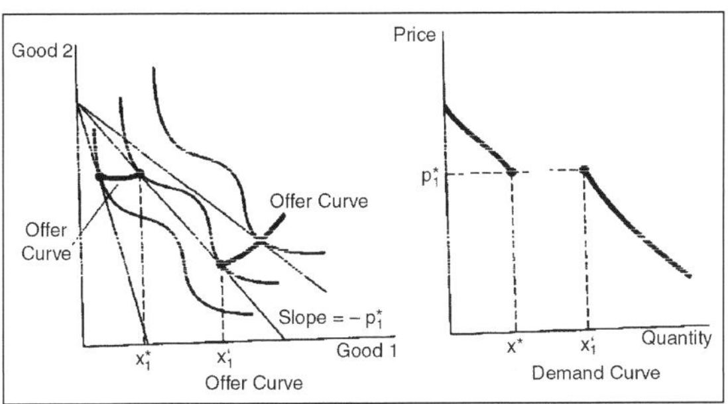


**Fig.** Discontinuous Demand. Demand is Discontinuous Due to Non-convex Preferences

Sometimes, we need to consider the slopes of demand curves and hence we would like a demand function is differentiable. What conditions can guarantee the differentiability? We give the following proposition without proof.

*Proposition: Suppose x > 0 solves the consumer's utility maximization problem at (p,m) > 0. If*

- *u is twice continuously differentiable on* $\mathbb{R}^L_{++}$,
- $\frac{\partial u(x)}{\partial x_l} > 0$ *for some* $l = 1,..., L$,
- The bordered Hessian of u has Non-zero determinant at x, *then x(p;m) is differentiable at (p;m).*

## INVERSE DEMAND FUNCTIONS

In many applications it is of interest to express demand behaviour by describing prices as a function of quantities. That is, given some vector of goods x, we would like to find a vector of prices p and an income *m* at which x would be the demanded bundle. Since demand functions are homogeneous of degree zero, we can fix income at some given level, and simply determine prices relative to this income level. The most convenient choice is to fix $m = 1$. In this case the first-order conditions for the utility maximization problem are simply,

$$\frac{\partial u(x)}{\partial x_i} - \lambda p_i = 0 \quad for\, i,....,k \quad \sum_{i=1}^{k} p_i x_i = 1.$$

We want to eliminate ¸ from this set of equations. To do so, multiply each of the first set of equalities by *xi* and sum them over the number of goods to get,

$$\sum_{i=1}^{k} \frac{\partial u(x)}{\partial x_i} x_i = \lambda \sum_{i=1}^{k} p_i x_i = \lambda.$$

Substitute the value of λ back into the first expression to find p as function of x:

$$p_i(x) = \frac{\dfrac{\partial u(x)}{\partial x_i}}{\sum_{i=1}^{k} \dfrac{\partial u(x)}{\partial x_i} x_j}.$$

Given any vector of demands x, we can use this expression to find the price vector p(x) which will satisfy the necessary conditions for maximization. If the utility function is quasi-concave so that these necessary conditions are indeed sufficient for maximization, then this will give us the inverse demand relationship.What happens if the utility function is not everywhere quasi-concave? Then there may be some bundles of goods that will not be demanded at any price; any bundle on a non-convex part of an indifference curve will be such a bundle.There is a dual version of the formula for inverse demands that can be obtained from the duality between direct utility function and indirect utility function we discussed earlier. The argument given there shows that the demanded bundle x must minimize indirect utility over all prices that satisfy the budget constraint. Thus x must satisfy the first-order conditions,

$$\frac{\partial \upsilon(p)}{\partial p_l} - \mu x_l = 0 \ for\ l = 1,....,L$$

$$\sum_{i=1}^{L} p_l x_l = 1.$$

Now multiply each of the first equations by $p_l$ and sum them to find that,

$$\mu = \sum_{l=1}^{L} \frac{\partial \upsilon(p)}{\partial p_l} p_l$$

Substituting this back into the first-order conditions, we have an expression for the demanded bundle as a function of the normalized indirect utility function:

$$x_i(p) = \frac{\dfrac{\partial \upsilon(p)}{\partial p_i}}{\sum_{j=1}^{k} \dfrac{\partial \upsilon(p)}{\partial p_j} p_j}.$$

Note the nice duality: the expression for the direct demand function, and the expression for the inverse demand function have the same form. This expression can also be derived from the definition of the normalized indirect utility function and Roy's identity.

## CONSUMER EQUILIBRIUM

The condition that exists when the last dollar spent on one good provides the same marginal utility as the last dollar spent on every other good. In consumer equilibrium, income is allocated between the purchase of different goods in such a way that the level of utility cannot be increased, that is, utility maximization has been achieved.Consumer equilibrium exists when a consumer selects or buys the combination of goods that maximizes utility.

This is achieved by equating the marginal utility-price ratio for each good consumed or by equating the ratio of prices and the ratio of marginal utilities. In other words, buyers are willing to pay relatively higher prices for goods that generate relatively more marginal utility.

**Consumption Options**

**Table. Pretzels and Sundaes.**

| Pretzels | Total | Marginal Utility (util) | Sundaes Utility (util) | Total Utility (util) | Marginal Utility (util) |
|---|---|---|---|---|---|
| 0 | 0 | | 0 | 0 | |
| 1 | 12 | 12 | 1 | 20 | 20 |
| 2 | 22 | 10 | 2 | 36 | 16 |
| 3 | 30 | 8 | 3 | 48 | 12 |
| 4 | 36 | 6 | 4 | 56 | 8 |
| 5 | 40 | 4 | 5 | 60 | 4 |
| 6 | 42 | 2 | 6 | 56 | -4 |
| 7 | 40 | -2 | 7 | 48 | -8 |

This table at the right presents utility information for Duncan Thurly, a regular human being consumer, who is pondering the purchase of two goods, Max Mulroney's Pretzel-on-a-Stick and Hot Momma Fudge Bananarama Ice Cream Sundae.The left half of the table summarises the utility numbers for Duncan's pretzel consumption.

As Duncan consumes up to 6 pretzels, his total utility rises to a peak of 42 utils before declining for the seventh. His marginal utility for pretzel consumption begins at 12 utils for the first pretzel, then declines (according to the law of diminishing marginal utility) until reaching -2 utils for the seventh one.

The utility story for Duncan's hot fudge sundae consumption in the right half of the table follows a similar pattern, albeit with different numbers. Duncan's total utility reaches a maximum of 60 utils for consuming 5 hot fudge sundaes before declining for the sixth and seventh sundaes. His marginal utility begins at 20 utils for the first hot fudge sundae then declines to -8 utils for the seventh (also following the law of diminishing marginal utility). Clearly overindulgence is not a good thing for Duncan.Duncan's challenge is to select the most satisfying, utility maximizing, combination of pretzels and hot fudge sundaes.

## No Limits

**Pretzels and Sundaes.**

| Pretzels | Total Utility (util) | Marginal Utility (util) | Sundaes | Total Utility (util) | Marginal Utility (util) |
|---|---|---|---|---|---|
| 0 | 0 | | 0 | 0 | |
| 1 | 12 | 12 | 1 | 20 | 20 |
| 2 | 22 | 10 | 2 | 36 | 16 |
| 3 | 30 | 8 | 3 | 48 | 12 |
| 4 | 36 | 6 | 4 | 56 | 8 |
| 5 | 40 | 4 | 5 | 60 | 4 |
| 6 | 42 | 2 | 6 | 56 | -4 |
| 7 | 40 | -2 | 7 | 48 | -8 |

In a world of unlimited income and without other constraints, Duncan maximizes utility by consuming 5 Hot Momma Fudge Bananarama Ice Cream Sundaes, giving him 60 utils of sundae satisfaction, and 6 Max Mulroney's Pretzels-on-a-Stick, giving him 42 utils of pretzel enjoyment. His grand satisfaction total is then 102 utils. Click the [Absolute Max] button to highlight this option.This result illustrates a simple, and to be quite honest, largely uninteresting consumer equilibrium. Duncan has simply consumed until he can consume no more. He has satiated his want (or need) for pretzels and hot fudge sundaes.

## Income and Prices

A more interesting analysis of consumer equilibrium occurs by recognising that people, including Duncan Thurly, do not live in a world of unlimited income. They face constrained utility maximization. For example, suppose Duncan has only $20 of income to spend on sundaes and pretzels. In this case, 5 sundaes at $4 each and 6 pretzels at $2 a piece requires $32 of income, which exceeds Duncan's $20 budget.

*Consider a couple of alternative ways Duncan could spend his $20 on sundaes and pretzels:*

- *Nothing But Sundaes*: Duncan could spend his entire $20 on sundaes. In this case, he could purchase 5 Hot Momma Fudge Bananarama Ice Cream Sundaes and generate 60 utils of total satisfaction. Unfortunately, no income remains to purchase any of Max Mulroney's tasty Pretzels-on-a-Stick. Duncan's utility total is maxed out at 60 utils. Click the [All Sundaes] button to highlight this option.
- *Mainly Pretzels*: Alternatively, Duncan could "go nuts" buying pretzels. Of course, once he purchases 6 of Max Mulroney's Pretzels-on-Sticks, reaching his maximum pretzel-based utility of 42 utils, he has no reason to buy the seventh. The seventh pretzel actually reduces his utility. However, these 6 pretzels use up only

$12 of Duncan's $20 budget. What might Duncan do with the remaining $8? How about buying 2 sundaes, which generates 36 utils? His total utility for this option is 78 utils--42 utils from 6 pretzels and 36 utils from 2 sundaes. Click the [Mostly Pretzels] button to highlight this option.

- *One More Sundae:* The second alternative certainly generates more total utility than the first, but can Duncan do even better? Suppose Duncan decides to buy one more sundae, bringing his sundae total to 3. However, to do so, he needs an extra $4. This can only come from cutting back on pretzel purchases. Duncan would have to buy two fewer pretzels (saving $2 each), bringing his new pretzel quantity to 4.

  On the sundae side of utility, Duncan obtains 48 utils of satisfaction from 3 sundaes. On the pretzel side, he has 36 utils from 4 pretzels. His grand utility total of 84 utils exceeds either of the two previous alternatives.
- Yet Another Sundae?: But can Duncan push his utility even higher? If a third sundae boosts total utility, maybe a fourth one does, too. Once again, though, an extra sundae means Duncan must give up two pretzels. Pursuing this option gives Duncan 78 utils of satisfaction--56 utils from 4 sundaes and 22 utils from 2 pretzels--which is clearly below the 84 utils from 3 sundaes and 4 pretzels. Click the [Too Many Sundaes] button to highlight this option.

As a matter of fact, Duncan's utility is maximized with 3 sundaes and 4 pretzels. He cannot buy any other combination of sundaes and pretzels with his $20 and receive a higher level of total utility.

**The Regulation of Consumer Equilibrium**

This combination of sundaes and pretzels satisfies what is termed the rule of consumer equilibrium. This rule states that utility is maximized by equating the marginal utility-price ratios for both goods.

- *The Sundae Ratio*: With a price of $4 each, the marginal utility of the third sundae (12 utils) means that the last dollar Duncan spends on sundaes generates 3 utils of satisfaction.
- *The Pretzel Ratio*: Moreover with a purchase price of $2, the marginal utility of the fourth pretzel (6 utils) means that the last dollar Duncan spends on pretzels also generates 3 utils of satisfaction.

The marginal utility-price ratio for both goods is 3 utils per dollar.

A quick comparison of the ratios of prices and marginal utilities also indicates equality. The price of hot fudge sundaes ($4) is twice the price of pretzels ($2). The marginal utility of hot fudge sundaes (12 utils) is also twice the price of pretzels (6 utils).

# CONSUMER BEHAVIOUR IN UNCERTAIN SITUATIONS

## ALTERNATIVE BASED ON EXPECTED VALUE

In some cases, buyers must make a purchase decision without knowing exactly what they're getting for their money. Deciding whether or not to buy a good without knowing exactly what the good is worth involves some degree of risk, as there is variation in the possible outcome.

To make these decisions, buyers have to evaluate, to their best ability, how much the goods are really worth, and then decide how much they are willing to pay for the goods. For example, if Jevan is interested in buying stock in a new startup, he can't be sure what will happen to the value of his stock as time passes.

The company could be a huge success, making his stock very valuable, it could be a moderate success, making his stock somewhat valuable, or it could be a failure, making his stock worthless.

Before he decides to buy any stock, Jevan has to decide what is the most likely outcome, and what his stock is going to be worth: that is, based on the probability of different outcomes, Jevan has to assign the stock an expected value to compare against the present price.

In order for Jevan to be able to calculate this expected value, he needs to account for all possible outcomes, so that the total probability will be equal to 1: let's assume that huge success, moderate success, and failure are the only possible outcomes, so the probability of at least one of them occurring is equal to 1.If Jevan thinks that there is a 1 in 8 chance that the startup will be a wild success, a 1 in 2 chance that it will be a moderate success, and a 3 in 8 chance that it will fail, then he has accounted for all possible outcomes, since the combined probabilities are equal to 1: (0.125 + 0.5 + 0.375) = 1

Next Jevan has to assign values to each outcome. In the event of huge success, Jevan thinks that each share of stock will be worth $20. In the event of moderate success, each share will be worth $5. In the event of failure, each share is worth $0. Combining all of Jevan's assumptions gives us the following chart of his expectations:

| Huge Success | Mod.Success | Failure |
|---|---|---|
| Probability = 1/8 | Probability = 1/2 | Probability = 3/8 |
| Stock Price = $20/Share | Stock Price = $5/Share | Stock Price = $0/Share |

**Fig.** Jevan's Expectations for the Startup Stock's Performance.

*To find out the expected value (EV) of the stock, multiply the probability of each event by the value of each event, and sum the results:*

$$EV = (0.125)(20) + (0.5)(5) + (0.375)(0)$$

$$EV = \$5 \text{ a share}$$

We find that Jevan expects the stock to be worth about $5, based on his assumptions about company performance. What this means is that Jevan will not be willing to pay more than $5 a share for this stock, since he believes it to be worth $5 a share. He will probably be willing to buy stock if the price is lower than $5, depending on how much he enjoys taking risks.

How would we explain it if the price is lower than $5, but Jevan decides not to buy any stock? We know that he believes the stock to be worth $5, so we would expect him to buy stock if it is priced lower than $5 a share. This can be explained by Jevan's openness to taking risks. Because the future price of the stock is uncertain, and Jevan's estimate is only an estimate, if Jevan doesn't like taking risks, that is, if he is risk-averse, then he may choose not to buy any stock, even if the expected returns are positive; he is not willing to invest in a "good" investment because he is still afraid of the possibility that he might lose money. Someone who is risk-averse will choose investments with little variation in possible outcomes, and a high degree of predictability.

On the other hand, if the price of the stock is over $5, and Jevan still decides he wants to buy stock, even though he believes it to be worth only $5 a share, then it may mean that he is risk-loving; he is willing to enter into an expected loss on the off chance that the company will make it big. This would be an extreme case; not all risk lovers will invest in stocks with negative expected values. More commonly, risk lovers will make investments that have positive expected values, but have very large variation in possible outcomes.

If Jevan is risk-neutral, then he will not buy stock with negative expected value, he will buy stock with positive expected value, and stock with 0 expected value makes no difference to him at all. Even if the risk is very high, if the expected returns are positive, he will make the purchase. Even if the risk is very low, if the expected returns are negative, he will refuse to buy stock.

This type of decision-making based on probable outcomes is used in many different situations: buyers decide how much they are willing to pay for a used car based on the different probabilities that it is in mint condition, that it needs minor repairs, or that it is a useless piece of junk. Students decide how much to study based on their expected performance after different amounts of studying.

Art lovers base their decisions on the probabilities that the pieces they are looking at are genuine or forged. In any case where the exact value of a good is unclear, buyers must make their decisions based on probable outcomes and possible worth. After making an estimate of expected value and assessing the risk involved, buyers can then attempt to maximize their utility based on their individual preferences for goods.Risk usually varies inversely with expected returns. That is, a high risk investment will often yield a much higher potential payoff than a low risk investment. This difference in value can be seen as a "reward" for buyers' willingness to take a higher risk.

The "penalty" for taking a higher risk is the possibility of losing a lot of money if the investment fails. We can see this discrepancy in the high yields (and losses) in the stock market, which is relatively high risk, the moderate yields of mutual funds, which are relatively moderate risk, and the low yields of government bonds, which are relatively low risk. When a payoff is guaranteed, as with low risk investments, the payoff is usually small, and when a payoff is uncertain, as with high risk investments, the payoff is usually higher.

## HOUSEHOLD PREFERENCES IN CONSUMER BEHAVIOUR

Consider a household choosing consumer goods $x = (x_1, \ldots, xn) \in X$, where X is the feasible set for x, $X \subset \Re_n$. (Often, we will assume that $X = \Re_n$). The household has preferences represented by a utility function u(*x*). The utility function represents consumer preferences in the sense that, for any $x' \in X$ that is weakly (strongly) preferred to $x \in X$, we have $u(x') \geq (>)\ u(x)$.

The utility function u(x) is defined up to a monotonic increasing transformation. This means that for any strictly increasing function f(u), the functions u(x) and v(x) = f(u(x)) represent the same consumer preferences. To see that, consider any situation where $x' \in X$ is weakly (strongly) preferred to $x \in X$. Then, u(x') ³ (>) u(x) is equivalent to v(x') = f(u(x')) ³ (>) v(x) = f(u(x)), for any strictly increasing function f(u). Note that, under differentiability, the monotonic increasing transformation f(u) preserves the sign of the first derivative of v(x), but not of the second derivative of v(x). This means that the concept of "diminishing marginal utility" is not meaningful in the analysis of consumer behaviour.

Often, we will impose some structure on consumer preferences.

*This includes the following assumptions:*

- *Continuity*: Consumer preferences are continuous if for all $x \in X$, the sets $\{x': u(x') \geq u(x)\}$ and $\{x': u(x') \leq u(x)\}$ are closed.
  *Note*: Continuity guarantees the existence of indifference curves defined as the set of consumption goods yielding utility level U: $\{x: u(x) = U\}$.
- *Non-satiation*: Consumer preferences are non-satiated if for all $x \in X$, there is an $x' \in X$ such that $u(x') > u(x)$.
- *Local Non-satiation:* Consumer preferences are locally non-satiated if for any $x \in X$ and any $\varepsilon > 0$, there is an $x' \in X$ such that $||x - x'|| < \varepsilon$ and $u(x') > u(x)$.
  *Note*: Local non-satiation means that, for any point x, there always exists a nearby point that is strictly preferred to x.

- *Monotonicity* ("more is preferred to less"): With $X = \Re^n_+$, consumer preferences exhibit weak (strong) monotonicity if $x' \geq x$ and $x' \neq x$ implies that $u(x') \geq (>) u(x)$.
- *Convexity*: Consumer preferences are convex if the set $\{x: u(x) \geq U, x \in X\}$ is convex for every U.

Alternatively, when X is convex, the function u(x) is quasi-concave if and only if

$$u(q\ x + (1\text{-}q)\ x')\ ^3 \min\{u(x), u(x')\},$$

for all x and $x' \in X$, and all $\theta \in [0, 1]$.

**Marshallian Demands**

Consider a household facing market prices $p = (p1, \ldots, pn) \in \Re^n_{++}$ for consumer goods x, where $pi > 0$ denotes the market price of $x_i$, $i = 1, \ldots, n$. Let $r > 0$ denote household income. Then, the household face the budget constraint:

$$p.\ x \leq r,$$

or

$$\sum_{i=1}^{n} pi\, x_i \leq r$$

Assume that economic rationality means that the household makes consumption decisions so as to maximize its utility u(x) subject to a budget constraint. This is represented by the following utility maximization problem,

$$V(p, r) = \max_x \{u(x): p.\ x \leq r, x \in X\},$$

where,

$$V(p, r) = u(x^*(p, r))$$

is the indirect utility function, and

$$x^*(p, r) \in \text{argmaxx}\ \{u(x): p.\ x \leq r, x \in X\},$$

are Marshallian demands representing the utility-maximizing decision rules for household consumption under prices p and household income r.

Under local non-satiation, the budget constraint is necessary binding at the optimum $x^*(p, r)$, with $p.\ x^*(p, r) = r$. This means that, under local non-satiation, the utility maximization problem (1) can be alternatively written as,

$$V(p, r) = \text{Max}_x \{u(x): p.\ x = r, x \in X\}.$$

- *First-order Conditions:* Under local non-satiation, expression (2) is a standard constrained maximization problem. It can be analysed using the Lagrangean approach. Define the associated Lagrangean.

$$L(x, \lambda, p, r) = u(x) + \lambda\ [r - p.\ x],$$

where $\lambda \geq 0$ is a Lagrange multiplier corresponding to the budget constraint: $r - p.\ x = 0$. If the utility function u(x) is differentiable, the first-order necessary conditions (FOC) for an interior solution x* are,

$$\partial L/\partial x \equiv \partial u(x)/\partial x - \lambda\ p = 0,$$

$$\partial L/\partial \lambda \equiv r - p.\ x = 0.$$

This is a system of (n+1) equations in (n+1) unknowns: (x, $\lambda$). Denote the solution of this system of equations by $x^*(p, r)$ and $\lambda^*(p, r)$.

- *Second-order conditions*: If the utility function is twice continuously differentiable, the second order necessary conditions (SOC) evaluated at the optimum ($x^*(p, r)$, $\lambda^*(p, r)$) are,

$$v^T [\partial^2 u/\partial x^2]\, v \leq 0 \text{ for all } v \in \Re^n \text{ satisfying } p^T.v = 0,$$

where vectors are written as column vectors and "T" denotes the transpose. The second order necessary conditions in (4) state that the Hessian of the utility function $[\partial^2 u/\partial x^2]$ is negative semi-definite "subject to constraints."

Assume that the utility function is locally non-satiated in $x_i$, with $\partial u/\partial x_i >$ 0. Define the marginal rate of substitution between $x_i$ and $x_j$ by,

$$MRS_{ij} = (\partial u/\partial x_j)/(\partial u/\partial x_i),$$

for $i \neq j$. The $MRS_{ij}$ can be interpreted as the negative of the slope of the indifference curve $x_i = s_i(x_j, U.)$ obtained from solving the equation $u(x_i, x_j.) =$ U for $x_i$, where U is some reference utility level. Indeed, applying the implicit function theorem to $u(x_i, x_j.) = U$ yields $\partial s_i/\partial x_j = -(\partial_u/\partial x_j)/(\partial u/\partial x_i) = -MRS_{ij}$. Figure shows the indifference curve $s_i(x_j, U.)$ giving the set of points x that keep the household at a given utility level U.

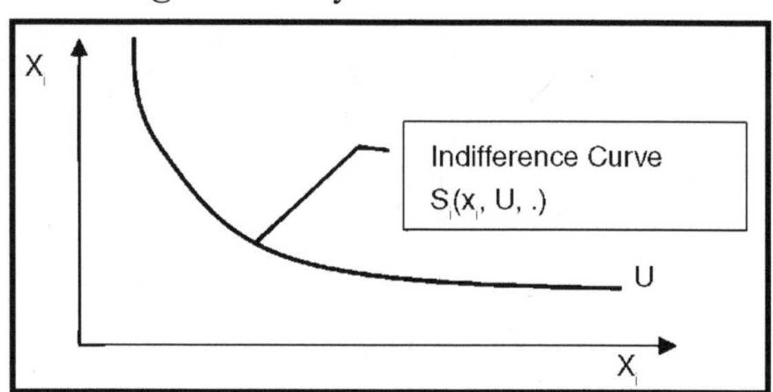


Given p > 0 and $\partial u/\partial x_i > 0$ (under local non-satiation with respect to $x_i$), equation implies that,

$$(\partial u/\partial x_j)/(\partial u/\partial x_i) = p_j/p_i, \text{ for } j \neq i.$$

This states that necessary conditions for an interior solution to the maximization problem are that the marginal rates of substitution, $MRS_{ij} = (\partial u/\partial xj)/(\partial u/\partial x_i)$, must equal the price ratio $p_j/p_i$, for all $j \neq i$.

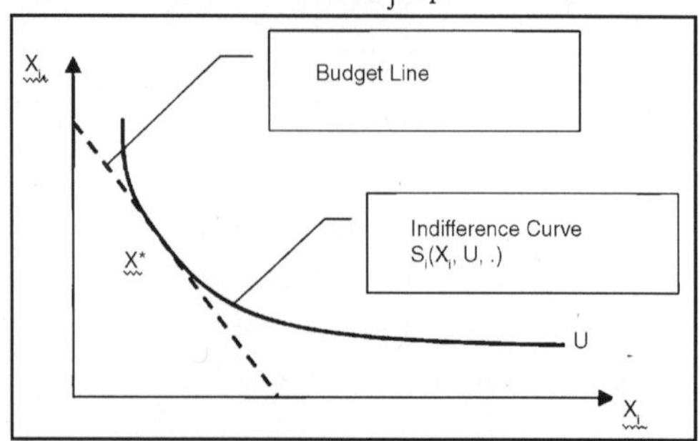

**Consumption Behaviour: Properties of the Marshallian Demands**

The analysis just presented can identify the utility maximizing demand x*(p, r). Here, we want to explore in more detail consumption behaviour and the properties of the decision rules x*(p, r). For convenience, we focus on the case where the decision rules x*(p, r) are differentiable functions.

**Comparative Statics**

Using a "primal approach", we can investigate the properties of the Marshallian demand functions x*(p, r) by applying the implicit function theorem.

*Given the Lagrangean:*

$$L = u(x) + \lambda\ [r - p.\ x],$$

denote the associated bordered Hessian by,

$$H = \partial^2 L/\partial(x, \lambda)^2 = \begin{bmatrix} \partial^2 u / \partial x^2 & -p \\ -p^T & 0 \end{bmatrix},$$

evaluated at (x*, λ*). Applying the implicit function theorem requires the non-singularity of the matrix H, where det(H) ≠ 0. Then, letting α = (p, r), the implicit function theorem applied to gives the comparative static results,

$$\begin{bmatrix} \partial x^* / \partial \alpha \\ \partial \lambda^* / \partial \alpha \end{bmatrix} = -H^{-1} \begin{bmatrix} \partial L / \partial x \partial \alpha \\ \partial L / \partial \lambda \partial \alpha \end{bmatrix},$$

or,

$$\begin{bmatrix} \partial x^* / \partial p & \partial x^* / \partial r \\ \partial \lambda^* / \partial p & \partial \lambda^* / \partial r \end{bmatrix} = -H^{-1} \begin{bmatrix} -\lambda I_n & 0 \\ -x^T & 1 \end{bmatrix}.$$

The implications of economic rationality for the properties of the (differentiable) Marshallian demand functions x*(p, r).

**Computation Restrictions**

That the under local non-satiation, the budget constraint is always binding. This implies that the following relationship always holds,

$$p.\ x^*(p, r) = r,$$

or,

$$\sum_{j=1}^{n} P_j X_j{}^*(p, r) = r.$$

*Differentiating this identity with respect to p gives:*

$$x^* + p.\ (\partial x^*/\partial p) = 0,$$

or,

$$x_i^* + \sum_{j=1}^{n} \left[ P_j \left( \partial x_j^* / \partial p_i \right) \right] = 0, \ i = 1, \ldots, n.$$

And differentiating this identity with respect to r gives,

$$p. (\partial x^* / \partial r) = 1,$$

or,

$$\sum_{j=1}^{n} \left[ P_j \left( \partial x_j^* / \partial r \right) \right] = 1.$$

The "adding-up" or "aggregation" restrictions, which must be satisfied if the budget constraint is always binding. Sometimes called the "Cournot aggregation restriction", is called the "Engel aggregation restriction."

*The Cournot aggregation restriction can alternatively be expressed in terms of demand elasticities:*

$$(p_i \, x_i^*/r) + \sum_{j=1}^{n} [(p_j \, x_j^*/r)(\partial \ln(x_j^*)/\partial \ln(p_i))] = 0, \ i = 1, \ldots, n,$$

where $p_i \, x_i^*/r$ is the budget share for the i-th commodity, and $\partial \ln(x_j^*)/\partial \ln(p_i) = (\partial x_j^*/\partial p_i)(p_i/x_j^*)$ is the Marshallian price elasticity of $x_j^*$ with respect to $p_i$. Similarly, the Engel aggregation restriction can be alternatively expressed as,

$$\sum_{j=1}^{n} [(p_j \, x_j^*/r) \, (\partial \ln(x_j^*)/\partial \ln(r))] = 1,$$

where $\partial \ln(x_j^*)/\partial \ln(r) = (\partial x_j^*/\partial r)(r/x_j^*)$ is the income elasticity for the j-th commodity. Then, the Engel adding-up restriction states that the weighted sum of the income elasticities across all commodities must be equal to 1, with budget shares as weights.

**Homogeneity Possessions**

Consider the case where there is proportional change in all prices p and income r. Then, the budget constraint becomes $(k \, p). \, x \leq k \, r$ for some $k > 0$, which is equivalent to $p. \, x \leq r$.

This makes it clear that a proportional change in (p, r) has no effect on the budget constraint. But (p, r) show up only in the budget constraint. It follows that a proportional change in (p, r) would have no effect on consumption behaviour, *i.e.*, that,

$$x^*(p, r) = x^*(k \, p, k \, r) \text{ for all } k > 0.$$

This implies that the Marshallian demand functions $x^*(p, r)$ are homogeneous of degree zero in (p, r). Intuitively, it means that only changes in relative prices and income affect Marshallian consumption behaviour.

*If $x^*(p, r)$ is continuously differentiable, from Euler equation, this generates the following homogeneity restrictions:*

$$(\partial x^*/\partial r) \, r + (\partial x^*/\partial p) \, p = 0,$$

or,

$$(\partial x_i^*/\partial r)\ r + \sum_{j=1}^{n} [(\partial x_i^*/\partial p_j)\ p_j] = 0,\ i = 1, \ldots, n,$$

or,

$$\partial \ln(x_i^*)/\partial \ln(r) + \sum_{j=1}^{n} \partial \ln(x_i^*)/\partial \ln(p_j) = 0,\ i = 1, \ldots, n,$$

where $\partial \ln(x_i^*)/\partial \ln(r)$ is the income elasticity for the i-th commodity, and $\partial \ln(x_i^*)/\partial \ln(p_j)$ is the price elasticity of the i-th Marshallian demand with respect to $p_j$. Then, there are n homogeneity restrictions stating that, for each Marshallian demand function, the sum of the income and (own and cross) price elasticities must be equal to 0.

*Note:*

With $r > 0$, the homogeneity of degree zero of $x^*(p, r)$ can be imposed by writing $x^*(p, r)$ as $x^*(p/r)$. Indeed, this guarantees that a proportional change in (p, r) would have no effect on Marshallian demands. This suggests a simple way to impose the homogeneity restrictions on the specification of Marshallian demands: use normalised prices (p/r), where all prices are deflated by consumer income r.

## Equilibrium Properties

### *The Slutsky Matrix*

Assume that u(x) is quasi-concave, locally non-satiated, twice continuously differentiable and satisfies $\det(H) \neq 0$. Then, the $(n \times n)$ matrix,

$$S \equiv [\partial x^*/\partial p + (\partial x^*/\partial r)\ (x^*)^T]$$

is symmetric, negative semi-definite.

Proof: The second order necessary conditions (SOC) are,

$$v^T\ [\partial^2 u/\partial x^2]\ v \leq 0 \text{ for all } v \in \Re^n \text{ satisfying } p^T\ v = 0.$$

Given $H = \begin{bmatrix} \partial^2 u / \partial x^2 & -p \\ -p^T & 0 \end{bmatrix}$, the SOC can be alternatively written as

$$v_1^T\ H\ v_1 \leq 0, \text{ for all } v_1 = (v, v_0) \in \Re^{n+1} \text{ satisfying } p^T\ v = 0,$$

where H is a symmetric matrix when u(x) is twice continuously differentiable (from Young theorem).

Choose $v = [\partial x^*/\partial p]\ w + [\partial x^*/\partial r]\ w_0$, and $v_0 = [\partial \lambda^*/\partial p]\ w + [\partial \lambda^*/\partial r]\ w_0$, where $w_1 = (w, w_0) \in \Re^{n+1}$. Then, $p^T\ v = 0$ implies that $w_0 = x^{*T}\ w$. Then, with $\alpha = (p, r)$ becomes

$$w_1^T\ [\partial(x^*,\lambda^*)/\partial\alpha]^T\ H\ [\partial(x^*,l^*)/\partial a]\ w_1 \leq 0,$$
$$\text{for all } w_1 = (w, w_0) \in \Re^{n+1} \text{ satisfying } w_0 = x^{*T}\ w,$$

or,

$$w^T \begin{bmatrix} I_n & x^* \end{bmatrix} \begin{bmatrix} \partial x^*/\partial p & \partial x^*/\partial r \\ \partial \lambda^*/\partial p & \partial \lambda^*/\partial r \end{bmatrix}^T H \begin{bmatrix} \partial x^*/\partial p & \partial x^*/\partial r \\ \partial \lambda^*/\partial p & \partial \lambda^*/\partial r \end{bmatrix} \begin{bmatrix} I_n \\ x^{*T} \end{bmatrix} w \leq 0,$$

for all $w \in \Re^n$, or using (5),

$$w^T \begin{bmatrix} I_n & x^* \end{bmatrix} \begin{bmatrix} \lambda^* I_n & x^* \\ 0 & -1 \end{bmatrix} \begin{bmatrix} \partial x^*/\partial p & \partial x^*/\partial r \\ \partial \lambda^*/\partial p & \partial \lambda^*/\partial r \end{bmatrix} \begin{bmatrix} I_n \\ x^{*T} \end{bmatrix} w \leq 0,$$

or,

$$w^T \lambda^* [\partial x^*/\partial p + (\partial x^*/\partial r)\, x^{*T}]\, w \leq 0, \text{ for all } w \in \Re^n.$$

Given $\lambda^* > 0$ under local non-satiation, this implies that $S \equiv [\partial x^*/\partial p + (\partial x^*/\partial r)\, x^{*T}]$ is a symmetric, negative semi-definite matrix.

The matrix $S \equiv [\partial x^*/\partial p + (\partial x^*/\partial r)\, x^{*T}]$ is called the Slutsky matrix. The symmetry and negative semi-definiteness of the Slutsky matrix are called the integrability conditions of consumer demand.

They are implications of utility maximizing behaviour for the properties of the Marshallian demand function $x^*(p, r)$. Such conditions must be satisfied for consumer decision rules to be consistent with utility maximization. For example, finding empirical evidence against the symmetry or negative semi-definiteness of the Slutsky matrix would be sufficient to conclude that observed household decisions rules are inconsistent with utility maximization.

*The two sets of restrictions on Marshallian demands:*

1. The symmetry in (9) implies $n\times(n-1)/2$ symmetry restrictions,

$$\partial x_i^*/\partial p_j + (\partial x_i^*/\partial r)\, x_j^* = \partial x_j^*/\partial p_i + (\partial x_j^*/\partial r)\, x_i^*, \text{ for all } i \neq j.$$

2. The negative semi-definiteness implies the sign restrictions,

$$\partial x_i^*/\partial p_\iota + (\partial x_i^*/\partial r)\, x_i^* \leq 0, \; i = 1.., n.$$

*The imposes restrictions on cross-price effects. It can alternatively be expressed in terms of elasticities:*

$$\partial \ln(x_i^*) \partial \ln(p_j) + (\partial \ln(x_i^*)/\partial \ln(r))\, (p_j\, x_j^*/r)$$

$$= \partial \ln(x_j^*)/\partial \ln(p_i) + (\partial \ln(x_j^*)/\partial \ln(r))\, (p_i\, x_i^*/r), \text{ for all } i \neq j,$$

where $\partial \ln(x_i^*)/\partial \ln(p_j)$ is the price elasticity of $x_i^*$ with respect to $p_j$, $\partial \ln(x_i^*)/\partial \ln(r)$ is the income elasticity of $x_i^*$, and $(p_i\, x_i^*/r)$ is the budget share for the i-th commodity.

Equation (10b) imposes restrictions on own-price effects. It can be expressed alternatively in terms of elasticities,

$$\partial \ln(x_i^*)/\partial \ln(p_i) + (\partial \ln(x_i^*)/\partial \ln(r))\, (p_i\, x_i^*/r) \leq 0, \; i = 1.., n.$$

Equation (10b) implies that $\partial x_i^*/\partial p_i \leq -(\partial x_i^*/\partial r)\, x_i^*$. This means that Marshallian own-price effects $\partial x_i^*/\partial p_i$ are necessarily negative if $\partial x_i^*/\partial r > 0$.

*This gives the following important result:*

Positive income effects ($\partial x_i^*/\partial r > 0$) are sufficient to guarantee that Marshallian own price effects are negative $\partial x_i^*/\partial p_i < 0$, i = 1, ..., n (*i.e.*, that Marshallian demands are "downward sloping").

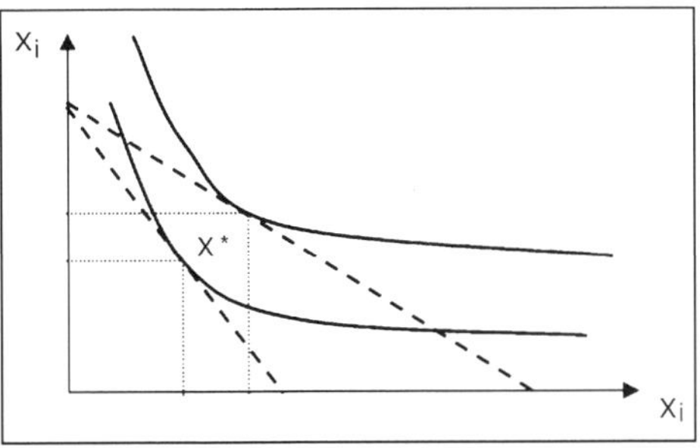


However, in general, the theory doe not imply that Marshallian own-price effects are always negative. Indeed, there are situations where a higher price can stimulate demand, $\partial x_i^*/\partial p_i > 0$. The commodities exhibiting this property are called Giffen goods. Giffen goods (satisfying $\partial x_i^*/\partial p_i < 0$) can exist only if income effects $\partial x_i^*/\partial r$ are negative and sufficiently large.

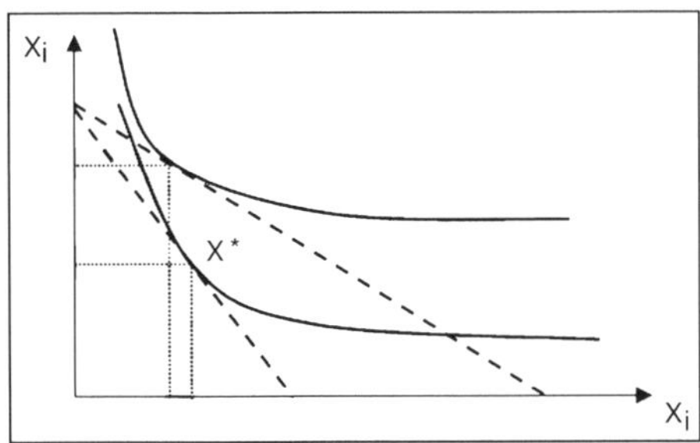


While the theory indicates that Giffen goods can exist, the empirical evidence suggests that they are rather rare. In other words, while the theory does not imply that all Marshallian demand functions are necessarily "downward sloping," it appears that most Marshallian demands exhibit negative own-price effects...

## The Advantage Function

We now explore other functions that will prove useful in the analysis of consumer behaviour. First, we consider the benefit function.

Consider some reference bundle $g \in \Re^n$, satisfying $g \geq 0$ and $g \neq 0$. Define the benefit function b(x, U, g) as follows,

$$b(x, U, g) = \sup_\beta \{\beta: u(x - \beta\, g) \geq U, (x - \beta\, g) \in X\},$$

if there is a $(x - \beta\, g) \in X$ such that $u(x - \beta\, g) \geq U$,

$$= -\infty \text{ otherwise.}$$

The benefit function b(x, U, g) measures the largest number of units of the reference bundle g that the household is willing to give up to reach point x starting from the utility level U. In the special case where the bundle g has a unit price (*i.e.*, where p. g = 1), then b(x, U, g) can be interpreted as a measure of the household willingness-to-pay to reach point x starting from utility level U.

Let $X^*(U) = \{x: u(x) \geq U, x \in X\} \subset X$ be the feasible set in the definition of the benefit function. Assuming that the set X*(U) is non-empty and closed, the benefit function b(x, U, g) has the following properties.

- *Continuity:* If the set X*(U) is closed, then the benefit function b(x, U) is upper-semi continuous in (x, U).

Assume that $u(x + \alpha g)$ is strictly increasing in $\alpha$ for all $x \in X$. Then,

$$u(x) = U \text{ implies that } b(x, U, g) = 0.$$

Proof: If u(x) = U, then $b(x, U, g) \geq 0$. If $u(x + \alpha g)$ is strictly increasing in $\alpha$, $(x - \beta g)$ being feasible implies that $u(x - \beta g) < u(x) = U$ for any $\beta > 0$. Thus, $b(x, U, g) > 0$ would imply that $u(x - b(x, U, g) g) < U$, a contradiction. This implies that b(x, U, g) = 0.

If x is in the interior of X, then,

$$b(x, U, g) = 0 \text{ implies that } u(x) = U.$$

Proof: If x is in the interior of X, b(x, U, g) = 0 implies that $u(x) \geq U$. It also implies that $u(x - \beta g) < U$ for $\beta > 0$. By continuity, letting $\beta \to 0$ gives $u(x) \leq U$. It follows that u(x) = U.

*Monotonicity: b(x, U, g) is non-increasing in U:*

$$b(x, U', g) \leq b(x, U, g) \text{ for all } U' > U.$$

Proof: Consider U and U' such that U' > U. Then $X^*(U') \subset X^*(U)$. Since the benefit function involves a supremum, it follows that $b(x, U', g) \leq b(x, U, g)$.

- *Translation:* If $x \in \Re^n_+$ and $(x + \alpha g) \in \Re^n_+$, then,

$$b(x + \alpha g, U, g) = \alpha + b(x, U, g).$$

Proof:

$$\begin{aligned} b(x + \alpha g, U, g) &= \sup_\beta \{\beta: u(x + (\alpha - \beta) g) \in U, (x + (\alpha - \beta) g) \in X\}, \\ &= \sup_\gamma \{\gamma + \alpha: u(x - \gamma g) \geq U, (x - \gamma g) \in X\}, \text{ where } \gamma = \alpha - \beta, \\ &= \alpha + b(x, U, g). \end{aligned}$$

- *Homogeneity in g:* The benefit function is homogeneous of degree -1 in g.

Proof: For any scalar k > 0,

$$\begin{aligned} b(x, U, k g) &= \sup_\beta \{\beta: u(x - \beta k g) \geq U, (x - \beta k g) \in X\}, \\ &= \sup_\alpha \{\alpha/k: u(x - \alpha g) \geq U, (x - \alpha g) \in X\}, \text{ where } \alpha = \beta k, \\ &= (1/k)\, b(x, U, g). \end{aligned}$$

Concavity in x: If the set X is convex and the utility function u(x) is quasi-concave in x, then the benefit function b(x, U, g) is concave in x.

Proof: Consider any two points x and x' $\in$ X. Since X is convex, $[\theta x + (1-\theta) x'] \in X$ for any $\theta \in [0, 1]$.

First, consider the case where b(x, U, g) > -∞ and b(x', U, g) > -∞. It follows that $u(x - b(x, U, g)\, g) \geq U$ and $u(x' - b(x', U, g)\, g) \geq U$.

By the quasi-concavity of u(x), we obtain,

$$u(\theta x - \theta b(x, U, g) g + (1-\theta) x' - (1-\theta) b(x', U, g) g) \geq U,$$

or,

$$u(\theta x + (1-\theta) x' - [\theta b(x, U, g) + (1-\theta) b(x', U, g)] g) \geq U,$$

for any $\theta \in [0, 1]$. By definition of the benefit function, this implies that

$$b(\theta x + (1-\theta) x', U, g) \geq \theta b(x, U, g) + (1-\theta) b(x', U, g) \text{ for any } \theta \in [0, 1].$$

Next, consider the case where b(x, U, g) = -∞ and/or b(x', U, g) = -∞. Then, the above inequalities always hold. These inequalities are the definition of b(x, U, g) being concave in x.

**The Distance Function**

Define the distance function D(x, U) as

$$D(x, U) = \sup_\alpha \{\alpha: \alpha > 0, u(x/\alpha) \geq U, (x/\alpha) \geq X\}$$

if there is a $(x/\alpha) \in X$ such that $u(x/\alpha) \geq U$,

$$= -\infty \text{ otherwise.}$$

The distance function D(x, U) measures the proportional rescaling in consumption x that will generate the reference utility level U.

Again, let $X^*(U) = \{x: u(x) \geq U, x \in X\}$. Assuming that the set X*(U) is non-empty and closed, the input distance function D(x, U) satisfies the following properties:

- *Continuity:* If the set X*(U) is closed, then the distance function D(x, U) is upper semi-continuous in (x, U).

*Proof:* The set X*(U) being closed means that $x_k \in X^*(U_k)$ and $(x_k, U_k) \to (x, U)$ implies that $x \in X^*(U)$. Thus, $D(x_k, U_k) \geq 1$, and $D(x, U) \geq 1$. The sequence $a_k = \sup\{D(x_k, U_k), D(x_{k+1}, U_{k+1}), \ldots\}$ being non-increasing and D(x, U) being a supremum, it follows that $\lim_{K\to\infty} a_k = \lim \sup_{K\to\infty} D(x_k, U_k)$ cannot be greater than D(x, U).

- *Homogeneity in x*: The distance function D(x, U) is homogeneous of degree 1 in x.

Proof: For any k > 0,

$$D(k x, U) = \sup_\alpha \{\alpha: \alpha > 0, u(k x/\alpha) \geq U, (k x/\alpha) \in X\},$$

$$= \sup_b \{k b: b > 0, u(x/b) \geq U, (x/b) \in X\}, \text{ with } b = \alpha/k,$$

$$= k D(x, U).$$

- *Concavity in x:* The function D(x, U) is concave in x if the set X*(U) is convex.

Proof: Consider two points (x, U) and (x', U).

First, consider the case where D(x, U) > -∞ and D(x', U) > -∞. Then, x/D(x, U) ∈ X*(U) and x'/D(x, U) ∈ X*(U). If the set X*(U) is convex, it follows that θ x/D(x, U) + (1-θ) x'/D(x', U) ∈ X*(U) for any θ ∈ [0, 1]. Choose θ = γ D(x, U)/[γ D(x, U) + (1-γ) D(x', U)], γ ∈ [0, 1]. It follows that (γ x + (1-γ) x')/[γ D(x, U) + (1-γ) D(x', U)] ∈ X*(U), implying that D[(γ x + (1-γ) x')/[γ D(x, U) + (1-γ) D(x', U), U] ≥ 1. The function D(x, U) being homogeneous of degree 1 in x, this gives

$$D(\gamma x + (1-\gamma) x', U) \geq \gamma D(x, U) + (1-\gamma) D(x', U).$$

Second, note that this inequality always holds when D(x, U) = -∞ and/or D(x', U) = -∞. This inequality is the definition that D(x, U) is concave in x.

- *Monotonicity:* The function D(x, U) is non-increasing in U:

$$D(x, U') \leq D(x, U) \text{ for all } U' > U.$$

Proof: Consider U and U' such that U' > U. Then X*(U') ⊂ X*(U). Since the distance function involves a supremum, it follows that D(x, U') ≤ D(x, U).

$$X^*(U) \subset \{(x: D(x, U) \geq 1\}.$$

Proof: Assume that D(x, U) < 1. By definition of the distance function, this implies that x ∉ X*(U), *i.e.*, that x ∉ X*(U). Thus, x ∈ X*(U) implies D(x, U) ≥ 1.

**THE INDIRECT USEFULNESS FUNCTION**

The indirect utility function V(p, r) is,

$$V(p, r) = u(x^*(p, r)) = \text{Max}_X \{u(x): p. x \leq r, x \in X\}.$$

It is the utility level obtained by a utility maximizing household facing prices p and household income r. Below, we investigate its properties, assuming that $X = \Re^n_+$.

- *Homogeneity:* The indirect utility function V(p, r) is homogeneous of degree 0 in (p, r).

Proof: For any k > 0,

$$V(k\,p, k\,r) = \text{Max}_X \{u(x): k\,p. x \leq k\,r, x \in X\},$$

$$= \text{Max}_X \{u(x): p. x \leq r, x \in X\},$$

$$= V(p, r).$$

- *Monotonicity:* When $X = \Re^n_+$, the indirect utility function V(p, r) is
  - Non-increasing in prices p
  - Non-decreasing in income r.

Proof: Consider p' ≥ p. When $X = \Re^n_+$, it follows that $\{x: p'. x \leq r, x \in \Re^n_+\} \subset \{x: p. x \leq r, x \in \Re^n_+\}$. Thus, in the utility maximization problem, the feasible set is larger under p than under p', implying that V(p', r) ≤ V(p, r).

Consider r' > r. Then, {x: p. x ≤ r, x ∈ X} ⊂ {x: p. x ≤ r', x ∈ X}. Thus, in the utility maximization problem, the feasible set is larger under r' than under r, implying that V(p, r') ≥ V(p, r).

- *Quasi-convexity*: The indirect utility function V(p, r) is quasi-convex in p.

Proof: V(p, r) is quasi-convex in p if the set {p: V(p, r) ≤ k} is convex for every r > 0 and k. Consider two prices $p_1$ and $p_2$ satisfying $V(p_1, r) \le k$ and $V(p_2, r) \le k$. Let $p = \theta\, p_1 + (1-\theta)\, p_2$, for any θ ∈ (0, 1). Let $C_1 = \{x: p_1. x \le r\}$, $C_2 = \{x: p_2. x \le r\}$, and C = {x: p. x ≤ r}. Consider an $x \notin C_1 \cup C_2$. This means that $p_1. x > r$ and $p_2. x > r$. It follows that $[\theta\, p_1 + (1-\theta)\, p_2]. x > \theta\, r + (1-\theta)\, r = r$, *i.e.*, that x ∉ C. Thus, x ∈ C implies that $x \in C_1 \cup C_2$, *i.e.*, that $C \subset C_1 \cup C_2$. Since x ∈ C implies that x must belong to either $C_1$ or $C_2$, it follows from utility maximization that $V(p, r) \le \max\{V(p_1, r), V(p_2, r)\}$ and thus V(p, r) ≤ k. This means that the set {p: V(p, r) ≤ k} is convex for every r > 0 and k.

Note that the quasi-convexity of V(p, r) in p does not require that the utility function u(x) be quasi-concave in x.

- *Roy's Identity*: If the utility function u(x) exhibits local non-satiation and the indirect utility function is differentiable in (p, r), then,

$$x^*(p, r) = -[\partial V(p, r)/\partial p]/[\partial V(p, r)/\partial r],$$

or,

$$xi^*(p, r) = -[\partial V(p, r)/\partial p_i]/[\partial V(p, r)/\partial r],\ i = 1, \ldots, n.$$

Proof: (another version of the envelope theorem). Under local non-satiation, note that at the optimum, the Lagrangean is,

$$L(x^*(p, r), \lambda^*(p, r), p, r) = u(x^*(p, r)) + \lambda^*(p, r)\,[r - p\ ?\ x^*(p, r)],$$

$$= u(x^*(p, r)),\ \text{since } [r - p.\ x^*(p, r)] = 0 \text{ under local non-satiation,}$$

$$= V(p, r).$$

Taking the derivative of the above identity with respect to (p, r) yields,

$$\partial V/\partial p = (\partial L/\partial x)(\partial x^*/\partial p) + (\partial L/\partial \lambda)(\partial \lambda^*/\partial p) - \partial^*(p, r)\, x^*(p, r),$$

$$\partial V/\partial r = (\partial L/\partial x)(\partial x^*/\partial r) + (\partial L/\partial \lambda)(\partial \lambda^*/\partial r) + \partial^*(p, r).$$

Using the first order condition (3a)-(3b), we obtain,

$$\partial V/\partial p = -\lambda^*(p, r)\, x^*(p, r),$$

$$\partial V/\partial r = \lambda^*(p, r).$$

Since λ*(p, r) > 0 under local non-satiation, this gives,

$$x^*(p, r) = -[\partial V(p, r)/\partial p]/[\partial V(p, r)/\partial r].$$

Roy's identity provides a simple and convenient way of obtaining the Marshallian demands x*(p, r) from the indirect utility function V(p, r).

**The Expenditure Purpose**

Consider the smallest expenditure that can support a reference utility level U. This corresponds to the following minimization problem, holding the household at a utility level U:

$$E(p, U) = \min_x \{p. x: u(x) \geq U, x \in X\},$$

where,

$$E(p, U) = p. x^c(p, U)$$

is the expenditure function, and,

$$x^c(p, U) \in \text{argmin}_x \{p. x: u(x) \geq U, x \in X\}$$

are Hicksian demands. The expenditure function is the smallest household expenditure required to reach the utility level U. The Hicksian demands $x^c(p, U)$ are sometimes called "compensated demands" (as they hold the household at a utility level U).

Again, let $X^*(U) = \{x: u(x) \geq U, x \in X\}$. Assuming that the feasible set $X^*(U)$ is non-empty and closed, the properties of the expenditure function E(p, U) are presented next.

- *Homogeneity:* The expenditure function E(p, U) is linear homogeneous in p:

$$E(t\,p, U) = t\,E(p, U) \text{ for all } t > 0.$$

Proof: For any $t > 0$,

$$E(t\,p, U) = \min_x \{t\,p. x: u(x) \geq U, x \in X\},$$

$$= t \min_x \{p. x: u(x) \geq U, x \in X\},$$

$$= t\,E(p, U).$$

- *Monotonicity:* Assuming that $X = \Re^n_+$, the expenditure function E(p, U) is
  - Non-decreasing in p
  - Non-decreasing in U.

Proof: Consider $p' \geq p$. Given $x \in \Re^n_+$, it follows that $p'. x \geq p. x$, implying that $E(x', U) \geq E(x, U)$.

Next, consider $U' \geq U$. This implies that $\{x: u(x) \geq U', x \in X\} \subset \{x: u(x) \geq U, x \in X\}$. Under expenditure minimization, this yields $E(x, U') \geq E(x, U)$.

Concavity in p: For $p \in \Re^n_+$, the expenditure function E(p, U) is concave (hence continuous) in p.

Proof: Consider any two prices $p_1 \in \Re^n_+$ and $p_2 \in \Re^n_+$. Let $p = \theta\,p_1 + (1\text{-}\theta)\,p_2$, for any $\theta \in [0, 1]$. We have,

$$E(p_1, U) \leq p_1. x^c(p, U)$$

and

$$E(p_2, U) \leq p_2 . x^c(p, U).$$

Multiplying the first equation by θ, the second one by (1-θ), and summing yields,

$$\theta\, E(p_1, U) + (1-\theta)\, E(p_2, U) \leq [\theta\, p_1 + (1-\theta)\, p_2] . x^c(p, U) = E(p, U).$$

This implies that E(p, U) is concave in p.

Shephard's lemma: If E(p, U) is differentiable in p, then,

$$\partial E(p, U)/\partial p = x^c(p, U).$$

Proof: Define g(p, p', U) = E(p, U) - p. xc(p', U). Expenditure minimization implies that g(p, p', U) ≤ 0 for all p and p' $\in \Re^n_{++}$, and g(p', p', U) = 0. Thus, the function g(p, p', U) is maximized with respect to p when p = p'. The function g(p, p', U) is differentiable in p when E(p, U) is differentiable in p. Then, the first-order necessary condition for a maximum of g(p, p', U) with respect to p (evaluated at p = p') are: $\partial E(p, U)/\partial p - x^c(p, U) = 0$, yielding the desired result.

**Properties of the Hicksian Demands**

Consider the case where the expenditure minimization problem has a unique solution.

$x^c(p, U)$ is homogeneous of degree zero in prices p.

Proof: for any t > 0,

$x^c(t\, p, U) \in \text{argmin}_x \{t\, p. x: u(x) \geq U, x \in X\} = \text{argmin}_x \{p. x:: u(x) \geq U, x \in X\}$, implying that,

$$x^c(t\, p, U) = x^c(p, U).$$

Note: When the Hicksian demands $x^c(p, U)$ are continuously differentiable in p, applying Euler theorem generates the following n homogeneity restrictions,

$$\sum\nolimits_{j=1}^{n} [\partial x_i^c(p, U)/\partial p_j]\, p_j = 0, i = 1, \ldots, n,$$

or, when $x^c(p, U) > 0$ and p > 0,

$$\sum\nolimits_{j=1}^{n} \partial \ln(x_i^c(p, U))/\partial \ln(p_j) = 0, i = 1, \ldots, n.$$

This states that, for each Hicksian demand, the sum of the own price elasticity, $\partial \ln(x_i^c(p, U))/\partial \ln(p_i)$, and cross-price elasticities $(\partial \ln(x_i^c(p, U))/\partial \ln(p_j)$, $j \neq i)$ must equal zero.

If the Hicksian demands xc(p, U) are continuously differentiable in p, then,

$$\partial x^c(p, U)/\partial p = \text{a (n×n) symmetric, negative semi-definite matrix.}$$

Proof: From Shephard's lemma, $\partial E(p, U)/\partial p = x^c(p, U)$. If $x^c(p, U)$ is continuously differentiable in p, Young theorem implies that $\partial^2 E(p, U)/\partial p^2 = \partial x^c(p, U)/\partial p$ is a (n×n) symmetric matrix. And E(p, U) being twice continuously differentiable and concave in p implies that $\partial^2 E(p, U)/\partial p^2$ is a (n×n) negative semi-definite matrix.

Note: The symmetry of the matrix $[\partial x^c(p, U)/\partial p^2]$ implies the following $n\times(n-1)/2$ symmetry restrictions,

$$\partial x_i^c(p, U)/\partial p_j = \partial x_j^c(p, U)/\partial p_i, \text{ for all } i \neq j,\ i, j = 1, \ldots, n.$$

The negative semi-definiteness of the matrix $[\partial x^c(p, U)/\partial p]$ implies the following inequality restrictions,

$$\partial x_i^c(p, U)/\partial w_i \leq 0,\ i = 1, \ldots, n.$$

This simply states that Hicksian demands are downward sloping: any increase in a price provides an incentive to reduce the use of the corresponding Hicksian quantity demanded.

Note: The homogeneity restrictions imply that $\sum_{j\neq 1}^{n} \partial\ln(x_i^c(p, U))/\partial\ln(p_j) = 0$, $i = 1, \ldots, n$. Given that $\partial x_i^c(p, U)/\partial p_i \leq 0$, it follows that,

$$\sum_{j\neq 1}^{n} \partial\ln(x_i^c(p, U))/\partial\ln(p_j) = -\partial\ln(x_i^c(p, U))/\partial\ln(p_i) \geq 0,\ i = 1, \ldots, n.$$

This implies that, for each Hicksian demand, the sum of the cross-price elasticities must be non-negative.

**Indirect Utility Function and the Expenditure Function**

Let $X = \Re_+^n$.

Assume that the utility function u(x) is continuous and exhibits local non-satiation. If x* solves the utility maximization problem (1), $V(p, r) = \max_x \{u(x): p.\, x \leq r,\ x \in X\}$, then x* also solves the expenditure minimization problem (13), $\min_x \{p.\, x: u(x) \geq U,\ x \in X\}$, when $U = V(p, r)$.

Proof: Suppose that x*. Then, there is an $x \geq 0$ satisfying $p.\, x < p.\, x^*$ and $u(x) \geq U$. By local non-satiation, there is an $x' \geq 0$ near x satisfying $p.\, x' \leq p.\, x^* \leq r$ and $u(x') > u(x) \geq U$. This x' is feasible in (1) and yields $u(x') > V(p, r)$, which contradicts (1).

This implies that

- $E(p, V(p, r)) = r$,

and

- $x^c(p, V(p, r)) = x^*(p, r)$.

The expenditure function E(p, U) and the indirect utility function V(p, r) are inverse functions of each other. When both are differentiable in p, differentiating with respect to p yields,

$$\partial E(p, U)/\partial p = -[\partial E(p, U)/\partial U]\ [\partial V(p, r)/\partial p].$$

The Hicksian demands $x^c(p, U)$ and the Marshallian demands $x^*(p, r)$ are closely related. When both are differentiable in p, differentiating with respect to p yields,

$$[\partial x^c(p, U)/\partial p] + [\partial x^c(p, U)/\partial U]\ [\partial V(p, r)/\partial p] = \partial x^*(p, r)/\partial p.$$

Assume that $p.\, x^c > 0$. If $x^c$ solves the expenditure minimization problem,

$E(p, U) = \min_x \{p. x: u(x) \geq U, x \in X\}$, $x^c$ also solves the utility maximization problem (1), $\max_x \{u(x): p. x \leq r, x \in X\}$, when $r = E(p, r)$.

Proof: Let $r = p. x^c > 0$. Suppose that $x^c$ solves. Consider an $x \geq 0$ satisfying $p. x \leq r$, and an $x' = \alpha x$ for some $\alpha \in (0, 1)$. It follows that $p. x' < r$. This implies that x' must be infeasible, *i.e.*, that $u(x') < u(xc)$. The utility function u(x) being continuous, letting $\alpha \to 1$ implies that $u(x) \leq u(x^c)$. Thus, any $x \geq 0$ satisfying $p. x \leq r$ implies that $u(x) \leq u(x^c)$. Thus, $x^c$ solves (1).

This implies that

- $V(p, E(p, U)) = U$,

and

- $x^*(p, E(p, U)) = x^c(p, U)$.

The indirect utility function V(p, r) and the expenditure function E(p, U) are inverse functions of each other. When both are differentiable in p, differentiating (15a) with respect to p yields,

$$\partial V(p, r)/\partial p = -[\partial V(p, r)/\partial r]\ [\partial E(p, U)/\partial p].$$

The Hicksian demands $x^c(p, U)$ and the Marshallian demands $x^*(p, r)$ are closely related. When both are differentiable in p, differentiating (15b) with respect to p yields,

$$[\partial x^*(p, r)/\partial p] + [\partial x^*(p, r)/\partial r]\ [\partial E(p, U)/\partial p] = \partial x^c(p, U)/\partial p.$$

Using Shephard's lemma, $[\partial E(p, U)/\partial p] = [x^c(p, U)]^T$, this gives,

$$[\partial x^*(p, r)/\partial p] + [\partial x^*(p, r)/\partial r]\ [x^c(p, U)]^T = \partial x^c(p, U)/\partial p,$$

or, using (15b),

$$[\partial x^*(p, r)/\partial p] + [\partial x^*(p, r)/\partial r]\ [x^*(p, r)]^T = \partial x^c(p, U)/\partial p,$$

when $r = E(p, U)$.

The instant Slutsky equation. The left-hand side is the Slutsky matrix $S = [\partial x^*(p, r)/\partial p] + [\partial x^*(p, r)/\partial r]\ [x^*(p, r)]^T$. The right-hand side is the price slope of the Hicksian demands, $\partial x^c(p, U)/\partial p$.

Slutsky matrix is symmetric and negative-semi definite. Also, we have shown above that the Hicksian price slope $[\partial x^c(p, U)/\partial p]$ is symmetric and negative semi-definite. The instant Slutsky equation establishes several important results:

- The Slutsky matrix S measures the Hicksian (or compensated) price slope:

$$S = \partial x^c(p, U)/\partial p,$$

- Knowing that the matrix of Hicksian price slope $[\partial x^c(p, U)/\partial p]$ is symmetric, negative semi-definite provides a quick proof of the integrability conditions of Marshallian demands: the Slutsky matrix is symmetric, negative semi-definite.
- Equation (16) can be alternatively written as,

$$[\partial x^*(p, r)/\partial p] = \partial x^c(p, U)/\partial p - [\partial x^*(p, r)/\partial r]\ [x^*(p, r)]^T,$$

when r = E(p, U). The Marshallian price effects [$\partial x^*(p, r)/\partial p$] into two additive terms: the Hicksian price effect (also called substitution effect) [$\partial x^c(p, U)/\partial p$], and the income effect, -[$\partial x^*(p, r)/\partial r$] [$x^*(p, r)]^T$.

**The Direct and Indirect Utility Function**

By definition, given $p \in \Re^n_{++}$, we have,

$$V(p, r) = \max_x \{u(x): p.\, x \leq r, x \in X\}.$$

where V(p, r) is the indirect utility function. This shows how the indirect utility function V(p, r) can be obtained from the direct utility function u(x), where V(p, r) = u(x*(p, r)), x*(p, r) being the (quantity dependent) Marshallian demands.

Assume that $X = \Re^n_+$ and that u(x) is continuous, quasi-concave and strongly monotonic. Then, for x > 0,

$$u(x) = \min_p \{V(p, 1): p.\, x \leq 1, p \in \Re^n_+\}.$$

*Proof:* From (17), we have V(p, 1) ≥ u(x) for all x > 0 and all p > 0 satisfying p. x ≤ 1. Thus, u(x) ≤ V(p, 1) for all p > 0 satisfying p. x ≤ 1. Since V(p, 1) is non-increasing in p, this implies that,

$$u(x) \leq \min_p \{V(p, 1): p.\, x \leq 1, p \geq 0\}.$$

Next, we need to show that, for each x > 0, we can find a p ≥ 0 such that p. x ≤ 1 and u(x) = V(p, 1). Consider the set $F(x) = \{x': u(x') \geq u(x), x' \in \Re^n_+\}$. When u(x) is continuous and quasi-concave, the set F(x) is closed and convex. Under strong monotonicity, x is necessarily on the lower bound on F(x). By the supporting hyperplane theorem, there is a non-zero p ≥ 0 such that p. x ≤ p. x' for all x' ∈ F(x). Normalising p such that p. x = 1, this implies that for each x > 0, there is a p ≥ 0 such that $x \in \text{argmin}_x' \{p.\, x': u(x') \geq u(x), x' \in \Re^n_+\}$. With r = 1, this implies $x \in \text{argmax}_x' \{u(x'): p.\, x' \leq 1, x' \in \Re^n_+\}$ and V(p, 1) = u(x).

The direct utility function u(x) can be obtained from the indirect utility function V(p, r). Let $p^*(x, 1) \in \text{argmin}_p \{V(p, 1): p.\, x \leq 1, p \in \Re^n_+\}$. Then, p*(x, 1) can be interpreted as price-dependent Marshallian demands, and u(x) = V(p*(x, 1), 1).

**The Expenditure and the Benefit Function**

Assume that $p \in \Re^n_+$ with p. g > 0. Then,

$$E(p, U) = \inf_x \{p.\, x - b(x, U, g)\, (p.\, g): x \in X\}.$$

Proof: First, we show that the inequality E(p, U) ≤ p. x - b(x, U, g) (p. g) holds for any $x \in \Re^n$. The inequality always holds when b(x, U, g) = $-\infty$. When b(x, U, g) > $-\infty$, the definition of the benefit function implies that [x - b(x, U, g) g] $\in X^*(U)$. This implies that E(p, U) $\leq$ p. [x - b (x, U, g) g] = p. x - b(x, U, g) (p. g). Thus, E(p, U) $\leq \inf_x$ {p. x - b(x, U, g) (p. g): $x \in \Re^n$}.

Second, we show that the converse holds. For any $x \in X^*(U)$, we have b(x, U, g) $\geq$ 0. This implies that E(p, U) = $\inf_x$ {p. x: $x \in X^*(U)$} $\geq \inf_x$ {p. x - b(x, U, g) (p. g): $x \in X^*(U)$} $\geq \inf_x$ {p. x - b(x, U, g) (p. g): $x \in \Re^n$}, *i.e.*, that E(p, U) $\geq \inf_x$ {p. x - b(x, U, g) (p. g): $x \in \Re^n$}.

Note: When prices are normalised such that that p. g = 1, equation becomes,

$$E(p, U) = \inf_x \{p.\ x - b(x, U, g): x \in X\}.$$

An alternative way of defining the expenditure function from the benefit function. Note that it is an unconstrained optimisation problem. An alternative way of defining the (quantity dependent) Hicksian demands as $x^c(p, U) \in \text{argmin}_x$ {p. x - b(x, U, g) (p. g): $x \in X$}. Finally, note that, under differentiability, the associated first-order necessary conditions (FOC) for an interior solution are the familiar marginal conditions: p = (p. g) $\partial b(x, U, g)/\partial x$. When p. g = 1, this implies that marginal cost p must equal marginal benefit $\partial b(x, U, g)/\partial x$. This illustrates that, when p. g = 1, the benefit function b(x, U, g) provides a monetary measure of consumer benefit.The utility function u(x) is continuous, quasi-concave and strongly monotonic. Let x > 0, $X = \Re^n_+$, and $g \in \Re^n_+$ with $g \neq 0$. Then,

$$b(x, U, g) = \inf_p \{p.\ x - E(p, U): p.\ g = 1, p \in \Re^n_+\}.$$

Proof: We present the proof in the case where b(x, U, g) is finite. When the utility function u(x) is continuous and quasi-concave and $X = \Re^n_+$, the set $X^*(U)$ = {x: u(x) $\geq$ U, $x \in X$} is closed and convex. Under strong monotonicity, [x - b(x, U, g) g] is on the lower boundary of $X^*(U)$. By the supporting hyperplane theorem, there is a non-zero $p \in \Re^n_+$ satisfying p. x' $\geq$ p. [x - b(x, U, g) g] for all $x' \in X^*(U)$. Normalising p such that p. g = 1, it follows that p. x' $\geq$ p. x - b(x, U, g) for all $x' \in X^*(U)$. First, since the hyperplane defined by p supports $X^*(U)$ at [x - b(x, U, g) g], it follows that E(p, U) = p. [x - b(x, U, g) g] = p. x - b(x, U, g). Second, for any p' $\geq$ 0 satisfying p'. g = 1, with u(x - b(x, U, g) g) $\geq$ U, we have E(p', U) $\leq$ p'. [x - b(x, U, g) g] = p'. x - b(x, U, g). Thus, b(x, U, g) $\leq$ p'. x - E(p', U) for all $p' \in \Re^n_+$.

An alternative way of defining the benefit function from the expenditure function. It is worth noting that, except for the price normalisation rule p. g = 1, the minimization problem is an unconstrained optimisation problem. Let $p^c(x, U) \in \text{argmin}_p$ {p. x - E(p, U): p. g = 1, $p \in \Re^n_+$}. Then, $p^c(x, U)$ can be interpreted as price-dependent Hicksian (or compensated) demands, expressing prices p as a function of quantities x, holding utility constant at level U. Note that, under differentiability, the associated first-order necessary conditions (FOC) for an interior solution are the marginal conditions: $x = \partial E(p, U)/\partial p$.

**The Expenditure and the Distance Function**

Recall the definition of the distance function

$$D(x, U) = \sup_{\alpha} \{\alpha: \alpha > 0, u(x/\alpha) \geq U, (x/\alpha) \in X\} \text{ if there is a } (x/\alpha) \in X, u(x/\alpha) \geq U,$$

$$= -\infty \text{ otherwise.}$$

Assume that the utility function u(x) is continuous, quasi-concave and strongly monotonic.Let x > 0, and $X = \Re^n_+$. Then the following results hold (the proof is similar to the one obtained using the cost function):

- $E(p, U) = \inf_x \{p. x: D(x, U) \geq 1\}, x \in \Re^n\}$, for $p \in \Re^n_{++}$.
- $D(x, U) = \inf_p \{p. x: E(p, U) \geq 1, p \in \Re^n_+\}$.

A way of defining the expenditure function $E(p, U) = [p. x^c(p, U)]$ from the distance function D(x, U), where $x^c(p, U) \in \text{argmin}_x \{p. x: D(x, U) \geq 1\}, x \in \Re^n\}$ are the quantity-dependent Hicksian demands.

Alternatively, a way of defining the distance function $D(x, U) = [p^c(x, U). x]$ from the expenditure function E(p, U), where $p^c(x, U) \in \text{argmin}_p \{p. x: E(p, U) \geq 1\}, p \in \Re^n_+\}$ are the price-dependent Hicksian demands.

**Family Production**

So far, we have considered households involved only in consumption activities. We now extent this analysis by considering that households can also get involved in production activities. Let $y \in \Re^m$ denote a vector of netputs involved in household production activities, where outputs are positive and inputs are negative. Let $y = (y_m, y_n)$, where ym is a vector of market goods with corresponding market price $p_m$, and $y_n$ is a vector of non-market goods (*i.e.*, goods that are not exchanged on a market place). The household production technology is represented by the set F, where $(y, x) \in F$. In the presence of market activities in production, household total income becomes: $r + p_m. y_m$, where r denotes exogenous income, and $p_m. y_m$ denotes the profit from marketed production activities. Then, the household budget constraint becomes: px ? x ? r + pm ? ym.

The household utility maximization problem becomes,

$$V(p_x, p_m, r) = \text{Max}_{x,y} \{u(x): p_x. x \leq r + p_m. y_m, (y, x) \in F\},$$

which has for solution the Marshallian decision rules $x+(p_x, p_m, r)$ and $y^+(p_x, p_m, r)$.

Note that this optimisation problem can be decomposed into two stages: first choose $y_m$; second, choose $(x, y_n)$. Then, the household utility maximization can be equivalently written as,

$$V(p_x, p_m, r) = \text{Max}_{x, yn} \{\text{Max}_{ym} \{u(x): px. x \leq r + p_m. y_m, (y, x) \in F\}\}.$$

The first stage maximization is,

$$\text{Max}_{ym} \{u(x): p_x. x \leq r + p_m. y_m, (y, x) \in F\}.$$

But under local non-satiation, this must necessarily imply the following profit maximization problem,

$$\pi(p_m, y_n, x) = \text{Max}_{ym} \{p_m. y_m: (y, x) \in F\},$$

which has for solution the profit maximizing decision rules $y_m^*(p_m, y_n, x)$, where $\pi(p_m, y_n, x) = p_m. y_m^*(p_m, y_n, x)$ is the indirect profit function. Indeed, if the choice of $y_m$ did not satisfy, this would necessarily be inconsistent since there would exist alternative production decisions that can increase household income, thus making the household better off. Then, under local non-satiation, the second stage maximization becomes,

$$\text{Max}_{x,yn} \{u(x): px. x \leq r + \pi(p_m, y_n, x), x \geq 0\},$$

which has for solution $x^+(p_x, p_m, r)$ and $y_n^+(p_x, p_m, r)$. Note that $(y_n, x)$ appear in the budget constraint, through the indirect profit function $\pi(p_m, y_n, x)$. This implies that the consumer goods x have an explicit market price px as well as an implicit or shadow price $\partial\pi/\partial x$. Similarly, the non-market goods $y_n$ have a shadow price $\partial\pi/\partial y_n$. This illustrates that the household production model is relevant in analysing the allocation of non-market goods.

*This has important implications:*

- Under local non-satiation, household utility maximization implies profit maximization with respect to the market production activities. This indicates that profit maximization is a relevant economic concept for households, even in the presence of non-market goods. This is an intuitive result: as long as the marginal utility of income is positive, the household have an incentive to maximize income, and thus to maximize profit (assuming that it is the "residual claimant").
- The solution to the first stage profit-maximization problem $y_m^*(p_m, y_n, x)$ is independent of consumer prices px and of consumer income r. This indicates that, in a household context, production decisions for marketed production activities are separable from the consumption decisions.
- The equivalence implies that

$$y_m^+(p_x, p_m, r) = y_m^*(p_m, y_n^+(p_x, p_m, r), x^+(p_x, p_m, r)).$$

- Non-market goods have a shadow price represented by $\partial\pi/\partial y_n$ measuring their opportunity cost and the extent of resource scarcity.

# FACTORS OF CONSUMER DECISION-MAKING

## STAGES OF THE CONSUMER BUYING PROCESS

Six Stages to the Consumer Buying Decision Process (For complex decisions). Actual purchasing is only one stage of the process. Not all decision processes lead to a purchase. All consumer decisions do not always include all 6 stages, determined by the degree of complexity...discussed next.

*The 6 stages are:*

1. *Problem Recognition(Awareness of Need)*: Difference between the desired state and the actual condition. Deficit in assortment of products. Hunger--Food. Hunger stimulates your need to eat.
   Can be stimulated by the marketer through product information--did not know you were deficient? *I.E.*, see a commercial for a new pair of shoes, stimulates your recognition that you need a new pair of shoes.
2. Information search:
   - Internal search, memory.
   - External search if you need more information. Friends and relatives (word of mouth). Marketer dominated sources; comparison shopping; public sources, etc.

   A successful information search leaves a buyer with possible alternatives, the evoked set.
   Hungry, want to go out and eat, evoked set is
   - Chinese food
   - Indian food
   - Burger king
   - Klondike kates etc
3. *Evaluation of Alternatives:* Need to establish criteria for evaluation, features the buyer wants or does not want. Rank/weight alternatives or resume search. May decide that you want to eat something spicy, indian gets highest rank, etc.
   If not satisfied with your choice then return to the search phase. Can you think of another restaurant? Look in the yellow pages, etc. Information from different sources may be treated differently. Marketers try to influence by "framing" alternatives.
4. *Purchase Decision*: Choose buying alternative, includes product, package, store, method of purchase, etc.
5. *Purchase:* May differ from decision, time lapse between 4 and 5, product availability.
6. *Post-Purchase Evaluation—Outcome*: Satisfaction or Dissatisfaction. Cognitive Dissonance, have you made the right decision. This can be reduced by warranties, after sales communication, etc. After eating an indian meal, may think that really you wanted a chinese meal instead.

## Supply and Demand

Although economists all agree that the price of a product or service is a major factor in the consumer decision-making process, it's not the only factor, and it may not always be the deciding factor. But a principle of microeconomics assumes that, if all other factors are equal, as the price of a product or service goes up, demand for that product or service declines. Conversely, if the price declines, demand goes up.

Based on pricing, therefore, microeconomics can forecast with reasonable accuracy what a consumer may buy, and how much of that product or service will be bought. Consumer demand - what a consumer wants and in what quantity - is called a demand curve and may be graphically plotted in a chart, like the one below.

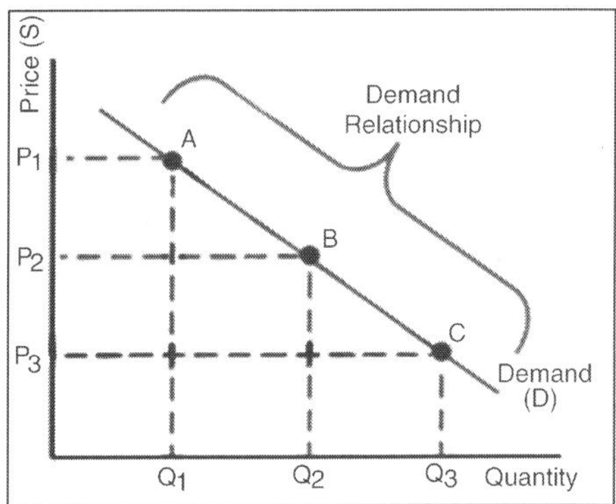


**Fig.** Demand Curve.

Another way to represent the demand curve is in a table like the example below. The table simply shows that demand for a product, in this case an apple pie, declines as the price for it goes up.

| A Demand Curve | |
|---|---|
| Price of an Apple Pie | Number of Apple Pies, People Want to Buy |
| $1.00 | 5 |
| $2.00 | 4 |
| $3.00 | 2 |
| $4.00 | 1 |

The demand curve for apple pies may change if a factor in the decision-making process changes. Let's say a competing bakery offers cherry pies that are bigger and cheaper than the apple pies. The demand curve for apple pies may then change, with demand falling off as demand for the cherry pies goes up. Consumer demand for both apple pies and cherry pies will depend on this price and size relationship - cherry pies are bigger and cheaper than apple pies. If the apple pie baker makes a new batch of apple pies as big as his competitor's cherry pies and offers to sell them at the same price or lower than the cherry pies, then demand for apple pies should go up.

## Chance Cost and Elasticity

Another price or cost to the consumer which must be calculated as part of consumer buying patterns is what microeconomics calls the opportunity cost. This "expense" or cost represents what consumers must give up in order to buy something - in other words, the tradeoff factor. If a consumer has a dollar to spend and buys a cup of coffee for a buck, then there's no money left for a donut. Conversely, if the consumer buys the donut, he or she has nothing to dunk it in. What the consumer gives up, or trades off, to buy one thing and not another is the opportunity cost. Prices changes in a product or service, either up or down, will influence the opportunity cost to consumers. A steep increase in the price of coffee for a confirmed coffee drinker may not prevent that consumer from buying the same amount of coffee. But for the random drinker of coffee who does not need a cup or two to start the day, the price increase may cut that consumer's coffee buying.

The change in the quantity of coffee bought by the consumer as the price changes is called demand elasticity. Demand may expand like a stretched rubber band - reflecting its elasticity - if the price of coffee goes down. Or demand may contract, or become inelastic, if the price goes up.

*Microeconomics measures the demand elasticity for a product or service as its price changes using this formula:*

$$\text{Elasticity} = \frac{\text{\% Change in Quantity Demanded}}{\text{\% Change in Price}}$$

These microeconomic formulae and theories illustrate the core influences that account for consumer decision-making: price, utility and opportunity costs. Other economic factors, of course, may also influence consumer buying choices. These may include the spending patterns of wealthy consumers for whom price considerations may not be as important as they are for the average consumer.

Or a consumer with an average income may be predisposed to spend more money on a product or service because of a preference for quality over price. Beyond the factors discussed above, several other elements also enter into the decision-making equations; these are less quantifiable.

## Extraneous Factors and Promotion

Consumer buying choices are also driven by psychological, cultural and social factors, all of which play a role in influencing preferences. The convenience factor is also a major influence on consumer buying. Some consumers patronise certain stores and retail outlets because they're in the neighbourhood. Some ethnic consumers may prefer to buy from retailers that speak their language.

Other consumers may buy from stores that provide easy credit. In some instances, these factors may be more important than considerations of price.What marketing executives refer to as brand loyalty and brand recognition are also important elements that propel consumer choices. A consumer who has had a beneficial experience with a specific brand of product or service will most likely continue to purchase it, despite increases in its price - up to a point.

So every significant development in the study of consumer decision-making, and every aspect of the process are of great interest to the businesses community. The data and insights provided by this microeconomic research are studied by marketers and frequently employed in a firm's pricing, marketing strategies, advertising, packaging, product research and development, quality and quantity considerations, and in other factors designed to stimulate sales.Accurate data on some aspects of consumer buying patterns and preferences can be found in print sources and on government and trade association web sites. Some of this data is also available from various business associations and individual firms who conduct their own surveys and research programmes to develop consumer data unique to their own businesses.

## CONSUMER'S FIRST ORDER-CONDITIONS

We can characterize optimizing behaviour by calculus, as long as the utility function is differentiable. As suggested, analyse this constrained maximization problem using the method of Lagrange multipliers. The Lagrangian for the utility maximization problem can be written as

$$\mathcal{L} = u(\mathrm{x}) - \lambda(\mathrm{px} - m),$$

where $\lambda$ is the Lagrange multiplier. Suppose preference is locally non-satiated. Differentiating the Lagrangian with respect to $x_i$, gives us the first-order conditions for the interior solution

$$\frac{\partial u(x)}{\partial x_i} - \lambda p_i = 0$$

$$px = m$$

Using vector notation, we can also write equation as,

$$\mathrm{D}u(\mathrm{x}) = \lambda\mathrm{p}.$$

Here,

$$Du(x) = \left(\frac{\partial u(x)}{\partial x_1}, \ldots, \frac{\partial u(x)}{\partial x_L}\right)$$

is the gradient of $u$: the vector of partial derivatives of $u$ with respect to each of its arguments.

In order to interpret these conditions we can divide the $i^{th}$ first-order condition by the $j^{th}$ first-order condition to eliminate the Lagrange multiplier. This gives us,

$$\frac{\frac{\partial u(x^*)}{\partial x_i}}{\frac{\partial u(x^*)}{\partial x_j}} = \frac{p_i}{p_j}$$

for $i,j, =1,...,L.$

The fraction on the left is the marginal rate of substitution between good $i$ and $j$, and the fraction on the right is economic rate of substitution between goods $i$ and $j$. Maximization implies that these two rates of substitution should be equal. Suppose they were not; for example, suppose

$$\frac{\frac{\partial u(x^*)}{\partial x_i}}{\frac{\partial u(x^*)}{\partial x_j}} = \frac{1}{1} \neq \frac{2}{1} = \frac{p_i}{p_j}.$$

Then, if the consumer gives up one unit of good $i$ and purchases one unit of good $j$, he or she will remain on the same indifference curve and have an extra dollar to spend. Hence, total utility can be increased, contradicting maximization.The argument geometrically. The budget line of the consumer is given by $\{x: p_1x_1 + p_2x_2 = m\}$. This can also be written as the graph of an implicit function: $x_2 = m/p_2-(p_1=p_2)x_1$. Hence, the budget line has slope$-p_1/p_2$ and vertical intercept $m/p_2$.

The consumer wants to find the point on this budget line that achieves highest utility. This must clearly satisfy the tangency condition that the slope of the indifference curve equals the slope of the budget line so that the marginal rate of substitution of $x_1$ for $x_2$ equals the economic rate of substitution of $x_1$ for $x_2$.

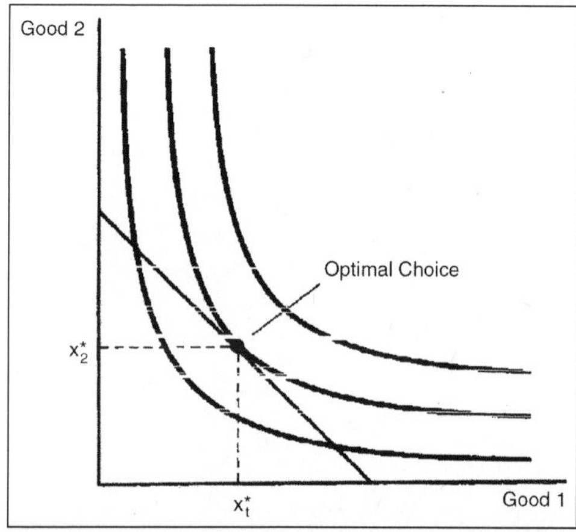


**Fig**: Preference Maximization. The Optimal Consumption Bundle will be at a Point where an Indifference Curve is Tangent to the Budget Constraint.

The calculus conditions derived make sense only when the choice variables can be varied in an open neighbourhood of the optimal choice and the budget constraint is binding. In many economic problems the variables are naturally Non-negative. If some variables have a value of zero at the optimal choice, the calculus conditions described may be inappropriate. The necessary modifications of the conditions to handle boundary solutions are not difficult to state. The relevant first-order conditions are given by means of the so-called Kuhn-Tucker conditions:

$$\frac{\partial u(x)}{\partial x_i} - \lambda p_i \leqq 0$$

with equality if $x_i > 0$ $i = 1,...., L$.

$$px \leqq m \text{ with equality if } \lambda > 0$$

Thus the marginal utility from increasing $xi$ must be less than or equal to $\lambda p_i$, otherwise the consumer would increase $xi$. If $x_i = 0$, the marginal utility from increasing $x_i$ may be less than $\lambda p_i$—which is to say, the consumer would like to decrease $x_i$. But since $x_i$ is already zero, this is impossible. Finally, if $x_i > 0$ so that the Non-negativity constraint is not binding, as suggested, have the usual conditions for an interior solution.

**SUFFICIENCY OF CONSUMER'S FIRST-ORDER CONDITIONS**

The first-order conditions are merely necessary conditions for a local optimum. However, for the particular problem at hand, these necessary first-order conditions are in fact sufficient for a global optimum when a utility function is quasi-concave. We then have the following proposition.

*Proposition*: Suppose that u(x) is differentiable and quasi-concave on $\mathbb{R}^L_{++}$ and (p,m) > 0. If (x, λ) satisfies the first-order conditions, then x solves the consumer's utility maximization problem at prices p and income m.

*Proof:* Since the budget set $B(p,m)$ is convex and $u(x)$ is differentiable and quasi-concave on $\mathbb{R}^2_{++}$ we know $x$ solves the consumer's utility maximization problem at prices $p$ and income $m$.

With the sufficient conditions in hand, it is enough to find a solution $(x, \lambda)$ that satisfies the first-order conditions. The conditions can typically be used to solve the demand functions $x_i(p,m)$ as we show in the following examples.

*Example*: Suppose the preference ordering is represented by the Cobb-Douglas utility function:

$$u(x_1, x_2) = x_1^{\alpha} x_2^{1-\alpha},$$

which is strictly quasi-concave on $\mathbb{R}^2_{++}$. Since any monotonic transform of this function represents the same preferences, we can also write,

$$u(x_1, x_2) = a \ln x_1 + (1–a) \ln x_2.$$

The demand functions can be derived by solving the following problem:

$$\max a \ln x_1 + (1–a) \ln x_2$$
$$\text{such that } p_1x_1 + p_2x_2 = m:$$

The first–order conditions are,

$$\frac{a}{x_1} - |\lambda p_1 = 0$$

or,

$$\frac{a}{p_1x_1} = \frac{1-a}{p_2x_2}.$$

Cross multiply and use the budget constraint to get,

$$ap_2x_2 = p_1x_1–ap_1x_1$$
$$am = p_1x_1$$

$$x_1(p_1, p_2, m) = \frac{am}{p_1}.$$

*Substitute into the budget constraint to get the demand function for the second commodity*:

$$x_2(p_1, p_2, m) = \frac{(1-a)m}{p_2}.$$

Example Suppose the preference ordering is represented by the Leotief utility function: $u(x_1, x_2) = \min\{ax_1, bx_2\}$. Since the Leontief utility function is not differentiable, so the maximum must be found by a direct argument. Assume $p > 0$.

The optimal solution must be at the kink point of the indifference curve. That is,

$$ax_1 = bx_2.$$

Substituting,

$$x_1 = \frac{b}{a}x_2$$

into the budget constraint $px = m$, we have,

$$p_1\frac{b}{a}x_2 + p_2x_2 = m$$

and thus the demand functions are given by,

$$x_2(p_1, p_2, m) = \frac{am}{bp_1 + ap_2}$$

and,

$$x_1(p_1,p_2,m)=\frac{am}{bp_1+ap_2}$$

*Example Now suppose the preference ordering is represented by the linear utility function*:

$$u(x,\ y) = ax + by.$$

Since the marginal rate of substitution is $a/b$ and the economic rate of substitution is $px/py$ are both constant, they cannot be in general equal. So the first-order condition cannot hold with equality as long as $a/b \neq px/py$. In this case the answer to the utility-maximization problem typically involves a boundary solution: only one of the two goods will be consumed. It is worthwhile presenting a more formal solution since it serves as a nice example of the Kuhn-Tucker theorem in action. The Kuhn-Tucker theorem is the appropriate tool to use here, since as suggested, almost never have an interior solution.

The Lagrange function is,

$$L(x,\ y,\ \lambda) = ax + by + \lambda(m - p_x x - p_y y)$$

and thus,

$$\frac{\partial L}{\partial x}=a-\lambda p_x$$

$$\frac{\partial L}{\partial y}=b-\lambda p_t$$

$$\frac{\partial L}{\partial \lambda}=m-p_x-p_y$$

*There are four cases to be considered:*

1. *Case* 1: $x > 0$ and $y > 0$. Then we have,

$$\frac{\partial L}{\partial x}=0 \text{ and} \frac{\partial L}{\partial y}=0 .$$

Thus,

$$\frac{a}{b}=\frac{p_x}{p_y} .$$

Since,

$$\lambda=\frac{a}{p_x}>0 ,$$

we have $pxx + pyy = m$ and thus all $x$ and $y$ that satisfy $p_x x + p_y y = m$ are the optimal consumptions.

2. *Case* 2. $x > 0$ and $y = 0$. Then we have,

$$\frac{\partial L}{\partial x}=0 \text{ and} \frac{\partial L}{\partial x}\leqq 0 .$$

Thus,

$$\frac{a}{b} \geqslant \frac{p_x}{p_y}.$$

Since,

$$\lambda = \frac{a}{p_x} > 0,$$

we have $p_x x + p_y y = m$ and thus,

$$x = \frac{m}{p_x}$$

is the optimal consumption.

3. *Case* 3: $x = 0$ and $y > 0$. Then we have,

$$\frac{\partial L}{\partial x} \leqq 0 \text{ and } \frac{\partial L}{\partial y} = 0.$$

Thus,

$$\frac{a}{b} \leqq \frac{p_x}{p_y}.$$

Since,

$$\lambda = \frac{b}{p_y} > 0,$$

we have $p_x x + p_y y = m$ and thus,

$$y = \frac{m}{p_y}$$

is the optimal consumption.

4. *Case* 4. $x = 0$ and $y = 0$. Then we have,

$$\frac{\partial L}{\partial x} \leqq 0 \text{ and } \frac{\partial L}{\partial y} \leqq 0.$$

Since,

$$\lambda \geqq \frac{b}{p_y} > 0,$$

we have $p_x x + p_y y = m$ and thus $m = 0$ because $x = 0$ and $y = 0$.

In summary, the demand functions are given by,

$$\left(x\left(p_x, p_y, m\right), y\left(p_x, p_y, m\right)\right) = \begin{cases} m/p_x, 0 & \text{if } a/b > p_x/p_y \\ \left(0, m/p_y\right) & \text{if } a/b < p_x/p_y \\ \left(x, m/px - p_y/p_x x\right) & \text{if } a/b = p_x/p_y \end{cases}$$

for all $x \in [0, m/p_x]$. In fact, it is easily found out the optimal solutions by comparing relatives steepness of the indifference curves and the budget line. For instance, when $a/b > p_x/p_y$, the indifference curves become steeper, and thus the optimal solution is the one the consumer spends his all income on good $x$. When $a=b < px/py$, the indifference curves become °atter, and thus the optimal solution is the one the consumer spends his all income on good $y$. When $a/b = px/py$, the indifference curves and the budget line are parallel and coincide at the optimal solutions, and thus the optimal solutions are given by all the points on the budget line.

# 3

# Production, Cost and Supply

## PRODUCTION

Economic activity not only involves consumption but also production and trade. Production should be interpreted very broadly, however, to include production of both physical goods–such as rice or automobiles{and services–such as medical care or financial services.

A firm can be characterized by many factors and aspects such as sectors, production scale, ownerships, organization structures, etc. But which are most important features for us to study producer's behaviour in making choices? To grasp the most important features in studying producer behaviour and choices in modern producer theory, it is assumed that the key characteristic of a firm is production set. Producer's characteristic together with the behaviour assumption are building blocks in any model of producer theory.

The production set represents the set of all technologically feasible production plans. The behaviour assumption expresses the guiding principle the producer uses to make choices. It is generally assumed that the producer seeks to identify and select a production that is most profitable. As suggested, first present a general framework of production technology.

By itself, the framework does not describe how production choices are made. It only specifies basic characteristic of a firm which defines what choices can be made; it does not specify what choices should be made. We then will discuss what choices should be made based on the behaviour assumptions on firms. A basic behaviour assumption on producers is profit maximization. After that, as suggested, describe production possibilities in physical terms, which is recast into economic terms—using cost functions.

## FACTORS OF PRODUCTION

Naturally, in a literal sense anything contributing to the productive process is a factor of production. However, economists seek to classify all inputs into a few broad categories, so standard usage refers to the categories themselves as factors. Earlier only three factors making up the *"classical triad"* were recognized: *land, labour,* and *capital*. Entrepreneurship is a fairly recent addition.

The concept of these factors is used to construct models illustrating general features of the economic process without getting caught up in inessential details. These include models purporting to explain growth, value, choice of production method, income distribution, and social classes. A major conceptual application is in the theory of production functions.

One intuitive basis for the classification of the factors of production is the manner of payment for their services: rent for land, wages for labour, interest for capital, and profit for entrepreneurship. Each of the factors is discussed in the following.

**Land**

Sometimes this factor however, extends over all natural resources. It is intended to represent the contribution to production of Non-human resources as found in their original, unimproved form. For the French physiocrats led by Francois Quesnay in the 1750s and 1760s, land was the only factor yielding a reliable gain to its owner. In their view, labourers and artisans were powerless and in excess supply, and hence they earned on average only a subsistence-level income; and in the same way what they produced outside of agriculture fetched enough to cover only their wages and input costs with no margin for profit.

Only in agriculture, due to soil fertility and other *"gifts of nature,"* could a labourer palpably produce more than required to cover subsistence and other costs, so only in agriculture could proprietors collect surplus. Thus the physiocrats explained land rent as coming from surplus produced by the land. They recommended taxes on land as the only sound way to raise revenue and land-grabbing as the best means to increase the government's revenue base.

In 1821, David Ricardo, in *The Principles of Political Economy and Taxation*, stated what came to be known as the classical view: that rent reflects scarcity of good land. The value of a crop depends on the labour required to produce it on the worst land under cultivation. This worst land yields no rent—as long as some of it remains unused—and rent collected on better land is simply its yield in excess of that on the worst land. Ricardo saw rent as coming from differences in land quality (including accessibility) and scarcity. The classical economists assumed only land—understood as natural resources—could be scarce in the long term.

In 1899, John Bates enlarge Marginalism in *The Distribution of Wealth*, takes a different approach. It declares that rent reflects the marginal productivity of land—not, as with Ricardo, the productivity of good versus marginal land. Marginal productivity is the extra output obtained by extending a constant amount of labour and capital over an additional unit of land of uniform quality.

Marginalists held that any factor of production could be scarce. Their theory is based on the possibility of substituting among factors to design alternative production methods, whereby the optimal production method allocates all the factors to equalize their marginal productivity with their marginal costs. Long thought of as a self-sustaining input, land might depreciate just like produced assets do.In 1989 Herman Daly and Jonathan Cobb, in *For the Common Good*, distinguished between Non-renewable resources that are consumed or depreciate irretrievably and renewable resources where the rate of natural renewal is important. One consequence of this work in environmental economics is that natural resource accounting increasingly resembles capital accounting.

**Labour**

In this factor the classical *"labour theory of value"* was an innovative theory in response to the physiocratic doctrine that only land could yield surplus. In 1776 Adam Smith, in *The Wealth of Nations*, observed that with expansion of production and trade, enterprises were making profits over long periods of time, although they either had nothing to do with agriculture or else as agricultural enterprises. Classical economists tried to answer the question: Where does profit come from? Their answer was that it came from labour.

In various industries, labour can yield a surplus over subsistence costs at prevailing prices. The question arises of why proprietors, but not labourers, earn profit. Ricardo arrived at one answer: Technical innovation increases labour productivity. Owners of innovative equipment, until its general adoption, get the premium from reduced costs. In 1867 Karl Marx in *Capital*, added that wages reflect the cost of subsistence, not what labourers can produce, and that profit is the difference between the two. Even without innovation proprietors would reap surpluses, Marx held, since labourers lack market power and cannot afford their own equipment.

Why wages are differ for different types of labour? Marx's answer was that higher wages cover costs, beyond personal subsistence, of training and cultivation of skills, acknowledging that one kind of *"equipment"* now known as human capital, was available at least to some labourers. Marginalist economists noticed the advance of technology, which according to classical and Marxist views made labour ever more productive, continually throws labourers out of work. This led them to attribute productivity to equipment rather than only to labour. Referring to equipment as capital, they developed production functions featuring labour and capital as substitutes for each other. In marinalist growth theory, choice among production techniques involving different combinations of labour and capital became a major theme.

**Capital**

This most controversial of factors is variously defined as produced equipment; as finance used to acquire produced equipment; as all finance used to begin and carry on production, including the "*wage fund*"; and as the assessed value of the whole productive enterprise, including intangibles such as "*goodwill.*" In 1960 Piero Sraffa, in *Production of Commodities by Means of Commodities*, showed that capital in the sense of produced equipment can fail to behave as expected in marginalist production functions when an entire economy is modeled. Specifically, equipment adopted to replace labour after wages rise from a low level, relative to interest on capital, may be abandoned again in favour of labour as wages rise still higher. This counterintuitive "*reswitching*" can happen because the equipment used is itself a product of labour and equipment, and because the ratio of labour to equipment varies for different products.

Frequently capital is treated as finance, associated with the payment of interest. Yet the connection with equipment, in spite of Sraffa's demonstration, has never been severed entirely. One still studies capital depreciation, distinguishing wear-and-tear from obsolescence, and from the present value of investments in capital. Increasingly, theory has come to treat any investment as a capital investment. Furthermore, acquired skills (as opposed to "know-how," an attribute of society rather than individuals) have come to be viewed as analogous to physical equipment, capable of yielding their owners a return. This analogy suggests their current designation as human capital. Thus capital is a concept still mired in confusion, and care must be taken in its use to be sure what it means.

**Entrepreneurship**

Before the twentieth century, this function was assigned to the capitalist and frequently conflated with capital. In the classical view, profit rather than interest was attributed to ownership of capital. In the marginalist view, capital earned interest, and profit was a mere residual after all the factors of production were compensated. In his *Principles of Economics*, first published in 1890, Alfred Marshall made extensive references to "*organization*" and "*management,*" referring to the coordination function of entrepreneurship but to neither risk-assuming nor innovation. But in 1912 Joseph Schumpeter, in *The Theory of Economic Development*, featured the revolutionary role of organizer and innovator and contrasted it with that of the conservative financier, thus vividly distinguishing the entrepreneur from the capitalist. In this view, the entrepreneur's role is not merely that of manager and risk-taker, but also of visionary—someone who seeks as much to destroy the old order as to create something new. Since innovation usually requires destroying old ways of doing things, Schumpeter gave it the name "*creative destruction.*" Profit is now assigned to entrepreneurship, to innovation. With the rise of "*venture capitalists*" and other financiers willing to take on more risk and do more for innovation in the hope for supernormal returns, the distinction between capitalist and entrepreneur has again become fuzzier. Instantly, there are entrepreneurial financiers as well as entrepreneurial producers and distributors.

Although in business usage stock dividends are distributed profits, in economic analysis they figure as returns to capital, a kind of interest payment, since they are a return to finance rather than to entrepreneurship. The fact that stocks are legally equity rather than debt shares are thereby ignored. Similarly, salaries of corporate executive officers are treated as profit, a return to entrepreneurship, rather than as wages for labour services.

## FUNCTION OF PRODUCTION

Let us begin with the production function, a function summarising the process of conversion of factors into a particular commodity. We might propose a production function for a good y of the following general form, first proposed by Philip Wicksteed (1894):

$$y = f(x_1, x_2..., x_m)$$

which relates a single output y to a series of factors of production $x_1, x_2..., x_m$. Note that in writing production functions in this form, we are excluding joint production, *i.e.*, that a particular process of production yields more than one output (*e.g.*, the production of wheat grain often yields a co-product, straw; the production of omelettes yields the co-product broken egg shells). Using Ragnar Frisch's (1965) terms, we are concentrating on "single-ware" rather than "multi-ware" production.For heuristic purposes, the production technology for the one-output/two-inputs case is (imperfectly). Output (Y) is measured on the vertical axis. The two inputs, which we call L and K which, for mnemonic purposes, can be called labour and capital,, are depicted on the horizontal axes. We ought to now warn that henceforth, throughout all our sections on the theory of production, all capital is assumed to be endowed, *i.e.*, there are no produced means of production. Notice that it includes all the area on the surface and in the interior of the hill. The production set is essentially the set of technically feasible combinations of output Y and inputs, K and L.

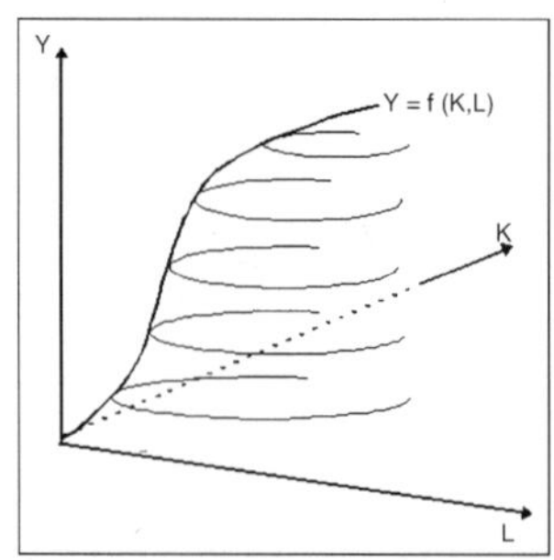


**Fig.** Production Function for One-output/Two-inputs.

A production decision -- a feasible choice of inputs and output - is a particular point on or in this "hill". It will be "on" the hill if it is technically efficient and "in" the hill if it is technically inefficient. Properly speaking, theproduction function $Y = f(K, L)$ is only the surface (and not the interior) of the hill, and thus denotes the set of technologically efficient points of the production set (*i.e.*, for a given configuration of inputs, K, L, output Y is the maximum feasible output).

Obviously, the hill-shape of the production function indicates that the more we use of the factors, the greater output is going to be (at least up to the some maximum, the "top" of the hill). The round contours along the production hill can be thought of as topographic contours as seen on maps and will serve as isoquants in our later analysis. The slope of the hill viewed from the origin captures the notion of returns to scale.Throughout the next few sections, we shall be outlining the technical properties of the production function. The representation of production functions in the diagrammatic form of "hills" and the corresponding analysis of production theory in terms of isoquant contours, etc., was initiated by Vilfredo Pareto (1906) and much of the analysis of its technical properties was largely advanced by the "Paretian" school of Hotelling, Frisch, Samuelson,Hicks, Shephard, etc., between the 1930s and the 1950s. In the 1950s, the Neo-Walrasians approached the analysis of the technical properties of production in a somewhat different spirit. Specifically, instead of focusing on the "production function" and its derivatives as the Paretians had done, the Neo-Walrasians preferred to analyse it via vector space methods and convex analysis.

On a more formal note, we should outline the properties of the production function, as normally assumed by Neo-classical economists. Let there be m factors of production and let vector $x = (x_1, x_2.., x_m)$ denote a bundle of factor inputs. We shall define an input space as the acceptable set of inputs for our economy. Commonly, a bundle of factor inputs x is deemed "acceptable" if every entry in that vector, *i.e.*, the quantity of every factor, is a non-negative, finite real number. Thus, any input bundle x lies in $R_+^m$, the non-negative orthant of m-dimensional Euclidian space. Thus, $R_+^m$ is our input space. Let y be output, which is assumed to be a single, finite number, *i.e.*, $y \in R$. Thus, a production function $f$ maps acceptable input bundles to output values, *i.e.*, $f: R_+^m \rightarrow R$. More specifically, $f(x)$ is the maximum output achievable for a given set of acceptable inputs, $x \in R_+^m$.

*The following assumptions are often imposed on any generic production function* $f: R_+^m \rightarrow R$:

- (A.1) $f(x)$ is finite, non-negative, real-valued and single-valued for all non-negative and finite x.
- (A.2) $f(0, 0.., 0) = 0$ (no inputs implies no output).
- (A.3) If $x \geq x`$, then $f(x) \geq f(x`)$ (monotonicity, *i.e.*, an increase in inputs does not decrease output)

- (A.4) $f$ is continuous and twice-continuously differentiable everywhere in the interior of the production set.
- (A.5) The set $V(y) = \{x \mid f(x) \geq y\}$ is a convex set (quasi-concavity of $f$)
- (A.6) The set V(y) is closed and non-empty for any $y > 0$.

These assumptions will be clarified as we go on. For the moment, let us just make the following notes. Assumption (A.1) simply defines the production function as a well-defined function of inputs $f$: $R_+^m \to R$. Nothing new there. Assumption (A.2) simply establishes that one cannot produce something from nothing. This is somewhat self-evident, at least for economists. Obviously, in other walks of life, one can produce something without inputs (*e.g.* "nice thoughts" can just be, well, "thought up" without inputs), but most examples of these things are outside the realm of economics. The monotonicity assumption (A.3) is also straightforward: increasing inputs leads to an increase in output (or, more precisely, no decrease in output). Although common, we will have more to say on this later. Assumption (A.4) is made largely for mathematical ease; later on, we shall relax this assumption somewhat. Assumption (A.5), the quasi-concavity of the production function $f$, is the more interesting one. We shall have much more to say on this later. Finally, (A.6) is imposed as a mathematical necessity.

**Marginal Efficiency**

The assumptions given earlier imply that, for any given production function $y = f(x_1, x_2.., x_m)$, it is a generally the case that, at least up to some maximum point:

$$\partial y/\partial x_i = f_i \geq 0$$

for all factor inputs i = 1, 2..., m. In other words, adding more units of any factor input will increase output (or at least not reduce it). This is the heart of assumption (A.3). However, it is also common in Neo-classical theory to also impose (A.5), *i.e.*, to assume "quasi-concavity" of the production function. It is often the case in economics that the quasi-concavity assumption implies that:

$$\partial^2 y/\partial x_i^2 = f_{ii} < 0$$

for all i = 1.., m, *i.e.*, diminishing marginal productivity of ith factor.

It is worthwhile to spend a few moments on the diminishing marginal productivity assumption. This means more we add of a particular factor input, all others factors remaining constant, the less the employment of an additional unit of that factor input contributes to output as a whole. This concept performs the same function in production functions as diminishing marginal utility did in utility functions. Conceptually, however, they are quite distinct.

**The Law of Diminishing Income**

The idea of diminishing marginal productivity was simultaneously introduced for applications of factors to a fixed plot of land by T.R. Malthus (1815), Robert Torrens (1815), Edward West (1815) and David Ricardo(1815). It was applied more generally to other factors of production by proto-marginalists such as J.H. von Th•Een (1826), Mountiford Longfield (1834) and Heinrich Mangoldt (1863). The apotheosis of the concept is found in the work of John Bates Clark (1889, 1891, 1899) and, more precisely, in Philip H. Wicksteed (1894). It was originally called the "Law of Diminishing Returns", although in order to keep this distinct from the idea of decreasing returns to scale.

Let us first be clear about the definition of the marginal productivity of a factor. Letting $\Delta x_i$ denote a unit increase in factor $x_i$, then the marginal product of that factor is $\Delta y/\Delta x_i$, *i.e.*, the change in output arising from an increase in factor i by a unit. Mathematically, however, it is more convenient to assume that $\Delta x$ is infinitesimal. This permits us to express the marginal product of the factor $x_i$ as the first partial derivative of the production function with respect to that factor -- thus the marginal product of the ith factor is simply $\partial y/\partial x_i = f_i$. If we do not wish to assume that factor units are infinitely divisible or if we do not assume that the production function is differentiable, we cannot express the marginal product mathematically as a derivative.

However, assuming marginal products exist and are well defined, then why diminishing?

*Taking Clark's famous analogy:*

- "Put one man only on a square mile of prairie, and he will get a rich return. Two laborers on the same ground will get less per man; and, if you enlarge the force to ten, the last man will perhaps get wages only."

The implication, then, is that as we increase the amount of labour applied to a particular fixed amount of land, each additional unit will increase total output but by smaller and smaller increments. When the field is empty, the first laborer has absolutely free range and produces as much as his body can reasonably do, say ten bushels of corn. When you add a second laborer to the same field, total output may increase, say to eighteen bushels of corn. Thus, the marginal product is eight.

The basic idea is that by adding the second man, the field gets "crowded" and the men begin to get in each other's way. If that explanation does not seem credible, think of the units of labour in terms of labour-hours for a single man: in the first hour, a particular man produces ten; in the second hour he produces eight, etc. The diminution can be explained in this case as an "exhaustion" effect.

Taking another example, suppose we apply a man to a set of shoe-making tools and a given swathe of leather; let us say he can produce ten pairs of shoes in a day. Add a second man to this without adding more shoe-making tools or increasing the leather, and one can easily envisage that more shoes get made in a day, but that the work of the shoe-makers slows down as they pick up the same tools in an alternating sequence of turns and perhaps fight over them a bit.

For other factors, different stories are told. In Ricardo's original story, the land is subject to diminishing marginal returns because of the assumption that land has different degrees of fertility and the most fertile acres are used first, and the less fertile ones added later. We can conceive this more simply in that increasing the amount of land without increasing the amount of labour that works on it will lead to less output per worker.

However it is justified, many Neo-classical theorists basically accept diminishing marginal productivity as an axiom - "the diminishing marginal productivity of labour, when it is used in connection with a fixed amount of capital, is a universal phenomenon. This fact shows itself in any economy, primitive or social.". However much early economists tried to claim it to be a natural law, this "axiom" turns out to be closer to a rather debatable assumption.

Non-etheless, it is important to clearly note a few matters in relation to this. Firstly, the idea that marginal product is always diminishing can be disputed (and will be disputed). Francis A. Walker (1891) took J.B. Clark to task for not recognising the possibility of increasing marginal productivity.

Secondly, as Pareto (1896, 1902) was quick to point out, it is not always true that if one adds a unit of a factor to an existing production process, output will increase. "If a pit has to be dug, the addition of one more man will make little difference to the day's output unless you give the man a spade". This difficulty is even more clear if we see the problem in terms of the marginal product of capital: if a pit has to be dug, the addition of one more spade will make no difference to output unless you add a man to use it. Thus, one must be very careful when pronouncing the idea of marginal productivity since we may need to produce in fixed, constant factor proportions.

Thirdly, it is important to underline that the marginal product is not, properly speaking, the contribution of the marginal unit by itself. Some commentators seem to have gone on to make arguments that seem to imply, in the context of our example, that the second man produces eight bushels of corn. Of course, this is not necessarily true.

The second man may very well produce nine or ten or eleven and still the total output increases only to eighteen because the first man reduces his output to nine, or eight or seven in the presence of the second. In our example, output increases from ten bushels to eighteen bushels when one adds the second man not because the second man only adds eight, but rather because his presence on the field makes the situation such that the total output of both men is eighteen. Notice that the contribution per man is reduced: the average product is actually nine. This may very well be how much each of the two laborers contributes. But this is not what interests us: what we wish to note is that by adding the second man, output was increased by eight. Thus, the marginal product of the second man is eight. But his actual contribution may be very different than this.

Finally, and above everything, it is very important to note that in deriving the marginal product of a factor, we are holding all other factors fixed. Specifically, in our earlier example, labour varied and land (and indeed all other factors) was fixed.

Thus, diminishing marginal productivity has nothing to do with "returns to scale", *i.e.*, the increase in output when we increase all factors. If we increased both land and labour in our example, then there might very well be no reduction in output per man (indeed, there is actually no reason for it, but we shall return to this later).

**The Law of Changeable Proportions**

Marginal productivity is not obvious in the production function Y = $f$ (L, K) as both inputs are varying there. We must first fix one of the factors and let the other factor vary. The "reduced" production function Y = $f$ (L, $K_0$), where only labour (L) varies while capital is held fixed at $K_0$. To obtain this from the former, we must figuratively "slice" the hill in vertically at the level $K_0$. Thus,, which represents the reduced production function Y = $f$ (L, $K_0$), is a vertical section of the hill. A reduced production function where all factors but one are held constant are often referred to as the "total product" curve.

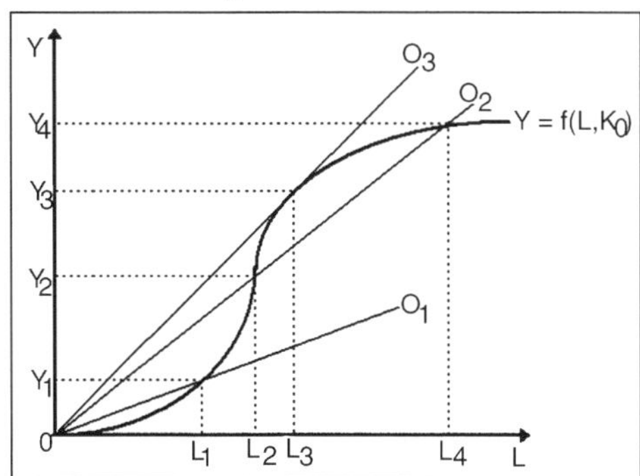


**Fig.** Total Product Curve.

The total product curve can be read in conjunction with the average and marginal product curves. The total product curve is originally due to Frank H. Knight (1921: p.100), and much of the subsequent analysis is due to him and John M. Cassels (1936). Although both these sets of curves have long been implicit in much earlier discussions (*e.g.* Edgeworth, 1911), average and marginal products were confused by early Neo-classicals with surprising frequency. The particular shape of the total product curve exhibits what has been baptised by John M. Cassels (1936) as the Law of Variable Proportions -- effectively what Ragnar Frisch (1965: p.120) quirkily renamed the ultra-passum law of production. The marginal product of the factor L is given by the slope of the total product curve, thus $MP_L = \partial Y/\partial L = df(L, K_0)/dL$. As we see, at low levels of L up to $L_2$, we have rising marginal productivity of the factor. At levels of L above $L_2$ we have diminishing marginal productivity of that factor. Thus, marginal productivity of L reaches its maximum at $L_2$. We can thus trace out a marginal product of L curve, $MP_L$. The labels there correspond. Thus the $MP_L$ curve rises until the inflection point $L_2$, and falls after it. It becomes negative after $L_5$ - which would be equivalent to the "top" of the reduced production function, what Frisch (1965: p.89) calls a "strangulation point". A negative marginal product is akin to a situation when one adds the fiftieth worker to a field whose only accomplishment is to get in everyone else's way - and thus does not increase output at all but actually reduces it.

The slope of the different rays through the origin ($O_1$, $O_2$, $O_3$, etc.) in reflect average products of the factor L, *i.e.*, $AP_L = Y/L$. The steeper the ray, the higher the average product. Thus, at low levels of output such as $Y_1$, the average product represented by the slope of $O_1$ is rather low, while at some levels of output such as $Y_3$, the average product (here the slope of $O_3$) is much higher. Indeed, as we can see, average product is at its highest at $Y_3$, what is sometimes called the extensive margin of production. Notice that at $Y_2$ and $Y_4$ we have the same average product (*i.e.*, the ray $O_2$ passes through both points). The average product curve $AP_L$ corresponding is also drawn.

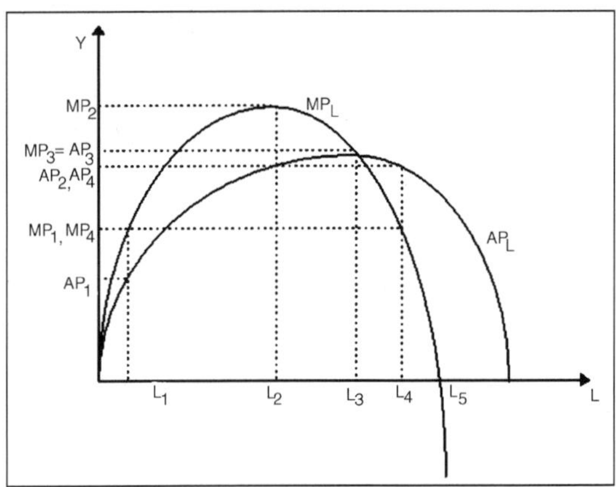


**Fig.** Marginal Product and Average Product Curves.

The slope of the total product curve is equal to the slope of the ray from the origin at $L_3$, thus average product and marginal product are equal at this point. We also know that as the ray from the origin associated with $L_3$ is the highest, thus average product curve intersects the marginal product curve, $MP_L = AP_L$, exactly where the average product curve is at its maximum. Notice that at values below $L_3$, $MP_L > AP_L$, marginal product is greater than average product whereas above $L_3$, we have the reverse, $MP_L < AP_L$. We shall make use of these results later on.

It seems that we can have increasing as well as diminishing marginal productivity of labour, as suggested by Walker (1891) and finally acknowledged by Clark (1899: p.164). However, we have already gone a long way in arguing for diminishing marginal productivity that it seems that we must be excluding points where there is rising marginal productivity, *i.e.*, those points to the left of L2.

How might such a restriction be justified? In effect, the argument is that in situations of increasing marginal productivity, one can always discard factors and increase output. Consider the following example. Assume we have an acre of ripened land to which we are going to apply various quantities of workers. The one lonely worker produces 10 bushels of wheat; two workers will produce 22 bushels of wheat; three workers will produce 36 bushels. Thus, we see:

| Qty. of Labor | Total Product | Average Product | Marginal Product |
|---|---|---|---|
| One Laborers | 10 | 10 | 10 |
| Two Laborers | 22 | 11 | 12 |
| Three Laborers | 36 | 12 | 14 |

Thus, there is increasing average product and increasing marginal product of labour in this example. Why? One can think of it as follows. When we apply one lonely worker to an entire acre of ripened land, his running around the entire acre trying to harvest it will produce a lower average product than if we had three workers, each working a third of the field by himself.

This should already reveal why we would never see a situation of increasing average product. Basically, when we are faced with a situation of a single worker on an acre of land, why should we force him to work on the entire acre and only produce 10 units of output? Average product (and total product) would be higher if instead of forcing that single worker to try to harvest the entire acre, we let him confine himself to a third of that acre, and let the other two-thirds of the plot lie untouched. In this case, the average product of the single worker is as it would have been had there been three harvesters, *i.e.*, 12 units of output. In other words, in situations of rising average and marginal product, total output is increased by discarding two-thirds of the land! Thus, situations of increasing marginal productivity will simply never be seen.

Of course, this logic is not unassailable. While the idea may apply naturally to some cases, it can be questioned in cases where division of labour is crucial as, say, we might have in an automobile factory. Suppose that the average productivity of a worker is highest when there are twenty men working on a factory floor, each worker specialising in fitting a special part of the automobile. We cannot subsequently do the same operation we did before. In other words, we cannot remove nineteen men and let 19/20ths of the car remain unbuilt. The only remaining man, whose productivity was highest when he only fitted wheels on axles, will not yield any output if he is permitted to perform only his specialised task bereft of the other nineteen men. Instead of having cars as output in that case, we would have axles-with-wheels.

Consequently, we see that in order to produce any cars whatsoever, the lone man must be forced to perform all the tasks, not only the fitting of wheels on axles. If this is true, his productivity by himself, where product is measured in number of cars produced rather than axles-with-wheels, will be lower than if he worked together with his nineteen colleagues.

The automobile case shows an example of indivisibility in production, a traditional explanation of increasing marginal productivity. Production is divisible if it "permits any particular method of production, involving certain proportions between factors and products, to be repeated in exactly the same way on larger or on a smaller scale.". In other words, in a perfectly divisible world, there cannot be changes in method when increasing or decreasing the scale of production. In our automobile example we have indivisibility: when we remove the nineteen men, the remaining man who previously only placed axles on wheels must change his method and do all the tasks in the construction of the automobile. In contrast, our agricultural example was divisible: a laborer working exclusively on his portion of the field will not change his method of harvesting that third of the field when the other laborers on the other the remaining two-thirds of the field are removed.

In sum, increasing marginal productivity, especially in cases where specialisation is vital, can be ostensibly encountered in the real world where there are indivisibilities in production. Nevertheless, much of the Neo-classical work on the production function omits this. This is, as noted earlier, is often taken axiomatically, but the question of whether one finds it an acceptable assumption is largely an empirical one.

**Isoquant Analysis of Production**

The contours along the production "hill" are the isoquants. A particular isoquant denotes the combinations of factors K and L which produce the same quantity of output. As we are assuming factors K and L are continuously substitutable (on which we will have more to say later), then every point on a particular isoquant represents a particular feasible technique, or factor combination, that can be used to produce a particular level of output. The isoquants play the same topographic role to the production "hill" as indifference curves played in the the "utility hill". As the isoquants ascend to the northeast, the amount of output produced increases, thus Y` < Y* < Y``.

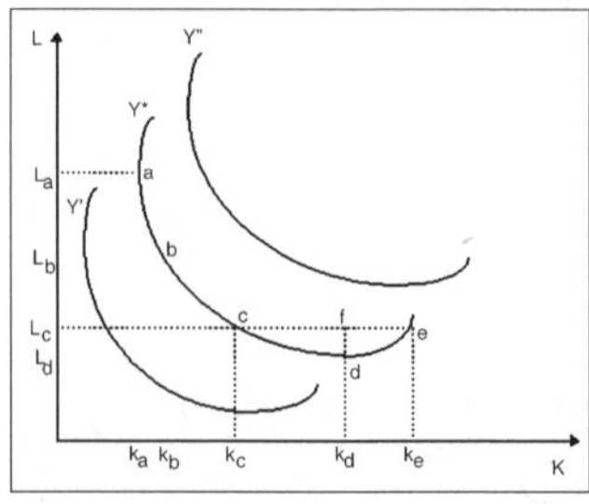


**Fig.** Isoquants.

It is an elementary matter to derive the slope of an isoquant. For our two-factor case, we had a production function Y = $f$ (L, K). Now, for the production of a given fixed quantity of output (call it Y*), it follows that Y* =$f$ (L, K). This is the formula for a particular isoquant.

*Totally differentiating this:*

$$dY^* = f_L dL + f_K dK$$

where $f_L = \partial Y/\partial L$ and $f_K = \partial Y/\partial K$ are the marginal products of labour and capital respectively, evaluated around Y*. Since on any isoquant, output is fixed at Y*, then dY* = 0. This implies that $f_L dL = -f_K dK$, or simply:

$$-dL/dK|_{Y^*} = f_K/f_L$$

The term on the left is the negative of the slope of the isoquant corresponding to output level Y*. This is known as the marginal rate of technical substitution (MRTS), *i.e.*, the rate at which capital can be susbstituted for labour while holding output constant along an isoquant. (note that dL/dK by itself is already negative, thus the MRTS will be a positive number). Provided our isoquants are smoothly differentiable, we will be able to define the MRTS at any point. Thus, the MRTS depends not only on the level of output (which isoquant we are on), but also the amounts of capital and labour (where on the isoquant we are). The equality of the MRTS with the ratio of marginal products of capital and labour,$f_K/f_L$, is a fundamental feature of production theory and helps us capture the concept of diminishing marginal productivity to a factor. In Figure, on isoquant Y*, as we move from point a to b to c to d, we are moving towards greater employment of K and less employment of L to produce a given level of output Y*, thus we are moving from labour-intensive techniques (*i.e.*, low capital-labour ratios) towards capital-intensive techniques (high capital-labour ratios). Notice also that the isoquant becomes flatter as we move from a to d, thus the marginal rate of technical substitution is higher at a than at d, *i.e.*, $MRTS_a > MRTS_b > MRTS_c > MRTS_d$. Thus, there is diminishing marginal rates of technical substitution as we move from a towards d.

Notice that this declining MRTS arises because of the convexity of the isoquants. As we can notice, the declining MRTS effectively can capture something akin to (but not exactly) of the assumption of diminishing marginal productivity to a factor we spoke of earlier. Compare only the points b and c. As $MRTS_b > MRTS_c$, then $f_K/f_L|b > f_K/f_L|_c$. But point b represents a lower capital-labour ratio than point c, *i.e.*, $K/L|_b < K/L|_c$. Thus, we can interpret the declining MRTS as saying that as we move from lower capital-intensity to higher capital intensity (b to c), the marginal product of capital decreases. Reciprocally, as we move from higher labour-intensity to lower labour-intensity (b to c), the marginal product of labour increases.

Note that we cannot derive diminishing MRTS from the assumption of diminishing marginal productivity of factors. To see this, consider the production function, Y = $f$ (K, L). The MRTS at any point is $f_K/f_L$. In order to have diminishing MRTS, then it must be that dMRTS/dK < 0. But as dMRTS/dK = $d(f_K/f_L)/dK$ and $f_K$ and $f_L$ vary with K and L, then we must take total derivatives.

*Thus:*

$$dMRTS/dK = d(f_K/f_L)/dK$$

$$= [(f_{KK} + f_{KL} \cdot dL/dK)f_L - (f_{LK} + f_{LL} \cdot dL/dK)f_K]/f_L^2$$

as $dL/dK = -f_K/f_L$ along any isoquant and given that $f_{KL} = f_{LK}$ by Young's Theorem, then:

$$dMRTS/dK = [f_{KK} f_L - 2f_{LK} f_K + f_{LL} \cdot f_K^2/f_L]/f_L^2$$

*or simply:*

$$dMRTS/dK = [f_{KK} f_L^2 - 2f_{LK} f_K f_L + f_{LL} \cdot f_K^2]/f_L^3$$

Now, by assumption, $f_K, f_L > 0$ and, by diminishing marginal productivity, $f_{KK} < 0$ and $f_{LL} < 0$. This is obviously not sufficient to determine the sign of dMRTS/dK. Specifically, the numerator will only be negative if, in addition, we assume that $f_{LK} > 0$, and the theory of diminishing marginal productivity implies no such thing. Thus, a diminishing MRTS is, in itself, an separate assumption.

We should note, however, that not every point along the isoquant is relevant. The isoquants, after all, are contours of our "production" hill and thus are actually "circular". We show the isoquants in their full topographic glory as a horizontal section of the production hill. Notice that the isoquant labels represent increasing output levels, Y < Y` < Y`` < Y```, etc. The "top of the hill", the highest output achievable, is represented by point M in the center, achieved by factor combination LM and KM. Notice that if we are the top of the hill, if we increase factor inputs (above KM or LM), output will actuallydecline.

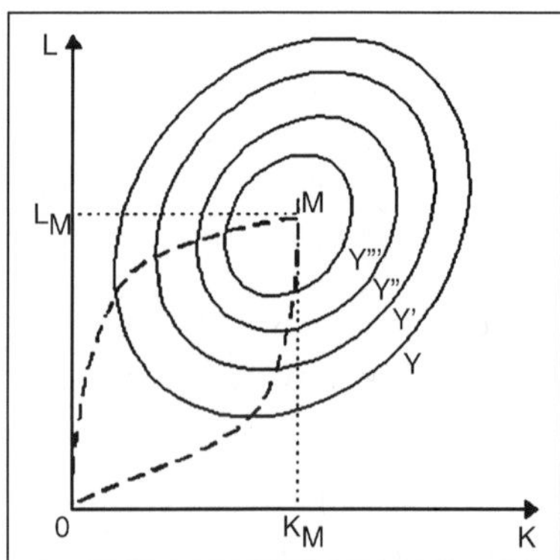


**Fig.** Isoquants with Ridge Lines.

We have also added dashed "ridge lines" to the topographic. Only those points within the ridge lines, in the lightly shaded region, are of economic relevance. To see why, return and notice that at point a, the isoquant has a vertical slope and a point d, the isoquant has a horizontal slope. Thus, $MRTS_a = f_K/f_L|_a = \infty$ and $MRTS_d = f_K/f_L|_d = 0$. But our isoquants seem to continue beyond them, yet we assert that points beyond them are economically irrelevant.

Why? Consider a factor combination such as at point e. Obviously, here, the slope of the isoquant is positive, *i.e.*, $dL/dK|_e > 0$, which implies, in turn, that $MRTS_e = f_K/f_L < 0$, thus the marginal product of one of the factors is negative. This violates the first assumption we made about the production function: namely, that $f_i > 0$ for all i, *i.e.*, increasing the employment of any factor in a production process will always increase output. Thus, we ought to exclude all regions where marginal products are negative.

Is this assumption reasonable? Well, notice that at point e, we are employing factors $K_e$ and $L_e$ to produce output level Y*. Yet, we could decrease the amount of capital employed to $K_d$ and leave labour at $L_e$ in order to achieve a combination at point f. But notice that as point f is above the isoquant Y*, it effectively represents a higher level of output.

Thus, if we are at a point such as e, then by reducing factor inputs we can increaseoutput: such factor combinations are therefore not "economical". Consequently we can rule out point e - and, indeed, all factor combinations on the isoquant Y* beyond d. Similarly, we exclude points on the isoquant beyond point a for the same reason.

The "ridge lines" drawn, pass through limiting points of the various isoquants akin to points a and d. In other words, at any point on the upper ridge line, MRTS $= \infty$ for the relevant isoquant, while at any point on the lower ridge line, MRTS $= 0$ for the relevant isoquant. Thus, we exclude all regions above the upper ridge line and below the lower ridge line as economically irrelevant.

Only the lightly shaded area is "relevent". Notice that the ridge lines meet at point M, the "top" of the production "hill". On a more formal note, we should connect the quasi-concavity of the production function to the convexity of the isoquants in general. A function ? is quasi-concave if, for any two input bundles x, $x` \in R_+^m$

$$\text{if } f(x) \geq f(x`), \text{ then } f(\lambda x + (1-\lambda)x`) \geq f(x`) \text{ for any } \lambda \in (0, 1).$$

In other words, the output produced from a convex combination (*i.e.*, weighted average) of two bundles of inputs is at least as great as the smaller of the two outputs produced using only one or the other input bundles. A special case of quasi-concave function is simply a concave function, namely for any two input bundles x, $x` \in R_+^m$:

$$f(\lambda x + (1-\lambda)x`) \geq \lambda f(x) + (1-\lambda) f(x`) \text{ for any } \lambda \in (0, 1).$$

which states that the output produced from a convex combination of inputs is at least as great as the convex combination of the outputs produced by the input bundles independently.

The definition of quasi-concavity we used in (A.5) states that V(y) = {x | *f* (x) ≥ y} is convex. In other words, a function is quasi-concave if the upper contour set V(y) is convex. As we see, this "upper contour set" V(y) is merely the isoquant defined by y and the area above that isoquant. Y* is the isoquant of relevance, thus V(Y*), the shaded area, is the upper contour set.

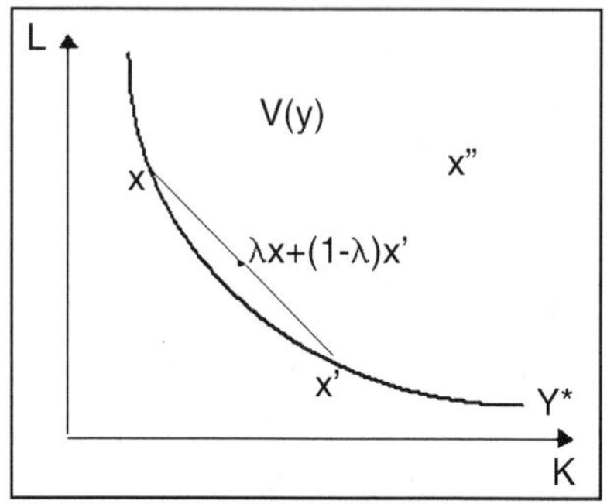


**Fig.** Upper Contour Set and Convexity.

It can be easily proven that if a function is quasi-concave in the sense defined earlier, then its upper contour set is necessarily convex. To see this intuitively, let x and x` be two points on the same isoquant, thus *f* (x) = *f* (x`). Thus, quasi-concavity implies that the output produced by any convex combination of the two points x and x` is greater than the output produced by either point individually. In other words, the convex combination of two points on the same isoquant will lie on a higher isoquant.

We see that λ x + (1-λ)x` is indeed within V(y), thus it will lie on a higher isoquant. This implies precisely the convex shape of the isoquant curves which implies, in turn, the convexity of the upper contour set V(y). A final characterisation of quasi-concavity makes use of the bordered Hessian matrix. The bordered Hessian matrix of a twice-continuously differentiable function y = *f* ($x_1$, $x_2$.., $x_m$) is defined as follows:

| | | | | | | |
|---|---|---|---|---|---|---|
| | | 0 | 1 | 2 | ... | m |
| B | = | 1 | 11 | 12 | ... | 1m |
| | | 2 | 21 | 22 | ... | 2m |
| | | : | ... | ... | ... | ... |
| | | m | m1 | m2 | ... | mm |

where $f_i$ is the first partial derivative of the production function with respect to factor xi and ? ij are the second derivatives, all evaluated at a particular factor combination x.

If the production function is quasi-concave, then we know that the bordered Hessian of that function evaluated at any input bundle x ∈ $R_+^m$ will be negative semi-definite, *i.e.*, its principal leading minors will alternate in sign.

*Specifically:*

| | | |
|---|---|---|
| 0 | 1 | |
| 1 | 11 | 0 |

... etc.

Notice that the very first principal minor implies that $-f\ 1^2 \leq 0$, which is true whether $f_1 \geq 0$ or $f_1 \leq 0$, so quasi-concavity does not rule out negative marginal products. The second principal minor implies:

$$-f_1 [f_1 f_{22} - f_2 f_{21}] + f_2 [f_1 f_{12} - f_2 f_{11}] \geq 0$$

as, byYoung's Theorem, $f_{21} = f_{12}$, this is reducible to:

$$2f_1 f_2 f_{21} - f_{12} f_{22} - f_2^2 f_{11} \geq 0.$$

Now, even if $f_1 \geq 0$ and $f_2 \geq 0$ by assumption, there is little implied by this condition. In other words, quasi-concavity of the production function is not sufficient to guarantee diminishing marginal productivities, *i.e.*, $f_{11} \leq 0$, $f_{22} \leq 0$, etc.

In contrast, concavity of the production function is, indeed, enough to yield diminishing marginal productivity. We can verify this by just examining the Hessian for the production function. This is:

| H | = | 11 | 12 | ... | 1m |
|---|---|---|---|---|---|
| | | 21 | 22 | ... | 2m |
| | | ... | ... | ... | ... |
| | | m1 | m2 | ... | mm |

where, note, the border is omitted. Concavity implies that the Hessian matrix must be negative semi-definite, by which we mean that the principle leading minors alternate in sign.

*This implies that:*

$f_{11} \leq 0$

$f_{11}\ f_{12}$

$f_{21}\ f_{22} \geq 0$

... etc.

Notice that the very first principal leading minor states that $f_{11} \leq 0$, *i.e.*, negative marginal productivity for input 1. As we can order inputs anyway we wish, then this effectively generalises to stating that every factor exhibits diminishing marginal productivity, *i.e.*, $f_{ii} < 0$ for all i = 1, 2.., m. Thus, while quasi-concavity cannot guarantee diminishing marginal productivity to factor inputs, concavity does indeed guarantee it. However, we should note that there are special cases when quasi-concavity of the production function guarantees diminishing marginal productivity - namely, under constant returns to scale.

## PRODUCTION OF A MACHINE

If labour is invested in the production of a machine, imagined by economists, which lasts for ever or what comes to the same, an improvement, such as the draining of land or opening a mine, or cutting an isthmus, which is calculated to yield a constant income for an indefinitely long series of years, then the series of positions along the stream at which the labour is supposed to be invested must be carried back indefinitely (see the channel of which the mouth is b1b'1) up to that needle-point whose tapering dimensions correspond to the perspective of an indefinitely distant future. Eternal machines are not very common; but the conception may serve to illustrate a species of tool or implement of which the race remains immortal, though the individual is worn out and perishes. Of this kind are implements which are directed not only to produce goods immediately ready for consumption or implements of a kind different from their own, but also to reproduce their own kind. Hammers and axes are presumably of this kind in a primitive society; in an advanced state of industry, some more complicated engines. Such machines may be compared to horses, if used not only as beasts of burden, but also as stations. The demand for such creatures is presumably influenced by the expected series of future generations, so far as commercial prospectiveness may extend. In the stationary state of steady motion, here provisionally contemplated, reproductive machines would be illustrated by beasts of burden of which the breed does not sensibly improve in successive generations.

Two channels only have been represented in the diagram, one of finite, the other of infinite length, with breadth exaggerated for the sake of clearness. Properly, there should be as many channels as there are categories of articles ready for immediate consumption, — *"goods of the first order,"* as the Austrians say; and the breadth should be such as to allow of the corresponding number of sectors being fitted into the circle. Another circumstance which must be left to the imagination is the introduction of one and the same article into several streams of production at different distances from the final stage. Coal, for instance, so far as it is used for warming dwelling-houses, is a good of the first order; so far as it is used to drive machines, — they perhaps used only to produce other machines, — coal is to be placed among the higher orders.

The distinction which has been drawn between work which is applied in the neighbourhood of and at a distance from the final stage of production is not coincident with the distinction between the saving and the non-saving classes. The shower of commodities apportioned to each spot according to its height above the littoral as well as to the volume of value which there took its rise, is not *"like the gentle rain from heaven."* It does not drop impartially on all who have been concerned with the work of eliciting the stream. Those who have done the common labour of pumping — the drawers of water-fare no better than if that work had been done at the littoral. In fact, it is proper to conceive that it was done at the littoral. As the energy generated at the Falls of Niagara is transmitted for use to a point higher up on the river, so on the stream of production the work of pumping is mostly done at the littoral, though it is applied at the heights. For instance, on the first stream an amount of work proportioned to a5a'5 might be done at the littoral, and be paid for in commodities at the rate current on the littoral; that is, without the augmentation of value which is due to defluxion.

The remainder of the volume of value which is discharged per unit of time flies off to those who occupy the height represented by a5a'5. If now it is asked where rent comes into this representation of distribution, the answer is to be found in the theory that from the point of view of the entrepreneur the use of land appears in the same light as the use of labourers, — as a factor of production. The idea of a steady cyclic flow which we are striving to win becomes not much more complicated when we imagine that those who, placed on the heights, preside over the origination of productive streams, obtain the material that is to form the current, the precious fluid which it is their office to start upon its downward flow, not solely from a pumping proletariat, but also from the fortunate owners of springs which gush spontaneously. However, there is difference between the labourer and the land-owner: that, whereas the former (even in the present age and still more when the classical economists flourished) has to spend a great proportion of his daily wage upon his daily necessaries, and therefore in respect of the bulk of his income must be placed at the littoral line, the latter may save a great part of his income, when it is greatly in excess of his daily necessaries, and in particular, with respect to that great portion, may defer fruition until the stream shall have flowed down from the point at which his contribution is applied to the point at which production becomes merged in consummation.

Another difference between land and labour in their relation to capital and enterprise arises from the circumstance that, unlike the labourer (in a free country), land itself, as well as its use, is sold. Whence arises a well-known correspondence between rent and interest in their relation to the capital value of land. This similarity will not be mistaken for identity by those who find the essential attribute of rent in the limitation of the objects for which rent is paid. To complete the analysis of the parties to Distribution, it may next be required to distinguish the capitalist from the entrepreneur. They are both easily distinguished from the salaried manager in that he is at the littoral, in that respect like the common workman, while they are both above that line. But to draw a line in the series of shades which intervene between the employer of Walker's type and the mere shareholder, to determine at what point the capitalist ends and the entrepreneur begins, appears to defy analysis. As Thought and Emotion are inseparably blended, though one may so far preponderate as to give its name to the state of consciousness at any time, such is the inseparable connection, such the intelligible but not exactly definable distinction, between Enterprise and Saving.

The indefiniteness of the relation is illustrated by the shifting use in economic literature of the term Profit. That profit other than remuneration for managerial work should be transmitted to those who occupy a position on the heights — often the easy position of a dormant shareholder – is certainly invidious and difficult. Yet it may be reflected that the condition of those below would have been worse if those above, or those from whom they purchased or inherited their position, had not been content to wait for future goods instead of grasping at immediate pleasure. The Flow so beneficial to all classes would never have been set up without abstinence. It could not continue in its present magnitude but for the continued abstinence of each one who has a right to dispose of wealth which is in course of production, make a bonfire of it, if he can get a momentary pleasure from that extravagance, or by some less simple, though more familiar increase of unproductive consumption "*eat up his capital.*"

The consequences of an increase in unproductive consumption may be contemplated by reversing the consequences of an increase in parsimony. The latter increase forms part of a larger subject, economic progress. The progressive change in the volume of value and channels of production cannot be understood until there has been attained what was the object of the preceding paragraphs, — the clear idea of a steady flow in channels for a time unchanged. The study of this stationary state is perhaps the part of economic science which principally deserves to be described as theory of Distribution. In these pages it is not attempted to go far beyond the comparatively narrow round of steady motion in fixed cycles of production and consumption.

It must suffice to indicate three species of progressive alteration in the economic mechanism. There is, first, a uniform increase in the number of both capitalists and labourers, or, more generally, capital and labour, other things being the same. This change presents no difficulty: it may be represented by an increase in the depth of all the channels. Second, the rate at which the breadth of the channels diminishes as one ascends from the littoral — in other words, the rate of interest — might be diminished. A limiting case of this species is put by Mill when he supposes unproductive expenditure of capitalists to be "*reduced to its lowest limit.*" Conceivably, this change might have no other effect than to reduce the portions accruing to the capitalists — such as a1a'1a2a'2 — to a minimum. The capitalists with new eagerness bid against each other for the service of the labourers; but, if the latter do not give more work for higher pay, the consequences might be a new equilibrium in which the same volume of value is steadily rolled down the same channels of trade, though the portion which flies back to the heights is a minimum. But, even if the quantity of value continued constant, it is hardly to be supposed that the quality of the commodities which make up the amount would remain unchanged. And, in fact, an increase of wages would probably be followed by an increase in the number and efficiency of the wage-earning classes.

And these results would favour the occurrence of a third kind of progress which may, however, be considered as arising independently of the others;

namely, the lengthening of the trains of production. It may be doubted whether any great lengthening of the trains is possible without a concomitant improvement in the arts of production; yet, as Sidgwick observes, invention is not necessarily followed by increase of capitalisation. The third head of progress even more surely than the second will be attended with changes in the channels of production. As already observed with reference to the portion of truth contained in the wage-fund theory, time will in general be required for the carrying out of such changes. The means of production which are rolling down the channels at the instant when the change begins must all or in great part be suffered to run out: otherwise there will probably be a considerable waste of labour, and interruption to consumption. One delicate adjustment which would be deranged can only be alluded to here – the monetary circulation, especially that form of it which consists of debts that are continually *"cleared,"* or cancelled.

We might imagine the flow of factors in the channels of production and the flight of finished products backward on the way to consumption to be attended each with a displacement of air in a direction opposite to the main movement, — light counter-currents which have their use in facilitating the movements of solid wealth, and in the fulfilment of their useful function continually meet and neutralise each other. But, evidently, we have reached the degree of complexity at which the illustration becomes more difficult to understand than the thing which is to be illustrated. For a more concrete embodiment of a more complete theory the student is referred to the Principles of Economics, — a reference of which the value is, if possible, enhanced by the solid work which Mr. N.G. Pierson has published under the same title.

The preceding hints and metaphors and warnings may assist the student to obtain a general idea of the process by which distribution of the national income is effected. An outline of theory so abstract is not to be despised as useless. It satisfies a legitimate curiosity. It is part of a liberal education. It is comparable in these respects with an elementary knowledge of astronomy. Such knowledge will not be of much use in navigation. And yet it has a certain bearing on real life. The diffusion of just notions about astronomy has rendered it impossible for astrologers any longer to practise on the credulity of mankind. Knowledge of first principles affords a test by which the authority of those who offer themselves as guides may be estimated. A little science has a further use: it is of assistance in obtaining more.

As the astronomer will proceed from a first approximation to a second, so economists should soften the hard outline of abstract theory by a regard to particular circumstances. As he in dealing with a new object will make certain of his first approximation, will consider, for example, whether an ellipse or a parabola fits better to the orbit of a new comet, — so it behaves us to consider whether the classical hypothesis presupposed in the preceding pages — two-sided competition — is appropriate to the conditions of modern industry. The hypothesis of two-sided monopoly is strongly suggested by what we see before us, — consolidated capital confronted by consolidated trade unions. But it is alleged that beneath that appearance the forces of competition are effectively at work; that the settlement which is apt to be, and ought to be, agreed to between a combination of Capital and a combination of Labour is no other than that which would have been determined by competition if the individuals now combined had been free to act competitively. No one has expressed this view with more authority and decision than Walker:

- Competition, perfect competition, affords the ideal condition for the distribution of wealth.
- Competition affords the only absolute security possible for the equitable and beneficial distribution of the products of industry.

To the same effect, Professor Clark, when he teaches that:

- The question whether the labourer is exploited and robbed depends on the question whether he gets his product.

What is meant by getting his product appears from the following passages:

- What we are able to produce by means of labour is determined by what a final unit of mere labour can add to the product that can be created without its aid.
- If each productive function is paid for according to the amount of its product [thus reckoned], then each man gets what he himself produces.

The ideal of just arbitration is that:

- Men should get something approximating the part of that joint product which they may fairly regard as solely the fruit of their own labour. The basis of the claim that a workman makes is that his presence in a mill causes a certain increase in the output of it.

If these views are generally accepted, the analysis of bargains in a regime of competition will retain its importance. But it may well be doubted whether these views will be generally accepted, even by the thoughtful few, much less by the more numerous of the concerned parties. First, it may be objected that the same principle will give very different results according to the relative numbers of the parties. Put a case which has actually existed, or at least may be well supposed to have existed, in order to test the general application of the principle, — the case in which the number of the employees is not much greater than, say not more than twice as great as, the number of the employers.

In such a case, if labour is sold by the hour, — openly, or virtually in a fashion that probably prevails at present, — there would be a determinate equilibrium of the labour market such that each labourer would earn an amount equal to the number of hours worked, multiplied by the final productivity of each hour. That arrangement might appear just, on a certain interpretation of the dictum that one's product "*is determined by what a final unit of mere labour can add to the product.*" But the arrangement would not be just if "*the basis of the claim that a workman makes is that his presence in the mill will cause a certain increase in the output of it.*" All turns on the unit employed. If it is allowable to take the hour as the unit, and find the wage of the individual man by multiplying the number of hours worked by the final productivity of the unit, why should it not be allowable to take a gang of men as the unit, and find the wage of the individual man by dividing the number of men in a gang into the final productivity of a gang? Not to rest the argument on supposed cases, take the case of the "*capitalist*" as he existed in Ricardo's time, or even the modern entrepreneur who is not a salaried manager. If such a one is to be paid on the basis that "*his presence in a mill causes a certain increase in the output of it,*" it is quite possible that he would be justified in claiming a much larger share of the joint product than he now obtains.

The assertion that the entrepreneur receives just as much as he adds to product is at best an empirical law, not possessing the sort of universality proper to a general canon of distributive justice. Thus the coincidence of perfect competition with ideal justice is by no means evident to the impartial spectator: much less is it likely to be accepted by the majority of those concerned, whose views must be taken into account by those who would form a theory that has some relation to the facts. One who has closely observed popular movements in America testifies to "*the growing belief that mechanical science and invention applied to industry are too closely held by private interests.*" "*An enormous private ownership of industrial mechanism, especially if coupled with lands and mines,*" forms the gravamen of the complaints. To advert for a moment to the accessory grievance with the view of understanding the main one, can we suppose that in a case such as Ireland was supposed to constitute before the Gladstonian land legislation, the land leaguers would have been content if they had obtained a perfect market in land, an equation of supply and demand undisturbed by hustling or delay, intimidation or cornering? This perfection of the market might have served only to bring out the disadvantage at which the many were placed by the vesting of the complete ownership of land in the hands of a few. The prevailing sentiment about the "*enormous private ownership of industrial mechanism*" may well be similar. It is true that the expediencies governing "judicial rents" are very different from those which are opposed to the legal regulation of wages. But we are now considering how the matter appears to the many, what regime they can be got to accept. It seems not to be competition pure and simple.

Are we, then, to abandon the guidance of competition, and follow a higher, an ethical, standard? Does the theory of distribution require a definition of distributive justice? What is justice? The result of Plato's prolonged inquiry would not be satisfactory to the modern asserter of the rights of labour. If a new Socrates were to go about inquiring, what is the ideally just distribution between the employing and employed classes, he would probably find the wisest to be those who confessed their ignorance. As Jevons says, nothing at first sight can seem more reasonable and just than the "*favourite saying that a man should have a fair day's wages for a fair day's work.... But, when you examine its meaning, you soon find that there is no real meaning at all. There is no way of deciding what is a fair day's wages*."

It has been well observed that an intuition as to the just rate of wages, the labourer's share of the total product, involves an intuition as to the capitalist's share, — a share which depends on the rate of interest. Can any one seriously pretend that the dictates of a moral sense are clear and decisive in such a matter? Let it be remembered also that the path of justice is not only dark, but dangerous. Striving to secure the rights of labour, you are very likely to hurt the interests of labour. The action of trade unions by lowering interest and harassing employers may result, as pointed out by Professor Marshall, in checking the accumulation of capital and the supply of business power. The increase in personal capital may indeed compensate for this check, but also it may not. Greater efficiency does not follow higher wages as the night the day.

In view of these considerations it is doubtful whether in the near future an influential majority will aim at setting aside competition. Moreover, even if this consummation were aimed at, it is not likely to be attained. So invincible in human nature is the "*propensity to truck,*" so true is it that, "*when one person is willing to sell a thing at a price which another is willing to pay for it, the two manage to come together in spite of prohibitions of King or Parliament, or of the officials of a Trust or Trade Union*" competition is like the air we breathe, which it is not only dangerous, but difficult to exclude. Between two guides, of who neither can be followed implicitly, let us walk warily. On the one hand, let us not aim at impossible ideals. But, on the other hand, let us not deserve the criticism which the advocates of trade unionism have with too much truth directed against "*the verdict of the economists*" respecting trade unions. Let us not be as trenchant in act as we have been in thought. Let us be cautious in applying our abstract theory to flesh and blood. To one seeking a representation at once clear and appropriate, the actual conditions of industry present the appearance of a viscous and deliquescent body, not so easy to be treated by simple formulae as a perfect liquid or a perfect solid.

An adequate theory of Distribution must in these days take some account of the action proper to combinations, effecting collective treaties between employers and employed: competition pure and simple no longer constitutes an adequate hypothesis. Exactly how these two principles are to be conceived as coexistent it is premature to state dogmatically: the economist whose aim is to "*teach, not preach,*" to show what is or will be rather than what ought to be, may well hesitate to pronounce on this question.He can at best invent hypotheses which may facilitate the conception of a compromise between the opposed principles of competition and combination. For example, the required compromise might be attained if it were arranged that the agreement between employers and employed under some heads might be settled by collective treaty between combinations, but under other heads by competitive bargaining between individuals, — as the German students in their duels expose only certain parts, not all parts, of the body to the brunt of the combat.

To determine what matters should be the subject of treaty would indeed it requires some sort of treaty. But it would be a kind of treaty for which there is good precedent in laws and institutions. For instance, there might grow up, or be enacted by law, the practice that the hours of labour in a trade should be a matter for collective treaty between a trade union and a combination of employers, the particular number of hours to be settled by such treaty, while other terms, such as the rate of wages, should be settled by the play of competition. So far as competition has free play, the received theory of supply and demand, even in its severest mathematical form, would be applicable. Indeed, the severer forms would be peculiarly appropriate in that they do not lend themselves to the contemplation of cornering and other dodges of the market, but assume the *"true price"* to be worked out honestly. Presumably, the competition which all parties agreed to retain would have to be conducted in a similar spirit. The conditions of the duel, already prescribed, would be further limited by forbidding certain strokes.

A similar regulation may be suggested for the working of an imaginary sort of competition which seems to be contemplated by some who are conversant with the practical problems of industry. Their view appears to be that two combinations might, without resorting to actual competition, agree to accept those terms which would probably result from the play of free competition. In playing this sort of Kriegspiel, it might be laid down as a rule of civilised industrial warfare that the workman should not be treated as living from hand to mouth. Suppose him freed from the imminence of starvation for a time at least, and then consider what sort of arrangement of the terms to be settled would constitute a steady flow of the type above described, in which each individual's final sacrifice is normally equivalent to the final utility which he procures thereby. Other rules might be suggested for the working of such imaginary competition. But it may be questioned whether the method admits of precision, for a reason urged by Mr. L.L. Price with reference to a proposed principle of arbitration, "that the arbitrator should endeavour to award such wages as would be attained if combination on either side were absent." "Where is the arbitrator to discover this ideal standard?" pertinently asks Mr. Price. The terms forming the subject of a collective treaty would be settled by a method essentially different from competition.

For instance, in the case above proposed, the length of a working day, let there be a law removing this article from the category of terms which are to be settled by the play of competition between individuals. Those who hold that such a law is based on the utilitarian first principle, the greatest happiness of those concerned, — here the citizens who have enacted the law, — will be prepared for the further suggestion that the particular number of hours to be settled will also be regulated by the utilitarian first principle, only that those concerned, whose maximum advantage constitutes the criterion, are not now the citizens, — if the citizens generally have no interest in the particular number of hours in the trade, but only the parties to the distribution, the members of the contracting combination. That this undergrowth of utilitarianism may, like the parent tree, prove fruitful, has been argued elsewhere.

Here it need only be repeated that, when the utilitarian arrangement is defined as the basis of conciliation between self-interested parties to a contract, it is presupposed that both parties gain by the contract: that it does not seem to either party to be their interest, rather than accept such an arrangement, to give up dealing at all with the other party — seek, it may be, some third party, some other employment of their capital and labour, or at least to defer agreement with the other party, in view of the probability that they will reduce their terms. The rationale of conciliation thus presented will doubtless not commend itself to many who accept substantially identical principles invested in a different form. Uniformity is not to be expected in the enunciation of first principles. The vital tenet is that each party must take account of and enter into the wants and motives of the other party.

When competition is no longer umpire, the economist must abandon — if he ever maintained — the position of extreme solipsism which Jevons in a solitary but remarkable passage has propounded: — Every mind is thus inscrutable to every other mind, and so no common denomination of feeling seems to be possible.... The motive in one mind is weighed only against other motives in the same mind, never against the motives in other minds. Each person is to other persons a portion of the outward world.... Hence the weighing of motives must always be confined to the bosom of the individual.

On this pinnacle of solitude, it has not remain consistently by Jevons himself. it is abandoned by economists in general in the received theory of taxation, founded, as Mill says, on "*human wants and feelings*." Self-regarding self-interest, the gospel of Adam Smith, is not alone sufficient for industrial salvation: a leaf must be taken from his older and less familiar testament, of which the cardinal doctrine was sympathy. Sympathy does not necessarily imply sentimental attachment: sympathy, according to Adam Smith, is the basis of a not very sociable emotion, — ambition. A distinguished psychologist has not hesitated to pronounce "*sympathy compatible with dislike*."

It is, then, no counsel of perfection to cultivate sympathy, in the sense of mutual understanding, between the parties to distribution. No Utopian eradication of self-love is contemplated.

It may be hoped, indeed, that through the practice of conciliation, in the course of generations, the dispositions of which the gratification constitutes self-interest may become more social, so that, for instance, an advantage founded on the extreme privation of others would not appear desirable to the capitalist employer of the future. But such "moralisation" of the saving classes, though it may be expected, need not be postulated for the working of conciliation. intellectual sympathy alone might effect much. The arts by which the sympathetic imagination may be cultivated form a supremely important topic, but one which hardly falls under the theory of Distribution.

## PRODUCTION AND COSTS: THE THEORY OF THE FIRM

### THE CIRCULAR FLOW MODEL

Recall that in our initial discussion of the economy we identified two broad groups of economic actors (or units); they were households and firms. In our study of demand we looked at households as consumer units effectingdemand for goods and services in the product market. On the supply side of the product market are the economic (or business) firms. They are the producers (and sellers) of goods and services. In this section we are going to look the behaviour of an economic firm.

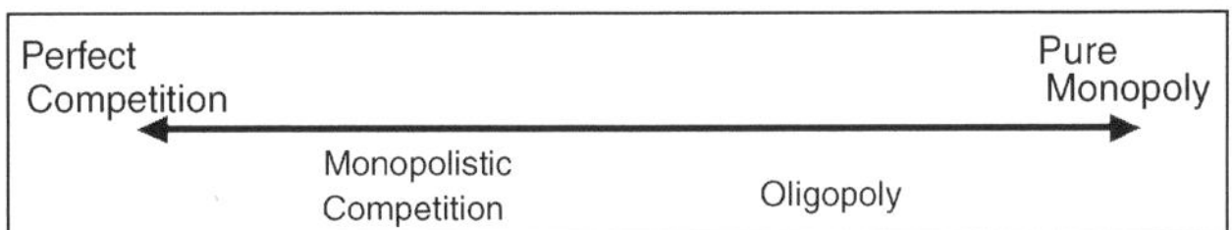


### Production and Costs

To produce a good or a service a firm needs economic resources or factors of production. In economics, the factors of production used by a firm in the production of a good or a service are generally referred to asinputs. What a firm produces is called output.

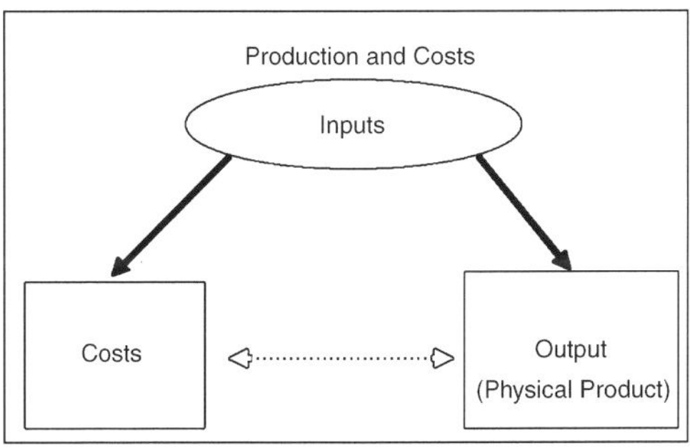


A firm has to pay for the inputs it needs. Therefore, inputs, on the one hand, generate costs and, on the other hand, generate output.We first study the relationship between inputs and the output; that is "production function".

Then we look at the relationship between the output and costs; that is cost function.

*Note:*

Studying the relationship between costs and inputs without regard to the output produced from the inputs is not useful. That is why we study the relationship between costs and output.

**Inputs: Factors of Production**

*Factors of production:*

- The primary factors of production are land and labour.
- Capital is another important factor of production.

*In economics we distinguish between physical capital and financial capital:*

- *Physical Capital:* Tools, machinery, equipment, buildings
- *Financial Capital:* Financial assets representing physical capital (stocks) or used to acquire physical capital are financial capital.
  In addition to land, labour and capital businesses often use intermediate goods (raw materials and supplies) in the production process.
- *Entrepreneurial Services:* In market economies the function of entrepreneurs is also very important. The function of an entrepreneur is to acquire and combine all the needed factors of production to produce a good. An entrepreneur takes chances (risks) in the hope of making profits.

*Cost of production is simply the sum of the costs of all inputs used in production:*

Production Costs = Costs of Inputs

**Production in the Long Run**

- In the theory of the firm the distinction between short run and long run is not necessarily based on the length of time. It is rather based on the degree of the variability of inputs.
- In the short run at least one of the factors of production remains unchanged (fixed).
- In the long run all factors of production are variable.
- In a two-input production process, in the short run, only one input is variable.
- In a two-input production model, in the short run, the changes in the output (physical product) are the result of changes in the variable input.

**Production in the Long Run**

- In the long run all inputs used in the production process by the firm are variable.
- In a two-input production model, in the long run, both inputs (say, capital and labour) are variable.

- In the long run the level of the output of a firm can change as a result of changes in any or all inputs.

## FUNCTIONS OF COST

Cost functions summarise information in the production function and they can along with total revenue be used to find the output level (Q) that maximizes profit (= TR-TC). They are functions of output that defines an isoquant, and the cost (C) associated with this isoquant is the minimum cost.

$$C = F(Q).$$

## SHORT RUN COSTS

Short-run: is the time period during which at least one of the inputs is fixed. This means that there is a fixed cost which is the cost of the fixed input, usually capital..

### Fixed Cost (FC)

Expenditures for plant maintenance, insurance, minimal number of employees, principal and interest payments, property taxes. FC does not change with output.

- *Variable Cost (VC):* Expenditures for wages, salaries and raw materials. VC increases with the size of output. It starts from the origin.
- *Total Cost (TC): Sum of VC and FC:* In the short run, TC starts where FC starts. When output is zero, TC = FC. In the graph, the difference between TC and VC is FC and, thus constant at all output levels.

The cost of producing with the same technology, as can be seen in the first three columns. Price of capital = $1000 per hour and w = $400.

**Table. The Cost Functions.**

| (1) K Fixed Input (Capital) [Given] | (2) L Variable Input (Labor) [Given] | (3) Q Output [Given] | (4) FC Fixed Cost [$1,000*(1)] | (5) VC Variable Cost [$400*(2)] | (6) TC Total Cost [(4)+(5)] |
|---|---|---|---|---|---|
| 2 | 0 | 0 | $2,000 | $0 | $2,000 =FC |
| 2 | 1 | 76 | $2,000 | 400 | 2,400 |
| 2 | 2 | 248 | $2,000 | 800 | 2,800 |
| 2 | 3 | 492 | $2,000 | 1,200 | 3,200 |
| 2 | 4 | 784 | $2,000 | 1,600 | 3,600 |
| 2 | 5 | 1,100 | $2,000 | 2,000 | 4,000 |
| 2 | 6 | 1,416 | $2,000 | 2,400 | 4,400 |
| 2 | 7 | 1,708 | $2,000 | 2,800 | 4,800 |
| 2 | 8 | 1,952 | $2,000 | 3,200 | 5,200 |
| 2 | 9 | 2,124 | $2,000 | 3,600 | 5,600 |
| 2 | 10 | 2,200 | $2,000 | 4,000 | 6,000 |
| 2 | 11 | 2,156 | $2,000 | 4,400 | 6,400 |

The relations among total cost (TC), variable cost (VC) and fixed cost (FC). FC is a horizontal line because it does not change with output even if output is zero. On the other hand, variable cost is zero if output is zero and it increases with the increase in the level of output. Total cost equals fixed cost when output is zero and then it increases with output, as does variable cost.

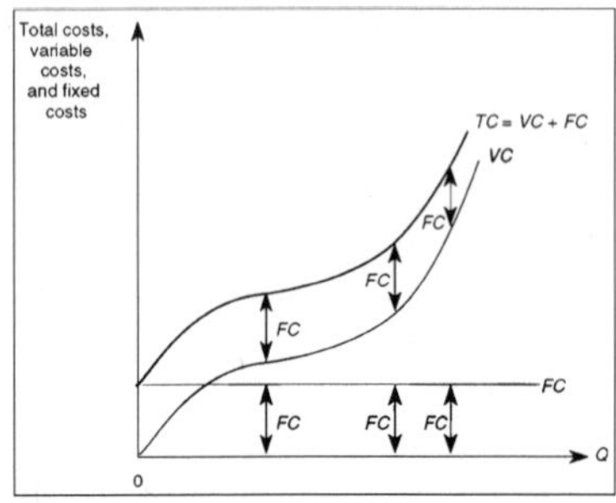


**Fig.** The Relationship among Costs.

## COSTS AND SUPPLY

In the field of business it can be looked by us in two points of view: productivity, inputs, and outputs (as we have just done) or outputs and costs. In advanced microeconomics, these two points of view are called *"duals."* They are equally valid, but they point up different things.

They are also opposites from a certain point of view — the higher the productivity, the lower the costs. By looking at the firm from the point of view of costs, we shift our perspective somewhat, and gain a much more direct understanding of supply. We also look more directly at the difference between the long and short run. In the short run, we have two major categories of costs:

- Fixed costs, and
- Variable costs

However, all costs are variable in the long run. Thus, we must study costs under two quite different headings. Costs will vary quite differently in the long run and in the short.

## FIXED AND VARIABLE COSTS

Variable costs can be defined as the costs that can be varied flexibly as conditions change. In the John Bates Clark model of the firm that we are studying, labour costs are the variable costs. Fixed costs are the costs of the investment goods used by the firm, on the idea that these reflect a long-term commitment that can be recovered only by wearing them out in the production of goods and services for sale.

Here, the view is that labour is a much more flexible resource than capital investment. People can change from one task to another flexibly (whether within the same firm or in a new job at another firm), while machinery tends to be designed for a very specific use.

If it isn't used for that purpose, it can't produce anything at all. Thus, capital investment is much more of a commitment than hiring is. In the eighteen-hundreds, when John Bates Clark was writing, this was pretty clearly true. Over the past century,

- Education and experience have become more important for labour, and have made labour more specialized, and
- Increasing automatic control has made some machinery more flexible. So the differences between capital and labour are less than they once were, but all the same, it seems labour is still relatively more flexible than capital. It is this (relative) difference in flexibility that is expressed by the simplified distinction of long and short run. Of course, productivity and costs are inversely related, so the variable costs will change as the productivity of labour changes.

**Fixed and Variable Costs 2**

Here is a picture of the fixed costs (FC), variable costs (VC) and the total of both kinds of costs (TC) for the productivity example in the last unit:

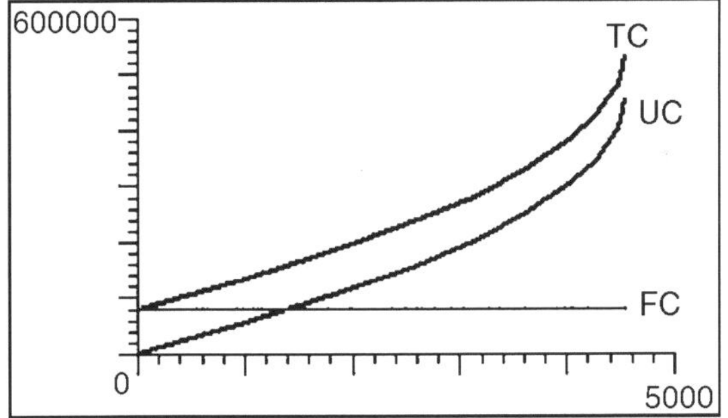


**Fig.** Output Produced is Measured toward the right on the Horizontal axis.

The cost numbers are on the vertical axis. Notice that the variable and total cost curves are parallel, since the distance between them is a constant number — the fixed cost.

**Opportunity Cost, Again**

What is the connection between the distinctions we have just made — fixed vs variable costs — and opportunity cost, the key concept in some earlier units?

In economics, all costs are included — whether or not they correspond to money payments. If we have opportunity costs with no corresponding money payments, they are called implicit costs. The implicit costs (as well as the money costs) are included in the cost analysis we have just given.There is some correlation between implicit costs and fixed or variable costs, but this correlation will be different in such different kinds of firms as a factory owned by an absentee investorThis is the easiest case to understand. All of the labour costs to the absentee investor are money costs, including the manager's salary. If the investor has borrowed some of the money he invested in the factory, then there is some money costs of the capital invested — interest on the loan.

However, we must consider the opportunity cost of invested capital as well. The investor's own money that he has used to buy the factory is money that she could have invested in some other business.

The return she could have gotten on another investment is the opportunity cost of her own funds invested in the business. This is an implicit cost, and in this case the implicit cost is part of the cost of capital and probably a fixed cost.

### A "Mom-and-Pop" Store

A store in which family members are self-employed and supply most of the labour is called a *"mom-and-pop"* store (family proprietorship or partnership). Typically, *"Mom"* and *"Pop"* don't pay themselves a salary — they just take money from the till when they need it, since it is their property anyway. As a result, there are no money costs for their labour.

But their labour has an opportunity cost — the salary or wages they could make working similar hours in some other business — and so, in this case, the implicit costs include a large component of variable labour costs.

### A Large Modern Corporation

Relatively, few implicit costs are have by the corporation but some will have generally. All labour costs will be expressed in money terms (though benefits and bonuses have to be included), since the shareholders doesn't supply labour to the corporation as *"Mom and Pop"* do in a family proprietorship. It will pay interest to bondholders and dividends to shareholders.

But the dividends aren't really a cost item — they include profits distributed to the shareholders. Moreover, the typical corporation will retain some profits and invest them within the business, a *"plowback"* investment.On the other hand, a broad part of their payout might be taken by shareholders in appreciation of the stock value — and plowback investment is one reason for the appreciation.

Thus we would say that the corporation has a net equity value, that is, that the corporation *"owns"* a certain amount of capital that it invests in its own business (very much like the absentee owner in the first example).

This capital has an opportunity cost and that opportunity cost is an implicit cost. The stockholders, who own the corporation, ultimately receive (as dividends or appreciation) both the opportunity cost of the equity capital and any profit left over after it is taken out.

## Unit Cost

It may be more meaningful if costs are expressed on a per-unit basis, as averages per unit of output. In this way, we again distinguish

*Average fixed cost (AFC)*

This is the quotient of fixed cost divided by output. In the numerical example we are using, when output is 4020 (in the table) fixed cost is 80000, so AFC is 80000/4020=19.9

*Average variable cost (AVC)*

This is the quotient of average cost divided by output. In the example, at an output of 4020 the variable cost is 350000, giving AVC of 350000/4020=87.06.

*Average total cost (ATC or AC)*

This is the quotient of total cost divided by output. In the example, with 4020 of output total cost is 430000, so AC is 430000/4020 = 106.96 = 87.06+19.90.

## Unit Cost Example

Here are the average, average variable, and average fixed costs for our example firm.

| Q | AC | AFC | AVC |
|---|---|---|---|
| 945 | 138 | 85 | 53 |
| 1780 | 101 | 45 | 56 |
| 2505 | 92 | 32 | 60 |
| 3120 | 90 | 26 | 64 |
| 3625 | 91 | 22 | 69 |
| 4020 | 95 | 20 | 75 |
| 4305 | 100 | 19 | 81 |
| 4480 | 107 | 18 | 89 |
| 4545 | 117 | 18 | 99 |

## A Picture of Unit Costs

Here is the average cost (AC), average variable cost (AVC) and average fixed cost (AFC) in a diagram. This is a good representative of the way that economists believe firm costs vary in the short run.

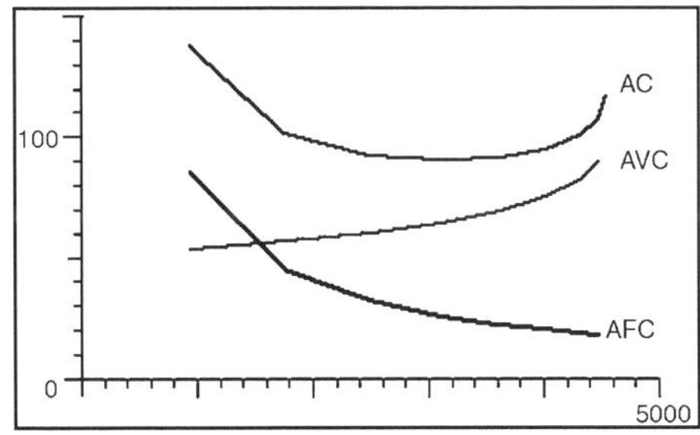


Notice how the average fixed costs decline as the fixed costs are "*spread over more units of output.*" For large outputs, however, average variable costs

rise pretty steeply. The idea is that with a limited capital plant and thus limited productive capacity — in the short run — costs would rise much more than proportionately to output as output goes beyond *"capacity."* The average total cost, dominated by fixed costs for small output, declines at first, but as output increases, fixed costs become less important for the total cost and variable costs become more important, and so, after reaching a minimum, average total cost begins to rise more and more steeply.

**Marginal Cost**

Marginal cost is defined as

$$MC = \frac{\Delta C}{\Delta Q}$$

As usual, Q stands for (quantity of) output and C for cost, so$\Delta Q$ stands for the change in output, while $\Delta C$ stands for the change in cost. As usual, marginal cost can be interpreted as the additional cost of producing just one more ("marginal") unit of output.To clear the definition of Marginal costs, let's have a numerical example. In the John Bates Clark style example we have been using, total cost is 280000 for an output of 3120, and it is 33000 for an output of 3625. So we have

$\Delta C = 330000 - 280000 = 50000$

And

$\Delta Q = 3625 - 3120 = 505$

So that

$$\frac{\Delta C}{\Delta Q} = \frac{50000}{505} = 99.01$$

for a marginal cost of \$99.01 for the next unit produced. As usual, this is an approximation, and the smaller the change in output we use, the better the approximation is.

**Marginal Cost Example**

Here is an example of marginal cost along with output and average cost.

| | Output | AverageCost | Marginal Cost |
|---|---|---|---|
| | 0 | 09.45 | |
| | 945 | 137.57 52.91 | |
| 1780 | 101.12 | 59.88 | |
| 2505 | 91.82 | 68.97 | |
| 3120 | 89.74 | 81.30 | |
| 3625 | 91.03 | 99.01 | |
| 4020 | 94.53 | 126.58 | |
| 4305 | 99.88 | 175.44 | |
| 4480 | 107.14 | 285.71 | |
| 4545 | 116.61 | 769.23 | |

### A Picture of Marginal Cost

Here is a picture of marginal cost for our example firm, together with average cost as output varies.

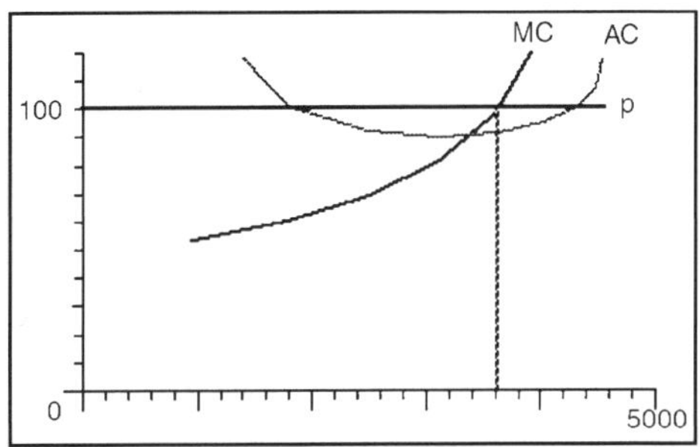


As before, the output produced is measured by the distance to the right on the horizontal axis. The average and marginal cost are on the vertical axis. Average cost is shown by the curve in yellow and marginal cost in red. Notice how the marginal cost rises to cross average cost at its lowest point.

### Maximization of Profits, Again

Instantly, some other rule for the maximization of profits can be given by us. The new rule is really just the same rule as we saw before, only now we state it in terms of price and costs. It is the equimarginal principle in yet another form.

*The question is*: *"I want to maximize profits. How much output should I sell, at the given price?"*

The answer is: increase output until p=MC

In the following table the point is illustrated which extends the marginal cost table in an earlier page to show the price and the profits for the example firm.

| Output | Average Cost | | Marginal Cost | Price | Profit |
|---|---|---|---|---|---|
| 0 | 0 | 9.45 | 100 | 0 | 945 |
| 137.57 | 52.91 | 100 | -35503.65 | | |
| 1780 | 101.12 | 59.88 | 100 | -1993.60 | |
| 2505 | 91.82 | 68.97 | 100 | 20490.90 | |
| 3120 | 89.74 | 81.30 | 100 | 32011.20 | |
| 3625 | 91.03 | 99.01 | 100 | 32516.25 | |
| 4020 | 94.53 | 126.58 | 100 | 21989.40 | |
| 4305 | 99.88 | 175.44 | 100 | 516.60 | |
| 4480 | 107.14 | 285.71 | 100 | -31987.20 | |
| 4545 | 116.61 | 769.23 | 100 | -75492.45 | |

Notice how profits are greatest at 32516.25 when the marginal cost is almost exactly equal to the price of $100. This occurs at an output of 3625, with marginal cost at 99.01. The profit-maximizing output would be very slightly more than 3625.

## SUPPLY AND DEMAND CONNECTION

Now that we know the laws of supply and demand, let's turn to an example to show how supply and demand affect price.

Imagine that a special edition CD of your favourite band is released for $20. Because the record company's previous analysis showed that consumers will not demand CDs at a price higher than $20, only ten CDs were released because the opportunity cost is too high for suppliers to produce more.

If, however, the ten CDs are demanded by 20 people, the price will subsequently rise because, according to the demand relationship, as demand increases, so does the price. Consequently, the rise in price should prompt more CDs to be supplied as the supply relationship shows that the higher the price, the higher the quantity supplied.

If, however, there are 30 CDs produced and demand is still at 20, the price will not be pushed up because the supply more than accommodates demand. In fact after the 20 consumers have been satisfied with their CD purchases, the price of the leftover CDs may drop as CD producers attempt to sell the remaining ten CDs. The lower price will then make the CD more available to people who had previously decided that the opportunity cost of buying the CD at $20 was too high.

### EQUILIBRIUM OF SUPPLY AND DEMAND

When supply and demand are equal (*i.e.*, when the supply function and demand function intersect) the economy is said to be at equilibrium.

At this point, the allocation of goods is at its most efficient because the amount of goods being supplied is exactly the same as the amount of goods being demanded. Thus, everyone (individuals, firms, or countries) is satisfied with the current economic condition. At the given price, suppliers are selling all the goods that they have produced and consumers are getting all the goods that they are demanding.

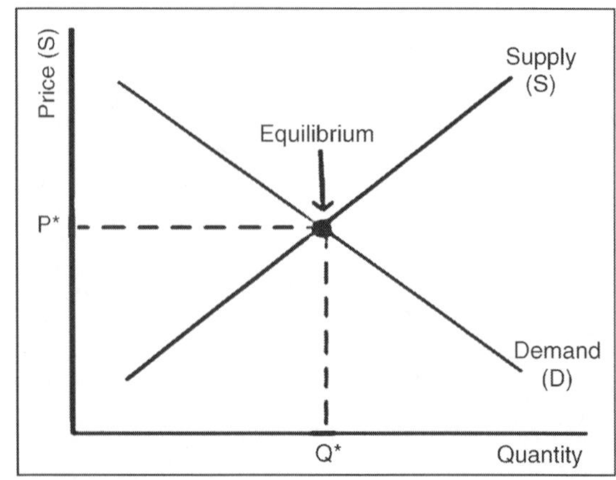

As you can see on the chart, equilibrium occurs at the intersection of the demand and supply curve, which indicates no allocative inefficiency. At this point, the price of the goods will be P* and the quantity will be Q*. These figures are referred to as equilibrium price and quantity.In the real market place equilibrium can only ever be reached in theory, so the prices of goods and services are constantly changing in relation to fluctuations in demand and supply.

**Disequilibrium of Price**

Disequilibrium occurs whenever the price or quantity is not equal to P* or Q*.

***Excess Supply***

If the price is set too high, excess supply will be created within the economy and there will be allocative inefficiency.

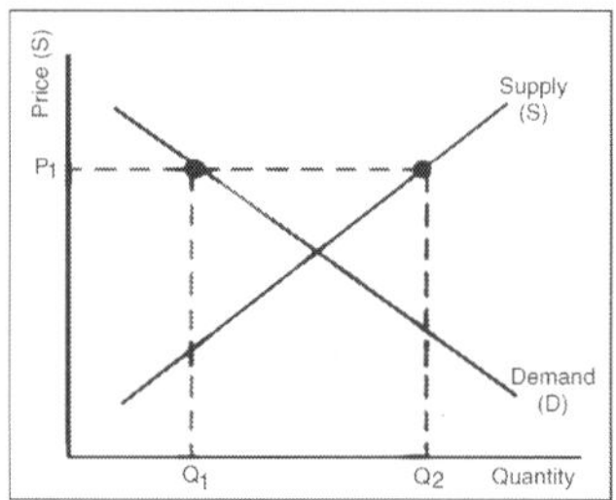


At price P1 the quantity of goods that the producers wish to supply is indicated by Q2. At P1, however, the quantity that the consumers want to consume is at Q1, a quantity much less than Q2. Because Q2 is greater than Q1, too much is being produced and too little is being consumed. The suppliers are trying to produce more goods, which they hope to sell to increase profits, but those consuming the goods will find the product less attractive and purchase less because the price is too high.

***Excess Demand***

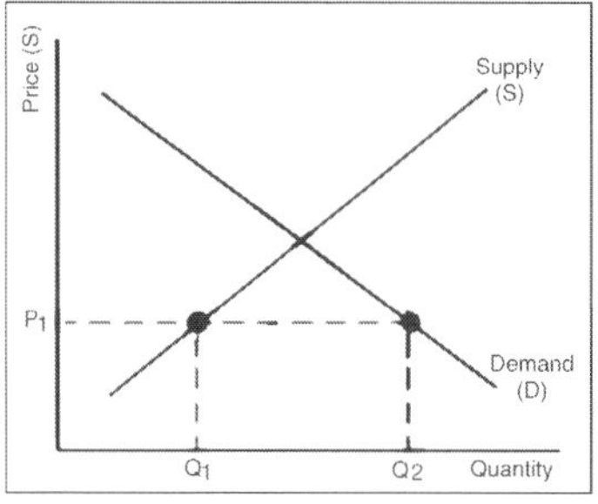


Excess demand is created when price is set below the equilibrium price. Because the price is so low, too many consumers want the good while producers are not making enough of it.In this situation, at price P1, the quantity of goods demanded by consumers at this price is Q2. Conversely, the quantity of goods that producers are willing to produce at this price is Q1. Thus, there are too few goods being produced to satisfy the wants (demand) of the consumers.

However, as consumers have to compete with one other to buy the good at this price, the demand will push the price up, making suppliers want to supply more and bringing the price closer to its equilibrium.

**Shifts vs. Movement**

For economics, the "movements" and "shifts" in relation to the supply and demand curves represent very different market phenomena:

***Movements***

A movement refers to a change along a curve. On the demand curve, a movement denotes a change in both price and quantity demanded from one point to another on the curve.

The movement implies that the demand relationship remains consistent. Therefore, a movement along the demand curve will occur when the price of the good changes and the quantity demanded changes in accordance to the original demand relationship.

In other words, a movement occurs when a change in the quantity demanded is caused only by a change in price, and vice versa.

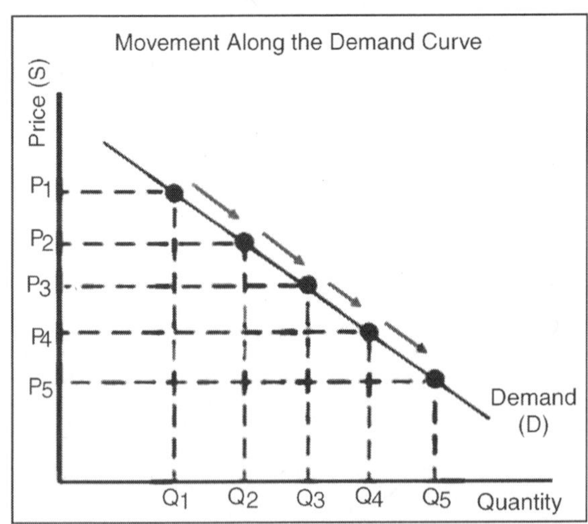


Like a movement along the demand curve, a movement along the supply curve means that the supply relationship remains consistent. Therefore, a movement along the supply curve will occur when the price of the good changes and the quantity supplied changes in accordance to the original supply relationship. In other words, a movement occurs when a change in quantity supplied is caused only by a change in price, and vice versa.

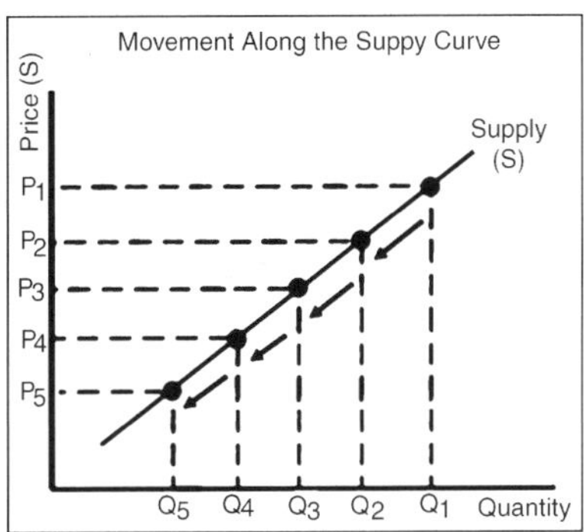


**Shifts Demand**

A shift in a demand or supply curve occurs when a good's quantity demanded or supplied changes even though price remains the same. For instance, if the price for a bottle of beer was $2 and the quantity of beer demanded increased from Q1 to Q2, then there would be a shift in the demand for beer.

Shifts in the demand curve imply that the original demand relationship has changed, meaning that quantity demand is affected by a factor other than price. A shift in the demand relationship would occur if, for instance, beer suddenly became the only type of alcohol available for consumption.

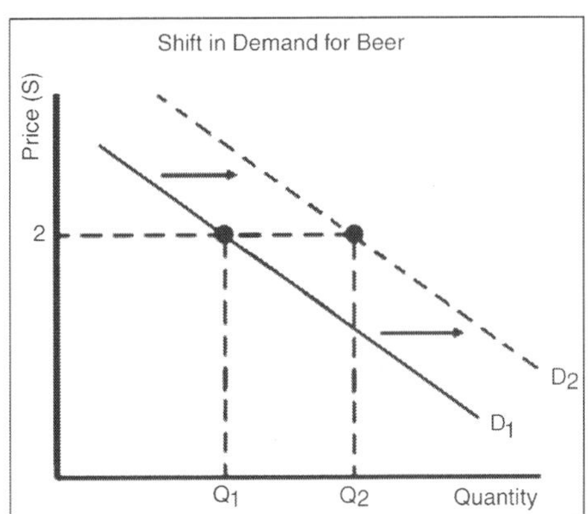


Conversely, if the price for a bottle of beer was $2 and the quantity supplied decreased from Q1 to Q2, then there would be a shift in the supply of beer. Like a shift in the demand curve, a shift in the supply curve implies that the original supply curve has changed, meaning that the quantity supplied is effected by a factor other than price. A shift in the supply curve would occur if, for instance, a natural disaster caused a mass shortage of hops; beer manufacturers would be forced to supply less beer for the same price.

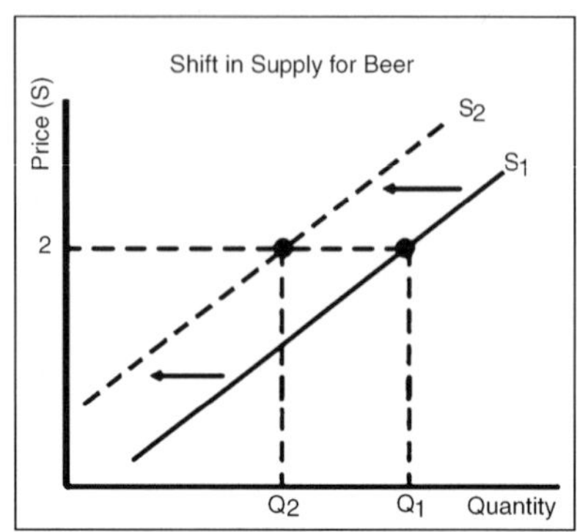


## SUPPLY FUNCTION AND SHIFTS IN MARKET SUPPLY

- *Supply Specification:* The simple supply equation is defined as:

$$Q^s = a + bP$$

and the slope with the respect to the price ΔQ/ΔP is positive. That is the supply curve is upward sloping.

*The general (direct) market supply equation can be expressed as a function:*

$$Q^S = f\,(P;\ \text{Production cost, Taxes, Expected Price}).$$

where "P" is the current period price for this good and is different from the expected future price. Change in current price causes a change in quantity supplied or a movement along the curve. The other factors (after the semi colon) are the shifters which cause a change or a shift in the entire supply.

Production cost includes the cost of labour, represented by the wage rate "$P_W$", capital cost represented by "$P_R$", the rental price of capital (equipment), and the price of raw materials "$P_M$". "T" will represent taxes and $P^{ex}$ represents the expected future price for this good. Then the general (direct) supply function can be rewritten as $Q^S = f\,(P;\ P_W, P_R, P_M, T, P^{ex})$

For example,

$$Q^s = 2000 + 3P - P_W - 4P_R - 2P_M - T + - P^{ex}.$$

where (direct) slope of supply with respect to (w. r. t.) current price P, ΔQ/ΔP, is +3, and the slope w.r.t., $P_W$, $\Delta Q/\Delta P_W$, is -1, and w. r. t. $P_R$, $\Delta Q/\Delta P_R$, is -4, $\Delta Q/\Delta P^{ex} > 0$ or $<0$.

If $P_W$ = \$20, $P_R$ = \$40, $P_M$ = \$10, T = \$100 and $P^{ex}$ = \$15, then after substitution for the constant shifters, the general (direct) supply equation collapses to the simple (direct) supply equation:

$$Q^s = 1715 + 3P, \text{ which is generally written as } Q^s = a + bP.$$

All the "other variables" have been lumped with the intercept and the simple direct slope is $\Delta Q/\Delta P = +3$. In the simple (direct) supply equation, all the variables after the "; " are the factors that are held constant and are usually lumped together to form the intercept a. They are the "Shifters".

*As indicated above, simple direct supply equation is given by:*

$$Q^s = a + bP.$$

(Here, a is the horizontal intercept and b is the direct slope).

*The simple "inverse" supply function is:*

$$P = -a/b + (1/b)Q^s$$

where +1/b is the inverse supply slope and -a/b is the vertical intercept.

A graph of the simple supply function is given by S1 below (P is placed on the vertical axis). Using the above example, $P = -1715/3 + 1/3{*}Q^s$ where 1/3 is the inverse slope.

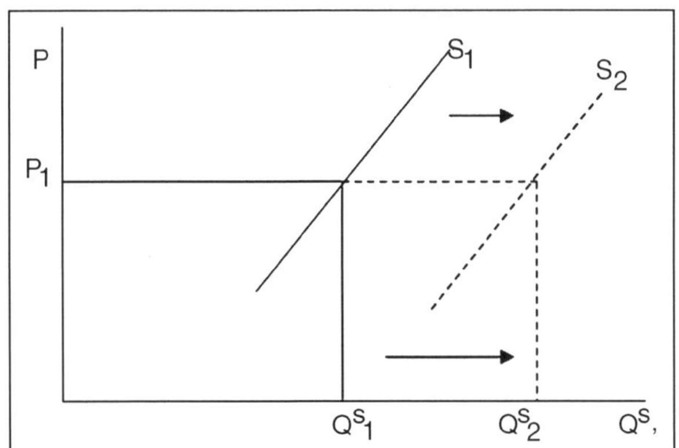


*Examples of shifts in Supply*: Suppose labour production cost decreases and also assume no changes in the other variables including the current price "P". A reduction in production cost implies an increase in profit (the difference between total revenues and costs), which should increase quantity supplied. The increase in the quantity supplied while the current price is assumed constant implies a right shift (an increase) in the supply curve from $S_1$ to $S_2$ in the graph below. The sign for wage rate should be -.

In conclusion, a decrease in the wage rate (W) implies an increase in the quantity supplied $Q^S$, assuming P is constant, which means a rightward shift in supply curve, and vice versa for an increase in (W), which implies a shift in supply to the left.

The same logic applies to decreases or increases in $P_R$ and $P_M$.

**Changes in Predictable Future Price (Pex)**

These changes are applied to the price expected to prevail in the next period. Their effect on quantity supplied in this period depends on the storability of the good in question.

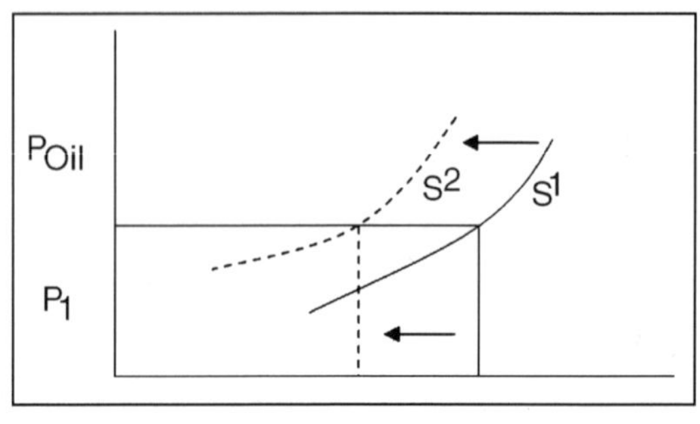


$Q^S_{21}$ $Q^S_1$ $Q^S_{oil}$

In the special case when the good is storable (*e.g.*, oil, gold, ... etc) then an increase in the expected price implies storing the good instead of producing more of it. Then at the current price, current quantity supplied decreases, representing a shift to the left in the supply curve. In general, an increase in expected price should shift the supply curve to the right, which is the normal case. This is particularly true for non-storable goods.

If the good is non-storable such as milk, then an increase in $P^{ex}$ leads to an increase in current QS because the production of non-storable goods does not take much time to bring them on stream and thus, the firms worry about maintaining their market shares. Therefore, the supply curve shifts to the right, assuming the other variables are constant.

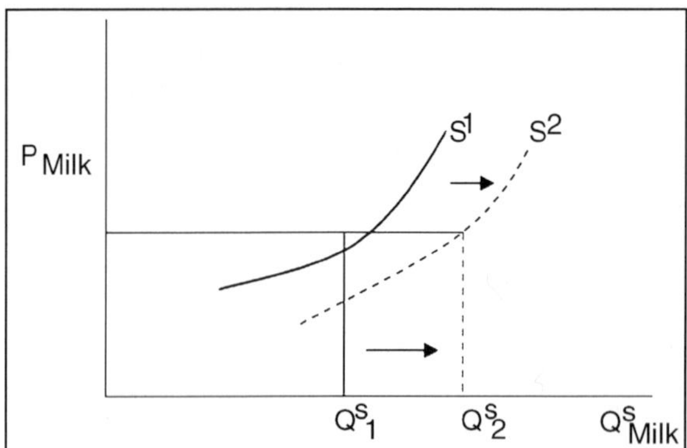


*Taxes: There are basically two types of taxes:*

1. Specific and
2. Ad valorem.

The specific tax is a fixed amount of money per unit sold (*e.g.*, 10 cents per pound), while ad valorem is proportional to the value or the price (*e.g.*, 10 per cent of the price) which may not be constant. An example of a specific tax is the excise tax, which is a constant $ tax on each unit sold and the tax revenue is collected from the supplier. In this case the (inverse) supply curve shifts up in a parallel fashion by the amount of the tax.

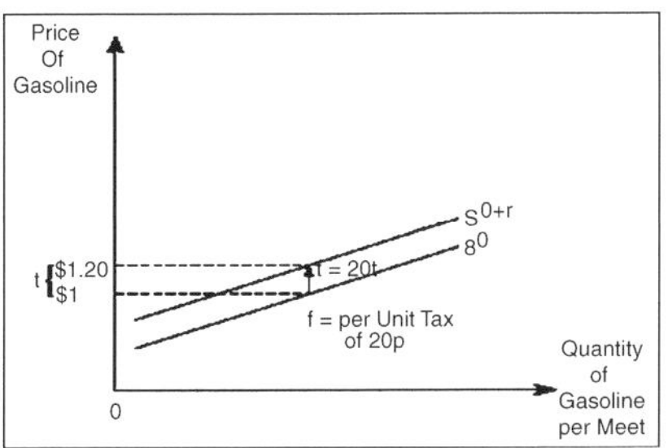


**Fig.** A per Unit (Excise) Specific Tax.

If the tax is ad valorem, then if the price increases, the amount of the proportional tax increases with the price. Suppose the tax rate =20 per cent. If P =\$10 then the tax amount is \$2. If P=\$20, then the tax is \$4. In this case the shift in supply is really an upward rotation.

Note that after tax, $P^1 = S^1 = (1+t\%)*S^0$ where supply $S^0 = P^0$ is expressed as an inverse supply equation:

$P^0 = -a/b + (1/b)Q^{s0}$ which is $S^0$, *where* $P^0$ *is price before tax.*

Then $S^1$ is

$P^1 = (1+t\%)*P^0 = (1+t\%)^*[-a/b + (1/b)^{Qs0}]$, where $P^1$ is price after tax.

Solve for $Q^{s1}$ as a function of $P^1$.

Direct supply after tax: $Q^{s1} = a + (b/(1+t\%))P_1 = a + bP^1 + t*bP^1$

(note that $(1+t\%) = 1+20\%) = 1.20$ in the above example)

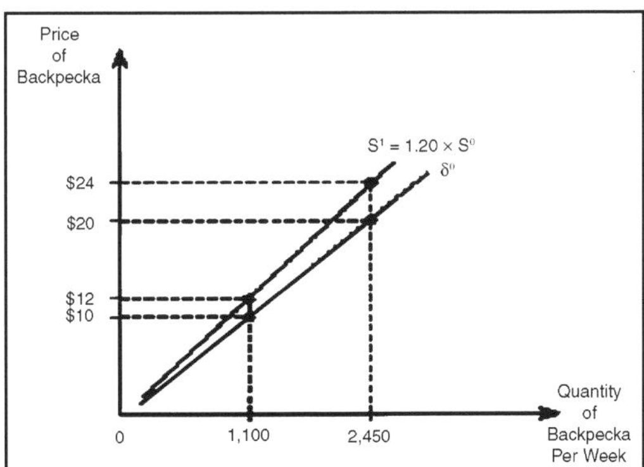


**Fig.** 2-8 An Ad Valorem Tax (t=20%).

That is, inverse $S^0$ rotates upward to $S^1$.

## Producer Surplus

The points on the supply curve measure the minimum amounts (or prices) the producers are willing to "accept" for producing the good because the supply curve is a cost curve. Those amounts are tantamount to minimum costs necessary to produce different levels of the good, and these costs are usually lower than the market price. Supply price is a minimum price.

*Suppose the (direct) supply equation for TVs is given by:*

$$Q^s = 2000 + 3P - P_W - 4P_R = 2000 + 3P - 2000 - 4*100 = -400 + 3P.$$

where $P_R$ is the rental price of monitors (a complement) per unit representing capital cost and $P_W$ is the price of an input like labour or the wage rate.

Suppose $P_R$ = \$100 and $P_W$ = \$2000.

*Then the simple (direct) supply equation is:* $Q^s = -400 + 3P$ (where -400 is *horizontal* intercept).

*The inverse supply equation is:* $P = 400/3 + (1/3)\ Q^s$ (400/3 is *vertical* intercept).

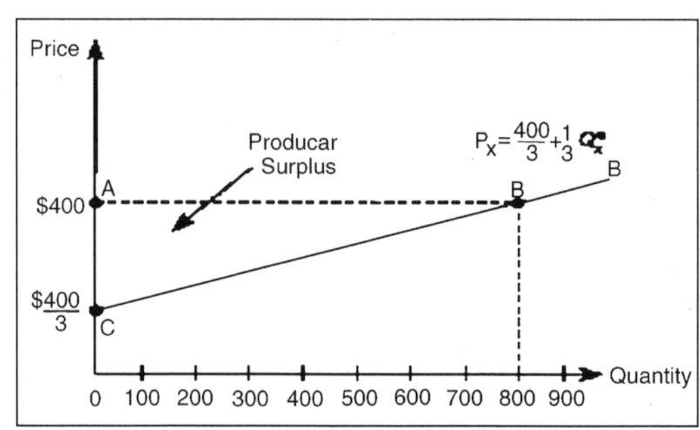


**Fig.** Producer Surplus.

The cost per unit to produce the first unit of the good is \$400/3 (point C) and to produce the 800 units per unit is \$400 (point B).In this figure, suppose the market price is \$400 and this market price applies to all units. Upon substitution, the quantity is 800 units Then the sales revenues received by the producers are P*Q = \$400 * 800 = \$320,000. This is the area of rectangle [0 A B 800].

The area under the supply curve up to the point where the price line intersects the supply curve is the minimum cost associated with producing 800 units (an integral). Then

Producer Surplus = Revenues received – minimum amount necessary to produce the good or PS = TR –VC where VC is variable cost.

= Area of the triangle ABC

= ½ * H * B

= ½ *(\$400 – 400/3)*800

= \$106,668. (for the wholesaler A)

Graphically, PS is the area below the price line and above the supply curve. It is a powerful tool for managers. In the above figure, suppose that the 800 units are 800 pounds of meat supplied by the meat wholesaler to the retailer which is the producer of steak (the restaurant).

In this case, the restaurant manager (the retailer) can bargain with the meat wholesaler over the producer surplus (a maximum of \$106,668) to capture some of it in the form of a lower price. Thus, the retailer can use the PS against the wholesaler.

# 4

# Demand Analysis

Transportation demand, simply stated, is the demand for trips that exist in any area. All of this demand, however, may or may not materialize into physical trips —and some of it generally remains latent and is referred to as hidden demand.

The importance of analyzing the transportation demand in order to be able to predict the expected number of trips in a given network cannot be overstated.The demand for transportation forms the primary input in any decision related to creation and management of transportation and traffic facilities, such as roads, intersections, parking lots, transit system, and so on.

The lecture is divided into three parts. The first part describes the nature of transportation demand and how it can be analysed.

Then it presents the sequential demand analysis technique — the most frequently used method of determining transportation demand. Finally it briefly describes some of the data collection mechanisms employed in travel demand analysis.

Transportation demand, unlike demand for other commodities, such as wheat, coffee, housing, clothing, etc., is a derived demand.

That is, one demands to be transported not because he/she just wants to move but because he/she wants to achieve some other purpose such as reaching school, or office or a movie theater.

In other words, the need for achieving some goal creates the need to travel. Hence, travel demand is primarily generated by the population's need to work, entertain, socialize, study, etc. Therefore, it is not surprising that two of the major aspects in travel demand analysis are land use and trip purpose.Land use refers to the pattern of land usage in an area. Land use affects transportation demand through generation and distribution of trips.

The effect of land use on transportation demand is not necessarily a one-way effect but rather a part of cycle in which land use changes transportation needs which in turn change land use. Figure shows a simple schematic of how land use and transportation demand are related.

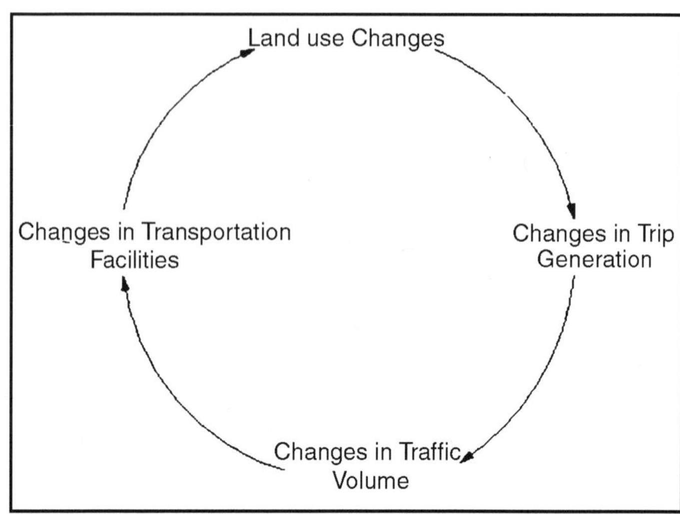


**Fig.** Relationship Between Land use and Transportation Demand.

Trip purpose refers to the purpose for which the trip is being undertaken. Travel demand behaviour changes with the trip purpose. For example, a person hardly exercises any choice for work trips; i.e. does not necessarily decide every time whether to go to work or not.

A person obviously does not decide where to go to work, even the choice of route and mode are not daily decisions. On the other hand, for recreational trips, an individual makes a large number of decisions, such as whether to go or not, where to go, how to go.Consequently, the travel demand behaviour for work trips varies considerably from that of recreational trips. This example, can obviously be extended to other types of trips such as shopping trips, etc. Given the effect of trip purpose on travel demand behaviour, the analysis of travel demand is done separately for different trip-purposes.

Although, the discussion throws light on some of the factors which affect travel demand, some more understanding of travel demand is necessary before one can analyse the demand and can, with some degree of confidence, predict the volume on various links of a network. Generally, a trip materializes after the trip-maker makes certain decisions.

*These decisions can be broadly classified as follows*:

- The decision to travel. The trip-maker, given his/her requirements, makes a conscious decision to travel so that the requirements can be met.
- The decision on the choice of destination. The trip maker also makes a decision as to where he/she wants to go; for certain kinds of trip purpose, such as work trips, this decision may not exist; yet for other kinds of trips, such as shopping trips, there may be certain alternative locations to choose from.

- The decision on the choice of mode. The trip-maker also takes a decision as to what mode of transport to use for a given trip. This decision, however, is only available to those who have access to different modes and are not captive users of any particular mode.
- The decision on the choice of route. The trip-maker on any given trip takes a definite decision on which route to take so as to reach the destination. Again, this decision is available to only those trip - makers who have access to modes which can use different routes as per the wishes of the trip maker. Such modes would generally include personal automobiles or two wheelers.

Although, there is unanimity on the fact that the decisions can aptly capture the entire trip-making behaviour of an individual and hence can be used to analyse travel demand pattern of an area, it is difficult to ascertain whether there exists any definite sequence in which these decisions are made.

Generally it is assumed, primarily for the ease of analysis rather than anything else, that the decisions are made in a strict sequence as shown in Figure Analysis techniques which assume that such a sequence exists are referred to as sequential demand analysis techniques.

Although, even today transportation demand is analysed sequentially, the assumption that the four major decisions of a trip-maker follow a strict sequence is possibly not the most appealing.

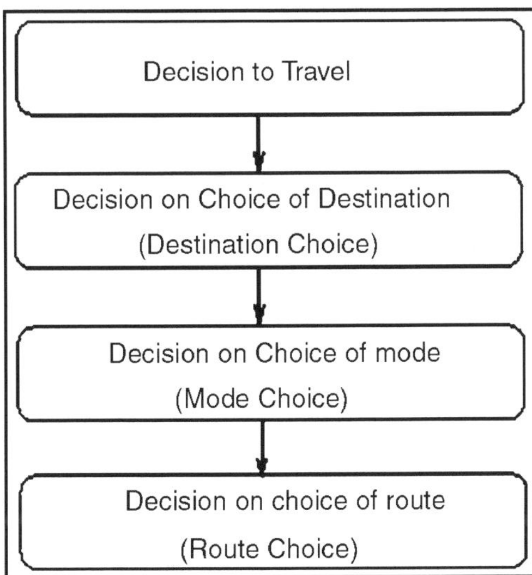


**Fig.** Schematic Representation of the Assumption of Sequential Decision Making.

Quite often, the *decision to travel* is changed because an appropriate destination does not exist; or an *initial choice of destination* is changed because it cannot be reached by the desirable mode of transport. It is possibly a truer picture of reality if the decision making framework is assumed to have feedback loops. One such possible structure is shown in Figure.In this structure, unlike in Figure, there are feedback loops indicating that decisions taken earlier can be changed based on a latter decision.

For example, the decision to travel may be aborted because at the *mode choice* stage if it is realised that none of the available modes suit the requirements.

As stated earlier, even though the assumption of the existence of a strict sequence in the decision-making process of a potential trip-maker may be debatable, generally sequential demand analysis is used to determine the travel demand. As will be seen throughout this lecture, even with this simplifying assumption of sequential decision making, the analysis of transportation demand remains sufficiently complex.

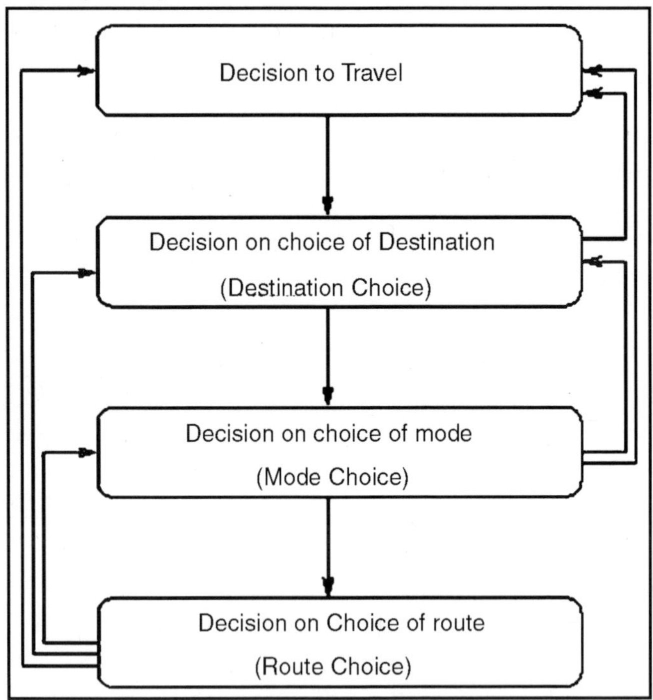


**Fig.** An Example of the Assumption of Non-sequential Decision Making

Figure shows a schematic of the sequential demand analysis procedure. The figure attempts to not only illustrate the logic of the analysis procedure but also gives the names of the different classes of models used to mathematically describe each decision-making phase of the analysis procedure. Before presenting the models, a general overview of the entire process is provided.

In this analysis procedure, first the entire study area is divided into various zones. These zones are generally obtained from the land-use pattern of the area. Next, for each zone the total number of trips generated in that zone are estimated using the trip-generation models. The outputs of the trip-generation models are then used to determine the number of trips between all zone pairs using the trip-distribution models. Given the trip-distribution pattern, the relative shares of these trips for the different modes are estimated using the mode-choice models. Finally, the traffic-assignment models estimate the volume on each link of the network by determining the routes that will be used by the trips.

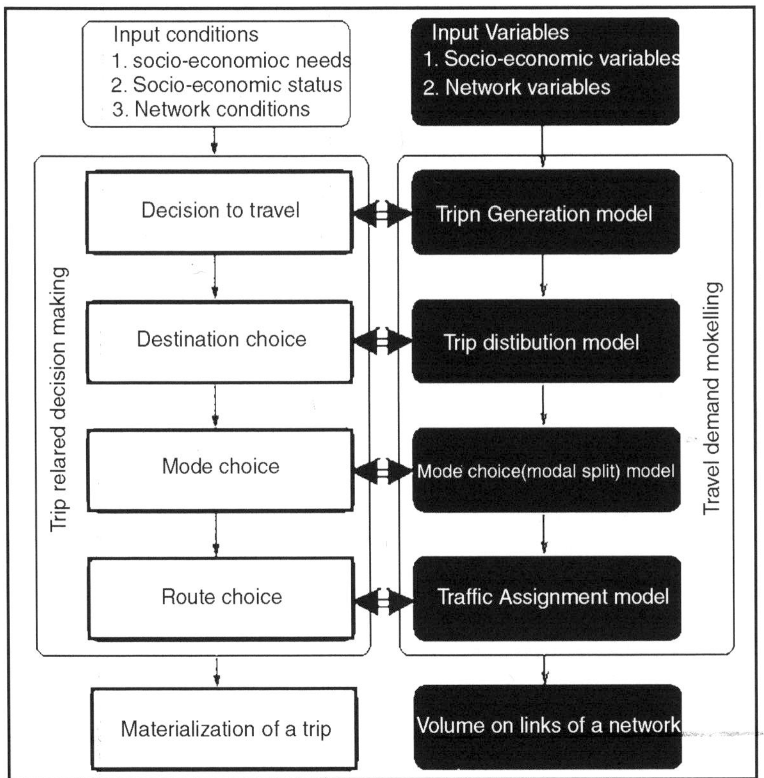


**Fig.** Sequential Demand Analysis Procedure

## DEMAND FORECASTING

A demand forecast is the prediction of what will happen to your company's existing product sales. It would be best to determine the demand forecast using a multi-functional approach.

The inputs from sales and marketing, finance, and production should be considered. The final demand forecast is the consensus of all participating managers. You may also want to put up a Sales and Operations Planning group composed of representatives from the different departments that will be tasked to prepare the demand forecast.

*Determination of the demand forecasts is done through the following steps*:

- Determine the use of the forecast
- Select the items to be forecast
- Determine the time horizon of the forecast
- Select the forecasting model(s)
- Gather the data
- Make the forecast
- Validate and implement results

*The time horizon of the forecast is classified as follows*:

| **Description** | **Forecast Horizon** | | |
|---|---|---|---|
| **Short-range** | **Medium-range** | **Long-range** | |
| Duration | Usually less than 3 months, maximum of 1 year | 3 months to 3 years | More than 3 years |
| Applicability | Job scheduling, worker assignments | Sales and production planning, budgeting | New product development, facilities planning |

## HOW IS DEMAND FORECAST DETERMINED?

*There are two approaches to determine demand forecast*:

- The qualitative approach,
- The quantitative approach.

*The comparison of these two approaches is shown*:

| **Description** | **Qualitative Approach** | **Quantitative Approach** |
|---|---|---|
| Applicability | Used when situation is vague & little data exist | Used when situation is stable & historical data exist |
| Considerations | Involves intuition and experience | Involves mathematical techniques |
| Techniques | Jury of executive opinion<br>Sales force composite<br>Delphi method<br>Consumer market survey | Time series models<br>Causal models |

## QUALITATIVE FORECASTING METHODS

Your company may wish to try any of the qualitative forecasting methods if you do not have historical data on your products' sales.

| Qualitative Method | Description |
|---|---|
| Jury of executive opinion | The opinions of a small group of high-level managers are pooled and together they estimate demand. The group uses their managerial experience, and in some cases, combines the results of statistical models. |
| Sales force composite | Each salesperson is asked to project their sales. Since the salesperson is the one closest to the marketplace, he has the capacity to know what the customer wants. These projections are then combined at the municipal, provincial and regional levels. |
| Delphi method | A panel of experts is identified where an expert could be a decision maker, an ordinary employee, or an industry expert. Each of them will be asked individually for their estimate of the demand. An iterative process is conducted until the experts have reached a consensus. |
| Consumer market survey | The customers are asked about their purchasing plans and their projected buying behavior. A large number of respondents is needed here to be able to generalize certain results. |

### Quantitative Forecasting Methods

*There are two forecasting models here*:

(1) The time series model and

(2) The causal model.

A time series is a s et of evenly spaced numerical data and is o btained by observing responses at regular time periods. In the time series model, the forecast is based only on past values and assumes that factors that influence the past, the present and the future sales of your products will continue.

On the other hand, t he causal model uses a mathematical technique known as the regression analysis that relates a dependent variable to an independent variable in the form of a linear equation.

## INTEREST RATES AND DEMAND

Using borrowed money various product are bought on credit using borrowed money, thus the demand for them may be sensitive to the rate of interest charged by the lender. Therefore if the Bank of England decides to raise interest rates – the demand for many goods and services may fall. Examples of "interest sensitive" products include household appliances, electronic goods, new furniture and motor vehicles. The demand for housing is affected by changes in mortgage interest rates.

## EXCEPTIONS TO THE LAW OF DEMAND

Does the demand for a product always vary inversely with the price? There are two possible reasons why more might be demanded even when the price of a good or service is increasing. We consider these briefly – ostentatious consumption and the effects of speculative demand.

### Ostentatious Consumption

Several goods are the items of luxurious where satisfaction comes from knowing both the price of the good and being able to flaunt consumption of it to other people! The demand for the product is a direct function of its price. A higher price may also be regarded as a reflection of product quality and some consumers are prepared to pay this for the "*snob value effect*".

Such examples might include perfumes, designer clothes, and top of the range cars. Consider the case of VI which is considered to be the most exclusive perfume in the world. Only 475 bottles have been produced and bottles have been selling for £47,500 each – a classic case of paying through the nose for an exclusive good. Goods of ostentatious consumption are known as Veblen Goods and they have a high-income elasticity of demand. That is, demand rises more than proportionately to an increase in income.

### Speculative Demand

Speculative demand affect the demand for a product. Here, potential buyers are interested not just in the satisfaction they may get from consuming the product, but also the potential rise in market price leading to a capital gain or profit. When prices are rising, speculative demand may grow, adding to the upward pressure on prices. The speculative demand for housing and for shares might come into this category and we have also seen, in the last few years, strong speculative demand for many of the world's essential commodities.

### Speculation Drives the Prices ofCommodities to Fresh Highs

In the global economy, the prices of world commodity have reached new highs this year helped by an increase in the rate of economic growth. Among the metals that have achieved record price levels are copper, zinc, gold and platinum; prompting sceptics to question how much longer prices can continue rising. Many market experts believe that the demand for commodities has been spurred by heavy speculator activity. For example, pension funds and hedge funds have been investing in commodity mutual funds over recent years leading to increased demand for precious metals. Firstly, there is high in prices because commodity producers are unable to raise output sufficiently to meet unexpectedly strong demand.

### The Non-Linear Demand Curve and the Idea of Price Points

Until now, in our introductory theory of demand we have drawn the demand curve for a product to be linear (a straight line). In many real world markets this assumption of a linear relationship between price and quantity demanded is not realistic. Many price-demand relationships are non-linear and an example of this is provided in the chart above, used to illustrate the idea of price-points.

Price points are points on the demand curve where demand is relatively high, but where a small change in price may cause a sizeable contraction in demand leading to a loss of total revenue for the producer. Price points can be justified in a number of ways:

- A price rise at the price point may make the product more expensive than a close substitute causing consumers to change their preferences
- Customers may have become used to paying a certain price for a type of product and if they see a further price rise, this may cause them to revalue how much satisfaction they get from buying and consuming something, leading to a decline in demand
- There may be psychological effects at work, supermarkets for example know the importance of avoiding price points - ≤2.99 somehow seems cheaper than ≤3.00 despite the tiny price difference

For AS level economics, you will be expected to draw and use linear demand curves in your basic analysis. But it is important to realise that in the real world of business, price-demand relationships can be complex and often a business does not have enough information about the behaviour of consumers for them to actually construct an accurate demand curve.

As with many aspects of economic theory, we are constructing curves to illustrate economic relationships. They are simplifications of reality.

**Elasticity**

The concept in economics that measures the responsiveness of one variable in response to another variable is elasticity. The best measure of this responsiveness is the proportional or percent change in the variables. This gives the most usable results for any type or range of data. Thus elasticity is the proportional (or percent) change in one variable relative to the proportional change in another variable.

The general formula for elasticity is:

*E = percent change in x / percent change in y*

There are five cases of elasticity. (Elasticity is almost always referred to as a positive value even thought it can be negative.)

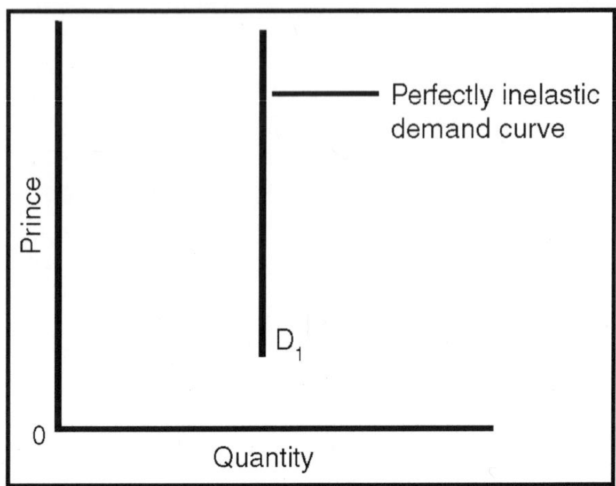


**Fig.** Perfectly Inelastic

- E = 1

Unit elasticity. The proportional change in one variable is equal to the proportional change in another variable.

- E > 1

Elastic. The proportional change in x is greater than the proportional change in y.

- E = infinity

Perfectly elastic. Any change in y will effect no change in x.

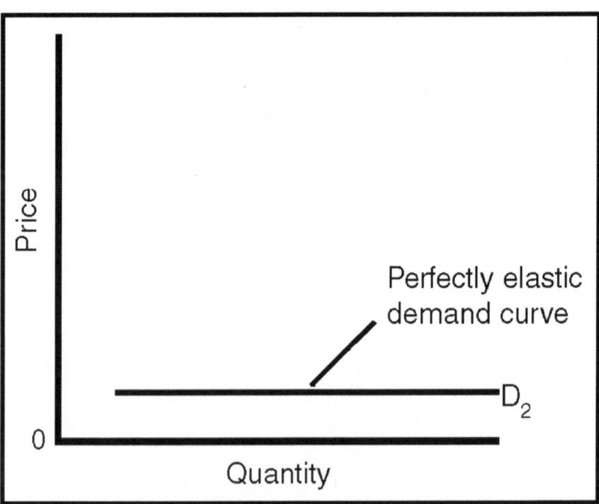


**Fig.** Perfectly Eastic

- E < 1

Inelastic. The proportional change in x is less than the proportional change in y.

- E = 0

Perfectly inelastic. Any change in y will have an infinite effect in x. The degree to which a demand or supply curve reacts to a change in price is the curve's elasticity. Elasticity varies among products because some products may be more essential to the consumer. Products that are necessities are more insensitive to price changes because consumers would continue buying these products despite price increases.

Conversely, a price increase of a good or service that is considered less of a necessity will deter more consumers because the opportunity cost of buying the product will become too high. A good or service is considered to be highly elastic if a slight change in price leads to a sharp change in the quantity demanded or supplied. Usually these kinds of products are readily available in the market and a person may not necessarily need them in his or her daily life. On the other hand, an inelastic good or service is one in which changes in price witness only modest changes in the quantity demanded or supplied, if any at all. These goods tend to be things that are more of a necessity to the consumer in his or her daily life.

To determine the elasticity of the supply or demand curves, we can use this simple equation:

Elasticity = (per cent change in quantity / per cent change in price)

If elasticity is greater than or equal to one, the curve is considered to be elastic. If it is less than one, the curve is said to be inelastic.

As we mentioned previously, the demand curve is a negative slope, and if there is a large decrease in the quantity demanded with a small increase in price, the demand curve looks flatter, or more horizontal. This flatter curve means that the good or service in question is elastic.

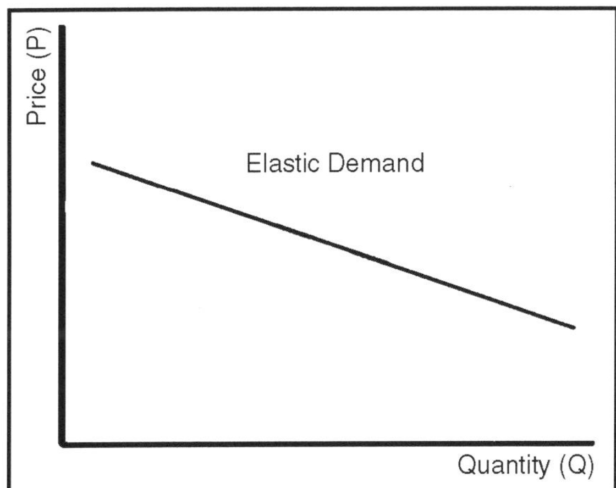


Meanwhile, inelastic demand is represented with a much more upright curve as quantity changes little with a large movement in price.

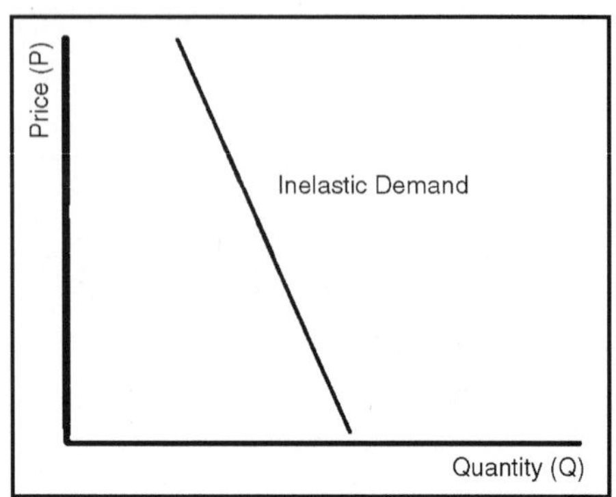


Elasticity of supply works similarly. If a change in price results in a big change in the amount supplied, the supply curve appears flatter and is considered elastic. Elasticity in this case would be greater than or equal to one.

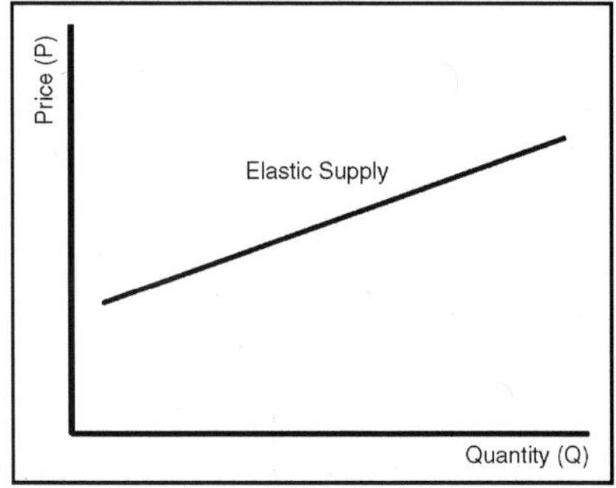


On the other hand, if a big change in price only results in a minor change in the quantity supplied, the supply curve is steeper and its elasticity would be less than one.

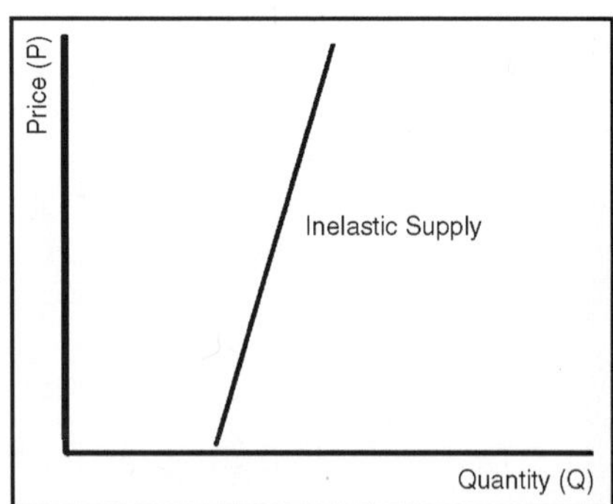


## FACTORS AFFECTING DEMAND ELASTICITY

Three main factors are there that influence a demand's price elasticity: The availability of substitutes - This is probably the most important factor influencing the elasticity of a good or service. In general, the more substitutes, the more elastic the demand will be. For example, if the price of a cup of coffee went up by $0.25, consumers could replace their morning caffeine with a cup of tea. This means that coffee is an elastic good because a raise in price will cause a large decrease in demand as consumers start buying more tea instead of coffee. However, if the price of caffeine were to go up as a whole, we would probably see little change in the consumption of coffee or tea because there are few substitutes for caffeine.

Most people are not willing to give up their morning cup of caffeine no matter what the price. We would say, therefore, that caffeine is an inelastic product because of its lack of substitutes. Thus, while a product within an industry is elastic due to the availability of substitutes, the industry itself tends to be inelastic. Usually, unique goods such as diamonds are inelastic because they have few if any substitutes.

- Amount of income available to spend on the good - This factor affecting demand elasticity refers to the total a person can spend on a particular good or service. Thus, if the price of a can of Coke goes up from $0.50 to $1 and income stays the same, the income that is available to spend on coke, which is $2, is now enough for only two rather than four cans of Coke. In other words, the consumer is forced to reduce his or her demand of Coke. Thus if there is an increase in price and no change in the amount of income available to spend on the good, there will be an elastic reaction in demand; demand will be sensitive to a change in price if there is no change in income.
- Time - The third influential factor is time. If the price of cigarettes goes up $2 per pack, a smoker with very few available substitutes will most likely continue buying his or her daily cigarettes. This means that tobacco is inelastic because the change in price will not have a significant influence on the quantity demanded. However, if that smoker finds that he or she cannot afford to spend the extra $2 per day and begins to kick the habit over a period of time, the price elasticity of cigarettes for that consumer becomes elastic in the long run.

## INCOME ELASTICITY OF DEMAND

In the second factor outlined above, we saw that if price increases while income stays the same, demand will decrease. It follows, then, that if there is an increase in income, demand tends to increase as well. The degree to which an increase in income will cause an increase in demand is called income elasticity of demand, which can be expressed in the following equation:

$$EDy = \frac{((Q\,current - Q\,previous)/(Q\,previous))}{((Y\,current - Y\,previous)/Y\,previous))}$$

ED= Elasticity of Demand
Q = Quantiry
Y = Income
EDy = Income Elasticity of Demand

If EDy is greater than one, demand for the item is considered to have a high income elasticity. If however EDy is less than one, demand is considered to be income inelastic. Luxury items usually have higher income elasticity because when people have a higher income, they don't have to forfeit as much to buy these luxury items. Let's look at an example of a luxury good: air travel.

Bob has just received a $10,000 increase in his salary, giving him a total of $80,000 per annum. With this higher purchasing power, he decides that he can now afford air travel twice a year instead of his previous once a year. With the following equation we can calculate income demand elasticity:

$$EDy = \frac{((2\text{-}1)/(1)) = 1}{((80000 - 70000))/(70000) = 0.14}$$

$$EDy = 1/0.14 = 7$$

Income elasticity of demand for Bob's air travel is seven -highly elastic. With some goods and services, we may actually notice a decrease in demand as income increases.

These are considered goods and services of inferior quality that will be dropped by a consumer who receives a salary increase. An example may be the increase in the demand of DVDs as opposed to video cassettes, which are generally considered to be of lower quality. Products for which the demand decreases as income increases have an income elasticity of less than zero. Products that witness no change in demand despite a change in income usually have an income elasticity of zero - these goods and services are considered necessities.

## PRICE ELASTICITY

Price elasticity measures the proportional change in quantity with respect to a proportional change in price. There are two types of price elasticity:

- Price elasticity of demand
- Price Elasticity Of Supply.

Price elasticity of supply measures the change in quantity supplied with respect to the change in price.

$E_s$ = *percent change in* $Q_s$ / *percent change in P*

Price elasticity of demand measures the change in quantity *demanded* with respect to the change in price.

$E_d$ = *percent change in* $Q_d$ / *percent change in P*

## ARC ELASTICITY

Arc elasticity equation is the way to estimate the elasticity of a point. Two points that are equidistant along the supply or demand curve from the point desired are chosen. The averages from those two points are then used in the above equations:

$$E = \frac{\dfrac{\Delta Q}{\dfrac{Q_1 + Q_2}{2}}}{\dfrac{\Delta P}{\dfrac{R_1 + R_2}{2}}}$$

## INCOME ELASTICITY OF DEMAND

Income elasticity of demand is the responsiveness of the quantity demanded in response to the change in income.

$E_i$ = *percent change in* $Q_d$ / *percent change in I*

Two types of goods are defined by income elasticity: Normal goods and inferior goods. Inferior goods have negative elasticities ($E < 0$) which means that consumption of a good goes down as income goes up. Normal goods have positive elasticities ($E > 0$). Normal goods who's elasticity is greater than one ($E > 1$) are defined as luxuries. Normal goods who's elasticity is less than one but still positive ($E < 1$) are defined as necessities.

## ELASTICITY AND TOTAL REVENUE

Total revenue received for a supplier is the price charged times the quantity sold.

*Total revenue = total quantity sold * price of good*

Elasticity is used to determines whether total revenue will change when prices are raised or lowered. There are three cases:

- $E > 1$

If $E_d$ is elastic, a rise in price decreases total revenue.

- $E = 1$

If $E_d$ is unit elastic, a rise in price leaves total revenue unchanged.

- $E < 1$

If $E_d$ is inelastic, a rise in price increases total revenue.

The relationship between changes in elasticity along a demand curve and its relationship to total revenue. When quantity is zero, total revenue is zero. When price is zero, total revenue is also zero. For elastic demand, as price decreases, total revenue increases. For inelastic demand, as price increases, total revenue increases.

## Applications

One distinctive application of the concept of elasticity is to consider what happens to consumer demand for a goods (for example, apples) when prices increase. As the price of a goods rises, consumers will usually demand a lower quantity of that good, perhaps by consuming less, substituting other goods, and so on. The greater the extent to which demand falls as price rises, the greater the price elasticity of demand. Conversely, as the price of a good falls, consumers will usually demand a greater quantity of that good, by consuming more, dropping substitutes, and so forth. However, there may be some goods that consumers require, cannot consume less of, and cannot find substitutes for even if prices rise (for example, certain prescription drugs). Another example is oil and its derivatives such as gasoline. For such goods, the price elasticity of demand might be considered inelastic.

Further, in the short term as well as in long term elasticity will normally be different. For example, for many goods the supply can be increased over time by locating alternative sources, investing in an expansion of production capacity, or developing competitive products which can substitute. One might therefore expect that the price elasticity of supply will be greater in the long term than the short term for such a good, that is, that supply can adjust to price changes to a greater degree over a longer time.

This applies to the demand side as well. For example, if the price of petrol rises, consumers will find ways to conserve their use of the resource. However, some of these ways, like finding a more fuel-efficient car, take time. So consumers as well may be less able to adapt to price shocks in the short term than in the long term.

In economies, the concept of elasticity has an extraordinarily wide range of applications. Particularly, an understanding of elasticity is useful to understand the dynamic response of supply and demand in a market, in order to achieve an intended result or avoid unintended results. For example, a business considering a price increase might find that doing so lowers profits if demand is highly elastic, as sales would fall sharply. Similarly, a business considering a price cut might find that it does not increase sales, if demand for the product is price inelastic.

The equation $MR = P * (1+E)/E$ show an example of how elasticity can be useful in business situations, where $MR$ is marginal revenue, $P$ is price of the good, and $E$ is the own price elasticity of demand for the good. Notice that when $E$ is less than negative one, demand is elastic. When $E$ is between negative one and zero, demand is inelastic. And at $E=-1$, demand is unit elastic (or unitary elastic), and thus $MC=MB$ and $MNB=0$.

## Importance

Elasticity is an important concept in understanding the incidence of indirect taxation, marginal concepts as they relate to the theory of the firm, distribution of wealth and different types of goods as they relate to the theory of consumer choice and the Lagrange multiplier. Elasticity is also crucially important in any discussion of welfare distribution, in particular consumer surplus, producer surplus, or government surplus. The concept of elasticity was also an important component of the Singer-Prebisch thesis which is a central argument in dependency theory as it relates to development economics.

As it is mentioned that elasticity is necessarily dimensionless — meaning that it is independent of units of measurement. For example, the value of the price elasticity of demand for gasoline would be the same whether prices were measured in dollars or euros, or quantities in tonnes or gallons. This unit-independence is the main reason why elasticity is so popular a measure of the responsiveness of economic behaviour.

## DEMAND AND ECONOMIC EVOLUTION

The concepts of demand, supply and equilibrium are intended to help us underst and the evolution of prices and outputs in competitive markets. They can be applied to the underst anding of past and current events. While future events are always uncertain, they can also be used to forecast what is likely to happen in the future. But we will need more detail in order to put these concepts to work. in history, for example, we can find developments that seem at first to pose problems for the supply and demand theory. But, as we shall see, a careful look at the details will solve the problems.

Here are four developments in economic history that raise questions about demand:

- Agricultural prices have fallen fairly steadily since 1910. During that time, agricultural employment and incomes have declined steadily.
- Computer prices have fallen steadily at least since 1960. During that time, the computer industry has exp anded and become more and more important.
- The LP record industry cut prices in an experiment and profits increased, leading to industry growth.
- Public transportation services have to increase their prices to reduce their deficit by increasing fare revenues.

How can we sort these seeming contradictions out? We will explore the answer in the pages to come. We will see that a key to underst anding many market developments is the *elasticity of demand.*

### REVENUE AND DEMAND

We want to sort out the four examples given before—farming, computers, records and public transportation. A first step is to distinguish between sales *revenue* and price. Revenue is the amount the company or industry takes in, before the costs. In other words, revenue is the product of the average price and the quantity sold:

R=p*Q

When the record industry cut their prices, they sold more records. In fact, they sold so many more that the increase in sales more than offset the cut in price and their sales revenue increased. That worked for the computer industry, too. But it didn't work for agriculture and public transportation—if they cut prices, they only sell a little more and their sales revenues and incomes fall. If the public transportation service cuts its fare, there will be an increase in the number of tickets sold, but just a small increase and it won't be enough to make up for the price cut. Likewise farmers—a cut in price will lead to more sales of food, but not enough more to make up for the price cut and farm incomes (the farmers' sales revenues) went done.

Since the change in sales revenue depends on both the change in price and the change in quantity sold, we can underst and why a cut in the price can have different results depending on how the quantity sold changes.

## DEMAND IN GENERAL

To make sense of this—and, indeed, for any practical applications of the economics of demand—we need to know something about the numerical characteristics of the demand relationship. For example: we know that if the price is cut, quantity sold will increase. But how much will it increase?

We cannot say much about this *in general.* The answer will vary from industry to industry. The answer may be different for agriculture, for example, than for computers. and that, of course, is the reason why the experience of those industries has differed so much. What can we do to deal with these differences?

What we can do is define some general terminology and principles to underst and these differences. (That's why we call the course "economic principles.")

## ELASTICITY OF DEMAND

One thing that makes a difference in these four examples is the strength of the response when there is a change in price. In two cases a drop in price causes a big increase in quantity sold and in the other two cases the response, the increase in quantity sold, is small. This is what we want to underst and.

A key concept for this purpose is the *price elasticity of demand.* Elasticity of demand is

$$\varepsilon = -\frac{\text{Percent change in quantity}}{\text{Percent change in price}} = -\frac{\frac{\Delta Q}{Q}}{\frac{\Delta p}{P}}$$

Elasticity of demand is a measure of how strongly the quantity dem anded responds to a change in price.

Noticing that

$$-\frac{\frac{\Delta Q}{Q}}{\frac{\Delta p}{P}} = -\frac{p\Delta Q}{Q\Delta p} \cong -\left(\frac{p}{Q}\right)\left(\frac{dQ}{dp}\right)$$

We can see that the elasticity is related to the slope ( and the derivative) but is not quite the same as the slope of the demand curve. What we are doing is measuring the change in price and the change in quantity sold each in percentage terms. This is helpful for several reasons, as we will see. For one thing, it means that the elasticity is independent of the units of measurement of price and quantity.

Here is a real world, real number example, from Philadelphia. In fiscal year 1990, SEPTA raised their fares in two steps from $1.15 to $1.50, the number of riders decreased by 6%. Since the increase in fares was 30%, this would give an approximate elasticity of 6/30=0.2.

This is only approximate, since some other things were changing at the same time. In particular, SEPTA claimed that the ridership would have decreased by 3.5% just because of population decrease. That would leave 2.5% decrease because of the fare increase and that would give an elasticity of 2.5%/ 30%=0.083. In any case, it is clear that the elasticity of demand for demand for SEPTA services in the city is considerably less than one.

### The Sign of the Elasticity of Demand

Notice that in the definition of elasticity of demand, there is a minus sign before the quotient. In the public transportation example, the elasticity of demand is positive. Remember, demand is an inverse relationship. That means that whenever the price rises, the quantity demand drops (ceteris paribus) and vice versa.

In other words, the signs of the changes in price and quantity, P and Q, will have opposite signs. Thus, the minus sign before the quotient will be canceled by the minus sign either in the numerator or the denominator. and that's the point—we want the elasticity to measure the response of quantity dem anded to a change in price and measure that responsiveness by a positive number.

To get the positive number, we have to cancel out the negative by another negative and the definition (minus sign and all) does this.

## ELASTICITY AND SLOPE

While elasticity and slope are not the same thing, we can roughly correlate elastic demand with a shallow slope of the demand curve and conversely.

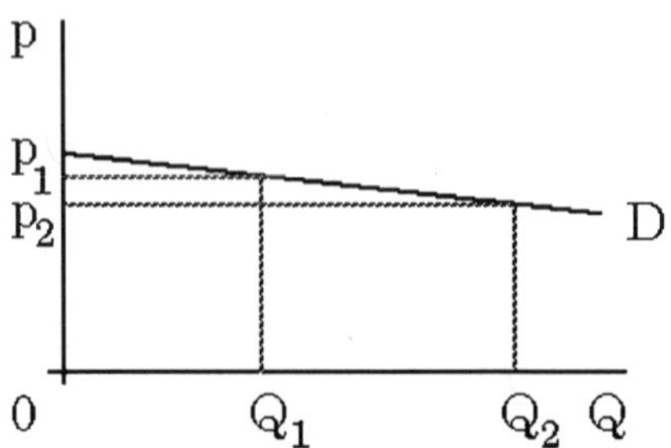


The figure above shows an example of high elasticity: a small decline in price (about 20%) leads to a large increase in quantity (about 120%), so that elasticity would be about 6.

## THE OTHER SIDE

Here is the other side of the example illustrating the relationship between the slope and elasticity:

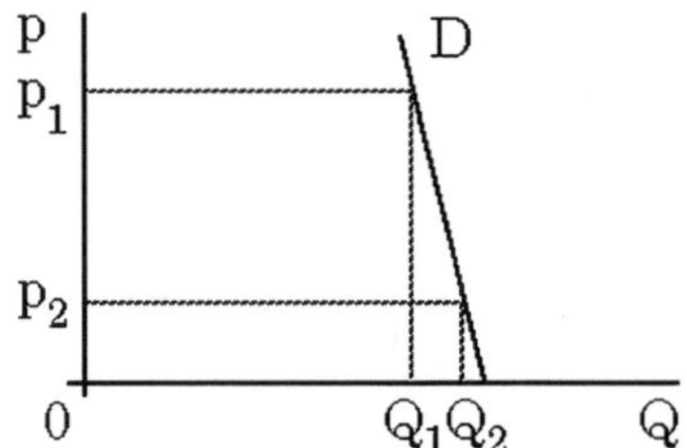


This figure shows an example of inelasticity: a large decrease in price (about 75%) leads to a small increase in quantity (about 25%), so that elasticity would be about 0.33.

## DETERMINANTS OF ELASTICITY

As we have noticed, there is only a little that can be said about the demand for goods *in general.* Different goods will have quite different demand relationships. In particular, the elasticity of demand will be different for different goods and services. What determines the demand for a particular good or service?

The most important thing in determining whether the demand will be elastic or inelastic is the availability of substitutes. For example, we have reason to believe that the demand for public transportation is less elastic in New York City than it is in some other cities. The reason could be that there are fewer good substitutes for public transportation in New York City than in some smaller cities. The private car is the most important substitute for public transportation for most local traffic and it is more expensive to keep a car in New York than it is most other places. Insurance is morecostly and parking places are harder to get. For these and other reasons, there are a larger proportion of the population in New York than in most cities who do not have cars. In all cities, in increase in the price of a ride on public transportation will cause some riders to switch to cars. In New York the proportion who make this substitution—car instead of subway—is smaller than in most American cities, for the reasons we have seen. Thus, a 1% increase in the fare in New York causes a smaller (percent) cut in the number of riders; in other words, elasticity is smaller.

In general, the more substitutes there are for the good and the better substitutes, the more elastic demand will be. The more substitutes, the more people switch and so, the more elastic demand is.

Another important thing that affects the elasticity of demand is the proportion of income spent on the good. An increase in the price of a good or service reduces the purchasing power of income and with less income (in purchasing power terms) people will cut back on purchases of all goods. If people spend a large part of their income on a particular good or service, then an increase in the price of that good or service reduces the purchasing power be a relatively great deal, causing a greater cutback than might otherwise occur. This means a bigger cutback when the price goes up—more elastic demand.It will also make a difference how much time people have to adjust to the change in price, but this can work out in several different ways. For cigarettes, for example—a good for which habit formation is important—the elasticity will probably be greater in the long run, since it will take a long time for people to break their habits and not be replaced by new smokers. For cars it would work the other way. In a short period of time, if car prices go up, people can just keep driving their old clunkers. That is, the cars already on the road are substitutes for new cars. But in a longer period of time the old cars wear out and the elasticity of demand is less.

Even after all these things are considered, there is still a lot of variation in the elasticity of demand from good or service to good or service. The only way to answer the question is to look at the numbers, do the statistics and let the evidence tell us what the elasticity of demand is for a particular good.

## APPLICATION

The most important influence on the elasticity of demand is the availability of substitutes for the product—the more and better substitutes readily available, the greater the elasticity. We can apply this idea to underst and a fundamental point about competitive industries. Why will farmers (for example) cut their prices when the result is that the sales revenue for the farm industry drops? The answer is that the individual firm faces a different demand curve, with a different elasticity, than the industry as a whole.

How will the individual firm's demand curve differ from the industry's demand curve? The elasticity of demand will be greater for the individual firm than for the entire industry. Here's why: The products of other firms in the industry are close substitutes for the product of any one particular firm. Each firm faces many, close substitutes—making for highly elastic demand. However, for the industry as a whole, the substitute products are not so close or numerous, so the elasticity is lower.

Taking potato farming as the example, the substitutes for the potato industry as a whole are rice, wheat, bread, pasta and such as that—not very good substitutes for a spud. But for Farmer Green's potatoes, the substitutes include farmer Brown's potatoes and potatoes from farmers Black, White, Blue,... and Jones, as well as rice and pasta and bread and wheat. Many more and better substitutes for Farmer Green's potatoes—so Farmer Brown's demand curve is more elastic than the demand curve for all potato farmers.

## DEMAND FOR BURGERS

We want to use the information so far to describe the consumer's demand for burgers. (We are still working on the theory of demand, after all). Remember, demand is a relationship between the price and the quantity a person wants to buy. So far we have quantity dem anded for just one price—quantity is 3 if the price is $1.98. So we need to generalize and get the quantity dem anded for the whole range of prices.

We can do that, using the rule MB=p (as nearly as possible with whole numbers). At any price, the consumer will adjust his consumption of burgers to make MB as nearly as possible equal to the price.

This means:

- When the price is less than $1, the consumer will buy four burgers.
- When the price is between $1 and $2, the consumer will buy three burgers.
- When the price is between $2 and $5, the consumer will buy two burgers.
- When the price is between $5 and $10, the consumer will buy one burger.
- When the price is above $10, the consumer will buy no burgers.

Using this information we can draw a picture of the individual's demand curve for burgers. Here it is.:

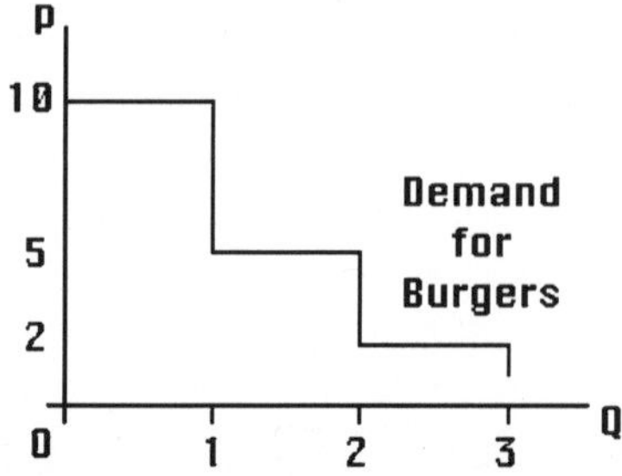


**Fig**: The Marginal Benefit of Burgers

## DEMAND IN GENERAL

This illustrates a general principle that applies to all consumer demand. In fact, it is so important and general that we might call it the fundamental principle of consumers' demand. Here it is:

*Fundamental Principle of Consumers' Demand*: The demand curve for any product or service is identical with the marginal benefit curve for that good or service.We remember the Law of Demand: a higher price means a lower quantity dem anded, ceteris paribus. We also remember the Law of Diminishing Marginal Utility: each additional unit of consumption adds less to utility than the previous one. Since benefits are approximately utility in money terms, that also applies to benefits—each additional unit of consumption adds less to total benefits than the previous one. So we have diminishing marginal benefits and we can now see that the Laws of Demand, Diminishing Marginal Utility and Diminishing Marginal Benefits all really are the same law, looked at from different points of view.

## INDIVIDUAL TO MARKET DEMAND

We now have a theory of the *individual's* demand curve. The theory tells us that the individual's demand curve is identical with the individual's marginal benefit curve. But, for supply and demand analysis, we need the *market* demand curve.

That's actually pretty easy. At any price, the market demand is the sum of the amounts dem anded by each of the individuals. That is, the market demand is the *horizontal sum* of the individual dem ands.

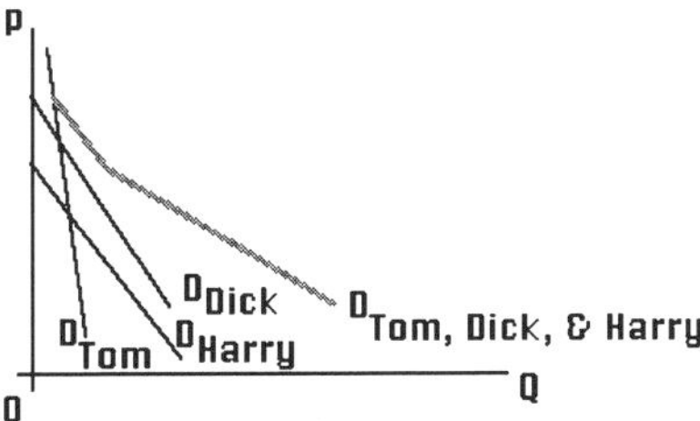


**Fig:** Individual and Market Demand

The diagram shows individual demand curves for Tom, Dick and Harry. The thick gray line is the demand curve for a market consisting of Tom, Dick and Harry.

In a market equilibrium, Tom, Dick and Harry will each pay the same price and adjust their purchases to the price. Each will be paying a price equal to his own marginal benefit. Thus

- The marginal benefit is the same for each of the consumers who buys the product.
- The market price measures the marginal benefit of one more unit of production, whoever may buy it.

We can see from this that the fundamental principle of consumers' demand applies to the market as a whole just as it applies to an individual consumer. For the market as for the individual consumer,

*Fundamental Principle of Consumers' Demand*: The demand curve for any product or service is identical with the marginal benefit curve for that good or service.

## MARGINAL BENEFIT AND CONSUMER'S SURPLUS

Now, let's see how to put these ideas to work in cost-benefit analysis. The first step will be to restate the relationship between the demand and the consumers' benefits. The consumer will buy just enough of any good so that the marginal benefit of the good is equal to its price. Conversely, the individual's demand curve is also her marginal benefit curve for the good.

The burgers example illustrates this. Let's forget about the pennies and suppose that the consumer bought three burgers at a price of $2, so that the price is exactly equal to the marginal benefit of the third burger.

But notice that the total benefit from three burgers is $17, while the consumer has paid only $6.00 for the three burgers. He has gotten a net benefit of $17-$6.00=$11.00 from the three burgers. This net benefit of $11.00 is called the "consumer's surplus."

How has this happened? The customer got a marginal benefit of $10 for the first burger, but paid only $2, for a net of $8. For the second burger, he got a marginal benefit of $5, but paid only $2, for a net of $3.

The consumer's surplus is the sum of the net benefits on the successive units bought: $8+$32=$11.

Price is equal to marginal benefit, which means the marginal benefit of the "last" unit bought. If the price had been higher, he would have bought fewer units. The "last" unit does not mean the last unit in time or space, but the unit the consumer would not have bought if the price were just a little higher. For the "previous" or "inframarginal" units, the person would be willing to pay more if he had to.

They must be worth more to him—but in a competitive market, he gets these "previous" or "inframarginal" units at the same price as the "last" unit. So he gets a net surplus on the "previous" or "inframarginal" units. In the example the surplus is $8 of benefits on the "first" burger and $3 on the "second" burger. This "consumers' surplus" is the benefit the consumer gets from buying in a competitive market.

## CONSUMER'S SURPLUS DIAGRAM

Consumer's surplus can be easily shown in a demand diagram. Let's take a graphic look at the consumers' surplus in the burger example.

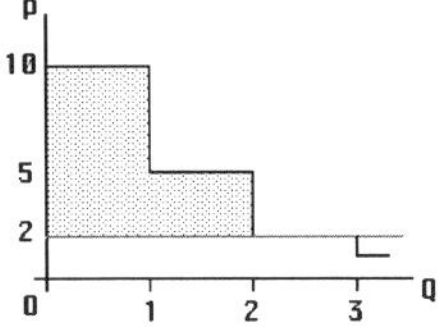

**Fig**: Individual Demand and Consumer's Surplus

In the figure, the demand for burgers is the stairstep "curve, " and the $2 price is the gray line. The lightly shaded area between the demand curve and the price line is the consumer's surplus. In general, we may visualize the "consumers' surplus" for any demand curve as the area between the demand curve and the price line, to the left of the quantity consumed.

## CONSUMER'S SURPLUS AND DEMAND IN GENERAL

In general, we identify the consumer's surplus in any demand diagram as the area between the demand curve and the price line, to the left of the quantity sold. With a linear approximation to the demand curve, the consumers' surplus is an area of triangular shape, as the shaded area in the diagram below.

We sometimes speak of this as "the consumers' surplus triangle" or "the welfare triangle." (The term "the welfare triangle" is used because this approach can be used to balance the benefits from buying one good against other aspects of the consumer's well-being or "welfare."

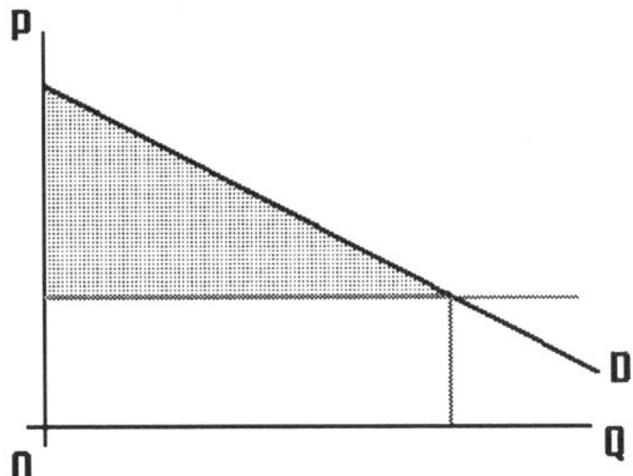

**Fig**: Consumers' Surplus in General

The demand curve gives more information for benefit-cost analysis. In an approximate sense, the area under the demand curve is the consumer's total benefit from consuming the good and the area between the demand curve and price line is her net benefit, that is, consumer's surplus.

### An Application of Consumers' Surplus

Let's have an example of an application of consumers' surplus in cost-benefit analysis. We might do a cost-benefit analysis of the introduction of a new good. The consumers' surplus from the good is the benefit to consumers from its introduction and so a major component of the total benefits. We could to a statistical estimated of the demand curve for the new product and derive the consumers' surplus from that and add that to the other benefits (business profits, perhaps increased pay and so on) to get the overall benefits from the introduction of the new good.

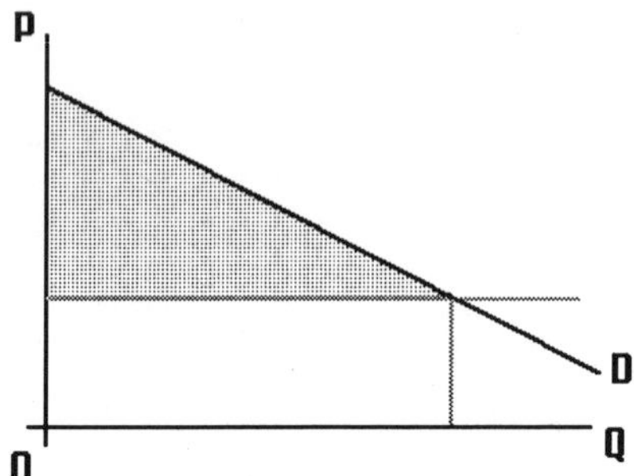


**Fig**: Consumers' Benefits from the Introduction of a New Good

As an example, we could use Video Cassette Recorders, VCR's. In fact VCR's were introduced a few years ago. How much do consumers benefit from the introduction of VCR's?

Suppose D is the demand for VCR's and p is the price for which they sell. Before VCR's were introduced, consumers of course got no benefit from them at all. After they are introduced, consumers get a surplus indicated by the area of the shaded triangle. That is their net benefit from buying VCR's and is the consumers' benefit from the introduction of the new good.

# 5

# Theory of Cost

## COST THEORY

### FIXED, VARIABLE, TOTAL, AVERAGE AND MARGINAL COSTS

Economists try to use language precisely. The words cost and prices are often confused. When we discuss costs we mean, how much did something cost to produce. This might be expressed as an opportunity cost, or in a currency such as dollars. When price is mentioned, economists mean the amount the consumer pays. Economists also try to explain the nature of costs. Why does one thing cost more to produce than another? Why does making an airplane cost so much less in a big factory than in a small factory.

To help explain, total costs are broken down into several parts and looked at in different ways. Before we start we make one basic assumption that the firm is operating in the short-run time period.

#### *Fixed Costs*

If aircraft are to be made then a factory is required. The land, the factory building, the machinery and office equipment must be bought or rented. These costs are called *fixed costs* and must be paid even when the factory has not produced anything. Fixed costs are costs that do not change, whatever the level of output is. Assuming an airplane factoryís fixed costs is a $60 million. See Table 1. A graph of the fixed costs (FC) would look like this;

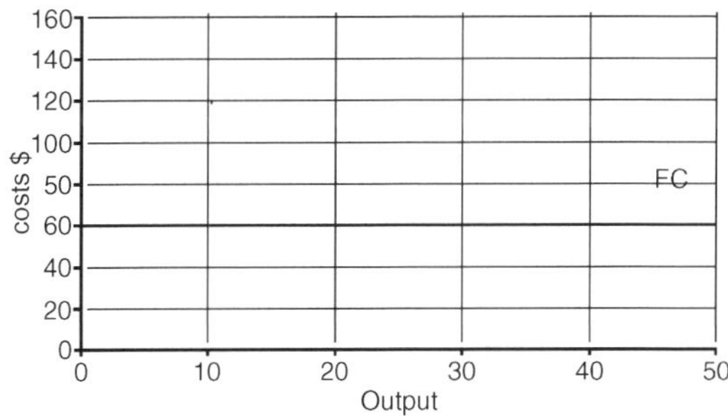

### *Variable Costs and Total Variable Costs*

Variable costs do change as the level of output changes. These costs are costs such as raw materials in production. In our example this would be the steel, components and labour needed to make each airplane.

If nothing were made the variable costs would of course be nothing. But as production rises the *total variable costs* (TVC) would rise. The variable cost is the cost per unit. The total variable cost is found by multiplying the variable cost (VC) by the level of output (Q), so TVC = VC x Q. Assuming that variable costs are constant at $1 million per airplane, a graph of TVC would look like this;

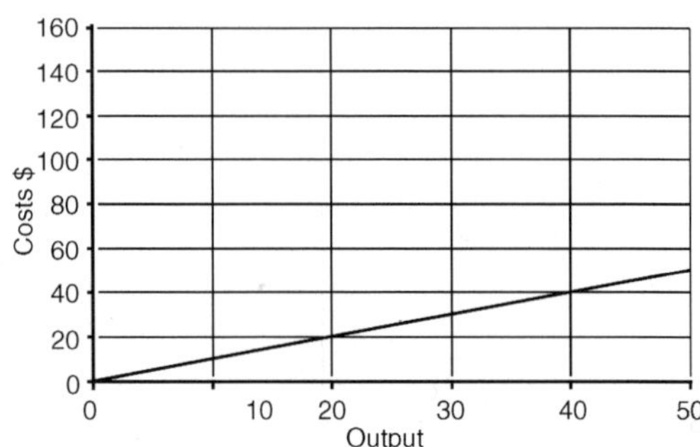


### Total Costs

Total costs are simply the sum of the total variable costs and the fixed costs. Note that the TC and TVC lines are parallel. The distance between the two lines is the amount of the fixed costs.

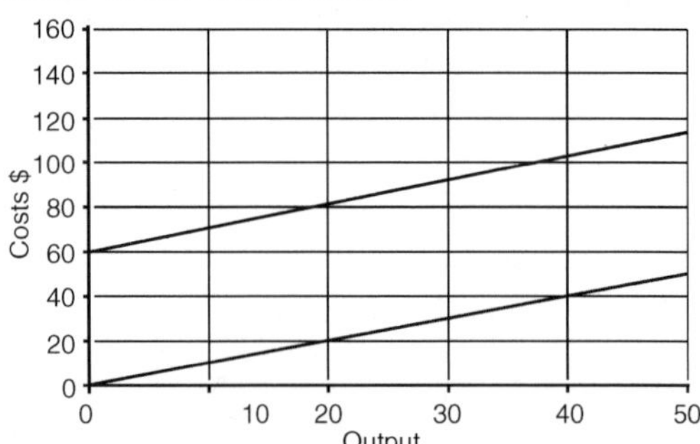


Table 1.

| Output *cost* | Fixed *variable* | Total cost | Total *cost* |
|---|---|---|---|
| 0 | 60 | 0 | 60 |
| 10 | 60 | 10 | 70 |
| 20 | 60 | 20 | 80 |
| 30 | 60 | 30 | 90 |
| 40 | 60 | 40 | 100 |
| 50 | 60 | 50 | 110 |

### Marginal Cost

Marginal cost is the cost of producing one extra unit.

marginal cost = the change in total costs the change in output

Using mathematical notation where the Greek letter delta is used to signify - change in.

$$MC = \frac{\Delta TC}{\Delta Q}$$

Notice that this equation is the same as the formula for the gradients of the variable cost and the total cost lines.

When output rises from 0 to 10 the change in output is 10.The corresponding change in total cost is 70 – 60 = 10. The cost of producing 10 extra units has been $10 million.

Therefore the cost of producing one extra unit is $1 million.

$$MC = \frac{\Delta TC}{\Delta Q} = \frac{10}{10} = 1$$

| *Output* | *Total cost* | *Marginal cost* |
|---|---|---|
| 0 | 60 | |
| 10 | 70 | 1 |
| 20 | 80 | 1 |
| 30 | 90 | 1 |
| 40 | 110 | 1 |
| 50 | 120 | |

Notice that the marginal cost in this example is the same as the variable cost.

This is because we assumed that variable costs are not always the same. In the later unit on the law of diminishing returns we will see that calculating and graphing marginal cost is a little more complicated than in this example.

### Average Costs

Average fixed costs (AFC) are the fixed costs divided by the level of output (FC/Q). So when output is 10 the AFC is 60/10 = 6.

Average total costs (ATC) are the total costs divided by the level of output (TC/Q). So when output is 10 the average fixed cost is 70/10 = 7.

So using the costs in table 1 above

| Output | Fixed cost | Total cost | Average fixed cost | Average total cost |
|---|---|---|---|---|
| 0 | 60 | 60 | - | - |
| 10 | 60 | 70 | 6 | 7 |
| 20 | 60 | 80 | 3 | 4 |
| 30 | 60 | 90 | 2 | 3 |
| 40 | 60 | 110 | 1.5 | 2.5 |
| 50 | 60 | 120 | 1.2 | 2.2 |

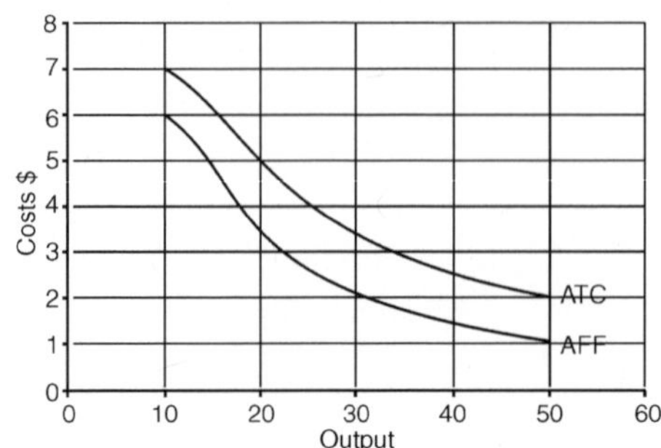


Understanding cost curves is best done by calculating and graphing examples yourself.

**The law of Diminishing (Marginal) Returns**

Although this is not needed for standard level when studying unit 2, the law of diminishing returns is important for unit 5 on development as a barrier to development. When one of the factors of production is held fixed in supply, successive additions of the other factors will lead to an increase in returns up to a point, but beyond this point returns will diminish.

This famous law was first written about by a Frenchman, Anne Robert Jacques Turgot and then alluded to by Thomas Malthus in his *Essay on the Principle of Population* (1798). The law was discussed in England during debates on free trade and the Corn Laws. Sometimes textbooks call it the law of decreasing (marginal) returns or the law of variable proportions.

Imagine a farm growing wheat. There are a number of jobs that need doing at harvest time and these must be done quickly before weather ruins the crop. First the wheat must be cut and gathered, the wheat and chaff must then be separated. The wheat has then to be carted to a barn, weighed, dried out in some instances, and then stored. All the farm machinery needs maintained, the paperwork completed and last but not least breakfast, lunch and dinner prepared. One man working alone will have difficulty doing all these tasks. By dividing the labour there will be gains in productivity.

If a second worker is employed the tasks can be shared. This means that productivity increases. They each become more skilled in the tasks that they specialise in and save time previously wasted by switching between tasks. However both have to stop when a piece of machinery breaks down or one of them stops for lunch.

Employing yet another person may once again improve their productivity. The harvest may continue as they take their lunch in rotation for example. But employing a fourth worker might mean productivity begins to fall (diminish). The gains made by employing the 4th are not as great as employing the 3rd worker. Eventually adding more employees might even lead to an overall decrease in production as they become bored with nothing to do and begin to interfere with production. The table below shows what happens as each extra worker is employed. Marginal means the next unit. So the marginal physical product (MPP) is the amount by which production rises when one extra worker is employed. MPP is calculated by measuring the change in total physical production per worker. The average physical product (APP) is simply the total physical product (TPP) divided by the number of workers

| **Number of** *workers* | **Total** Physical *Product (TPP)* | **Marginal** Physical *Product (MPP)* | **Average** Physical *Product (APP)* |
|---|---|---|---|
| 1 | 10 | 10 | 10 |
| 2 | 30 | 30 – 10 = 20 | 15 |
| 3 | 90 | 90 – 30 = 60 | 30 |
| 4 | 120 | 120 – 90= 30 | 30 |
| 5 | 130 | 130 – 120 = 10 | 26 |
| 6 | 120 | 120 – 130 = –10 | 20 |

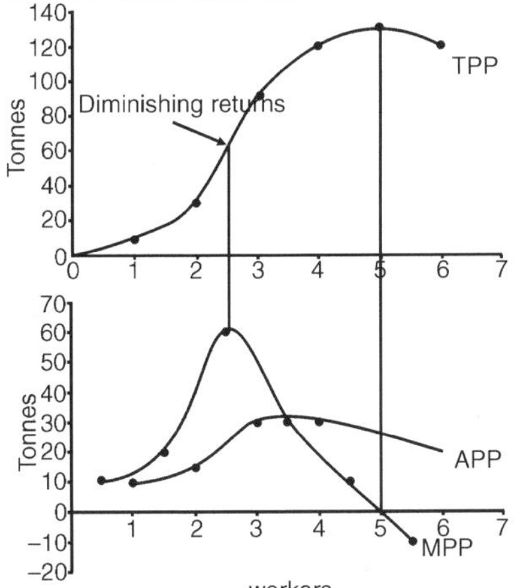


In the example the factors of production land and capital are constant but the amount of labour is being varied. The marginal physical product, (MPP) increases to start. When the 4th worker is employed the total still increases from 90 to 120 tonnes, but the increase of 30 tonnes is not as great as the previous increase of 60. It as this point that we say the marginal return diminishes.

The diagram and table shows that when the marginal physical product curve reaches its peak and then changes direction downwards that this is the point of diminishing marginal returns. On the total physical product curve diminishing returns do not occur at the peak of the curve (a common mistake), but where the gradient of the curve instead of becoming steeper changes and becomes less steep (known in maths as the point of inflection). When MPP becomes negative this means that additional workers are causing a reduction in the total production and the TPP curve changes direction downwards.The relationship between the marginal and average curves is important to understand. Notice that MPP intersects the APP when APP is at its maximum point. The reason is merely a simple mathematical relationship between marginal and averages. Think of a class of students.

The average age in the class is 17. If another student comes in the room and they are 18, what will happen to the average? – It will of course increase. On the other hand if the student were 16 the average age in the class would fall. So in the graph, as long as the marginal is higher than the average the average curve goes up and when the marginal is below the average. The average falls.The demonstration of the law above rests on a couple of assumptions. First we assume that each unit of labour is homogenous. That is that each worker has the same skills and works equally hard. Second, all the other factors of production are held fixed in quantity.The law of diminishing marginal returns has two main applications for IB students.

- The shape of the short run cost curve is determined by the principles above and,
- Diminishing marginal returns in agriculture act as a barrier to economic development

**The Importance of Costs for Decision-making**

Costs are a major concern in the decision making process of all firms. However, sometimes, those involved in the decision making process may get too concerned with only the costs of a proposal and forget that there is another side to the production, and hence the profit, equation. This is the benefit of the proposal. In the profit equation, total costs (TC) are subtracted from total revenues (TR). Thus, P$\Pi$ =TR–TC where $\Pi$ is profit. However, one has to remember that there is another equation that is directly related to profit and underlies the business structure. This is the production equation, called a production function, where inputs are combined to create an output or set of outputs.In some cases, added costs can come from changes in the price of an input. This is an instance where there will be no change in the output levels and no additional revenue (benefit) is gained. Other added costs may occur as a result of a change in inputs or the addition of inputs. These changes are likely to have an effect on the output production and, hence, on the revenue total as well. This is where cost-benefit analysis becomes important to the firm's decision making process.

***Illustrative Examples***

To further illustrate this, let us examine a couple of scenarios in a cattle enterprise:

- A producer is looking at two sources for dewormer. Once product is fifty cents cheaper than the other. They work nearly identically. On a 100 head cow herd, the difference in cost will be over $50.

- A producer is considering her veterinarian's recommendation to adopt a managed her-health Programmeme. The Programmeme will cost her about $15 more per brood cow. If we assume the producer has 100 brood cows, the additional annual cost it $1,500. Also, let us assume that her current weaning rate is 70 percent on her herd. This weaning rate is based solely on her 100 exposed cows and heifers from the previous breeding season. The veterinarian assures her that her herd's weaning rate will improve to 80 percent and possibly 90 percent due to improved health and efficiency in her cows. This 10 percent improvement in weaning rate will also translate to an improvement in revenue. In table 1, we explore the impacts of this new Programme. We will make a few additional assumptions for this analysis. The producer sells her calves at 350 pounds average, and the prices used will be a steer and heifer average price.

Table 2.

| | | *Without the Programmeme* | | *With the Programmeme* | |
|---|---|---|---|---|---|
| Weaning Rate | 70% | 70% | 75% | 80% | 90% |
| Additional # of Calves | 0 | 0 | 5 | 10 | 20 |
| Additional Costs | None | $!,500 | $1,510 | $1,520 | $1,540 |
| Additional Revenues | | | | | |
| @ $100/cwt. | None | None | $1,750 | $3,500 | $7,000 |
| @ $95/cwt. | None | None | $1,663 | $3,325 | $6,650 |
| @ $90/cwt. | None | None | $1,575 | $3,150 | $6,300 |
| @ $85/cwt. | None | None | $1,488 | $2,975 | $5,950 |
| Change in P$\Pi$ | | | | | |
| @ $100/cwt. | $0 | ($1,500) | $240 | $1,980 | $5,460 |
| @ $95/cwt. | $0 | ($1,500) | $153 | $1,805 | $5,110 |
| @ $90/cwt. | $0 | ($1,500) | $65 | $1,630 | $4,760 |
| @ $85/cwt. | $0 | ($1,500) | ($22) | $1,455 | $4,410 |

### *Analysis*

In Scenario 1, it is clear that a simple cost analysis would yield the same result as a cost-benefit analysis since there are no clear benefits to the more costly of the two products. Revenue is not improved in anyway while costs are increased. The net result would be to decrease profit. So, in the cost-benefit framework, there is negative benefit to the increased cost of the more expensive product. With Scenario 2, cost-benefit analysis yields a dramatically different result than simply looking a the cost of the Programmeme. With scientific backing that healthier animals are more efficient, one could reasonably expect significant performance gains in this situation. Therefore, simply considering the cost of the Programmeme would leave out some important considerations to the bottom line of the business enterprise. In fact, a further analysis would show that any improvement in the weaning rate above four percent would make the Programmeme profit enhancing above an $87 per hundredweight average steer and heifer price given the assumptions used in this example.

## COST FUNCTIONS

The cost function measures the minimum cost of producing a given level of output for some fixed factor prices. As such it summarizes information about the technological choices available to the firms. It turns out that the behaviour of the cost function can tell us a lot about the nature of the firm's technology.As suggested, first investigate the behaviour of the cost function $c(w; y)$ with respect to its price and quantity arguments. We then define a few related functions, namely the average and the marginal cost functions.

### PROPERTIES OF COST FUNCTIONS

You may have noticed some similarities here with consumer theory. These similarities are in fact exact when one compares the cost function with the expenditure function. Indeed, consider their definitions.

1. Expenditure Function:

$$e(p,u) = \min_{x \in \mathbb{R}^n_+} px$$

such that $u(x) \geqq u$

2. *Cost Function*:

$$+c(w,y) = \min_{x \in \mathbb{R}^n_+} wx$$

Such that $f(x) \geqq y$

Mathematically, the two optimization problems are identical. Consequently, for every theorem we proved about expenditure functions, there is an equivalent theorem for cost functions. We shall state these results here, but we do not need to prove them. Their proofs are identical to those given for the expenditure function.

*Proposition*: Suppose the production function f is continuous and strictly increasing.

*Then the cost function has the following properties:*

1. c(w, y) is nondecreasing in w.
2. c(w, y) is homogeneous of degree 1 in w.
3. c(w, y) is concave in w.
4. c(w, y) is continuous in w, for w > 0.

5. For all w > 0, c(w, y) is strictly increasing y.
6. Shephard's lemma: If x(w, y) is the cost-minimizing bundle necessary to produce production level y at prices w, then

$$x_i(w,y)=\frac{\partial c(w,y)}{\partial w_i}$$

*for i = 1,..., n assuming the derivative exists and that xi* > 0.

**PROPERTIES OF CONDITIONAL INPUT DEMAND**

As solution to the firm's cost-minimization problem, the conditional input demand functions possess certain general properties. These are analogous to the properties of Hicksian compensation de+9

*Proposition*: *The matrix of substitution terms* ($\partial x_j$(w, $y$)/$\partial w_i$) *is negative semi-definite.*

Again since the substitution matrix is negative semi-definite, thus it is symmetric and has non-positive diagonal terms. We then particularly have

*Proposition*: *The matrix of substitution terms* is symmetric, *i.e.*,

$$\frac{\partial x_j(w,y)}{\partial w_i}=\frac{\partial^2 c(w,y)}{\partial w_j \partial w_i}=\frac{\partial^2 c(w,y)}{\partial w_i \partial w_j}=\frac{\partial x_i(w,y)}{\partial w_j}.$$

*Proposition*: *The compensated own-price* effect is non-positive; that is, the input demand curves slope downward:

$$\frac{\partial x_j(w,y)}{\partial w_i}=\frac{\partial^2 c(w,y)}{\partial w_i^2}\leqq 0,$$

Using the cost function, we can restate the firm's profit maximization problem as,

$$\max_{y\geqq 0} py-c(w,y).$$

The necessary first-order condition for $y^*$ to be profit-maximizing is then, $p-\dfrac{\partial c(w,y^*)}{\partial y}\leqq 0,$

with equality if $y^* > 0$:

In other words, at an interior optimum (*i.e.*, $y^* > 0$), price equals marginal cost. If $c(w, y)$ is convex in $y$, then the first-order condition is also sufficient for $y^*$ to be the firm's optimal output level.

**AVERAGE AND MARGINAL COSTS**

Let us consider the structure of the cost function. Note that the cost function can always be expressed simply as the value of the conditional factor demands.

$$c(\mathrm{w}, y) \equiv \mathrm{wx}(\mathrm{w}, y)$$

In the short run, some of the factors of production are fixed at predetermined levels.

Let $\mathrm{x}_f$ be the vector of fixed factors, $\mathrm{x}_v$, the vector of variable factors, and break up w into $\mathrm{w} = (\mathrm{w}_v, \mathrm{w}_f)$, the vectors of prices of the variable and the fixed factors. The short-run conditional factor demand functions will generally depend on $\mathrm{x}_f$, so we write them as $\mathrm{x}_v(\mathrm{w}, y, \mathrm{x}_f)$. Then the short-run cost function can be written as

$$c(\mathrm{w}, y, \mathrm{x}_f) = \mathrm{w}_v\mathrm{x}_v(\mathrm{w}, y, \mathrm{x}_f) + \mathrm{w}_f\mathrm{x}_f.$$

The term $\mathrm{w}_v\mathrm{x}_v(\mathrm{w}, y, \mathrm{x}_f)$ is called short-run variable cost (SVC), and the term $\mathrm{w}_f\mathrm{x}_f$ is the fixed cost (FC). We can define various derived cost concepts from these basic units:

$$Short-run\,total\,cost = STC = w_v x_v\left(w, y, x_f\right) + w_f x_f$$

$$Short-run\,average\,cost = SAC = \frac{c\left(w, y, x_f\right)}{y}$$

$$Short-run\,average\,variable\,cost = SAVC = \frac{w_v x_v\left(w, y, x_f\right)}{y}$$

$$Short-run\,average\,fixed\,cost = SAFC = \frac{w_f x_f}{y}$$

$$Short-run\,marginal\,cost = SMC = \frac{\partial c\left(w, y, x_f\right)}{\partial y}.$$

When all factors are variable, the firm will optimize in the choice of $\mathrm{x}_f$. Hence, the long-run cost function only depends on the factor prices and the level of output as indicated earlier. We can express this long-run function in terms of the short-run cost function in the following way. Let $\mathrm{x}_f(\mathrm{w}, y)$ be the optimal choice of the fixed factors, and let $\mathrm{x}_v(\mathrm{w}, y) = \mathrm{x}_v(\mathrm{w}, y, \mathrm{x}_f(\mathrm{w}, y))$ be the long-run optimal choice of the variable factors.

Then the long-run cost function can be written as,

$$c(\mathrm{w}, y) = \mathrm{w}_v\mathrm{x}_v(\mathrm{w}, y) + \mathrm{w}_f\mathrm{x}_f(\mathrm{w}, y) = c(\mathrm{w}, y, \mathrm{x}_f(\mathrm{w}, y)).$$

*Similarly, we can define the long-run average and marginal cost functions*:

long-run average cost = $LAC$

$$= \frac{c(w, y)}{y}$$

long-run marginal cost = $LMC$,

$$= \frac{\partial c(w, y)}{\partial y}.$$

Notice that "long-run average cost" equals "ong-run average variable cost" since all costs are variable in the long-run; "long-run fixed costs" are zero for the same reason.

*Example*: Suppose the second factor in a Cobb-Douglas technology is restricted to operate at a level $k$. Then the cost-minimizing problem is,

$$\min w_1x_1 + w_2k$$

such that,

$$y = x_1^a k^{1-a}.$$

Solving the constraint for $x_1$ as a function of $y$ and $k$ gives,

$$x_1 = \left(yk^{a-1}\right)^{\frac{1}{b}}.$$

Thus,

$$c(w_1, w_2, y, k) = w_1\left(yk^{a-1}\right)^{\frac{1}{a}} + w_2k.$$

*The following variations can also be calculated*: Short-run average cost

$$= w_1\left(\frac{y}{k}\right)^{\frac{1-a}{a}} + \frac{w_2k}{y}$$

short-run average variable cost,

$$= w_1\left(\frac{y}{k}\right)^{\frac{1-a}{a}}$$

short-run average fixed cost,

$$= \frac{w_2k}{y}$$

short-run marginal cost,

$$= \frac{w_1}{a}\left(\frac{y}{k}\right)^{\frac{1-a}{a}}$$

*Example*: If the production function exhibits constant returns to scale, then it is intuitively clear that the cost function should exhibit costs that are linear in the level of output: if you want to produce twice as much output it will cost you twice as much. This intuition is verified in the following proposition.

*Proposition*: *If the production function exhibits constant returns to scale, the cost function may be written as* $c(\mathrm{w}, y) = yc(\mathrm{w}, 1)$.

*Proof*: Let x* be a cheapest way to produce one unit of output at prices w so that $c(\mathrm{w}, 1) = \mathrm{wx}^*$. We want to show that $c(\mathrm{w}, y) = \mathrm{w}y\mathrm{x}^* = yc(\mathrm{w}, 1)$. Notice first that $yx^*$ is feasible to produce $y$ since the technology is constant returns to scale. Suppose that it does not minimize cost; instead let x' be the cost-minimizing bundle to produce $y$ at prices w so that wx' < w$y$x*. Then wx'/$y$ < wx* and x'=$y$ can produce 1 since the technology is constant returns to scale. This contradicts the definition of x*: Thus, if the technology exhibits constant returns to scale, then the average cost, the average variable cost, and the marginal cost functions are all the same.

## THE GEOMETRY OF COSTS

Let us first examine the short-run cost curves. In this case, as suggested, write the cost function simply as $c(y)$, which has two components: fixed costs and variable costs. We can therefore write short-run average cost as,

$$SAC = \frac{c(w,y,x_f)}{y} = \frac{w_f x_f}{y} + \frac{w_v x_v(w,y,x_f)}{y} = SAFC + SAVC.$$

As we increase output, average variable costs may initially decrease if there is some initial region of economies of scale. However, it seems reasonable to suppose that the variable factors required will eventually increase by the low of diminishing marginal returns, as depicted in Figure. Average fixed costs must of course decrease with output, as indicated in Figure. Adding together the average variable cost curve and the average fixed costs gives us the $U$-shaped average cost curve in Figure.

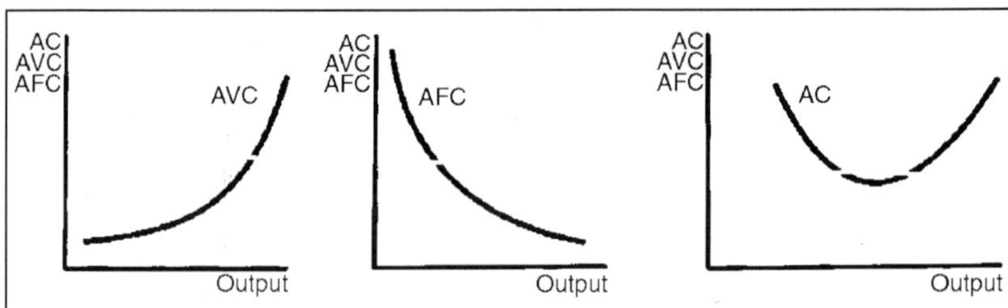


**Fig**: Average Variable, Average Fixed, and Average Cost Curves.

The initial decrease in average costs is due to the decrease in average fixed costs; the eventual increase in average costs is due to the increase in average variable costs. The level of output at which the average cost of production is minimized is sometimes known as the minimal efficient scale.

In the long run all costs are variable costs and the appropriate long-run average cost curve should also be $U$-shaped by the facts that variable costs usually exhibit increasingv returns to scale at low lever of production and ultimately exhibits decreasing returns to scale.

Let us now consider the marginal cost curve. What is its relationship to the average cost curve? Since

$$\frac{d}{dy}\left(\frac{c(y)}{y}\right)=\frac{yc'(y)-c(y)}{y^2}=\frac{1}{y}\left[c'(y)-\frac{c(y)}{y}\right],$$

$$\frac{d}{dy}\left(\frac{c(y)}{y}\right)\leqq(0\geqq)$$

if and only if

$$c'(y)-\frac{c(y)}{y}\leqq 0(\geqq 0).$$

Thus, the average variable cost curve is decreasing when the marginal cost curve lies the average variable cost curve, and it is increasing when the marginal cost curve lies the average variable cost curve. It follows that average cost reach its minimum at $y^*$ when the marginal cost curve passes through the average variable cost curve, *i.e.*,

$$c'(y)-\frac{c(y^*)}{y^*}.$$

All of the analysis just discussed holds in both the long and the short run. However, if production exhibits constant returns to scale in the long run, so that the cost function is linear in the level of output, then average cost, average variable cost, and marginal cost are all equal to each other, which makes most of the relationships just described rather trivial.

## LONG-RUN AND SHORT-RUN COST CURVES

Let us now consider the relationship between the long-run cost curves and the short-run cost curves. It is clear that the long-run cost curve must never lie any short-run cost curve, since the short-run cost minimization problem is just a constrained version of the long-run cost minimization problem.

Let us write the long-run cost function as $c(y) = c(y, z(y))$. Here we have omitted the factor prices since they are assumed fixed, and we let $z(y)$ be the cost-minimizing demand for a single fixed factor. Let $y^*$ be some given level of output, and let $z^* = z(y^*)$ be the associated long-run demand for the fixed factor. The short-run cost, $c(y, z^*)$, must be at least as great as the long-run cost, $c(y, z(y))$, for all levels of output, and the short-run cost will equal the long-run cost at output $y^*$, so $c(y^*, z^*) = c(y^*, z(y^*))$. Hence, the long-and the short-run cost curves must be tangent at $y^*$.

This is just a geometric restatement of the envelope theorem. The slope of the long-run cost curve at $y^*$ is

$$\frac{dc(y^*,z(y^*))}{dy}=\frac{\partial c(y^*,z^*)}{\partial y}+\frac{\partial c(y^*,z^*)}{\partial z}\frac{\partial z(y^*)}{\partial y}.$$

But since $z^*$ is the *optimal* choice of the fixed factors at the output level $y^*$, we must have,

$$\frac{\partial c(y^*,z^*)}{\partial z}=0.$$

Thus, long-run marginal costs at $y^*$ equal short-run marginal costs at ($y^*$, $z^*$). Finally, we note that if the long-and short-run cost curves are tangent, the long-and short-run *average* cost curves must also be tangent.

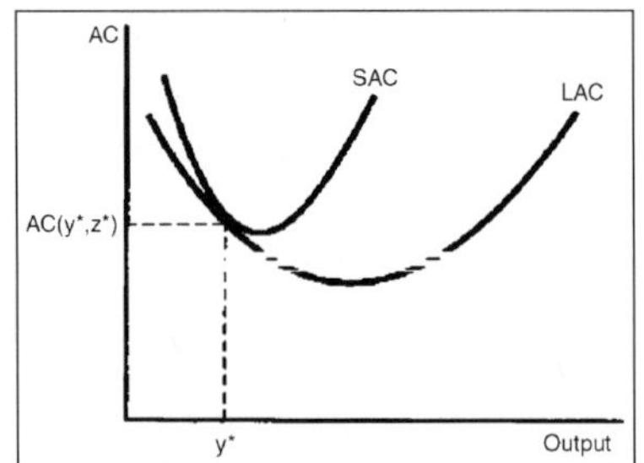


**Fig**: Long-run and Short-run Average Cost Curves. Note that the Long-run and the Short-run Average Cost Curves must be Tangent which Implies that the Long-run and Short-Run Marginal Cost must Equal.

## COST MINIMIZATION

An important implication of the firm choosing a profit-maximizing production plan is that there is no way to produce the same amounts of outputs at a lower total input cost. Thus, cost minimization is a necessary condition for profit maximization.

This observation motives us to an independent study of the firm's cost minimization. The problem is of interest for several reasons.First, it leads us to a number of results and constructions that are technically very useful.Second, as long as the firm is a price taker in its input market, the results flowing from the cost minimization continue to be valid whether or not the output market is competitive and so whether or not the firm takes the output price as given as.Third, when the production set exhibits nondecreasing returns to scale, the cost function and optimizing vectors of the cost minimiztion problem, which keep the levels of outputs fixed, are better behaved than the profit function.

To be concrete, we focus our analysis on the single-output case. We assume throughout that firms are perfectly competitive on their input markets and therefore they face fixed prices.

Let $w = (w_1, w_2, ...., w_n) \geqq 0$ be a vector of prevailing market prices at which the firm can buy inputs $x = (x_1, x_2, ..., x_n)$.

## FIRST-ORDER CONDITIONS OF COST MINIMIZATION

*Let us consider the problem of finding a cost-minimizing way to produce a given level of output:*

$$\min_{x} wx$$

$$\text{such that } f(x) = y$$

*We analyse this constrained minimization problem using the Lagrangian function:*

$$\mathcal{L}(\lambda, x) = wx - \lambda_{\text{¸}} (f(x) - y)$$

where production function $f$ is assumed to be differentiate and $\lambda_{\text{¸}}$ is the Lagrange multiplier.

The first-order conditions characterizing an interior solution $x^*$ are,

$$w_i - \lambda \frac{\partial f(x^*)}{\partial x_i} = 0, \; i = 1, ..., n$$

$$f(x^*) = y$$

or in vector notation, the condition can be written as,

$$w = \lambda Df(x^*):$$

We can interpret these first-order conditions by dividing the $j^{th}$ condition by the $i^{th}$ condition to get,

$$\frac{w_i}{w_j} = \frac{\frac{\partial f(x^*)}{\partial x_i}}{\frac{\partial f(x^*)}{\partial x_j}} \; i, j = 1, ..., n,$$

which means the marginal rate of technical substitution of factor $i$ for factor $j$ equals the economic rate of substitution factor $i$ for factor $i$ at the cost minimizing input bundle. This first-order condition can also be represented graphically.

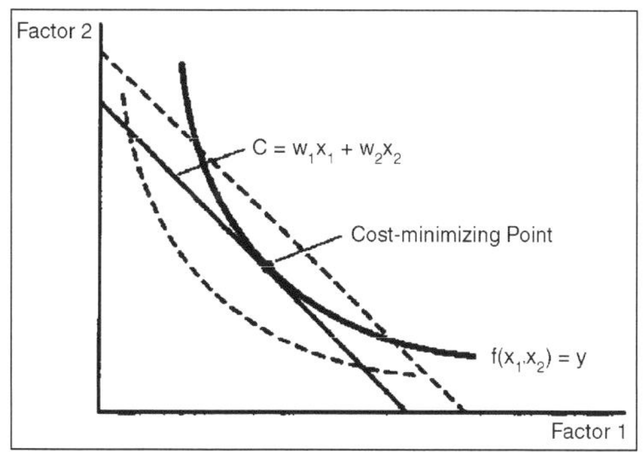


**Fig.** Cost Minimization. At a Point that Minimizes Costs, the Isoquant must be Tangent to the Constant Cost Line.

In Figure, the curved lines represent iso-quants and the straight lines represent constant cost curves. When $y$ is fixed, the problem of the firm is to find a cost-minimizing point on a given iso-quant. It is clear that such a point will be characterized by the tangency condition that the slope of the constant cost curve must be equal to the slope of the iso-quant.

Again, the conditions are valid only for interior operating positions: they must be modified if a cost minimization point occurs on the boundary. The appropriate conditions turn out to be,

$$\lambda \frac{\partial f(x^*)}{\partial x_i} - w_i \leqq 0$$

with equality if $x_i > 0$; $i = 1, 2, \ldots, n$

It is known that a continuous function achieves a minimum and a maximum value on a closed and bounded set. The objective function wx is certainly a continuous function and the set $V(y)$ is a closed set by hypothesis. All that we need to establish is that we can restrict our attention to a bounded subset of $V(y)$. But this is easy. Just pick an arbitrary value of x, say x'. Clearly the minimal cost factor bundle must have a cost less than wx'. Hence, we can restrict our attention to the subset,

$$\{x \text{ in } V(y): wx \leqq wx'\},$$

which will certainly be a bounded subset, as long as $w > 0$. Thus the cost minimizing input bundle always exists.

## SUFFICIENCY OF FIRST-ORDER CONDITIONS FOR COST MINIMIZATION

Again, like consumer's constrained optimization problem, the first-order conditions are merely necessary conditions for a local optimum.

However, these necessary first-order conditions are in fact sufficient for a global optimum when a production function is quasi-concave, which is formerly stated in the following proposition.

*Proposition: Suppose that $f(x)$:*

$$\mathbb{R}^n_+ \to \mathbb{R}$$

is differentiable and quasi-concave on $\mathbb{R}^n_+$ and $w > 0$. If $(x, \lambda) > 0$ satisfies the first-order conditions, then x solves the firm's cost minimization problem at prices w.

*Proof*: Since

$$f(x) :\to \mathbb{R}^n_+$$

is differentiable and quasi-concave, the input requirement set $V(y) = \{x: f(x) \geqq y\}$ is a convex and closed set. Further the object function $wx$ is convex and continuous, then by the Kuhn-Tucker theorem, the first-order conditions are sufficient for the constrained minimization problem.

Similarly, the strict quasi-concavity of $f$ can be checked by verifying if the naturally ordered principal minors of the bordered Hessian alternative in sign, *i.e.*,

$$\begin{vmatrix} 0 & f_1 & f_2 \\ f_1 & f_{11} & f_{12} \\ f_2 & f_{21} & f_{22} \end{vmatrix} > 0,$$

$$\begin{vmatrix} 0 & f_1 & f_2 & f_3 \\ f_1 & f_{11} & f_{12} & f_{13} \\ f_2 & f_{21} & f_{22} & f_{23} \\ f_3 & f_{31} & f_{32} & f_{33} \end{vmatrix} < 0,$$

and so on, where,

$$f_i = \frac{\partial f}{\partial x_i}$$

and,

$$f_{ij} = \frac{\partial^2 f}{\partial x_i \partial x_j}.$$

For each choice of w and $y$ there will be some choice of x* that minimizes the cost of producing $y$ units of output. As suggested, call the function that gives us this optimal choice the conditional input demand function and write it as x(w, $y$). Note that conditional factor demands depend on the level of output produced as well as on the factor prices.The cost function is the minimal cost at the factor prices w and output level $y$, that is.

$$c(\mathrm{w}, y) = \mathrm{wx}(\mathrm{w}, y).$$

*Example*: Consider the cost minimization problem

$$c(w, y) = \min_{x_1, x_2} w_1 x_1 + w_2 x_2$$

such that,

$$A x_1^a x_2^b = y.$$

Solving the constraint for $x2$, we see that this problem is equivalent to,

$$\min_{x_1} w_1 x_1 + w_2 A^{-\frac{1}{b}} y^{\frac{1}{b}} x_1^{-\frac{a}{b}}.$$

The first-order condition is,

$$w_1 - \frac{a}{b} w_2 A^{-\frac{1}{b}} y^{\frac{1}{b}} x_1^{-\frac{a+b}{b}} = 0,$$

which gives us the conditional input demand function for factor 1:

$$x_1(w_1, w_2, y) = A^{-\frac{a}{a+b}} \left[\frac{aw_1}{bw_2}\right]^{\frac{b}{a+b}} y^{\frac{1}{a+b}}.$$

The other conditional input demand function is,

$$x_2(w_1, w_2, y) = A^{-\frac{1}{a+b}} \left[\frac{aw_2}{bw_1}\right]^{\frac{a}{a+b}} y^{\frac{1}{a+b}}.$$

The cost function is thus,

$$c(w_1, w_2, y) = w_1, x_1(w_1, w_2, y) + w_2, x_2(w_1, w_2, y)$$

$$= A^{\frac{-a}{a+b}} \left[\left(\frac{a}{b}\right)^{\frac{b}{a+b}} \left(\frac{a}{b}\right)^{\frac{-a}{a+b}}\right] w_1^{\frac{a}{a+b}} w_2^{\frac{b}{a+b}} y^{\frac{1}{a+b}}.$$

When $A = 1$ and $a + b = 1$ (constant returns to scale), we particularly have,

$$c(w_1, w_2 y) = K w_1^a w_2^{1-a} y,$$

where,

$$K = a^{-a}(1-a)a^{-1}.$$

*Example*: Suppose that,

$$f(x_1, x_2) = \left(x_1^{\rho} + x_2^{\rho}\right)^{\frac{1}{\rho}}.$$

What is the associated cost function? The cost minimization problem is,

$$\min w_1 x_1 + w_2 x_2$$

such that,

$$x_1^{\rho} + x_2^{\rho} = y^{p}$$

The first-order conditions are,

$$w_1 - \lambda \rho x_1^{\rho-1} = 0$$

$$w_2 - \lambda \rho x_2^{\rho-1} = 0$$

$$x_1^{\rho} + x_2^{\rho} = y.$$

Solving the first two equations for $x_1^\rho$ and $x_2^\rho$ we have,

$$x_1^\rho = w_1^{\frac{\rho}{\rho-1}} (\lambda\rho)^{\frac{-\rho}{\rho-1}}$$

$$x_2^\rho = w_2^{\frac{\rho}{\rho-1}} (\lambda\rho)^{\frac{-\rho}{\rho-1}}.$$

Substitute this into the production function to find,

$$(\lambda\rho)^{\frac{-\rho}{\rho-1}} \left( w_1^{\frac{\rho}{\rho-1}} + w_2^{\frac{\rho}{\rho-1}} \right) = y^\rho.$$

Solve this for,

$$(\lambda\rho)^{\frac{-\rho}{\rho-1}}$$

and substitute into equation. This gives us the conditional input demand functions

$$x_1(w_1, w_2, y) = w_1^{\frac{1}{\rho-1}} \left[ w_1^{\frac{\rho}{\rho-1}} + w_2^{\frac{\rho}{\rho-1}} \right]^{-\frac{1}{\rho}} y$$

$$x_2(w_1, w_2, y) = w_2^{\frac{1}{\rho-1}} \left[ w_1^{\frac{\rho}{\rho-1}} + w_2^{\frac{\rho}{\rho-1}} \right]^{-\frac{1}{\rho}} y$$

Substituting these functions into the definition of the cost function yields,

$$c(w_1.w_2, y) = w_1 x_1(w_1, w_2, y) + w_2, x_2(w_1, w_2, y)$$

$$= y \left[ w_1^{\frac{\rho}{\rho-1}} + w_2^{\frac{\rho}{\rho-1}} \right] \left[ w_1^{\frac{\rho}{\rho-1}} + w_2^{\frac{\rho}{\rho-1}} \right]^{-\frac{1}{\rho}}$$

$$= y \left[ w_1^{\frac{\rho}{\rho-1}} + w_2^{\frac{\rho}{\rho-1}} \right]^{\frac{\rho-1}{\rho}}.$$

This expression looks a bit nicer if we set $r = \rho/(\rho-1)$ and write,

$$c(w_1, w_2, y) = y\left[w_1^r + w_2^r\right]^{\frac{1}{r}}.$$

Note that this cost function has the same form as the original CES production function with $r$ replacing ρ. In the general case where,

$$f(x_1, x_2) = \left[(a_1x_1)^\rho + (a_2x_2)^\rho\right]^{\frac{1}{\rho}},$$

similar computations can be done to show that,

$$c(w_1, w_2, y) = \left[(w_1/a_1)^r + (w_2/a_2)^r\right]^{\frac{1}{r}} y.$$

*Example*: Suppose $f(x_1, x_2) = \min\{ax_1, bx_2\}$. Since we know that the firm will not waste any input with a positive price, the firm must operate at a point where $y = ax_1 = bx_2$.

Hence, if the firm wants to produce $y$ units of output, it must use $y=a$ units of good 1 and $y/b$ units of good 2 no matter what the input prices are. Hence, the cost function is given by

$$c(w_1, w_2, y) = \frac{w_1 y}{a} + \frac{w_2 y}{b} = y\left(\frac{w_1}{a} + \frac{w_2}{b}\right).$$

*Example*: Suppose that $f(x_1, x_2) = ax_1 + bx_2$, so that factors 1 and 2 are perfect substitutes. What will the cost function look like? Since the two goods are perfect substitutes, the firm will use whichever is cheaper.

Hence, the cost function will have the form $c(w_1, w_2, y) = \min\{w_1/a, w_2/b\}y$.In this case the answer to the cost-minimization problem typically involves a boundary solution: one of the two factors will be used in a zero amount.

It is easy to see the answer to this particular problem by comparing the relative steepness of the isocost line and isoquant curve. If

$$\frac{a_1}{a_2} < \frac{w_1}{w_2},$$

the firm only uses $x_2$ and the cost function is given by,

$$c(w_1, w_2, y) = w_2 x_2 = w_2 \frac{y}{a_2}.$$

If,

$$\frac{a_1}{a_2} < \frac{w_1}{w_2},$$

the firm only uses $x_1$ and the cost function is given by,

$$c(w_1, w_2, y) = w_1 x_1 = w_1 \frac{y}{a_1}.$$

## COST STRUCTURE OF THE FIRM

We can look at the business firm from at least two points of view: productivity, inputs and outputs (as we have just done) or outputs and costs. In advanced microeconomics, these two points of view are called "duals." They are equally valid, but they point up different things. They are also opposites from a certain point of view—the higher the productivity, the lower the costs. By looking at the firm from the point of view of costs, we shift our perspective somewhat and gain a much more direct underst anding of supply.

We also look more directly at the difference between the long and short run. In the short run, we have two major categories of costs:

- Fixed costs and
- Variable costs

In the long run, however, all costs are variable. Thus, we must study costs under two quite different headings. Costs will vary quite differently in the long run and in the short.

## FIXED AND VARIABLE COSTS

Variable costs are costs that can be varied flexibly as conditions change. In the John Bates Clark model of the firm that we are studying, labour costs are the variable costs. Fixed costs are the costs of the investment goods used by the firm, on the idea that these reflect a long-term commitment that can be recovered only by wearing them out in the production of goods and services for sale.The idea here is that labour is a much more flexible resource than capital investment. People can change from one task to another flexibly (whether within the same firm or in a new job at another firm), while machinery tends to be designed for a very specific use. If it isn't used for that purpose, it can't produce anything at all. Thus, capital investment is much more of a commitment than hiring is. In the eighteen-hundreds, when John Bates Clark was writing, this was pretty clearly true. Over the past century, a) education and experience have become more important for labour and have made labour more specialized and b) increasing automatic control has made some machinery more flexible.So the differences between capital and labour are less than they once were, but all the same, it seems labour is still relatively more flexible than capital. It is this (relative) difference in flexibility that is expressed by the simplified distinction of long and short run.

Of course, productivity and costs are inversely related, so the variable costs will change as the productivity of labour changes.Here is a picture of the fixed costs (FC), variable costs (VC) and the total of both kinds of costs (TC) for the productivity example in the last unit:

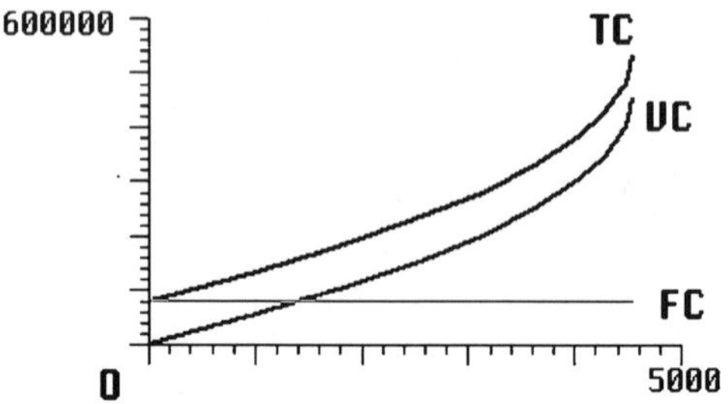


Output produced is measured Towards the right on the horizontal axis. The cost numbers are on the vertical axis. Notice that the variable and total cost curves are parallel, since the distance between them is a constant number—the fixed cost.

**OPPORTUNITY COST**

What is the connection between the distinction we have just made—fixed vs variable costs—and opportunity cost, the key concept in some earlier units? In economics, all costs are included—whether or not they correspond to money payments. If we have opportunity costs with no corresponding money payments, they are called implicit costs. The implicit costs (as well as the money costs) are included in the cost analysis we have just given.

There is some correlation between implicit costs and fixed or variable costs, but this correlation will be different in such different kinds of firms as:

*A factory owned by an absentee investor*: This is the easiest case to underst and. All of the labour costs to the absentee investor are money costs, including the manager's salary. If the investor has borrowed some of the money he invested in the factory, then there are some money costs of the capital invested—interest on the loan. However, we must consider the opportunity cost of invested capital as well.The investor's own money that he has used to buy the factory is money that she could have invested in some other business. The return she could have gotten on another investment is the opportunity cost of her own funds invested in the business. This is an implicit cost and in this case the implicit cost is part of the cost of capital and probably a fixed cost.

*A "mom- and-pop" store*: A "mom- and-pop" store (family proprietorship or partnership) is a store in which family members are self-employed and supply most of the labour. Typically, "Mom" and "Pop" don't pay themselves a salary—they just take money from the till when they need it, since it is their property anyway. As a result, there are no money costs for their labour. But their labour has an opportunity cost—the salary or wages they could make working similar hours in some other business—and so, in this case, the implicit costs include a large component of variable labour costs.

*A large modern corporation*: The corporation has relatively few implicit costs, but generally will have some. All labour costs will be expressed in money terms (though benefits and bonuses have to be included), since the shareholders don't supply labour to the corporation as "Mom and Pop" do in a family proprietorship. It will pay interest to bondholders and dividends to shareholders. But the dividends aren't really a cost item—they include profits distributed to the shareholders.Moreover, the typical corporation will retain some profits and invest them within the business, a "plowback" investment. Conversely, shareholders may take a large part of their payout in appreciation of the stock value—and plowback investment is one reason for the appreciation. Thus we would say that the corporation has a net equity value, that is, that the corporation "owns" a certain amount of capital that it invests in its own business (very much like the absentee owner in the first example). This capital has an opportunity cost and that opportunity cost is an implicit cost. The stockholders, who own the corporation, ultimately receive (as dividends or appreciation) both the opportunity cost of the equity capital and any profit left over after it is taken out.

## UNIT COST

Here are the average, average variable and average fixed costs for our example firm.

**Table.**

| Q | AC | AFC | AVC |
|---|---|---|---|
| 945 | 138 | 85 | 53 |
| 1780 | 101 | 45 | 56 |
| 2505 | 92 | 32 | 60 |
| 3120 | 90 | 26 | 64 |
| 3625 | 91 | 22 | 69 |
| 4020 | 95 | 20 | 75 |
| 4305 | 100 | 19 | 81 |
| 4480 | 107 | 18 | 89 |
| 4545 | 117 | 18 | 99 |

Here are the average cost (AC), average variable cost (AVC) and average fixed cost (AFC) in a diagram. This is a good representative of the way that economists believe firm costs vary in the short run.

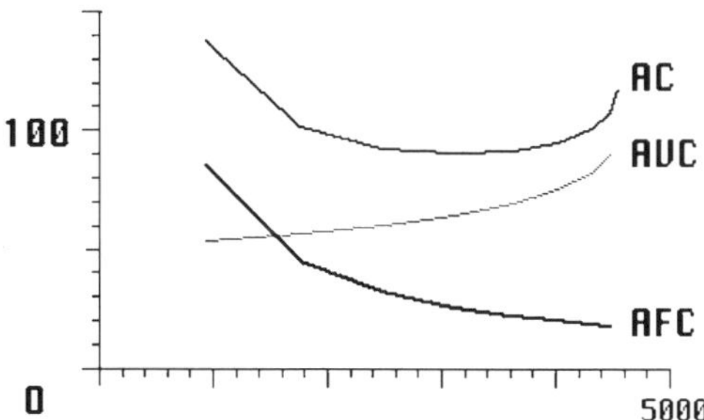


Notice how the average fixed costs decline as the fixed costs are "spread over more units of output." For large outputs, however, average variable costs rise pretty steeply. The idea is that with a limited capital plant and thus limited productive capacity—in the short run—costs would rise much more than proportionately to output as output goes beyond "capacity."

The average total cost, dominated by fixed costs for small output, declines at first, but as output increases, fixed costs become less important for the tótal cost and variable costs become more important and so, after reaching a minimum, average total cost begins to rise more and more steeply.

## MARGINAL COST

As before, we want to focus particularly on the marginal variation. In this case, of course, it is marginal cost. Marginal cost is defined as

$$MC = \frac{\Delta C}{\Delta Q}$$

As usual, Q st ands for (quantity of) output and C for cost, so Q st ands for the change in output, while C st ands for the change in cost. As usual, marginal cost can be interpreted as the additional cost of producing just one more ("marginal") unit of output.

Let's have a numerical example of the Marginal Cost definition to help make it clear.

In the John Bates Clark style example we have been using, total cost is 280000 for an output of 3120 and it is 33000 for an output of 3625. So we have $\Delta C = 330000 - 280000 = 50000$ and $\Delta Q = 3600 - 3120 = 505$

so that $\frac{\Delta C}{\Delta Q} = \frac{50000}{505} = 99.01$ for a marginal cost of $99.01 for the next unit produced. As usual, this is an approximation and the smaller the change in output we use, the better the approximation is. Here is the marginal cost for our example firm, along with output and average cost.

**Table**

| Output | Average | Marginal | Cost | Cost |
|---|---|---|---|---|
| 0 | 0 | 9.45 | | |
| 945 | 137.57 | 52.91 | | |
| 1780 | 101.12 | 59.88 | | |
| 2505 | 91.82 | 68.97 | | |
| 3120 | 89.74 | 81.30 | | |
| 3625 | 91.03 | 99.01 | | |
| 4020 | 94.53 | 126.58 | | |
| 4305 | 99.88 | 175.44 | | |
| 4480 | 107.14 | 285.71 | | |
| 4545 | 116.61 | 769.23 | | |

Here is a picture of marginal cost for our example firm, together with average cost as output varies.

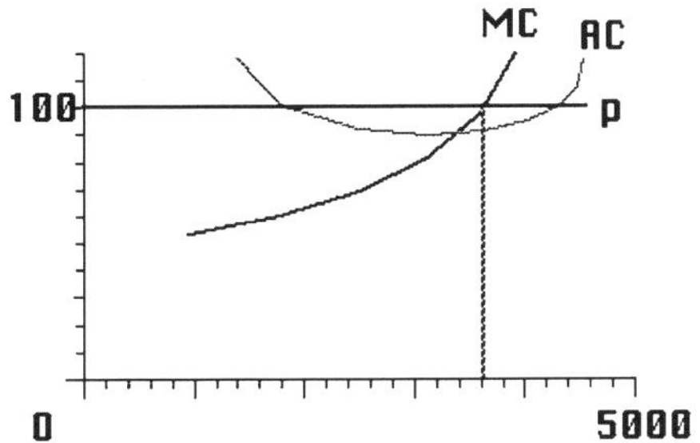


As before, the output produced is measured by the distance to the right on the horizontal axis. The average and marginal cost are on the vertical axis. Average cost is shown by the curve in yellow and marginal cost in red. Notice how the marginal cost rises to cross average cost at its lowest point.

## MAXIMIZATION OF PROFITS

We can now give another rule for the maximization of profits. The new rule is really just the same rule as we saw before, only now we state it in terms of price and costs. It is the equimarginal principle in yet another form.The question is: "I want to maximize profits. How much output should I sell, at the given price?"

The answer is: increase output until

p=MC

The point is illustrated by the following table, which extends the marginal cost table in an earlier page to show the price and the profits for the example firm.

**Table.**

| Output | Average | Marginal | price | profit | Cost | Cost |
|---|---|---|---|---|---|---|
| 0 | 0 | 100 | 0 | 9.45 | 945 | 137.57 100 |
| -35503.65 | 52.91 | 1780 | 101.12 | 100 | -1993.60 | 59.88 2505 |
| 91.82 | 100 | 20490.90 | 68.97 | 3120 | 89.74 100 | 32011.20 |
| 81.30 | 3625 | 91.03 | 100 | 32516.25 | 99.01 4020 | 94.53 100 |
| 21989.40 | 126.58 | 4305 | 99.88 | 100 | 516.60 175.44 | 4480 |
| 107.14 | 100 | -31987.20 | 285.71 | 4545 | 116.61 100 | -75492.45 |
| 769.23 | | | | | | |

Notice how profits are greatest (at 32516.25) when the marginal cost is almost exactly equal to the price of $100. This occurs at an output of 3625, with marginal cost at 99.01. The profit-maximizing output would be very slightly more than 3625.

## MARGINAL COST AND FIRM SUPPLY

We have discovered the principle of supply for the individual firm.

Remember: what is supply? It is the relation between the price and the quantity that people want to sell. For an individual firm, that is: the relation between the price and the quantity the firm wants to sell. So we ask: at a given price, how much will a (profit-maximizing) firm want to sell? The answer:

enough so that the price is equal to marginal cost. In other words, the marginal cost curve is the supply curve for the individual firm.

## SHUTTING DOWN AND BANKRUPTCY

As long as the firm produces something, it will maximize its profits by producing "on the marginal cost curve." But it might produce nothing at all. When will the firm shut down? The answer goes a bit against common sense. The firm will shut down if it cannot cover its variable costs. So long as it can cover the variable costs, it will continue to produce.

This is an application of the opportunity cost principle. Just because fixed costs are fixed, they are not opportunity costs in the short run—so they are not relevant to the decision to shut down. Even if the company shuts down, it must pay the fixed costs anyway. But the variable costs are avoidable—they are opportunity costs! So the firm will shut down it it cannot meet the variable (short run opportunity) costs. But as long as it can pay the variable costs and still have something to apply Towards the fixed costs, it is better off continuing to produce.

It is important not to confuse shut-down with bankruptcy. They are two different things. If a company cannot pay its interest and debt payments (usually fixed costs), then it is bankrupt. But that doesn't mean it will shut down. Bankrupt firms are often reorganized under new ownership and continue to produce—just because they can cover their variable costs and so the new owners do better to continue producing than to shut down.

## LONG RUN COST

Thus far we have not considered the long run in cost theory. We will now think a bit about the long run, using the concept of average cost. We have defined "the long run" as "a period long enough so that all inputs are variable." This includes, in particular, capital, plant, equipment and other investments that represent long-term commitments.

Thus, here is another way to think of "the long run:" it is the perspective of investment planning. So let's approach it this way: Suppose you were planning to build a new plant—perhaps to set up a whole new company—and you know about how much output you will be producing.

Then you want to build your plant so as to produce that amount at the lowest possible average cost. To make it a little simpler we will suppose that you have to pick just one of three plant sizes: small, medium and large. Here's the way they look in a picture:

### Envelope Curve

Here are the average cost curves for the small (AC1), medium (AC2) and large(AC3) plant sizes:

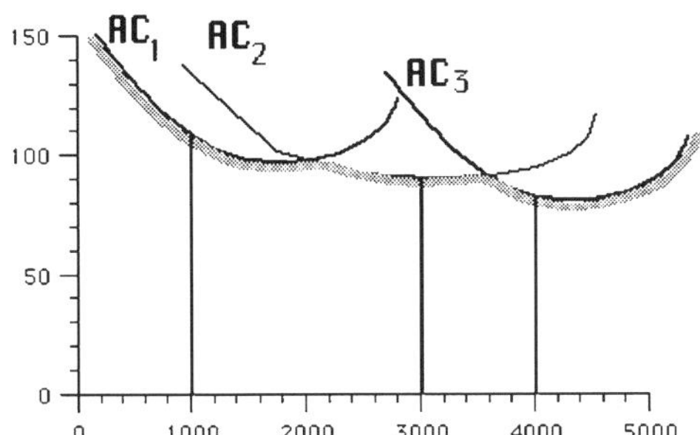


If you produce 1000 units, the small plant size gives the lowest cost. If you produce 3000 units, the medium plant size gives the lowest cost. If you produce 4000 units, the large plant size gives you the lowest cost.

Therefore, the long run average cost (LRAC)—the lowest average cost for each output range—is described by the "lower envelope curve, " shown by the thick, shaded curve that follows the lowest of the three short run curves in each range.

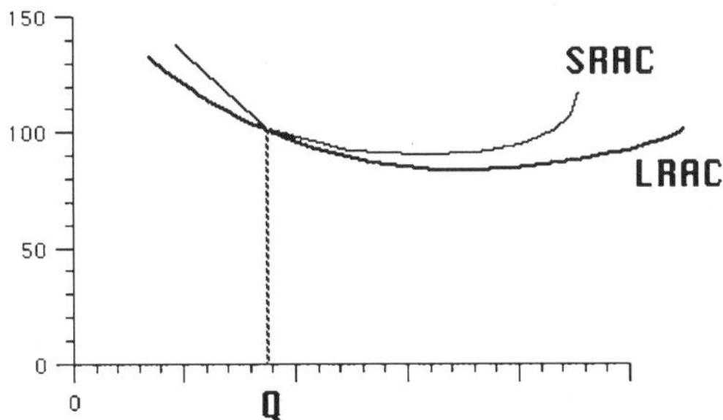


## LONG RUN AVERAGE COST IN GENERAL

More realistically, an investment planner will have to choose between many different plant sizes or firm scales of operation and so the long run average cost curve will be smooth, something like this:

As shown, each point on the LRAC corresponds to a point on the SRAC for the plant size or scale of operation that gives the lowest average cost for that scale of operation.

### Returns to Scale

cases: Increasing returns to scale = decreasing cost

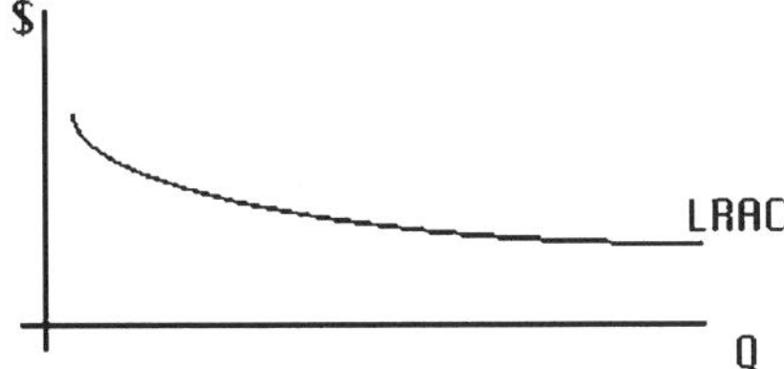


Constant returns to scale = constant costs

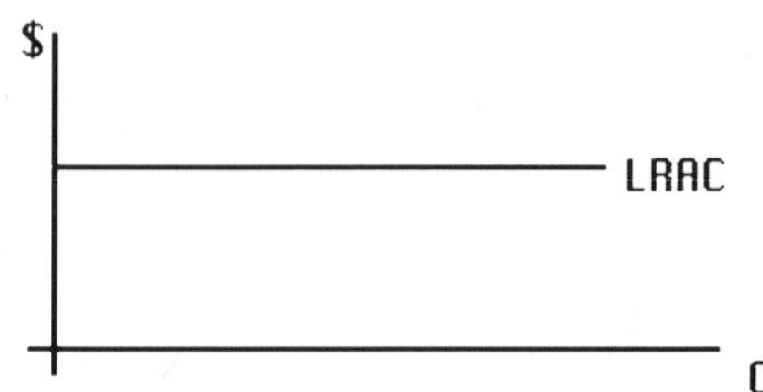


Decreasing returns to scale = increasing costs

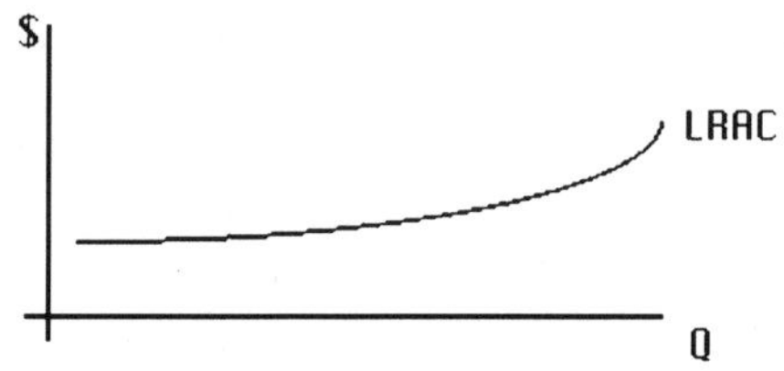


In our pictures of long run average cost, we see that the cost per unit changes as the scale of operation or output size changes. Here is some terminology to describe the changes: increasing returns to scale = decreasing cost average cost decreases as output increases in the long run constant returns to scale = constant costs average cost is unchanged as output varies in the long run decreasing returns to scale = increasing costs average cost increases as output increases in the long run Here are pictures of the average cost curves for the three

## INCREASING RETURNS TO SCALE

Economists usually explain "increasing returns to scale" by indivisibility. That is, some methods of production can only work on a large scale—either because they require large-scale machinery, or because they require a great deal of division of labour. Since these large-scale methods cannot be divided up to produce small amounts of output, it is necessary to use less productive methods to produce the smaller amounts.

Thus, costs increase less than in proportion to output—and average costs decline as output increases.

Increasing Returns to Scale is also known as "economies of scale" and as "decreasing costs." All three phrases mean exactly the same.

### Constant Returns to Scale

We would expect to observe constant returns where the typical firm (or industry) consists of a large number of units doing pretty much the same thing, so that output can be exp anded or contracted by increasing or decreasing the number of units. In the days before computer controls, machinery was a good example. Essentially, one machinist used one machine tool to do a series of operations to produce one item of a specific kind—and to double the output you had to double the number of machinists and machine tools.Constant Returns to Scale is also known as "constant costs." Both phrases mean exactly the same.

## DECREASING RETURNS TO SCALE

Decreasing returns to scale are associated with problems of management of large, multi-unit firms. Again with think of a firm in which production takes place by a large number of units doing pretty much the same thing—but the different units need to be coordinated by a central management. The management faces a trade-off. If they don't spend much on management, the coordination will be poor, leading to waste of resources and higher cost. If they do spend a lot on management, that will raise costs in itself. The idea is that the bigger the output is, the more units there are and the worse this trade-off becomes—so the costs rise either way.

Decreasing Returns to Scale is also known as "diseconomies of scale" and as "increasing costs." All three phrases mean exactly the same.

## THE LRAC CURVE

In our examples, the LRAC is (more or less roughly) u-shaped, like this:

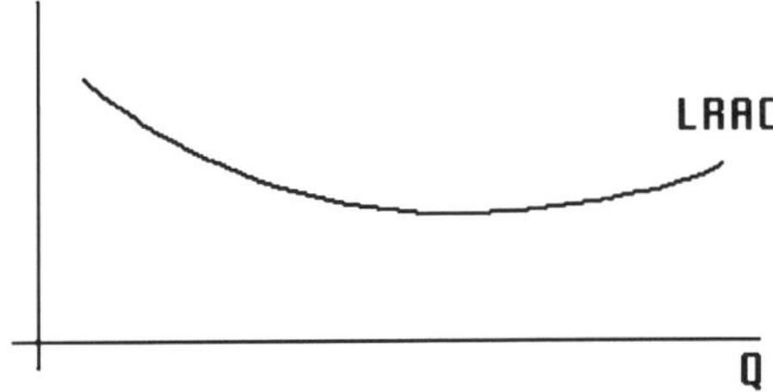


The idea is that:

- For small outputs, indivisibilities predominate and so long run average cost declines with increasing output
- For intermediate outputs, operations can be exp anded roughly proportionately, while tendencies to increasing and decreasing costs—if any—offset one another.
- For large outputs, the problems of management predominate and so long run average cost increases with increasing output.

That's reasonable—but we should recall that it is pretty much a guess and may or may not apply in a particular case!

# 6

# Perfect Competition

## INTRODUCTION TO PERFECT COMPETITION

Let us start to consider the case of pure competition in which there are a large number of independent sellers of some uniform product. In this situation, when each firm sets the price in which it sells its output, it will have to take into account not only the behaviour of the consumers but also the behaviour of the other producers.

### ASSUMPTIONS ON COMPETITIVE MARKET

*The competitive markets are based on the following assumptions*:

- Large number of buyers and sellers—price-taking behaviour
- *Unrestricted Mobility of Resources among Industries*: no artificial barrier or impediment to entry or to exit from market.
- *Homogeneous Product*: All the firms in an industry produce an identical production in the consumers' eyes.
- *Passion of all Relevant Information (all Relevant Information are Common Knowledge)*: Firms and consumers have all the information necessary to make the correct economic decisions.

### THE COMPETITIVE FIRM

A competitive firm is one that takes the market price of output as being given. Let $\overline{p}$ be the market price. Then the demand curve facing an ideal competitive firm takes the form

$$D(p)=\begin{cases} 0 & if\, p>\overline{p} \\ any\, amount & if\, p=\overline{p} \\ \infty & if\, p<\overline{p} \end{cases}$$

A competitive firm is free to set whatever price it wants and produce whatever quantity it is able to produce. However, if a firm is in a competitive market, it is clear that each firm that sells the product must sell it for the same price: for if any firm attempted to set its price at a level greater than the market price, it would immediately lose all of its customers. If any firm set its price at a level below the market price, all of the consumers would immediately come to it. Thus, each firm must take the market price as given, exogenous variable when it determines its supply decision.

## COMPETITION: THE STUDY OF INDUSTRIES

We have now built up enough background to study what economists call "industrial organization"—that is, the study of industries, including their organization and structure, how they conduct business, how they respond to change and evolve and how efficiently they perform.

Economists believe all these things are interrelated, so this is sometimes called a structure/conduct/performance approach.

As usual, the first step will be some terminology. Economists in general recognize four major types of market structures (plus a larger number of subtypes):

- "Perfect Competition"
- Monopoly
- Oligopoly
- Monopolistic competition

For now, I will just define the first of the four and then use concepts related to "Perfect Competition" to define the other three.

### WHAT IS A MARKET?

These are forms of markets. We might pause for a moment to think about just what a market is. A market consists of all the (potential) buyers and sellers of a particular good or service.

In order for a market to exist, though, these potential buyers and sellers must have some way to communicate offers to buy and sell with one another. One possibility is for them to come together and yell at one another (as at the New York Stock Exchange). In traditional societies, craftsmen in a particular trade may all be located on the same street, so that customers know where to go to buy.

Of course, many modern markets make use of a wide range of electronic communication methods, as do NASDAQ and the international currency markets.

Thus, it is natural to identify a market with the place where traders come together (as in the case of a stock market) or the means by which they communicate. But the market consists of the people willing to buy and sell.

### P-COMPETITION

What many economists call "Perfect Competition" is an idealized structure of an industry in which price competition is dominant—in fact the only form of competition possible. The terminology "Perfect Competition" is quite common but not quite universal. The term "Pure Competition" is also sometimes used. I will use the term "P-Competition, " where the P can st and for perfect, pure, or price competition—whichever you like.

A P-Competitive structure is defined by four characteristics. For an industry to have a P-competitive structure, it must have all four of these characteristics:

- Many buyers and sellers
- A homogenous product
- Sufficient knowledge
- Free entry

These are all characteristics that favour price competition. Each of these characteristics will be explained in turn.

**Many**

The idea is that the sellers and buyers are small relative to the size of the market, so that no one of them can "fix the price." If there are "many small sellers, " it makes it much harder for any seller or any group of sellers to "rig the price." Similarly, if there are "many small buyers, " there is little opportunity for buyers to "rig the price" in their own favour. Each seller reasons as follows: "If I try to charge a price above the market price, my customers will know that they can get a better price from my competitors. My own share of the market is so small that all of my customers will be able to buy what they want from the competition—and I won't have any customers left!" Thus, the seller treats the price as being given and determined by "the forces of the market" independently of her own output.

How many sellers? How small? There is no absolute answer to that question; but there must be enough sellers and they must each be small enough so that each regards the price as being determined by the market, so that none of the sellers sees any opportunity to push the price up by cutting back on his or her output.Similarly, there must be enough buyers and each small enough, that each one treats the price as being determined by the market and beyond her or his own ability to influence.

These conditions encourage the buyers and sellers in the market not even to try to control the price, but instead to compete against one another whenever quantity supplied differs from quantity dem anded, driving the price Towards the equilibrium of supply and demand.

**Homogeneity**

If the product (or service) of one seller differed significantly from that of another seller, then each seller would probably be able to retain at least some of the customers, even at a very high price. These would be the customers who just prefer this seller's product (or service) to that of someone else. The assumption of homogenous products serves to rule that out.

But this assumption should not be taken too literally. No two potatoes are exactly alike. We are not assuming that the goods are alike: only that the goods produced by one supplier are good substitutes for those offered by another seller. Thus, the potatoes don't need to be just alike—provided that, on the average, Farmer Jones' potatoes are just as good as Farmer Green's. This is especially important with respect to services. It would be hard to prove that two haircuts are just alike! But so long as the haircuts supplied by one barber are substitutable for the haircuts supplied by another—and their conversation is about equally amusing—then the "homogenous products" assumption is fulfilled.

"Homogenous products" means all suppliers sell products that are perfect substitutes. If different sellers sold different products, then customers might be reluctant to switch suppliers when one supplier raises the price. They might stick with the supplier even at the higher price, because, even at the higher price, they like the product of that firm better than the product of another firm. By ruling this out, the homogeneity of products encourages price competition.

**Knowledge**

Some versions of the "perfectly competitive" structure include "perfect knowledge" as one of its characteristics—but, of course, "perfect knowledge" never exists in reality.Perfect information is a little less clear than the other assumptions—we can hardly assume that people know everything there is to know! In practice, what is important is that each buyer and seller knows all about her or his opportunities to make deals, that is, knows the terms on which other market participants will buy and sell. Remember what we said in the paragraph on "many small sellers:" a seller would assume that her or his customers would know if the competition were selling more cheaply. If the customers didn't know that they had alternatives, then even a very small seller might get away with pushing the price up, without losing many customers.

Thus, the "perfect information" assumption complements the other assumptions. The assumptions that there are many small buyers and many small sellers and the assumption of free entry, all mean that buyers and sellers have many alternatives of potential buyers and sellers to choose among. The assumption of sufficient information says that they know what those alternatives are.Traders need to know quite a bit to compete effectively in markets. They need to know the terms on which other people are offering goods and services, or offering to buy; the quality of the goods and services offered and enough about costs to judge whether the trade is profitable or not. This is what I mean by "sufficient knowledge"

**Free Entry**

Remember Adam Smith's concept of the "natural price:" when the price of beer is high, so that brewing is especially profitable, people will enter the brewing trade and their competition with the established breweries will force the price down Towards the "natural" price. As Smith was aware, in the long run the entry of new competition—or the exist of unprofitable firms from the industry, to go into other trades—is one of the most important aspects of competition and is thus one of the four characteristics of the P-competitive structure.

Free entry means that new companies can set up in business to compete with established companies whenever the new competitors feel that the profits are high enough to justify the investment. This is, first and foremost, a legal condition. That is, in a "perfectly competitive" market there are no government restrictions on the entry of new competition. This legal status is often called by the French phrase "laissez faire, " meaning "let them make (whatever they want to make for sale)." But it could also be a practical condition. For example, if no-one could set up in business without enormous capital investments, that might prove an effective limit on the entry of new competition—especially if, for some reason, the capital cannot be raised by borrowing or issuing shares.

**Other Market Forms**

The other three market structure models can be defined in terms of the ways in which they deviate from the characteristics of P-Competition. In a Monopoly there is just one seller of a good or service for which there is no close substitute. In an oligopoly there are two or more, but only a few firms. In Monopolistic Competition, the products are not homogenous but are "differentiated."

We don't have a st andard model for "insufficient knowledge" but, at least in some cases, that seems to work similarly to "product differentiation."

**The Competitive Firm**

Our next step is to explore the operation of a firm in a P-Competitive industry. To be specific, what does the demand curve for the individual firm look like?

We have already noticed, some time back, that the individual firm's demand curve is different from that of the industry and is more elastic. This is because substitutes increase elasticity and the customer of the firm has many good substitutes for that firm's output—namely, the output of other firms in the industry.Let's go back through the four characteristics of the P-Competitive industry structure and see how they influence the elasticity of the individual firm's demand.

## THE FOUR CHARACTERISTICS OF P-COMPETITIVE MARKETS AND THE ELASTICITY OF FIRM DEMAND

Here are the basics:

Many small sellers

The more sellers there are, the more substitutes the consumer has

Homogenous product

When the product is homogenous, then the substitutes are "perfect substitutes."

Sufficient knowledge

When customers know the prices offered by other sellers, they will be better able to switch—increasing elasticity further.

Free entry

In the long run, companies may even enter the market to provide still more substitutes

## FIRM DEMAND

Since a P-Competitive structure is an idealization of these tendencies, we say that the demand curve for a P-Competitive firm is infinitely elastic.

In fact the demand curve for a P-Competitive Firm is a horizontal line corresponding to the going price.and that makes sense, because the price in a P-Competitive market is determined by supply and demand—not by the seller or the buyer. Conversely, so far as the seller or the buyer is concerned, the price must be a given, since it is determined by supply and demand.

The seller has no control over the price and to say that the seller has no control control over the price is to say that the price is given—a constant, a horizontal line—from the point of view of the seller.

Economists sometimes express this by saying that the price is "parametric, " meaning that while it may change from time to time, it does not change in response to the firm's output decision.

## FIRM SUPPLY AND DEMAND

Happily—but not by coincidence!—all of our examples of profit maximization to date are based on the assumption of given prices. Thus, we already know that the supply curve of a P-Competitive firm is the firm's marginal cost curve.Thus, marginal cost = price is the same as quantity supplied = quantity dem anded for the individual firm.

When marginal cost = price for each firm in the industry, we have quantity supplied = quantity dem anded in the industry as a whole.

Here's a picture:

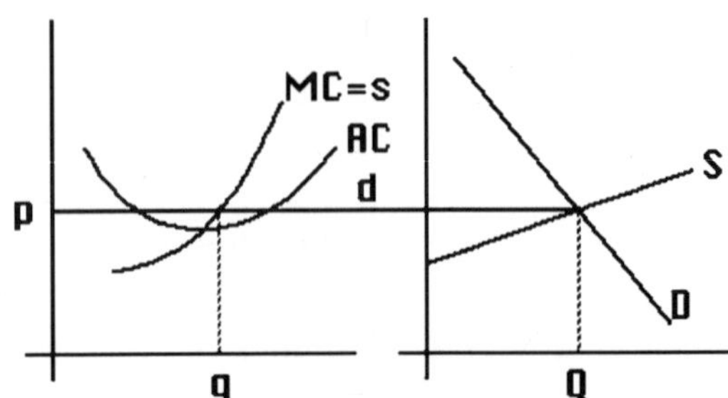


In the figure, the lower case q, s and d refer to output, supply and demand from the point of view of the individual firm, respectively and the capital S, D and Q are for the industry as a whole.

Cost and supply curves are shown in red and demand curves in green. Price (per unit sold) is the same from all points of view.

**PROFITS AND ENTRY**

We notice that, in the picture just shown, the firm is making an "economic profit." All costs, explicit and implicit, are included in the firm's Average Cost curve.

In particular, Average Cost includes the opportunity cost of capital investment—so another way of putting it is that investors in this industry are making more than their best alternative investment in any other industry.

These profit opportunities will attract new firms into the industry. With "free entry, " the (short run) supply curve of the industry shifts to the right, causing the price to drop until the economic profits are eliminated.

This process of entry and price change is known as the "long run equilibrium process" and it continues until "long run equilibrium" is attained. Here is a picture of the firm and industry in "long run equilibrium:"

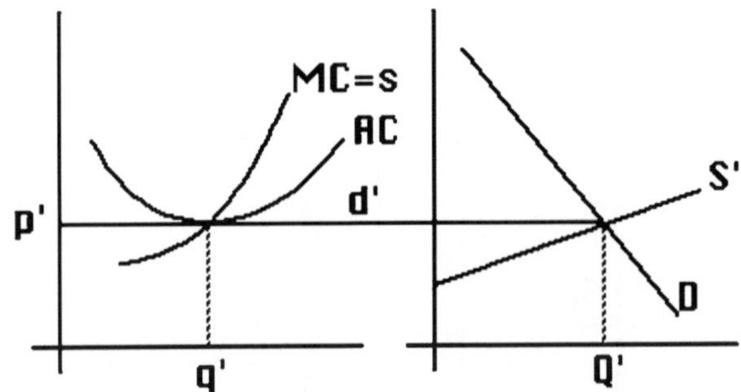


The new price, quantity, firm demand and short run supply are indicated by primes—p', q'. Q', d', S'. We see that, at a slightly lower price, the individual firm is lower on the MC curve and produces a little less, but since there are more firms in the industry, the industry as a whole produces more.

## P-COMPETITIVE EQUILIBRIUM AS AN IDEAL

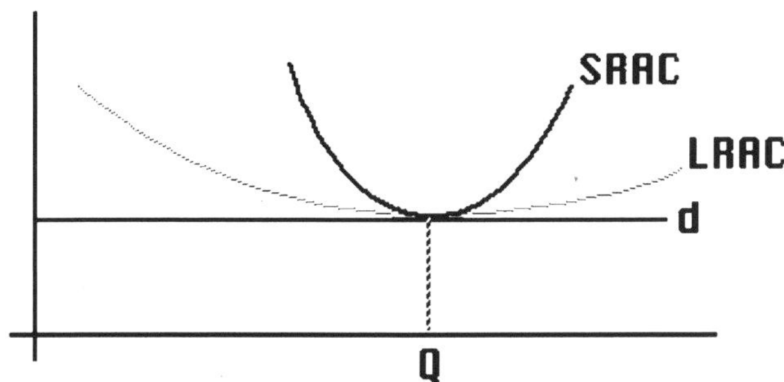


We notice something else about the long-run equilibrium of a P-Competitive industry: each firm chooses the plant and equipment and productive capacity that gives the lowest average cost overall. This is shown by the above figure.

To see what this means, we might ask the following hypothetical question:

If an industry is to produce a certain amount of output, how should the output it be divided up among the different firms?

More specifically, how many firms should share that production assignment? If there are very many firms, then each will be producing at a very small scale. They will not be taking advantage of the economies of scale and cost per unit will be high. On the other h and, if there are very few firms, each will be producing on a very large scale and suffering from diseconomies of scale, so, again, unit costs would be high.

It would be best to balance the disadvantages of too large scale against the disadvantages of too small scale and have just enough firms in the industry so that each is at the bottom of its average cost curve. The total cost of producing that output is then at a minimum.

What we see is that the equilibrium in a P-competitive industry does just that. That is one reason why economists often think of P-competition as an ideal.Remember the assumption behind this whole argument! The assumption is that the long run average cost curve is u-shaped as shown.

There may be some industries for which that is not true and the argument would not be applicable to those industries.

## POINTS ABOUT LONG RUN EQUILIBRIUM

We have seen that profits will lead to the entry of new firms into a P-competitive industry. This also works in the opposite direction: if firms in the industry were taking losses, supply in the industry will decrease.

Firms in the industry might continue to produce in the short run, despite the losses. Remember—that a profit-maximizing firm will continue to produce, in the short run, so long as it can cover its variable costs. However, in the long run, firms will drop out of the industry, if they continue to lose money. Thus, the supply curve of the unprofitable industry will shift to the left. But that in turn means prices will rise and the long run equilibrium comes where the price is equal to average cost, as shown in Figure.

This discussion could apply to any economic activity to which there is "free entry." Economic profits—profits over and above the opportunity cost of capital—will attract new entrants. Returns less than the opportunity cost of capital will cause firms to get out of the industry.

This will continue until the return to capital in that activity is the same as the opportunity cost of invested capital, that is, until profits are zero. We might call this principle "the Entry Principle."

It says that In the long run, with free entry, returns to invested capital in an industry are just enough to offset the opportunity cost. When there are economic profits or losses, entry into the industry or exit of firms from it will shift the industry supply until economic profits are zero.

**Long Run Supply**

We can use these principles to explore the long run supply curve of the industry. Remember, in the short run, the capital plant and productive capacity of the industry is given and the industry is made up of a certain group of firms. But in the long run, all of these things are variable.

By definition, capital plant is variable in the long run—in fact, all inputs are variable. and the number and identity of the firms in the industry is variable. As we have just seen, economic profits will bring more firms into the group and losses will result in the exit of firms.

Alfred Marshall expressed this by saying that a competitive industry is like a forest and the firms are like the trees. A forest does not grow by having bigger trees, but by having more trees. and similarly, a competitive industry grows or shrinks primarily by having more or fewer firms. Let's consider a simple case. The simplifying assumptions are

- All firms have identical cost curves
- The cost curves are u-shaped
- The cost curves remain stationary as the number of firms in the industry changes

Now, let's look at Figure. We start out in long run equilibrium with 10, 000 firms producing a total output of $Q_1$. Short run supply and demand curves are not shown.

The average and marginal cost curves shown represent approximately those for the 10, 000th firm with respect to its contribution to industry output, after the other 9999 firms have produced their parts. (These cost curves are very exaggerated. Drawn to scale they would be invisible).

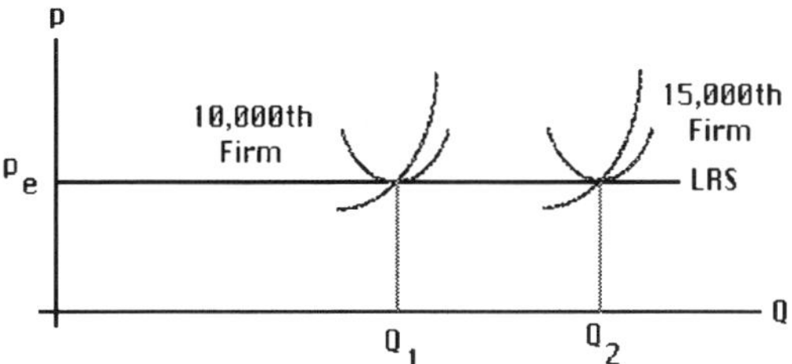


Now suppose there is an increase in demand (not shown) so that the price rises above $p_e$. The existing 10, 000 firms will enjoy economic profits. These profits will attract new firms, so the number of firms in the industry will grow, shifting the short run industry supply (not shown) to the right and thus depressing the price back Towards $p_e$. When will these new entries stop? Only when economic profits are back to zero. We suppose, for the example, that this happens when there are 15, 000 firms in the industry, producing $Q_2$ of output. As the (exaggerated) cost curves for the 15, 000th firm show, the price will be back at $p_e$.

*What this example shows us is that*: The long run supply curve in this case is a horizontal line corresponding to the bottom of the average cost curve of a firm in the industry.

This is a bit of a surprise. We have been thinking of supply curves as being upward sloping—there are some exceptions. In the long run, supply may or may not be upward sloping.

But first, let's define the long run supply curve a little more carefully.

For each industry output, the long run supply curve shows the lowest price at which that output can be produced, so that the price covers all costs including the opportunity cost of invested capital.

Thus the long run supply curve is a boundary—the boundary between profitable and unprofitable prices, given industry output. We have seen that, on the simplifying assumptions:

- All firms have identical cost curves
- The cost curves are u-shaped
- The cost curves remain stationary as the number of firms in the industry changes

The Long Run Supply curve (LRS) is a horizontal line. In economics, this special case is known as a constant cost industry, for reasons that are probably pretty obvious. But these simplifying assumptions can't always be applied. Assumption 3. is the tricky one. For example, agricultural industries would pretty clearly be exceptions to it.

Suppose, for example, that the demand for wheat increases, so wheat farming becomes profitable. Then more farmers switch from producing other crops to producing wheat. But that increases the demand for the best wheat l and, so the rental cost of that l and increases. New farms will have to pay the higher rental cost or make use of l and that is less well suited to producing wheat. Either way, the new firms will have higher costs. Thus, the cost curves will shift upward as the number of wheat farms increases and the new long run equilibrium price will be higher. Agricultural industries are not constant cost industries, but increasing cost industries.

For an increasing cost industry, the long run supply curve is upward sloping. Some economists believe there are also decreasing-cost industries, with downward-sloping long run supply curves. However, we will leave these complications for a course at a more advanced level.

Instead, let's look at another example of long run supply in a constant-cost industry: computer software.

One problem is that computer Programmes are not identical, so we would have to measure the output of the industry in some uniform units. Perhaps, to a rough approximation, the output can be measured in lines of code. Of course, not all lines are equal—some lines are wasted and some are inspired—but this measure may work OK on the average and, in fact, businessmen do use lines of code as a measure of programmer output. Let's assume, for the sake of the example, that software output can be measured on the average by lines of code and that the industry is a constant-cost industry. The example is illustrated by Figure:

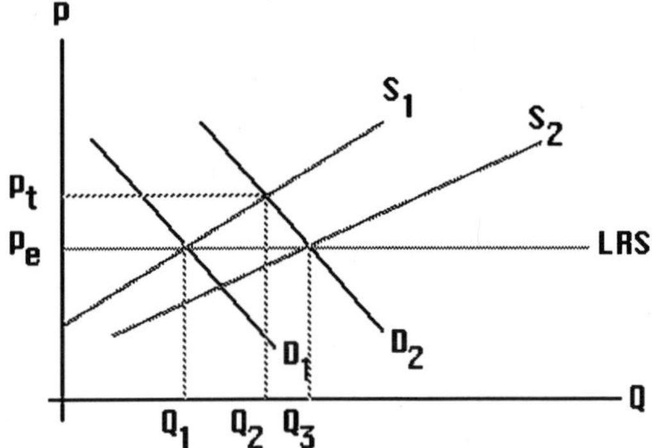


In the diagram, the long run supply of computer software is the gray line LRS. At the beginning, we have long run equilibrium at $p_e$ and $Q_1$. Demand is $D_1$ and short run supply is $S_1$.

Now a breakthrough in computer hardware, a complementary good, increases the usefulness of computer software and so increases the demand for software. (The invention of desk-top computers pretty clearly had this effect). In the short run, the price of computer software rises to $p_t$ with $Q_2$ lines of software produced. At this price, software is a profitable industry—the price is above the long run supply curve, which, by definition, is the boundary between profitable and unprofitable prices. Thus, there will be entry into the software industry ( and more programmers and software engineers will be trained, an investment in human capital) so that the short run supply curve shifts to the right. The shift continues until the new long run equilibrium is reached at price $p_e$ and production $Q_3$, with short run supply $S_2$.This two-stage adjustment process is characteristic of industries characterized by free entry and supply-and-demand pricing.

## THE COMPETITIVE FIRM'S SHORT-RUN SUPPLY FUNCTION

Since the competitive firm must take the market price as given, its profit maximization problem is simple. The firm only needs to choose output level $y$ so as to solve

$$\max_{y} py - c(y)$$

where $y$ is the output produced by the firm, $p$ is the price of the product, and $c(y)$ is the cost function of production.

*The first-order condition (in short, FOC) for interior solution gives*:

$$p = c'(y) \equiv MC(y).$$

The first order condition becomes a sufficient condition if the second-order condition (in short, SOC) is satisfied

$$c''(y) > 0.$$

Taken together, these two conditions determine the supply function of a competitive firm: at any price $p$, the firm will supply an amount of output $y(p)$ such that $p = c'(y(p))$.

By $p = c'(y(p))$, we have

$$1 = c''(y(p))y'(p)$$

and thus,

$$y'(p) > 0,$$

which means the law of supply holds.

Recall that $p = c'(y^*)$ is the first-order condition characterizing the optimum only if $y^* > 0$, that is, only if y¤ is an interior optimum. It could happen that at a low price a firm might very well decide to go out of business. For the short-run (in short, SR) case,

$$c(y) = c_v(y) + F$$

The firm should produce if

$$py(p) - c_v(y) - F \geqq -F,$$

and thus we have

$$p \geqq \frac{c_v(y(p))}{y(p)} \equiv AVC.$$

That is, the necessary condition for the firm to produce a positive amount of output is that the price is greater than or equal to the average variable cost. Thus, the supply curve for the competitive firm is in general given by: $p = c'(y)$

if

$$p \geqq \frac{c_v\left(y(p)\right)}{y(p)}$$

and,

$$p \leqq \frac{c_v\left(y(p)\right)}{y(p)}.$$

That is, the supply curve coincides with the upward sloping portion of the marginal cost curve as long as the price covers average variable cost, and the supply curve is zero if price is less than average variable cost.

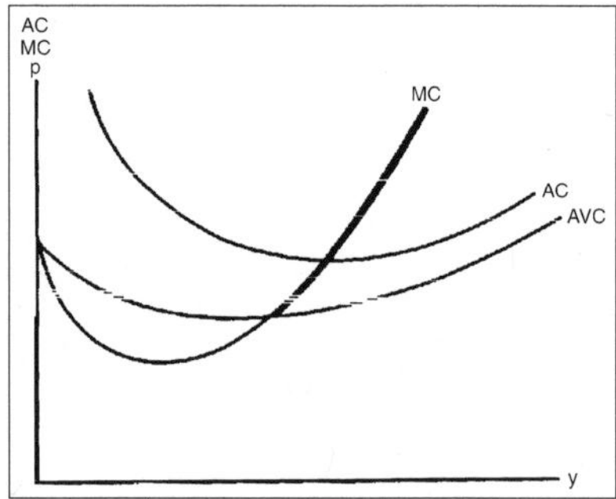


**Fig**: Firm's Supply Curve, and AC, AVC, and MC Curves.

Suppose that we have *j* firms in the market. (For the competitive model to make sense, *j* should be rather large.) The industry supply function is simply the sum of all individuals' supply functions so that it is given by

$$\hat{y}(p)=\sum_{j=1}^{J} y_i(p)$$

where $y_i(p)$ is the supply function of firm *j* for $j = 1,..., J$. Since each firm chooses a level of output where price equals marginal cost, each firm that produces a positive amount of output must have the same marginal cost. The industry supply function measures the relationship between industry output and the common cost of producing this output. The aggregate (industry) demand function measures the total output demanded at any price which is given by,

$$\hat{x}(p)=\sum_{i=1}^{n} x_i(p)$$

where $x_i(p)$ is the demand function of consumer *i* for $i = 1,...., n$.

## PARTIAL MARKET EQUILIBRIUM

How is the market price determined? It is determined by the requirement that the total amount of output that the firms wish to supply will be equal to the total amount of output that the consumers wish to demand. Formerly, we have

A *partial equilibrium price* $p^*$ is a price where the aggregate quantity demanded equals the aggregate quantity supplied. That is, it is the solution of the following equation:

$$\sum_{i=1}^{n} x_i(p) = \sum_{j=1}^{J} y_i(p)$$

Once this equilibrium price is determined, we can go back to look at the individual supply schedules of each firm and determine the firms level of output, its revenue, and its profits. In Figure, we have depicted cost curves for three firms. The first has positive profits, the second has zero profits, and the third has negative profits. Even though the third firm has negative profits, it may make sense for it to continue to produce as long as its revenues cover its variable costs.

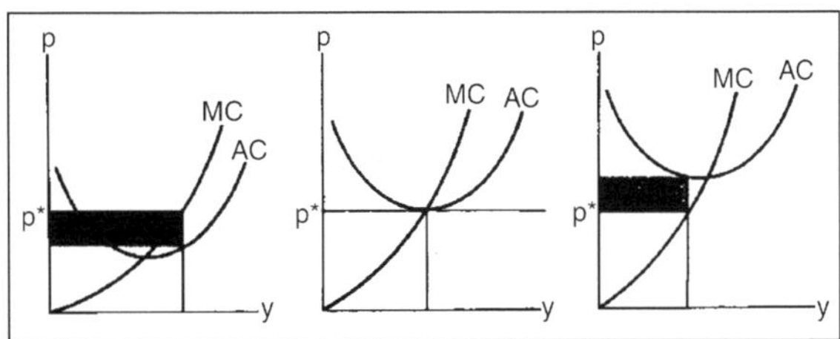


**Fig**: Positive, Zero, and Negative Profits.

*Example*: $\hat{x}(p) = a - bp$ and $c(y) = y^2 + 1$. Since $MC(y) = 2y$, we have

$$y = \frac{p}{2}$$

and thus the industry supply function is

$$\hat{y}(p) = \frac{Jp}{2}$$

Setting,

$$a - bp = \frac{Jp}{2},$$

we have,

$$p^* = \frac{a}{b + J/2}.$$

Now for general case of $D(p)$ and $S(p)$, what happens about the equilibrium price if the number of firms increases? From

$$D(p(J)) = Jy(p(J))$$

we have,

$$D'(p(J))p'(J) = y(p) + Jy'(p(J))p'(J)$$

and thus,

$$p'(J) = \frac{y(p)}{X'(p) - Jy'(p)} < 0,$$

which means the equilibrium price decreases when the number of firms increases.

## COMPETITIVE IN THE LONG RUN

The long-run behaviour of a competitive industry is determined by two sorts of effects. The first effect is the free entry and exit phenomena so that the profits made by all firms are zero. If some firm is making negative profits, we would expect that it would eventually have to change its behaviour. Conversely, if a firm is making positive profits we would expect that this would eventually encourage entry to the industry.

If we have an industry characterized by free entry and exit, it is clear that in the long run all firms must make the same level of profits. As a result, every firm makes zero profit at the long-run competitive equilibrium.

The second influence on the long-run behaviour of a competitive industry is that of technological adjustment. In the long run, firms will attempt to adjust their fixed factors so as to produce the equilibrium level of output in the cheapest way. Suppose for example we have a competitive firm with a long-run constant returns-to-scale technology that is operating at the position illustrated in Figure.

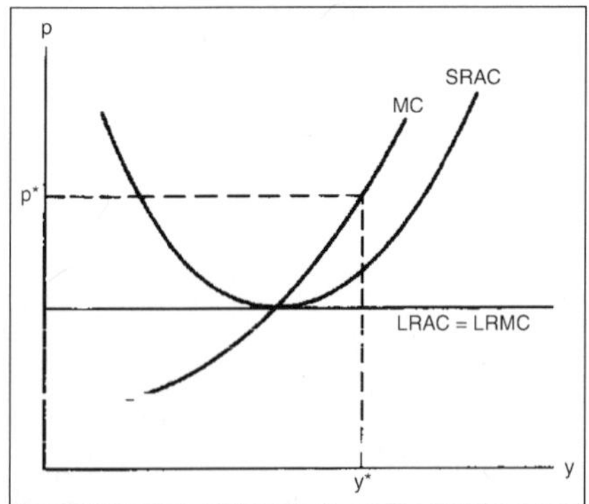


**Fig:** Long-run Adjustment with Constant Costs.

Then in the long run it clearly pays the firm to change its fixed factors so as to operate at a point of minimum average cost. But, if every firm tries to do this, the equilibrium price will certainly change.In the model of entry or exit, the equilibrium number of firms is the largest number of firms that can break even so the price must be chosen to minimum price.

*Example*: $c(y) = y^2 + 1$. The break-even level of output can be found by setting

$$AC(y) = MC(y)$$

so that $y = 1$, and $p = MC(y) = 2$.

Suppose the demand is linear: $X(p) = a-bp$. Then, the equilibrium price will be the smallest $p^*$ that satisfies the conditions

$$p^* = \frac{a}{b + J/2} \geqq 2.$$

As $J$ increases, the equilibrium price must be closer and closer to 2.

## FORCE OF COMPETITION

Generally, there would exist no force of competition by which any particular arrangement (as to the average mountain) initiated by custom and accident could be disturbed. That is, still supposing the service of a guide or porter to be sold as a whole. For, if the labour of the assistants can be sold by the hour, or other sort of differential dose, the phenomenon of determinate equilibrium will reappear. There seems no reason to think that the case of indeterminate equilibrium which has been illustrated is other than exceptional in the actual labour market, even where the bargain appears to be made for totals as distinguished from doses of labour, — situations rather than tasks.

In fact, for there is such a variety of situations attended with different amounts of work as probably in practice to realise that divisibility of the thing supplied — here labour — which, together with the divisibility of the thing demanded, — here money, — constitutes a condition of a perfect market with determinate equilibrium.

Still, the point of theory is worth notice. Perhaps the friction in the labour market would be less if labour were sold freely by the hour (or other small "*dose*"). It ought to be mentioned that a different view of Exchange has been taken by a high authority on Distribution. Professor Bohm-Bawerk presents as the general type of a market that very case which is here regarded as exceptional. On one side of the markets are put dealers each with a horse or it may be a batch of several horses — which he will not sell under a certain price, on the other side buyers each of which will not go beyond a certain price.In such a case some further datum is required to determine price. "*That this latitude should be narrowed down, the further circumstance must be present that the desire of the buyers is directed to an limited number of goods, while at the same time the total amount of means of purchase must be strictly limited, and the buyers must be determined to spend the whole of this sum in purchase of the commodities in question.*" This condition is fulfilled, according to Professor Bohm-Bawerk, by the "*general subsistence market.*" This example will hardly be accepted as typical of a market by the mathematical economists who walk in the way of Gossen. Agreeing with the

Austrian leader that value rests at bottom on subjective estimates, they will accept his scheme, just as they would accept the description of a common auction, as illustrative of that attribute. But they may complain that the illustration does not illustrate another attribute which they regard as essential to the determination of value in a market, — the circumstance that each party on the one side is free, in concert with some party or parties on the other side, to vary the amounts of those quantities on which depends his advantage — the quid and the pro quo — up to a limiting point, or margin at which he estimates his advantage to be a maximum.

The law of marginal utility was hardly exemplifies by the "*marginal pair*" of the Austrian scheme. We require knowing, not so much the least price which each horse dealer will take for his horse or stud, but how much horseflesh each individual or at least all collectively, will offer at each of several prices, with similarly graduated data for the would-be buyers. Granted data of this sort, the mathematical economist need not trouble himself much about a matter which is vital according to the Austrian scheme, — whether the "*subjective valuation*" of a horse is the same (or very similar) for all the sellers, while the dispositions of the buyers are likewise identical. The case of like dispositions does not constitute a special variety of the problem, one which is insoluble without additional data. Far from being anomalous, that case may be normally assumed as a harmless and convenient simplification, very proper to an introductory statement of the general theory.

"Nec Deus intersit, nisi dignus vindice nodus Inciderit"– The case of like dispositions does not present any peculiar difficulty calling for so very mechanical a Deus ex machina as the hypothesis that "*the total amount of means of purchase must be strictly limited and the buyers must be determined to spend the whole of this sum in purchase of the commodities in question.*" It is riding a one-horse illustration to death to put the accidents of an exceptional sort of auction as representative of the actual transactions by which the great mass of national income is distributed. This criticism, it must be freely admitted, involves an issue about which legitimate differences of opinion may exist; — what is the most appropriate conception of the process by which value is determined through the higgling of the market? Any simple conception must involve a considerable element of hypothesis, not admitting of decisive proof. The hypothetical character of the inquiry will appear if we look back to that model labour market in which guides or porters were supposed to be hired by amateur mountaineers. It was tacitly assumed that each party has certain dispositions as to the amount of money that he is willing to give or take in exchange for a certain amount of work, — a scale of subjective estimates which is supposed to be formed before the parties come into communication, and not to be modified by the chaffering of the market. The constancy of these dispositions being assumed, it is presumed that somehow a state of equilibrium will be brought about, such that the party on one side cannot improve his position by entering into new contracts with some party or parties on the other side. The better opinion is that only the position of equilibrium is knowable, not the path by which equilibrium is reached. As Jevons says, It is a far more easy task to lay down the conditions under which trade is completed and interchange ceases than to attempt to ascertain at what rate trade will go on when equilibrium is not attained.

Particular paths may be indicated by way of illustration, *"to fix the ideas,"* as mathematicians say. In this spirit two kinds of higgling may be distinguished as appropriate respectively to short and long periods. First, we may suppose the intending buyers and sellers to remain in communication without actually making exchanges, each trying to get at the dispositions of the others, and estimating his chances of making a better bargain than one that has been provisionally contemplated. By this preliminary tentative process a system of bargains complying with the condition of equilibrium is, as it were, rehearsed before it is actually performed. Or, second, one may suppose a performance to take place before such rehearsal is completed.

In our example, on the first day a set of hirings are made which prove not to be in accordance with the dispositions of the parties. These contracts terminating with the day, the parties encounter each other the following day, with dispositions the same as on the first day, — like combatants armis animisque refecti, — in all respects as they were at the beginning of the first encounter, except that they have obtained by experience the knowledge that the system of bargains entered into on the first occasion does not fit the real dispositions of the parties. The second plan of higgling was supposed in the example, — the plan which is more appropriate to *"normal"* value.

Contemplating the theory of exchange in the abstract, we may exclaim with Burke, *"Nobody, I believe, has observed with any rejection what market is without being astonished at the truth, the correctness, the celerity, the general equity, with which the balance of wants is settled."* But, when we come to the labour market, or any particular market, we must carefully inquire with what degree of approximateness the above-stated fundamental postulate holds good. When the bargaining extends over a considerable time, changes are apt to occur in the dispositions of the parties, whether independently of each other and sporadically, or in a manner even more fatal to the theory, by way of imitation. Also, where there occurs a series of encounters between buyers and sellers, the results of the earlier encounter may affect the dispositions with which the later ones are entered on. The terms which the labourer is ready to offer and accept are altered by the alteration in his habits and efficiency which is the consequence of previous bad bargains.

Professor Marshall pointed out the peculiarities of the labour market pointed out by go far to modify the general presumption in favour of laisser faire. But less careful writers are less successful in supporting the burden of proof which lies on those who profess to add to or take away from that outlined theory of Exchange which seems to express all that is known in general about the working of a market. A warning example of such modification not warranted by specific experience is the doctrine of the wage-fund, which is now universally discredited, and ought always to have excited suspicion and challenged proof because, as already intimated in another connection, it is a supposition repugnant to the general theory of Exchange that "*the total amount of means of purchase must be strictly limited, and the buyers must be determined to spend the whole of this sum in purchase of the commodities in question*." However, as Sir Leslie Stephen says with reference to the classical writers, "*the assumption slipped into their reasoning unawares*." Sometimes it may have been intended only to convey that early lesson which is contained in our opening paragraphs, — that no party to production can expect to earn more than the total produce. Sometimes there was contemplated a more definite statement true of short periods, — a truth which has been well stated by Professor Taussig in his article on "*The Employer's Place in Distribution*," and at greater length in his book on Wages and Capital —

The whole of the real income available for the community is not in any substantial sense at the disposal of the capitalists.... A large part of the commodities now on hand would not serve their turn. The supply of bread and flour and grain at any moment is adjusted to the expected needs of the whole mass of consumers.... The effective choice which the capitalists would have... would be thus confined, for the time being at least, within limits not very elastic. It might be assumes by us that the working classes live on bread only, while the capitalist classes consume buns also. On a day, after a conference between employers and employed, the partition of the national dividend is altered in favour of the capitalists. Yet they will be unable to benefit immediately by the change. On that day more buns will not be forthcoming, all the bakers' ovens being preoccupied with bread. For the purpose of illustration there has been chosen a especially simple case in which the articles consumed by the two classes are formed out of the same material, and by a process which is identical up to the penultimate stage. The stream of production does not bifurcate till it debouches into the mouths of the two parties to Distribution.When the longer tracts of that stream are consider by us, there comes into view a circumstance to be discussed under the head of Capital, the influence of time on value. To illustrate the distribution of produce between those who have contributed at different times to its production, let us at first make abstraction of other differences, and imagine economic men uniting the functions of workman and capitalist-entrepreneur, differing only in the amount of capitalisation, the length of time during which their labour is invested. One labours at proximate means, another at remote means, tending to the ultimate product out of which all the producers are remunerated. An idea of a train of production formed by successive operations directed to an ultimate product may be obtained by watching any factory.Here you have the raw cotton-wool put in, there you see a "*sliver*" of carded cotton flowing from one machine en route to another, until at the last stage there comes out the finished article. To illustrate the process of distribution, we must now conceive a backward flow of the ultimate product to the several producers. We might imagine each one's share to be conveyed to him by some contrivance like those wondrous little vehicles in the Boston Public Library, which, as if gifted with human intelligence, find their way about the building to the particular place where each book belongs.

In time of distribution to illustrate the result of distance, we must further modify the model presented by an ordinary factory. We must suppose the interval of time between the processes to be greatly magnified, months being substituted for minutes. Then there will come into view the circumstance to which attention is particularly directed, — that a larger share will be conveyed to each producer (other things being equal), the greater his distance from the final stage. There will thus be a continual flow of materials in process of manufacture onwards and of products ready for consumption backwards, if the work at each stage is steadily maintained, provided that there is a continual stream of raw material, and that the machines are continually renewed.

Considering the continuous round of production and consumption, we realise the important truth which Mill has thus expressed: — "*The miller, the reaper, the ploughman, the plough-maker, the wagoner and wagon-maker, and the sailor and ship-builder, when employed, derive their remuneration from the ultimate product, — the bread made from the corn on which they have severally operated or supplied the instruments for operating.*"

To represent the continual expansion of value as the present ripens into the future, a series of concentric circles has been happily employed by Professor Bohm-Bawerk. Varying his illustration, let us suppose the circles to be drawn on ground which rises uniformly from the outmost circle towards the centre O in the accompanying diagram at which the apex tapers to a needle-point. The circles are drawn at equal distances as measured on the surface, and therefore, in a bird's-eye view which the diagram is intended to represent, become huddled together in the neighbourhood of the central height.

Across the circles, down the hill, flow streams with uniform velocity, so as to pass from circle to circle in a unit of time. The breadth of a stream increases with its length, — not in direct proportion to the length, but according to the law of accumulated price.The volume of the stream is proportioned to its breadth and to its depth (not shown on the figure). The stream takes its rise at some position on the channel (e. g. at a5a'5), the flow per unit of time at that point being proportioned to the energy put forth in pumping from a certain source. As the volume thus originated rolls down the channel, it continually increases by infiltration from the neighbouring soil without any additional pumping, so that, the depth being preserved constant, the volume is proportioned to the increasing breadth. Besides this increase due to its defluxion, the volume may also in the course of its downward flow be increased by additional pumping from a second source. This second increase corresponds to an increase in depth (not shown in the figure); and this second contribution is augmented, like the first, by the infiltration which attends defluxion.

As there may be many sources as circles are cut by the descending stream. But there need not be a source at each interval. The equidistant circles correspond to successive lines, not always coincident with successive stages of production at each of which additional labour is applied. The train of production thus represented terminates in a product ready for consumption — it may be loaves or ribbons, wine or shoes – on the shore of a circumfluent sea of commodities. As in the natural world rivers are replenished by the melting of the snow, which is formed on mountains by the congelation of vapour, which is wafted up from the ocean, into which the rivers flow down, so in the mundus economicus, by a compensation carried into more just detail, labour is restored and re-created by a refreshing rain of commodities derived from that sea into which all finished commodities are discharged.

Volatile shoes and wine, and other commodities in due admixture up to a certain value, find their way to each point upon the heights from which a source has been tapped, the volume of this return corresponding to the volume of the original contribution, — not indeed the same, but the same increased by a factor of accumulation, the ratio which the breadth of the stream at the littoral bears to its breadth at the point of origin.

The flight of the commodities from the littoral to the heights need not be supposed to occupy an appreciable time. The idea of a Flow which has been illustrated is primary applicable to the case in which materials and consumable commodities aroused up once for all within a unit of time. But the case of labour invested for longer periods is easily assimilated. Suppose that a plough lasts five years, and that in each year of its existence it makes an equal addition to the consumable crop, the year being taken as the unit of time. Then, although the plough may have been made in a week or month, the labour of its production is to be considered as invested in five unequal portions at unequal distances in time from the epoch at which the invested labour meets with its return. The total labour of making the plough may be considered as applied at several positions (a'1a1, a2a'2,... a5a'5) in several contributions, respectively proportioned to the breadth of the stream at these points.

## MONOPOLISTIC COMPETITION

Recall that we assumed that the demand curve for the monopolist's product depended only on the price set by the monopolist. However, this is an extreme case. Most commodities have some substitutes and the prices of those substitutes will affect the demand for the original commodity. The monopolist sets his price assuming all the producers of other commodities will maintain their prices, but of course, this will not be true. The prices set by the other firms will respond—perhaps indirectly—to the price set by the monopolist in question. We imagine a group of $n$ "monopolists" who sell similar, but not identical products. The price that consumers are willing to pay for the output of firm $i$ depends on the level of output of firm $i$ but also on the levels of output of the other firms: we write this inverse demand function as $p_i(y_i, y)$ where $y = (y_1 ...... y_n)$.

Each firm is interested in maximizing profits: that is, each firm $i$ is wants to choose its level of output $y_i$ so as to maximize:

$$p_i(y_i, y)y_i - c(y_i)$$

Unfortunately, the demand facing the $i^{th}$ firm depends on what the other firms do. How is firm $i$ supposed to forecast the other firms behaviour?

As suggested, adopt a very simple behaviourial hypothesis: namely, that firm $i$ assumes the other firms behaviour will be constant. Thus, each firm $i$ will choose its level of output $y_i^*$ so as to satisfy:

$$p_i\left(y_i^*, y\right) + \frac{\partial p_i\left(y_i^*, y\right)}{\partial y_i} y_i^* - c_i'\left(y_i^*\right) \leqq 0$$

with equality if

$$y_i^* > 0$$

For each combination of operating levels for the firms $y_1,...,y_n$, there will be some optimal operating level for firm $i$. As suggested, denote this optimal choice of output by $Y_i(y_1,.., y_n)$. (Of course the output of firm $i$ is not an argument of this function but it seems unnecessary to devise a new notation just to reflect that fact.) In order for the market to be in equilibrium, each firm's forecast about the behaviour of the other firms must be compatible with the other firms actually do. Thus if,

$$\left(y_1^*, ..., y_n^*\right)$$

is to be an equilibrium it must satisfy:

$$y_1^* = Y_1\left(y_1^*, ...., y_n^*\right)$$

$$\vdots$$

$$y_n^* = Y_n\left(y_1^*, ...., y_n^*\right)$$

that is $y_1^*$ must be the optimal choice for firm $i$ if it assumes the other firms are going to produce $y_2^*, ...., y_n^*$, and so on. Thus a monopolistic competition equilibrium $y_1^*, \ldots, y_n^*$, must satisfy:

$$p_i\left(y_i^*, y\right) + \frac{\partial p_i\left(y_i^*, y^*\right)}{\partial y_i} y^* - c_i'\left(y_i^*\right) \leqq 0$$

with equality if $y_i^* > 0$ and $i = 1, \ldots, n$.

For each firm, its marginal revenue equals its marginal cost, given the actions of all the other firms. This is illustrated in Figure.

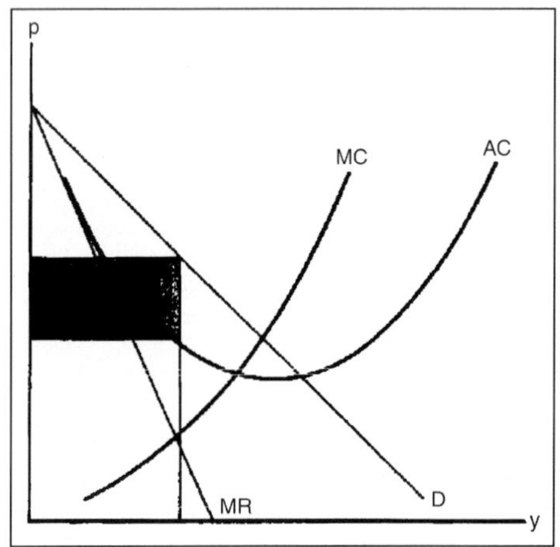


**Fig**: Short-run Monopolistic Competition Equilibrium

Now, at the monopolistic competition equilibrium depicted in Figure, firm $i$ is making positive profits. We would therefore expect others firms to enter the industry and share the market with the firm so the firm's profit will decrease because of close substitute goods. Thus, in the long run, firms would enter the industry until the profits of each firm were driven to zero. This means that firm $i$ must charge a price $p_i^*$ and produce an output $y_i^*$ such that:

$$p_i^* y_i^* - c_i\left(y^*\right) \leqq 0$$

with equality if $y_i^* > 0$

or

$$p_i^* - \frac{c_i\left(y^*\right)}{y^*} \leqq 0$$

With equality $y_i^* > 0$ $i = 1, 2, \ldots\ldots, n$

Thus, the price must equal to average cost and on the demand curve facing the firm. As a result, as long as the demand curve facing each firm has some negative slope, each firm will produce at a point where average cost are greater than the minimum average costs. Thus, like a pure competitive firms, the profits made by each firm are zero and is very nearly the long run competitive equilibrium. On the other hand, like a pure monopolist, it still results in inefficient allocation as long as the demand curve facing the firm has a negative slope.

## PROFIT MAXIMIZATION PROBLEM OF MONOPOLIST

At the opposite pole from pure competition we have the case of pure monopoly. Here instead of a large number of independent sellers of some uniform product, we have only one seller.

A monopolistic firm must make two sorts of decisions: how much output it should produce, and at what price it should sell this output. Of course, it cannot make these decisions unilaterally. The amount of output that the firm is able to sell will depend on the price that it sets.

We summarize this relationship between demand and price in a market demand function for output, $y(p)$. The market demand function tells how much output consumers will demand as a function of the price that the monopolist charges. It is often more convenient to consider the inverse demand function $p(y)$, which indicates the price that consumers are willing to pay for $y$ amount of output. The revenue that the firm receives will depend on the amount of output it chooses to supply. We write this revenue function as $R(y) = p(y)y$.

The cost function of the firm also depends on the amount of output produced. Here we have the factor prices as constant so that the conditional cost function can be written only as a function of the level of output of the firm.

*The profit maximization problem of the firm can then be written as*:

$$\max R(y)-c(y) = \max\, p(y)y-c(y)$$

The first-order conditions for profit maximization are that marginal revenue equals marginal cost, or,

$$p(y^*) + p'(y^*)y^* = c'(y^*)$$

The intuition behind this condition is fairly clear. If the monopolist considers producing one extra unit of output he will increase his revenue by $p(y^*)$ dollars in the first instance. But this increased level of output will force the price down by $p'(y^*)$, and he will lose this much revenue on unit of output sold. The sum of these two effects gives the marginal revenue. If the marginal revenue exceeds the marginal cost of production the monopolist will expand output. The expansion stops when the marginal revenue and the marginal cost balance out. The first-order conditions for profit maximization can he expressed in a slightly different manner through the use of the price elasticity of demand.

The price elasticity of demand is given by:

$$\in(y) = \frac{p}{y(p)}\frac{dy(p)}{dp}$$

Note that this is always a negative number since $dy(p)/dp$ is negative. Simple algebra shows that the marginal revenue equals marginal cost condition can be written as:

$$py^*\left[1+\frac{y^*}{p(y^*)}\frac{dp(y^*)}{dy}\right]=p(y^*)\left[1+\frac{1}{\in(y^*)}\right]=c'(y^*)$$

that is, the price charged by a monopolist is a markup over marginal cost, with the level of the markup being given as a function of the price elasticity of demand.There is also a nice graphical illustration of the profit maximization condition. Suppose for simplicity that we have a linear inverse demand curve: $p(y) = a–by$. Then the revenue function is,

$$R(y) = ay–by^2,$$

and the marginal revenue function is just

$$R'(y) = a–2by.$$

The marginal revenue curve has the same vertical intercept as the demand curve hut is twice as steep. We have illustrated these two curves in Figure, along with the average cost and marginal cost curves of the firm in question.

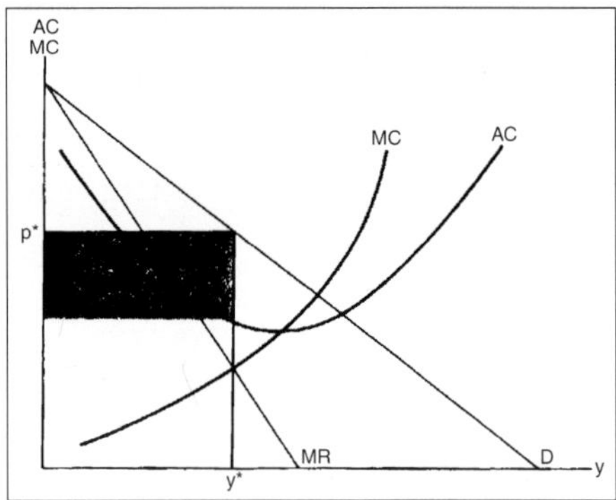


**Fig**: Determination of profit-maximizing Monopolist's Price and Output.

The optimal level of output is located where the marginal revenue and the marginal cost curves intersect. This optimal level of output sells at a price $p(y^*)$ so the monopolist gets an optimal revenue of $p(y^*)y^*$. The cost of producing $y^*$ is just $y^*$ times the average cost of production at that level of output. The difference between these two areas gives us a measure of the monopolist's profits.

## INEFFICIENCY OF MONOPOLY

We say that a situation is Pareto efficient if there is no way to make one agent better off and the others are not worse off. Pareto efficiency will be a major theme in the discussion of welfare economics, but we can give a nice illustration of the concept here.Let us consider the typical monopolistic configuration illustrated in Figure. It turns out a monopolist always operates in a Pareto inefficient manner. This means that there is some way to make the monopolist is better off and his customers are not worse off.

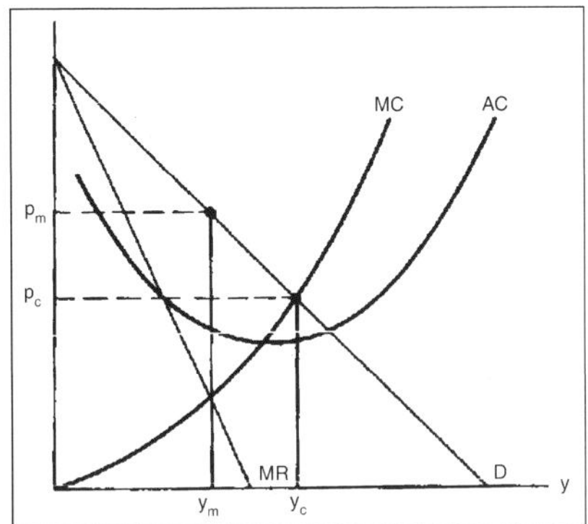


**Fig**: Monopoly Results in Pareto Inefficient Outcome.

To see this let us think of the monopolist in Figure after he has sold $y_m$ of output at the price $p_m$, and received his monopolist profit. Suppose that the monopolist were to produce a small unit of output $\Delta y$ more and offer to the public. How much would people be willing to pay for this extra unit? Clearly they would be willing to pay a price $p(y_m + \Delta y)$ dollars.

How much would it cost to produce this extra output? Clearly, just the marginal cost $MC(y_m+\Delta y)$. Under this rearrangement the consumers are at least not worse off since they are freely purchasing the extra unit of output, and the monopolist is better off since he can sell some extra units at a price that exceeds the cost of its production. Here we are allowing the monopolist to discriminate in his pricing: he first sells $y_m$ and then sells more output at some other price.

How long can this process be continued? Once the competitive level of output is reached, no further improvements are possible. The competitive level of price and output is Pareto efficient for this industry. As suggested, investigate the concept of Pareto efficiency in general equilibrium theory.

## MONOPOLY IN THE LONG RUN

We have seen how the long-run and the short-run behaviour of a competitive industry may differ because of changes in technology and entry. There are similar effects in a monopolized industry. The technological eddect is the simplest: the monopolist will choose the level of his fixed factors so as to maximize his long-run profits. Thus, he will operate where marginal revenue equals long-run marginal cost, and that is all that needs to be said. The entry effect is a bit more subtle. Presumably, if the monopolist is earning positive profits, other firms would like to enter the industry. If the monopolist is to remain a monopolist, there must be some sort of barrier to entry so that a monopolist may make positive profits even in the long-run. These barriers to entry may be of a legal sort, but often they are due to the fact that the monopolist owns some unique factor of production. For example, a firm might own a patent on a certain product, or might own a certain secret process for producing some item. If the monopoly power of the firm is due to a unique factor we have to be careful about we measure profits.

# 7

# Price and Output Determination

## PRICE DETERMINATION

The interaction of the broad forces of supply and demand which determine the market price level is known as price determination. For fed cattle, supply determinants or factors affecting the quantity of beef produced include input prices (feeder cattle and grain), technology (growth promotants, etc.), and price of outputs produced from those inputs (fed cattle). Broad demand forces or factors affecting the amount of beef consumed include the price of products produced from fed cattle (beef), price of competing products (pork and poultry), consumer income, and consumer tastes and preferences.

## COMPONENTS AND THEORIES OF DISTRIBUTION

In economics distribution refers to the way total output or income is distributed among individuals or among the factors of production (labour, land, and capital). In general theory and the national income and product accounts, each unit of output corresponds to a unit of income. One use of national accounts is for classifying factor incomes and measuring their respective shares, as in National Income. But, where focus is on income of *persons* or *households*, adjustments to the national accounts or other data sources are frequently used. Here, interest is often on the fraction of income going to the top (or bottom) $x$ per cent of households, the next $y$ per cent, and so forth (say in quintiles), and on the factors that might affect them (globalization, tax policy, technology, etc.).

### Descriptive, Theoretical, Scientific, and Welfare Uses

It can be describes by income distribution a prospectively observable element of an economy. It has been used as an input for testing theories explaining the distribution of income, for example human capital theory and the theory of economic discrimination. In welfare economics, a level of *feasible* output possibilities is commonly distinguished from the distribution of income for those output possibilities. But in the formal theory of *social* welfare, rules for selection from feasible distributions of income and output are a way of representing normative economics at a high level of generality.The species of Exchange by which produce is divided between the parties who have contributed to its production is distribution. Exchange being divided according as both, or one only, or neither of the parties have competitors, Distribution is similarly divided. The case in which both parties have competitors will here be first and principally considered. The simplest type of this distributive exchange would be of a kind which is effected once for all, without reference to a series of future productions and exchanges.

For example, Mr. Henry George used to adapt an illustration, let it be supposed that on a particular occasion each out of a number of white men hires one or more black men to assist in catching seals, on the agreement that each white man shall give his black assistants a certain proportion of the take, the terms having been settled in an open market in which any one white is free to bid against any other white and any one black against any other blacks.

A conception more appropriate to existing industry is that each white agrees to pay in exchange for a certain amount of service a definite quantity of produce, not in general limited to the result of a particular operation. On a particular day less seal may be taken than the employer has agreed to give the employee for the day. In this case, even if payment is not made till the end of the day, the employer must pay for help on a particular day in part with seal caught on a previous day. He must pay altogether out of past accumulations when payment is made before the work is one. When the employer agrees to pay a definite amount, he cannot expect to gain on each day's transaction, but on an average of days.

This example is suited to illustrate some general properties of Exchange which attach to Distribution as a species of Exchange. Such are the laws which connect a change in the supply or demand upon one side of the market with a change in the advantage resulting from the transaction to the parties on either side. Thus, competition on both sides being presupposed, a decrease of supply in a technical sense of the term on the one side is, ceteris paribus, universally attended with detriment to the other side, but is not universally attended with detriment to the side on which the supply is decreased.

Accordingly, a limitation of supply on one side may be advantageous to that side, though not to both sides. The case of Distribution compared with Exchange in general in respect to such limitation of supply has only this peculiarity, — that the danger of this policy defeating itself is in the case of Distribution specially visible and threatening. There is an evident limit to what the black man dealing with the white man can get in exchange for a certain amount of his service; namely, the total product which that service utilized by the white man will on an average produce. For a true decision, there is here but a case of the general principle that no one will give more for a thing, whether article of consumption or factor of production, than the equivalent of its total utility to him, which total diminishes as the quantity of the commodity is reduced. But this limit is less liable to escape attention when it is fixed by the material conditions of production rather than by the desires of consumers. Conspicuous warning is given to parties in the position of our black men not to attempt to benefit themselves by a considerable reduction in their supply of service; for, though they might possibly obtain a larger proportion, they would probably obtain a smaller portion, of the average product. The laws which have been stated and other general laws of Exchange are equally true in more complicated cases of Distribution.

Till now, only a single factor are supposed to have by us — the service of the black man, or, more generally, the factor beta – offered by the competitors B1, B2, etc., in exchange for some of the produce a offered by the competitors A1, A2, etc. Let us now introduce other kinds of factors, alpha, beta, etc. And let us no longer suppose payment to be made by parties of the type A, in the kind of commodity which is produced, namely, alpha. A more concrete conception is that, besides the group A, B, C, D, there is another and another group, — A', B', C', D'; A", B", C", D"; — where each capital letter typifies a set of competing individuals. It may be supposed that each A purchases out of the finished product that he turns out — namely, a — portions of the products a', a", etc., which he distributes according to the law of supply and demand among parties of the type B, C, D.

In fine, each A may pay for the factors of production altogether in some one product, a'", — *"numeraire,"* as happily conceived by M. Walras, or, less generally, money — which the purveyors of the factors can exchange for the articles which they want. These articles need not be all commodities ready for consumption: some of the parties may care to purchase factors of production wherewith to play the role which has been assigned to A.

It is now obtained a general idea of the machinery by which distribution in a regime of competition is effected, let us go on to consider in more detail the parts of the mechanism. And, first, of the party that takes factors of production in exchange for products or the means of purchasing the same, the party above represented by the white man and labelled A. The functions of this party may be investigated by an ancient method which Sidgwick has proposed to rehabilitate for the purposes of modern economics, — the search for a definition. What is an entrepreneur? Amid the diversified combinations of attributes which the industrial world presents — innumerable as the varieties in which vegetable nature riots — we ought to fix certain characters agreeably to the rule laid down by Mill under the head of Definition by Type. *"Our conception of the class" should be "the image in our minds which is that of a specimen complete in all the characteristics."*

Four such type-specimens may be distinguished, ranged in a descending order according to the extent of functions ascribed to the entrepreneur. First, there is the party whom the classical writers designate as the Capitalist, "*who from funds in his possession pays the wages of the labourers, or supports them during the work; who supplies the requisite buildings, materials, and tools, or machinery; and to whom, by the usual terms of the contract, the produce belongs to be disposed of at his pleasure*." This party will here be considered as devoting his care and savings to a single business. Second, there is the entrepreneur as portrayed by the late President Walker, "*not an employer because he is a capitalist, or in proportion as he is a capitalist.*"

Third, there is the party to whom Mr Hawley would wish to restrict the term "*entrepreneur,*" the man who undertakes risks, of which class the most prominent, though not the only, species is the investor in joint stock companies. Fourth, at the extreme degree of tenuity, is the entrepreneur who makes no profit. It might seem, indeed, as if this class did not call for special treatment, as differing only in the amount, not in the kind of remuneration. A fig-tree which bears no fruit is not therefore a tree of a distinct species. The horse which the Scotchman its owner had just trained to live upon a minimum, when the animal unfortunately died, was not therefore a new variety of the equine genus, requiring mention in a treatise on Natural History. However, as imposing theories have been connected with this last category, it comes within the scope of the present inquiry.

As our aim in comparing definitions should be, as Sidgwick says, far less to decide which we ought to adopt than to apprehend the grounds on which each has commended itself to reflective minds — the hunt for a definition being followed not so much for the sake of the quarry as of the views which are incidentally presented, — let us go on to consider the principal propositions which the several conceptions are adapted to bring under our notice. In this inquiry much assistance will be obtained from a series of articles on cognate subjects in the Quarterly Journal of Economics, which forms a sort of economic symposium.

The first definition is particularly suited to inquiries in which the parties who are in the habit of saving are contrasted as to their actions and interests with the parties who do not save, — approximately the working classes. Specimens of such inquiry may be found in the fifth chapter of Mill's first book, and in Professor Taussig's important article on "*The Employer's Place in Distribution.*" It sounds paradoxical to add that the classical conception is not particularly adapted to illustrate the Ricardian theory of rent. But the definition of the capitalist above given is not easily reconciled with the received representation, that the capitalist's remuneration is equal to the number of doses which he lays out, multiplied by the remuneration of the last dose, the ordinary rate of profit. For, as Sidgwick argues, there is no adequate reason for expecting that "*remuneration for management*" as well as interest should tend to be at the same rate for capitals of different sizes.

Probably, the proposition is accurate enough to support the practical consequences which have been deduced from it. But, while fully admitting this, one may still agree with Sidgwick that *"even Mill's exposition"* is *"highly puzzling."* For the idea of an economic person laying out doses up to the margin and obtaining the remuneration equal to the number of doses multiplied by the marginal productivity of each dose is only proper to the case in which the doses are for sale. But it is only in the conditions proper to our third definition that doses of capital are put on a market in exchange for profit. Perhaps the classical writers, having an eye to practice and not restricted by a sharp definition, often tacitly introduce the supposition that it is open to the *"capitalist"* to take part in some other business besides his own.

## TYPES OF PRICE DISCRIMINATION

### First Degree Price Discrimination

In first degree price discrimination, price varies by customer's willingness or ability to pay. This arises from the fact that the value of goods is subjective. A customer with low price elasticity is less deterred by a higher price than a customer with high price elasticity of demand. As long as the price elasticity for a customer is less than one, it is very advantageous to increase the price: the seller gets more money for fewer goods.

With an increase of the price elasticity tends to rise one. One can show that in the optimum the price, as it varies by customer, is inversely proportional to one minus the reciprocal of the price elasticity of that customer at that price. This assumes that the consumer passively reacts to the price set by the seller, and that the seller knows the demand curve of the customer. In practice however there is a bargaining situation, which is more complex: the customer may try to influence the price, such as by pretending to like the product less than he or she really does or by threatening not to buy it.

An alternative way to understand First Degree Price Discrimination is as follows: This type of price discrimination is primarily theoretical because it requires the seller of a good or service to know the absolute maximum price that every consumer is willing to pay. It is true that consumers have different price elasticities, but the seller is not concerned with such. The seller is concerned with the maximum willingness to pay of each customer. By knowing the reservation price, the seller is able to absorb the entire market surplus, thus taking all of the consumer's surplus from the consumer and transforming it into revenues. From a social welfare perspective though, first degree price discrimination is not necessarily undesirable. That is, the market is still entirely efficient and there is no deadweight loss to society. In a market with first degree price discrimination, the seller(s) simply captures all surplus. Efficiency is unchanged but the wealth is transferred. This type of market does not exist much in reality, hence it is primarily theoretical. Examples of where this might be observed are in markets where consumers bid for tenders, though still, in this case, the practice of collusive tendering undermines efficiency.

**Second Degree Price Discrimination**

In second degree price discrimination, price varies according to quantity sold. Larger quantities are available at a lower unit price. This is particularly widespread in sales to industrial customers, where bulk buyers enjoy higher discounts. Additionally to second degree price discrimination, sellers are not able to differentiate between different types of consumers. Thus, the suppliers will provide incentives for the consumers to differentiate themselves according to preference. Quantity "discounts", or non-linear pricing, is a means by which suppliers use consumer preference to distinguish classes of consumers. This allows the supplier to set different prices to the different groups and capture a larger portion of the total market surplus. In reality, different pricing may apply to differences in product quality as well as quantity. For example, airlines often offer multiple classes of seats on flights, such as first class and economy class. This is a way to differentiate consumers based on preference, and therefore allows the airline to capture more producer's surplus.

**Third Degree Price Discrimination**

In third degree price discrimination, price varies by attributes such as location or by customer segment, or in the most extreme case, by the individual customer's identity; where the attribute in question is used as a proxy for ability/ willingness to pay. Additionally to third degree price discrimination, the supplier(s) of a market where this type of discrimination is exhibited are capable of differentiating between consumer classes.

Examples of this differentiation are student or senior discounts. For example, a student or a senior consumer will have a different willingness to pay than an average consumer, where the reservation price is presumably lower because of budget constraints. Thus, the supplier sets a lower price for that consumer because the student or senior has a more elastic price elasticity of demand. The supplier is once again capable of capturing more market surplus than would be possible without price discrimination. Note that it is not always advantageous to the company to price discriminate even if it is possible, especially for second and third degree discrimination. In some circumstances, the demands of different classes of consumers will encourage suppliers to simply ignore one/some class(es) and target entirely to the other(s). Whether it is profitable to price discriminate is determined by the specifics of a particular market.

**Price Skimming**

In price skimming, price varies over time. Typically a company starts selling a new product at a relatively high price then gradually reduces the price as the low price elasticity segment gets satiated. Price skimming is closely related to the concept of yield management.These types are not mutually exclusive. Thus a company may vary pricing by location, but then offer bulk discounts as well.

*Airlines use several different types of price discrimination, including*:

- Bulk discounts to wholesalers, consolidators, and tour operators.
- Incentive discounts for higher sales volumes to travel agents and corporate buyers.
- Seasonal discounts, incentive discounts, and even general prices that vary by location. The price of a flight from say, Singapore to Beijing can vary widely if one buys the ticket in Singapore compared to Beijing. In online ticket sales this is achieved by using the customer's credit card billing address to determine his location.
- Discounted tickets requiring advance purchase and/or Saturday stays. Both restrictions have the effect of excluding business travellers, who typically travel during the workweek and arrange trips on shorter notice.
- First degree price discrimination based on customer. It is not accidental that hotel or car rental firms may quote higher prices to their loyalty programme's top tier members than to the general public.

## MODERN TAXONOMY

The first/second/third degree taxonomy of price discrimination is due to Pigou suggests an alternative taxonomy:

- *Complete Discrimination*: Where each user purchases up to the point where the user's marginal benefit equals the marginal cost of the item;
- *Direct Segmentation*: Where the seller can condition price on some attribute that directly segments the buyers; and
- *Indirect Segmentation*: Where the seller relies on some proxy to structure a choice that indirectly segments the buyers.

The hierarchy-complete/direct/indirect-is in decreasing order of:

- Profitability; and
- Information requirement.

Complete price discrimination is most profitable, and requires the seller to have the most information about buyers. Indirect segmentation is least profitable, and requires the seller to have the least information about buyers.

## EXPLANATION

The purpose of price discrimination is generally to capture the market's consumer surplus. This surplus arises because, in a market with a single clearing price, some customers would have been prepared to pay more than the single market price. Price discrimination transfers some of this surplus from the consumer to the producer/marketer.

Strictly, a consumer surplus need not exist, for example where some below-cost selling is beneficial due to fixed costs or economies of scale. An example is a high-speed internet connection shared by two consumers in a single building; if one is willing to pay less than half the cost, and the other willing to make up the rest but not to pay the entire cost, then price discrimination is necessary for the purchase to take place. It can be proved mathematically that a firm facing a downward sloping demand curve that is convex to the origin will always obtain higher revenues under price discrimination than under a single price strategy.

A single price (P) is available to all customers. The amount of revenue is represented by area P, A, Q, O. The consumer surplus is the area line segment P, A but below the demand curve (D). With price discrimination, the demand curve is divided into two segments.

A higher price is charged to the low elasticity segment, and a lower price is charged to the high elasticity segment. The total revenue from the first segment is equal to the area P1, B, Q1, O.

The total revenue from the second segment is equal to the area E, C, Q2, Q1. The sum of these areas will always be greater than the area without discrimination assuming the demand curve resembles a rectangular hyperbola with unitary elasticity.

The more prices that are introduced, the greater the sum of the revenue areas, and the more of the consumer surplus is captured by the producer. Note that the requires both first and second degree price discrimination: the right segment corresponds partly to different people than the left segment, partly to the same people, willing to buy more if the product is cheaper. It is very useful for the price discriminator to determine the optimum prices in each market segment. This is done where each segment is considered as a separate market with its own demand curve.As usual, the profit maximizing output (Qt) is determined by the intersection of the marginal cost curve (MC) with the marginal revenue curve for the total market (MRt).

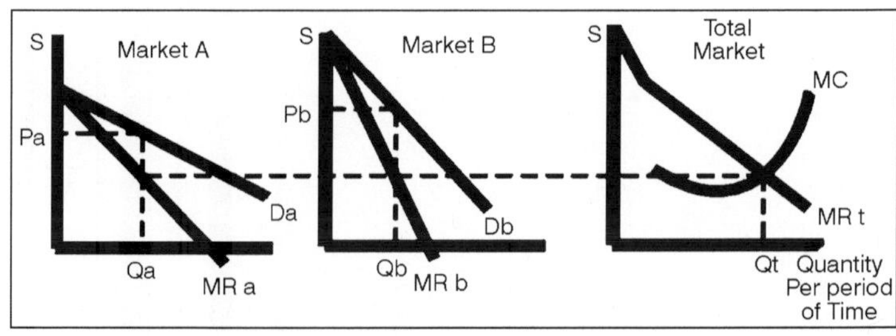


Multiple Market Price Determination

The firm decides what amount of the total output to sell in each market by looking at the intersection of marginal cost with marginal revenue. This output is then divided between the two markets, at the equilibrium marginal revenue level. Therefore, the optimum outputs are Qa and Qb. From the demand curve in each market we can determine the profit maximizing prices of Pa and Pb. It is also important to note that the marginal revenue in both markets at the optimal output levels must be equal, otherwise the firm could profit from transferring output over to whichever market is offering higher marginal revenue. Given that Market 1 has a price elasticity of demand of E1 and Market of E2, the optimal pricing ration in Market 1 *versus* Market 2 is P1 / P2 = [1 – 1 / E2] / [1 – 1 / E1].

## EXAMPLES OF PRICE DISCRIMINATION

### Retail Price Discrimination

In certain circumstances, it is a violation of the Robinson-Patman Act, for manufacturers of goods to sell their products to similarly situated retailers at different prices based solely on the volume of products purchased.

### Travel Industry

Airlines and other travel companies use differentiated pricing regularly, as they sell travel products and services simultaneously to different market segments. This is often done by assigning capacity to various booking classes, which sell for different prices and which may be linked to fare restrictions. The restrictions or "fences" help ensure that market segments buy in the booking class range that has been established for them.

For example, schedule-sensitive business passengers who are willing to pay $300 for a seat from city A to city B cannot purchase a $150 ticket because the $150 booking class contains a requirement for a Saturday night stay, or a 15-day advance purchase, or another fare rule that discourages, minimizes, or effectively prevents a sale to business passengers. Notice, however, that in this example "the seat" is not really always the same product. That is, the business person who purchases the $300 ticket may be willing to do so in return for a seat on a high-demand morning flight, for full refundability if the ticket is not used, and for the ability to upgrade to first class if space is available for a nominal fee. On the same flight are price-sensitive passengers who are not willing to pay $300, but who are willing to fly on a lower-demand flight or via a connection city, and who are willing to forgo refundability. On the other hand, an airline may also apply differential pricing to "the same seat" over time, *e.g.*, by discounting the price for an early or late booking.

This could present an arbitrage opportunity in the absence of any restriction on reselling. However, passenger name changes are typically prevented or financially penalised by contract. Since airlines often fly multi-leg flights, and since no-show rates vary by segment, competition for the seat has to take in the spatial dynamics of the product. Someone trying to fly A-B is competing with people trying to fly A-C through city B on the same aircraft. This is one reason airlines use yield management technology to determine how many seats to allot for A-B passengers, B-C passengers, and A-B-C passengers, at their varying fares and with varying demands and no-show rates.

With the rise of the Internet and the growth of low fare airlines, airfare pricing transparency has become far more pronounced. Passengers discovered it is quite easy to compare fares across different flights or different airlines. This helped put pressure on airlines to lower fares. Meanwhile, in the recession following the September 11, 2001, attacks on the U.S., business travellers and corporate buyers made it clear to airlines that they were not going to be buying air travel at rates high enough to subsidize lower fares for non-business travellers.

This prediction has come true, as vast numbers of business travellers are buying airfares only in economy class for business travel. There are sometimes group discounts on rail tickets and passes. This may be in view of the alternative of going by car together.

**Premium Pricing**

For certain products, premium products are priced at a level that is well beyond their marginal cost of production. For example, a coffee chain may price regular coffee at $1, but "premium" coffee at $2.50. Economists such as Tim Harford in the Undercover Economist have argued that this is a form of price discrimination: by providing a choice between a regular and premium product, consumers are being asked to reveal their degree of price sensitivity for comparable products.

Similar techniques are used in pricing business class airline tickets and premium alcoholic drinks, for example. This effect can lead to perverse incentives for the producer. If, for example, potential business class customers will pay a large price differential only if economy class seats are uncomfortable while economy class customers are more sensitive to price than comfort, airlines may have substantial incentives to purposely make economy seating uncomfortable. In the example of coffee, a restaurant may gain more economic profit by making poor quality regular coffee-more profit is gained from up-selling to premium customers than is lost from customers who refuse to purchase inexpensive but poor quality coffee.

In such cases, the net social utility should also account for the "lost" utility to consumers of the regular product, although determining the magnitude of this foregone utility may not be feasible.

**Segmentation by Age Group and Student Status**

Many movie theatres, amusement parks, tourist attractions, and other places have different admission prices per market segment: typical groupings are Youth, Student, Adult, and Senior. Each of these groups typically have a much different demand curve. Children, people living on student wages, and people living on retirement generally have much less disposable income.

**Discounts for Members of Certain Occupations**

Many businesses, especially in the Southern United States, offer reduced prices to active military members. In addition to increased sales to the target group, businesses benefit from the resulting positive publicity, leading to increased sales to the general public.

Less publicised are discounts to other service workers such as police; off-duty police customers in high-crime areas are said to constitute free security.

**Employee Discounts**

Discounts that businesses give to their own employees are also a form of price discrimination.

**Retail Incentives**

A variety of incentive techniques may be used to increase market share or revenues at the retail level. These include discount coupons, rebates, bulk and quantity pricing, seasonal discounts, and frequent buyer discounts.

**Incentives for Industrial Buyers**

Many methods exist to incentivise wholesale or industrial buyers. These may be quite targeted, as they are designed to generate specific activity, such as buying more frequently, buying more regularly, buying in bigger quantities, buying new products with established ones, and so on. Thus, there are bulk discounts, special pricing for long-term commitments, non-peak discounts, discounts on high-demand goods to incentivise buying lower-demand goods, rebates, and many others. This can help the relations between the firms involved.

**Two Necessary Conditions for Price Discrimination**

There are two conditions that must be met if a price discrimination scheme is to work. *First* the firm must be able to identify market segments by their price elasticity of demand and *second* the firms must be able to enforce the scheme. For example, airlines routinely engage in price discrimination by charging high prices for customers with relatively inelastic demand – business travellers – and discount prices for tourist who have relatively elastic demand, The airlines enforce the scheme by making the tickets non-transferable thus preventing a tourist from buying a ticket at a discounted price and selling it to a business traveller. Airlines must also prevent business travellers from directly buying discount tickets. Airlines accomplish this by imposing advance ticketing requirements or minimum stay requirements conditions that it would be difficult for average business traveller to meet.

## THE PRICE COMPETITION MECHANISM

Now the discussion of the *'price competition'* mechanism can formalize by us. We confine attention, for ease of exposition, to the class of *'symmetric'* produce differentiation models. In these models, each firm chooses some number n of distinct product varieties to offer, and incurs a setup cost $\varepsilon > 0$ for each one. The profit of firm i in an equilibrium of the final stage sub game can be written as S (n i / (n–i)). Now consider a family of such models, across which the form of price competition in the final stage sub game differs. We consider a one-parameter family of models that can be ranked in the following sense: we define a family of profit functions parameterized by $\theta$, denoted by (n i / (n – i ); $\theta$ ).

An increase in è shifts the profit function downwards, in the sense that, for any given configuration we have that if 1 2 $\theta > \theta$, then $\pi$ (ni/(n–i); $\theta$1) < $\pi$ (ni (n–i); $\theta$2) The parameter $\theta$ denotes the *'toughness of price competition'* in the sense that an increase in $\theta$ reduces the level of final stage profit earned by each firm, for any given form of market structure (*i.e.* configuration).

*We now proceed as follows*: For each value of S, we define the set of configurations satisfying the viability condition, viz. S$\pi$(ni (n–i);$\theta$) $\geq \varepsilon$ for all i – (2.2) For each configuration, we define an index of concentration. For concreteness, we choose the 1-firm sales concentration ratio 1 C, defined as the share of industry sales revenue accounted for by the industry's largest firm. We now select, from the set of configurations satisfying (2.2), the configuration with the lowest (or equal lowest) value of 1 C, and we define this level of concentration as 1 C (S; $\theta$ ). This construction defines the schedule 1 C (S; $\theta$), which forms a lower bound to concentration as a function of market size. Assuming that $\pi$ is increasing in C, 1 then it follows immediately from equation (2.2) that an increase in è shifts this schedule upwards.

Then, in some market we begin with an equilibrium configuration. Holding the size of the market constant, we introduce a change in the external circumstances of the market which implies a rise in $\theta$; for example, this might be a change in the rules of competition policy (a law banning cartels, say), or it might be an improvement in the transport system that causes firms in hitherto separated local markets to come into direct competition with each other (as with the building of national railway systems in the nineteenth century, for example).

If the associated shift in $\theta$ is large enough, then the current configuration will no longer be an equilibrium, and some shift in structure must occur in the long run. At this point, a caveat is in order: the theory is static, and we can not specify the dynamic adjustment path that will be followed once equilibrium is disturbed. All that can be said is that restoration of the stability and viability conditions requires a rise in concentration. We may distinguish two candidate mechanisms that may bring this about: the exit of some firm(s), and/or the consolidation of others via mergers and acquisitions. This argument relies upon the link between concentration and price (and so gross profit per firm).

## EMPIRICAL EVIDENCE

The most systematic test of this prediction is that of Symeonidis who takes advantage of an unusual *'natural experiment'* involving a change in competition law in the U.K. in the 1960s. As laws against the operation of cartels were strengthened, a general rise in concentration occurred across the general run of manufacturing industries. Symeonidis traces the operation of these changes in detail, and finds a process at work that is consistent with the operation of the response mechanisms postulated above.

In the late 19$^{th}$ century, Sutton reports some *'natural experiments'* affecting particular industries in the wake of the spread of the railways. The salt industry, both in the US and Europe, went through a process of consolidation in the wake of these changes. First prices fell, rendering many concerns unviable. Attempts to restore profitability via price coordination failed, due to *'free riding'* by some firms. Finally, a process of exit, accompanied by mergers and acquisitions, led to the emergence of a concentrated industry.

Sugar industry history offers some interesting illustrations of the way in which differences in the competition policy regime affected outcomes. In the U.S., it follows a similar pattern to that of the salt industry over the same period. In Continental European countries, on the other hand, a permissive competition policy regime allowed firms to coordinate their prices, thus permitting the continuance of a relatively fragmented industry into the twentieth century. The Japanese market provides an unusually informative natural experiment, in that it went through three successive regimes in respect of competition policy. A tight cartel operated in the period prior to the First World War, and concentration was low. In the inter-war years, the cartel broke down and concentration rose. However, in the years following the Second World War the authorities permitted the industry to operate under a permissive *'quota'* regime; and this relaxation in the toughness of price competition encouraged new entry, and a decline in concentration.

### The Escalation Mechanism

It is turn to a general statement of the *'Non-convergence'* result introduced in the *'quality choice'* by us and developed in two steps. The analysis is developed in two steps. In this section, we consider a *'classical'* setting in which each firm offers a (single) product within the same market, and all these products are substitutes. We will turn to a more complex setting in which the market comprises several distinct product groups, or *'submarkets'*. Here, then, each firm's action takes one of two forms, *'Don't Enter'* or *'Enter with quality ui'*, where ui is chosen from the interval [1,").

The outcome of firms' actions is described by a configuration u = (u1, ... ui, ... uN) We associate with every configuration u a number representing the highest level of quality attained by any firm, *viz.* u^ (u) = max $_i$ u i

We summarize the properties of the final-stage subgame in a pair of functions that describe the profit of each firm and the sales revenue of the industry as a whole. Firm i's final stage profit is written as Π(ui|(u–i)) ≡ Sπ(ui|(u–i)) ≥ 0 where u–i denotes the N–1 tuple of rivals' qualities, and S denotes the number of consumers in the market20. Total industry sales revenue is denoted by Y(u) ≡ Sy(u).

It is assumed that any firm entering the market incurs a minimum setup cost of F0 and that increases in the quality index above unity involve additional spending on fixed outlays such as R&D and Advertising. We choose to label this index so that the fixed outlay of firm i is related to the quality level ui according to = F(ui ) F0 u i$^b$, on ui [1, ∞), for some β ≥ 1.

We identify the level of spending on R&D and Advertising as R (u i ) = F 0 (ui ) – F The economics of the model depends only on the composite mapping from firms' fixed outlays to firms' profits, rather than on the separate mappings of fixed outlays to qualities and from qualities to profits. At this point, the labelling of u is arbitrary up to an increasing transformation. There is no loss of generality, therefore, in choosing this functional form for R(ui). (The form used here has been chosen for ease of interpretation, in that we can think of β as the elasticity of quality with respect to fixed outlays).

For avoiding trivial cases, we assume throughout that the market is always large enough to ensure that the level of sales exceeds some minimal level for any configuration, and that the market can support at least one entrant. With this in mind, we restrict S to the domain [1, ∞), and we assume, following Assumption 1 above,

*Assumption* 3:

The level of industry sales associated with any Non-empty configuration is bounded away from zero; that is, there is some η > 0 such that for every configuration u ≠ ∞, we have y(u) ≥ η > 0 for all u ≠ ∞. This assumption, together with Assumption 1(i), implies that the level of industry sales revenue Sy(u) ≥ Sη in any Equilibrium Configuration increases to infinity as S → ∞.

**A Non-convergence Theorem**

In what follows, we are concerned with examining whether some kinds of configuration u are unstable against entry by a *'high-spending'* entrant. With this in mind, we investigate the profit of a new firm that enters with a quality level k times greater than the maximum value û offered by any existing firm. More specifically, we ask: What is the minimum ratio of this high-spending entrant's profit to current industry sales that will be attained *independently* of the current configuration u and the size of the market?

For each k, we define an associated number a(k) as follows:

*Definition:*

a(k)= inf Π(ku^/u)/ y(U )

It follows from this definition that, given any configuration u with maximal quality û, the final-stage profit of an entrant with capability kû, denoted Sπ(ku^ u) , is at least equal to a(k)Sy(u) = a(k)Y(u) , where a(k) is independent of u and S. The intuition is as follows: k measures the size of the quality jump introduced by the new *'high spending'* entrant. We aim to examine whether such an entrant will earn enough profit to cover its fixed outlays, and so we want to know what price it will set, and what market share it will earn. This information is summarised by the number a(k), which relates the gross (final-stage) profit of the entrant, Sπ(ku^ u) , to pre-entry industry sales revenue, Sy(u) = Y(u) . Since we wish to develop results that are independent of the existing configuration, we define a(k) as an infimum over u.

*We are now in a position to state:*

Theorem 1 (Non- convergence) Given any pair (k,a(k)), a necessary condition for any configuration to be an equilibrium configuration is that a firm offering the highest level of quality has a share of industry sales revenue exceeding a(k) / kβ. PROOF Consider any equilibrium configuration u in which the highest quality offered is û. Choose any firm offering quality u^ and denote the sales revenue earned by that firm by $S\hat{y}$, whence its share of industry sales revenue is $S\hat{y}/SY(u) = \hat{y}/Y(u)$.

Consider the net profit of an entrant who attains quality kû. The definition of a(k) implies that the entrant's net profit is at least aSy(u) – F(ku^) = aSy(u) " kβF(u^ ) where we have written a(k) as a, in order to ease notation. The stability condition implies that this entrants' net profit is non-positive, whence F(u^ ) ≥ a / k β  Sy(u)

But the viability condition requires that each firm's final-stage profit must cover its fixed outlays. Hence the sales revenue of the firm that offers quality û in the proposed equilibrium configuration cannot be less than its fixed outlays:

Sy^ ≥ F(u^ ) e ≥ a/ k β Sy(u )

whence its market share

Sy^/ Sy(u) e ≥ a/ k β

This completes the proof.

The intuition underlying this result is as follows:

If the industry consists of a large number of small firms, then the viability condition implies that each firm's spending on R&D is small, relative to the industry's sales revenue. In this setting, the returns to a high-spending entrant may be large, so that the stability condition is violated. Hence a configuration in which concentration is *"too low"* cannot be an equilibrium configuration.

This result motivates the introduction of a parameter, which we call alpha, as the highest value of the ratio a/kβ that can be attained by choosing any value $k \geq 1$, as follows:

Definition $\alpha = \sup k\ a(k)/ k\beta$.

We can now reformulate the preceding theorem as follows: since the one-firm sales concentration ratio C1 is not less than the share of industry sales revenue enjoyed by the firm offering quality $\hat{u}$, it follows from the preceding theorem that, in any equilibrium configuration, C1 is bounded below by α, independently of the size of the market, *viz.*

$$C1 \geq \alpha \quad (2.3)$$

Equation (2.3) constitutes a restatement of the basic noncovergence result developed in the preceding theorem. In the light of this result, we see that alpha serves as a measure of the extent to which a fragmented industry can be destabilised by the actions of a firm who outspends its many small rivals in R&D or Advertising. The value of alpha depends directly on the profit function of the final stage subgame, and on the elasticity of the fixed cost schedule. Hence it reflects both the pattern of technology and tastes and the nature of price competition in the market. We noted earlier that the results do not depend on the way we label u, but only on the composite mapping from F to π.

To underline this point, we can re-express the present result as follows: Increasing quality by a factor k requires that fixed outlays rise by a factor kβ. For any given value of β, write kβ as K. We can now write any pair (k,a(k)) as an equivalent (K,a(K)) pair. The question: what if, as the quality level(s) of firms rise(s), we could always find a suitable pair k, a(k), Alpha can then be described as the highest ratio a(K)/K that can be attained by any choice of $K \geq 1$.

**An Ancillary Theorem**

Within our present context of a classical market in which all goods are substitutes, the interpretation of alpha is straightforward. The parameter a(k) measures the degree to which an increase in the (perceived) quality of one product allows it to capture sales from rivals. Thus the statement, within this context, that there exists some pair of numbers k and $a(k)>0$ satisfying the above conditions requires only very weak restrictions on consumer preferences.

*The question of interest is:* How costly is it, in terms of fixed outlays, to achieve this k-fold increase in u? This is measured by the parameter β. With this in mind, we proceed to define a family of models, parameterised by β, as follows: we take the form of the profit function, and so the function a(k), as fixed, while allowing the parameter β to vary. We assume, moreover, that for some value of k, a(k) > 0. The value of $\alpha$ = sup a(k) / k$\beta$ k varies with $\beta$. (The case $\alpha = 0$ can be treated as a limiting case as a(k) $\rightarrow$ 0 or $\beta \rightarrow \infty$.)

Now, we are in a place to an ancillary theorem whose role is to allow us to use the observed value of the R&D and/or Advertising to Sales ratio to proxy for the value of $\beta$. We are now in a position to develop The intuition behind the ancillary theorem is this: if the value of $\beta$ is high, this implies that the responsiveness of profit to the fixed outlays of the deviant firm is low, and under these circumstances we might expect that the level of fixed outlays undertaken by all firms at equilibrium would be small; this is what the theorem asserts.

It has been set up by us by showing that certain configurations must be unstable, in that they will be vulnerable to entry by a low-spending entrant. The idea is that, if spending on R&D and Advertising is ineffective, then a low spending entrant may incur much lower fixed outlays than (at least some) incumbent firm(s), while offering a product that is only slightly inferior to that of the incumbent(s). The ancillary theorem allows us to fix some threshold level for the ratio of R&D plus Advertising to sales, and consider the set of industries for which the ratio exceeds this threshold level: we may characterize this group as being *'low* $\beta$' and so *'high alpha'* industries, as against a control group of industries in which R&D and Advertising levels are (very close to) zero.

It is this result which leads to the empirical test of the non-convergence theorem. Before stating the theorem however, some preliminary development is necessary, since the proof of the ancillary theorem rests on an appeal to the entry of a low-spending firm. This raises a technical issue: suppose, for the sake of illustration, that the underlying model of the final stage sub game, whose properties are summarised in the profit function $\pi(\cdot)$, takes the form of the elementary *'Bertrand model'*. In this setting, if all firms offer the same quality level, once one firm is present in the market, no further entry can occur; for any entry leads to an immediate collapse of prices to marginal cost, and so the entrant can never earn positive margins, and so cover the sunk cost incurred in entering.

This excluding case must be excluded. To define and exclude this limiting case, we need to specify the relationship between the profit earned by an entrant, and the pre-entry profit of some active firm (the *'reference firm'*). Consider an equilibrium configuration in which the industry-wide R&D (or Advertising) to sales ratio is x (> 0). Within this industry, we select some reference firm whose R&D and Advertising outlays constitute a fraction x (or greater) of its sales revenue. There must be at least one such firm in the industry, and since this firm must satisfy the viability condition, it must earn a gross profit of at least fraction x of its sales revenues in order to sustain its level of R&D and Advertising.

Now consider an entrant that offers the same quality level as the reference firm. Insofar as entry reduces prices, this entrant will enjoy a lower price-cost margin than that earned by the reference firm in the pre-entry situation. But, for a sufficiently high value of x, we assume that the entrant will enjoy some strictly positive price-cost margin, so that its final stage profit is strictly positive.

The horizontal axis shows the ratio between the quality of the entrant's product, and that of the reference firm; k varies from 0 to 1, with a value of 1 corresponding to the entrant of equal quality. Our assumption states that for k = 1, the entrant's post-entry profit is strictly positive. On the vertical axis, we show the ratio of the entrant's profit to the pre-entry profit of the reference firm. Our exclusion of the Bertrand limit states that, for k = 1, this ratio is strictly positive. We further assume that the entrant's profit varies continuously with its quality, and so with k. It then follows that we can depict the entrant's profit as a function of k as a curve; the assumption states that this curve does not collapse inwards to the bottom right-hand corner of the diagram (the '*Bertrand limit*'). Specifically, it says that there is some value of x, such that if the pre-entry price-cost margin exceeds x, then there is some point in the interior of the square such that the curve we have just described lies above this point.

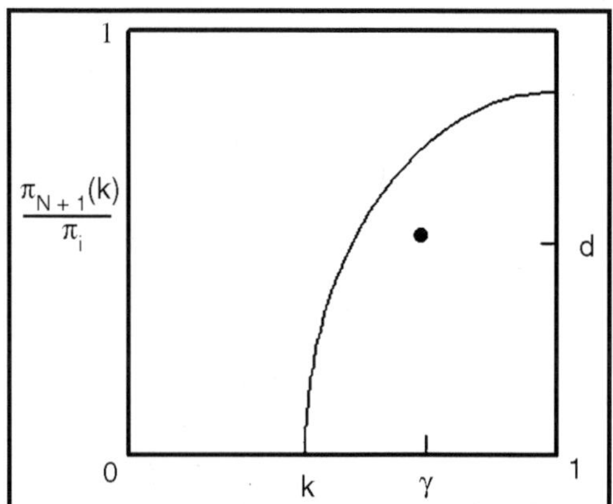


**Fig.** The Relative Profit of a Low-quality Entrant. The Incumbent Firm, Labelled i, Offers Quality ui and Earns (Pre-entry) Profit pi. The Entrant, Labelled Firm N+1, Offers Quality kui and Earns Profit pN+1(k).

We state this formally as follows:

*Assumption* 4:

There is some triple (x, γ, d) with 0 < x, γ < 1, and 0 < d < 1, with the following property: Suppose any firm i attains quality level ui and earns final-stage profit i π that exceeds a fraction x of its sales revenue. Then an entrant attaining a quality level equal to max(1, γui) attains a final-stage profit of at least dπi. The ancillary theorem linking the R&D (or advertising)/sales ratio to the parameter β now follows:Theorem 2 For any threshold value of the R&D (or advertising)/sales ratio exceeding max (x, 1–d), where x and d are defined as in Assumption 4, there is an associated value of $\beta^*$ such that for any $\beta > \beta^*$, no firm can have an R&D/sales ratio exceeding this threshold in any equilibrium configuration. A proof of this theorem is given in Sutton. An implication of Theorem 2 is that an industry with a high R&D (or advertising)/sales ratio must necessarily be a high-alpha industry.

With this result in place, we are now in a position to formulate an empirical test of the theory: Choose some ('sufficiently high') threshold level for the R&D (or advertising)/sales ratio (written as R/Y in what follows), and split the sample of industries by reference to this threshold.

All industries in which alpha is close to zero will fall in the low R/Y group, and so for this group the lower bound to the cloud of points in (C,S) space should converge to zero as $S \to \infty$. For all industries in the group with high R/Y, on the other hand, the value of β will lie below $\beta^*$, and so the lower bound to concentration will be bounded away from zero by $\beta\ C1 \geq a(k) / k$.

In pooling data across different industries, it is necessary to '*standardise*' the measure of market size by reference to some notion of the minimum level of setup cost ε. A practical procedure to represent this as the cost of a single plant of minimum efficient scale, and to write the ratio of annual industry sales revenue to minimum setup cost as ε. This leads to the prediction; tests of this prediction are reported in the next section.

It is interesting to consider the relationship between this prediction and the traditional practice of regressing concentration on a measure of scale economies to market size (essentially S/ε), together with a measure of advertising intensity and R&D intensity. Such regressions indicated that concentration fell with S/ε, and rose (weakly) with the advertising-sales ratio. It can be shown that, under the present theory, these results are predicted to emerge from the (mis-specified) regression relationship.

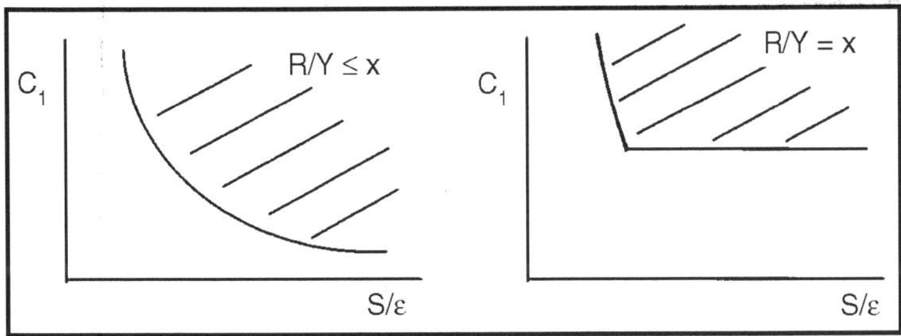


**Fig.** The '*Bounds*' Prediction on the Concentration-market Size Relationship.

## EMPIRICAL EVIDENCE

In a context we have developed this first version of the non-convergence theorem in which the classical market definition applies, *i.e.* the market comprises a single set of substitute goods, so that an increase in fixed and sunk outlays enhances consumers' willingness-to-pay for all its products in this market. Now this condition will apply strictly only in rather special circumstances. One setting in which it applies to a good approximation is that of certain groups of advertising-intensive industries. Here, even though the market may comprise a number of distinct product categories, the firm's advertising may support a brand image that benefits all its products in the market.

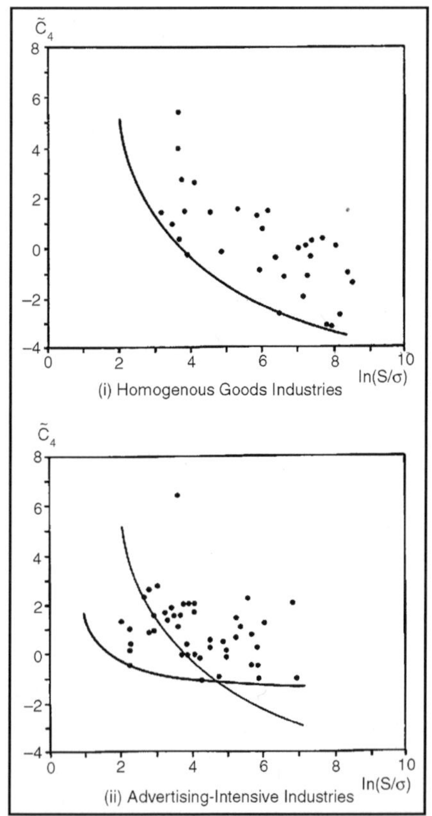


**Fig.** A Plot of 4 C ~ Versus S/e for Advertising-intensive Industries (Bottom Panel) and a Control Group (Top Panel).
The Fitted Bound for the Control Group is Reproduced in the Bottom Panel for Comparison Purposes.

Across the six largest Western economies, the first test of the non-convergence theorem was carried out on a dataset for 20 industries drawn from the food and drink sector. The industries were chosen from a single sector so as to keep constant as many extraneous factors as possible. The food and drink sector was chosen because, alone among the basic 2-digit SIC industry groups, it is the only one in which there is a nice split between industries that have little or no advertising (sugar, flour, etc.) and industries that are advertising-intensive (breakfast cereals, pet-food, etc.).

Data was compiled from market research reports, combined with company interviews. The industry definitions used are those which are standard in the market research literature, and these correspond roughly to 4-digit SIC definitions. All industries for which suitable data could be assembled were included. The size of each market was defined as the number of '*minimum efficient scale*' plants it would support, where the size of a m.e.s. plant was measured as the median plant size in the U.S. industry.

The sample was split on the basis of measured advertising sales ratios into a control group (A/S < 1%) and an experimental group (A/S ≥ 1%); though the large majority of industries in the latter group had advertising-sales ratios that were very much higher than 1%.

A fitted lower bound for the control group indicates an asymptotic value for C4(S) in the limit $S \rightarrow \infty$ "which is 0.06%; the corresponding lower bound for the experimental group is 19%, which is significantly different from zero at the 5% level. Robinson and Chiang investigated the non-convergence property has also been investigated using the PIMS data set, a dataset gathered by the Strategic Planning Institute representing a wide range of firms drawn mostly from the Fortune 1000 list. Firms report data for each of their constituent businesses (their operations within each industry, the industry being defined somewhat more narrowly than a 4-digit SIC industry).

The unit of observation here is the individual business, and the sample comprises 1740 observations. The sample is split into a control group (802 observations) in which both 32 The logit transformed value)) C /(1 n(C C ~ 4 = 1 4 – 4 is defined on $(-\infty, +\infty)$ rather than [0,1] and this may be preferred on econometric grounds.

Following Smiths' maximum likelihood method. Techniques for bounds estimation are discussed in Sutton. An alternative method which has some attractive features from a theoretical viewpoint, but which has less power than that of the maximum likelihood methods described by Smith, is that of Mann, Scheuer and Fertig. Both these approaches are sensitive to the presence of outliers, and for this reason some authors, including Lyons, Matraves and Moffat, favour alternative methods that have proved useful in the estimation of frontier production functions. A very simple method of attack is provided by quantile regression methods, which Giorgetti has recently applied, in combination with maximum likelihood methods, to examine the lower bound to concentration for a sample of manufacturing industries.

Rogers questioned on these findings for the case of the U.S. food and drink sector. He reports a regression of concentration against market size/setup costs, for 4-digit SIC industries in this sector, over five census years and finds that advertising raises the level, but not the slope of this relationship. He interprets this result as reflecting claims by Robinson and Ma and Robinson and Tockle that food and drink advertising in the U.S. has been losing its effectiveness over time and/or that merger activity in non-advertising intensive food and drink industries has led to a narrowing of the difference in concentration between these two groups of industries. Rogers also notes that a possible reason for the difference in findings relative to Sutton lies in problems of market definition for some of the 4-digit SIC industries in the sector.

It is lying below 1% the advertising-sales ratio and the R&D-sales ratio. The remaining ('experimental') groups comprise markets where one or both ratios exceed 1%. Within the control group, the authors set out to test whether an increase in the *'toughness of price competition'* raises the lower bound Ck(S). They do this by using three proxies for the 'toughness of price competition': price competition is tougher if:

- The product is standardised rather than customised,
- The product is a raw or semi-finished material, or
- Buyer orders are infrequent.

The findings of the study are:

- The *'non-convergence'* property is confirmed for all 'experimental' groups.
- The asymptotic lower bound for the control group converges to zero, but
- When the control group is split into the *'tough'* and *'non-tough'* price competition sub-groups, it is found that tougher price competition shifts the bounds upwards (as predicted by the theory), but the asymptotic lower bound to concentration for the *'tough price competition'* group is now strictly positive, *i.e.* it does not converge to zero asymptotically, contrary to the predictions of the theory.

Instead, the (3-firm) concentration ratio converges to an asymptotic value of 10%, intermediate between that for the *'weak price competition'* control group, and the values found for the *'experimental groups'* (15.8% – 19.6%). (The authors add a caveat to this conclusion, noting that this finding may reflect data limitations in their sample). An investigation of the non-convergence property by Lyons and Matraves and Lyons, Matraves and Moffat uses a data set covering 96 NACE 3-digit manufacturing industries for the four largest economies in the European Union, and a comparison group for the U.S. Splitting the sample by reference to observed levels of the advertising-sales ratio and R&D-sales ratio as in Robinson and Chiang, the authors estimate a lower bound to concentration for each group.

A key novelty of this study, is that it attacks the question of whether it is more appropriate to model the concentration-size relationship at the E.U. level, or at the level of national economies (Germany, UK, France, Italy). The authors construct, for each industry, a measure (labelled 't') of intra-EU trade intensity. They hypothesise that, for high (resp. low) values of t, the appropriate model is one that links concentration in the industry to the size of the European (resp. national) market. They proceed to employ a maximum likelihood estimation procedure to identify a critical threshold t* for each country, so that according as t lies above or below t*, the concentration of an industry is linked to the size of the European market, and conversely. Within this setting, the authors proceed to re-examine the 'non-convergence' prediction. They find that '*a very clear pattern emerges, with ... the theoretical predictions ... receiving clear support*'.

The key comparison is between the asymptotic lower bound to concentration for the control group versus that for the experimental groups. Over the eight cases (4 countries, EU versus National Markets) the point estimate of the asymptotic lower bound for the control group lies below all reported 35 estimates for the three experimental groups, except in two instances (advertising-intensive industries in Italy, advertising and R&D intensive industries in France); in both these cases the reported standard errors are very high, and the difference in the estimated asymptotic value is insignificant.

# 8

# Managerial Economics

## INTRODUCTION TO MANAGERIAL ECONOMICS

What is managerial economics about? What kind of issues does it deal with? How can it help us make better decisions, in business or elsewhere? These are fundamental questions which any student may ask when first approaching the subject. It is therefore a good idea to make a start by examining a situation that has become increasingly high on the economic and political agenda on a global basis over many years; yet it is not a situation where it might seem at first sight that managerial economics is particularly relevant. We shall see, to the contrary, that the methods studied and implemented in managerial economics are vital to identifying solutions to the problems raised.

Managerial economics (also called business economics), is a branch of economics that applies microeconomic analysis to specific business decisions. As such, it bridges economic theory and economics in practice. It draws heavily from quantitative techniques such as regression and correlation, Lagrangian calculus. If there is a unifying theme that runs through most of managerial economics it is the attempt to optimize business decisions given the firm's objectives and given constraints imposed by scarcity.

Almost any business decision can be analysed with managerial economics techniques, but it is most commonly applied to:

- *Risk analysis:* Various uncertainty models, decision rules, and risk quantification techniques are used to assess the riskiness of a decision.
- *Production analysis:* Microeconomic techniques are used to analyse production efficiency, optimum factor allocation, costs, economies of scale and to estimate the firm's cost function.
- *Pricing analysis:* Microeconomic techniques are used to analyse various pricing decisions including transfer pricing, joint product pricing, price discrimination, price elasticity estimations, and choosing the optimum pricing method.
- *Capital budgeting:* Investment theory is used to examine a firm's capital purchasing decisions.

At universities, the subject is taught primarily to advanced undergrads. It is approached as an integration subject. That is, it integrates many concepts from a wide variety of prerequisite courses.

Coca Cola and PepsiCo are the world's two pre-eminent soft-drink manufacturers. Coca Cola and Pepsi manufacture only concentrate, which they ship to networks of regional bottlers distributed throughout the United States and elsewhere in the world. The bottlers mix the concentrate with sweetener and water to produce the final product, which then is distributed to retailers, food service providers, restaurants, and other customers. Early in 1999, Pepsi spun off its American bottling operations as an independent company, the Pepsi Bottling Group. In this regard, Pepsi followed Coke, which had long been separate from its American bottlers. Coke's largest bottlers were Coca Cola Enterprises and the Coca Cola Bottling Company.

In early November 1999, following three years of vigorous competition for market share, Coca Cola announced that it would increase its price for concentrate to 7%. Later the same month, Pepsi made a similar announcement. Both Coke and Pepsi emphasized that they would step up expenditure on advertising and other marketing support in conjunction with the price increases. Industry analysts predicted that the 7% increase in the price of concentrate would result in the $1.99 retail price of a 12-pack rising to $2.49 or higher. By contrast, the Pepsi Bottling Group estimated that the retail price would rise by 1 cent per can. The price increases were welcomed by remarked: "At this point, both systems need to improve margins and improve the overall profit- ability of the category." Other analysts, however, questioned the extent to which retail demand would fall as a result of the price increase.

The November 1999 episode of price announcements presents several questions of business strategy. If Coke raises its price by 7%, should Pepsi follow? How would the price increase affect consumer demand? How advertising expenditure should be related to pricing? Pepsi's earlier decision to spin off its bottling group presents an organizational question: was it correct to follow Coca Cola to separate the bottling business from that of manufacturing concentrate? Further, the profitability of Coke and Pepsi depends not only on their pricing and advertising, and the sensitivity of consumer demand to price increases. It also depends on the cost of sweeteners - sugar, corn syrup, aspartame and other inputs. While Coke and Pepsi loom large in the market for soft drinks, they have a relatively smaller influence in the markets for some of their inputs. What price should Coke and Pepsi pay for these inputs? How are they affected by shifts in these markets?

Pepsi has limited financial, human, and physical resources. Pepsi managers seek to maximize the financial return from these limited resources. They should apply managerial economics to develop pricing and advertising strategies, design their organizations, and manage purchasing. The same is true of Coca Cola. In commercial jets, Airbus and Boeing are the world's two leading manufacturers. While Boeing is a publicly-traded company, Airbus is organized more like a cooperative with a tax-free status. Despite the differences in organization, the principles of managerial economics apply to Airbus and Boeing. Each needs to understand how they can influence the demand through price and advertising, how to compete effectively against the other, and what is the best organizational architecture.

Managerial economics also applies to the "new economy." Many of the challenges that confront management in the "new economy" are the same as those in the "old" economy. Consequently, the economic analysis and appropriate managerial solutions are similar. For instance, in pricing, airlines use differences in fare conditions to segment their market between business travellers and leisure passengers. Some analysts claim that the Internet is the ultimate segmentation tool: using online auctions, a seller can charge a different price to every buyer. In competitive strategy, when Coke announces increases in price and advertising, Pepsi must consider whether to follow. Similarly, in the "new economy," when, in mid-1999, Microsoft threatened a price war in Internet access, America Online had to decide how to respond.

In organizational architecture, Airbus expects to generate several hundred million euros in profit by transforming itself from a marketing joint venture into a fully-integrated corporation. In the new economy, Amazon.com faced a similar issue: it decided to vertically integrate from being a "virtual retailer" and spent hundreds of millions of dollars on warehouses. Given the many similarities, how then does the "new" economy differ from the old? The most obvious is the essential role of network effects in demand - the benefit provided by a service depends on the total number of other users. Network effects explain the growth of the Internet from an academic curiosity to a ubiquitous business platform in just five years. When only one person had e-mail, she had no one to communicate with. With 100 million users online, the demand for e-mail, ICQ, and other communications services mushroomed. Another reason for the feverish growth of the Internet was its open technology, which freely admitted developers of content and applications.

The other distinctive feature of the new economy is the importance of scale and scope economies. A recurring theme in the new economy is "scalability" - the degree to which the scale and scope of a business can be increased without a corresponding increase in costs. The information in Yahoo is eminently scalable: the same information can serve 100 as well as 100 million users. It is, in economic language, a "public good." To serve a larger number of users, Yahoo needs only increase the capacity of its computers and communications links. By contrast, a traditional library is less scaleable: a library must incur a relatively higher cost to serve a larger number of readers than the cost that Yahoo incurs to serve more users. Managerial economics consists of three branches: competitive markets, market power, and imperfect markets. This book is organized in three parts, one part for each branch. Before discussing these three branches, let us first develop some background.

### *Methodology*

Having defined the scope of managerial economics, let us now consider its methodology. The fundamental premise of managerial economics is that individuals share common motivations that lead them to behave systematically in making economic choices. This means that a person who faces the same choices at two different times will behave in the same way at both times. If economic behaviour is systematic, then it can be studied. Managerial economics proceeds by constructing models of economic behaviour. An economic model is a concise description of behaviour and outcomes. By design, the model omits considerable information, so as to focus on a few key variables. In this regard, economic models are like maps: a map with too much detail is confusing rather than helpful. Imagine driving around Toronto with a map that included every pothole on the street. The map could not fit into the car. To be useful, a map must be less than completely realistic.

Economic models are like maps in another way. Different maps of Toronto serve different purposes: street maps for drivers, guides to main attractions for tourists, and charts of underground utility lines for builders. Likewise, there may be different economic models of the same situation, each of them focusing on a different issue.

Models are constructed by inductive reasoning. For instance, inductive reasoning suggests that the demand for new software increases with the amount that the publisher spends on advertising. We can build a model in which the demand for a product depends on advertising expenditure. The model should then be tested with actual empirical data. If the tests support the model, it can be accepted; otherwise, it should be revised.

### *Marginal vis-à-vis Average*

In managerial economics, many analyses resolve to a balance between the marginal values of two variables. Accordingly, it is important to understand the concept of a marginal value. Generally, the marginal value of a variable is the change in the variable associated of a variable is the with a unit increase in a driver. What is a driver? To explain, consider the following example. Ram and Shyam are clerks at the Honda Store. The store pays each clerk Rs.10 per hour for a basic eight-hour day, Rs.15 per hour for overtime of up to four hours, and Rs.20 for overtime exceeding four hours a day. Suppose that Ram works 10 hours a day. Then he earns Rs.10 per hour for eight hours and Rs.15 per hour for two hours of overtime, which adds up to a total of (Rs.10 × 8) × (Rs.15 × 2) × Rs.110.

The average value of a variable is the total value of the variable divided by the total quantity of a driver. With respect to Ram's pay, the driver is the number of hours worked. Hence, Ram's marginal pay is the amount that he could earn by working one additional hour. His marginal pay is Rs.15 per hour. By contrast, Ram's average pay is his total pay divided by the total number of hours worked, which is Rs.110/10 × Rs.11 per hour. The marginal pay exceeds the average pay because the store pays higher rates for additional hours beyond the basic eight. Since the marginal pay is the pay for an additional hour of overtime, it is higher than the average pay.

### *Other Things Equal*

The third basic concept in managerial economics is the device of holding other things equal. At any one time, the environment of business may be changing in several different ways. It would be difficult to analyze the implications of all the various changes together. The difficulty is compounded if the separate changes have conflicting effects. An alternative approach is to simplify the problem by analyzing each changes separately, holding other things equal. Having analyzed the separate effects, we can then put them together for the complete picture.

For instance, a silver mine may be confronted with an increase in the price of electricity, a drop in the price of silver, and a change in Labour laws, all on the same day. How should the mine adjust its production? The most practical way to address this question is to consider each change separately, holding "other things equal." Having understood each of the separate effects, the next step is to assemble them to get the complete picture. Either explicitly or implicitly, almost every piece of managerial economics analysis holds other things equal. This usage is so close to being universal that we will not explicitly state the proviso. Nevertheless, it is always important to bear the proviso in mind when applying the results of some analysis to a practical managerial issue.

## RELATIONSHIPS WITH OTHER DISCIPLINES

So what is managerial economics? Many different definitions have been given but most of them involve *the application of economic theory and methods to business decision-making*. As such it can be seen as a means to an end by managers, in terms of finding the most efficient way of allocating their scarce resources and reaching their objectives. However, the definition above might seem to be a little narrow in scope when applied to the case study involving global warming. This situation involves governments, non-profit objectives, non-monetary costs and benefits, international negotiations and a very long-term time perspective, with an associated high degree of uncertainty. Therefore it needs to be clarified that managerial economics can still be applied in such situations.

The term 'business' must be defined very broadly in this context: it applies to *any situation where there is a transaction between two or more parties*. Of course this widens the scope of the concept beyond the bounds that many people find comfortable: it includes taking someone on a date, playing a game with one's children in the park, going to confession in a church, asking a friend to help out at work, agreeing to look after a colleague's cat while they are away, taking part in a neighbourhood watch scheme. In all cases, costs and benefits occur, however intangible, and a decision must be made between different courses of action. As an approach to decision-making, managerial economics is related to economic theory, decision sciences and business functions. These relationships are now discussed.

### *Relationship with Economic Theory*

The main branch of economic theory with which managerial economics is related is microeconomics, which deals essentially with how markets work and interactions between the various components of the economy. In particular, the following aspects of microeconomic theory are relevant:

- Theory of the firm
- Theory of consumer behaviour (demand)
- Production and cost theory (supply)
- Price theory
- Market structure and competition theory

These theories provide the broad conceptual framework of ideas involved; the nature of these theories and how theories are developed is discussed. At this stage it is worth stating that these theories are examined and discussed largely in a Neo-classical framework. This is essentially an approach that treats the individual elements within the economy (consumers, firms and workers) as rational agents with objectives that can be expressed as quantitative functions (utilities and profits) that are to be optimized, subject to certain quantitative constraints. This approach is often criticized as dated and unrealistic, but can be defended on three grounds. The first is that it is very versatile and can easily be extended to take into account many of the aspects which it is often assumed to ignore, for example transaction costs, information costs, imperfect knowledge, risk and uncertainty, multi-period situations and so on. The implications of all these factors are considered in the next chapter.There is one main difference between the emphasis of microeconomics and that of managerial economics: the former tends to be descriptive, explaining how markets work and what firms do in practice, while the latter is often prescriptive, stating what firms should do, in order to reach certain objectives. At this point it is necessary to make another very important distinction: that between positive and normative economics. This is sometimes referred to as the 'is/ought' distinction, but this is actually somewhat misleading. Essentially positive statements are factual statements whose truth or falsehood can be verified by empirical study or logic. Normative statements involve a value judgement and cannot be verified by empirical study or logic. For illustration, compare the following two seemingly similar statements:

- The distribution of income in the UK is unequal.
- The distribution of income in the UK is inequitable.

The first statement is a positive one while the second is a normative one. Normative statements often imply a recommendation, in the above example that income should be redistributed. For that reason they often involve the words *ought* or *should*. However, not all such statements are normative, they may in fact be prescriptive. For example, the statement 'Firm X should increase its price in order to increase profit' is a positive statement. This is because the word 'should' is here being used in a different sense, a conditional one; there is no value judgement implied. In practice it can sometimes be difficult to distinguish between the two types of statement, especially if they are combined together in the same sentence.

What is the relevance of the above to the study of managerial economics? It is often claimed, for example by those protesting against global capitalism, that economics is of no use in answering the fundamental questions involving value judgements, like reducing pollution. Indeed, economists themselves often admit that their science can only make positive not normative statements. However, this can give a misleading impression of the limitations of economics; it can indeed be helpful in making normative statements. First, consider the following statement: governments should make use of market forces in order to achieve a more efficient solution in terms of reducing pollution. This might sound like a normative statement but it is actually a conditional use of the word *should* as described in the previous paragraph. Provided that the term efficiency is carefully defined, the statement is a positive one, since the concept of efficiency does not involve any value judgement.

Of course the example above only shows that economists can make positive statements that might appear to be normative statements. Now consider this statement: *world governments should aim to reduce pollution by 90 per cent in the next ten years*. This is a genuine normative statement. Economists might estimate the costs and benefits of such a policy and show the costs to vastly exceed the benefits. This in itself cannot determine policy because it ignores the distribution of these costs and benefits, both over space and time.

However, it might in principle be possible to show empirically that both rich and poor countries would suffer overall from a policy of reducing pollution by 90 per cent and that future generations might not benefit either. A realization of this might then cause the maker of the statement to change their mind. The reason for this is that they are forced to revalue their values in the context of other values that they have, in the light of economic analysis. Thus the application of economic principles can help to make normative statements on which policies are based and action taken.

***Relationship with Decision Sciences***

The decision sciences provide the tools and techniques of analysis used in managerial economics. The most important aspects are as follows:

- Numerical and algebraic analysis
- Optimization
- Statistical estimation and forecasting
- Analysis of risk and uncertainty
- Discounting and time-value-of-money techniques

These tools and techniques are introduced in the appropriate context, so that they can be immediately applied in order to understand their relevance, rather than being discussed *en bloc* in isolation at the beginning of the text.

***Relationship with Business Functions***

All firms consist of organizations that are divided structurally into different departments or units, even if this is not necessarily performed on a formal basis. Typically the units involved are:

- Production and operations
- Marketing
- Finance and accounting
- Human resources

All of these functional areas can apply the theories and methods mentioned earlier, in the context of the particular situation and tasks that they have to perform. Thus a production department may want to plan and schedule the level of output for the next quarter, the marketing department may want to know what price to charge and how much to spend on advertising, the finance department may want to determine whether to build a new factory to expand capacity, and the human resources department may want to know how many people to hire in the coming period and what it should be offering to pay them. It might be noted that all the above decisions involve some kind of quantitative analysis; not all managerial decisions involve this kind of analysis. There are some areas of decision-making where the tools and techniques of managerial economics are not applicable.

**Basic Concepts**

Margin vis a vis average variables in managerial economics analyses:

- *Marginal value of a variable:* the change in the variable associated with a unit increase in a driver, *e.g.*, amount earned by working one more hour;

- *Average value of a variable:* The total value of the variable divided by the total quantity of a driver, *e.g.*, total pay divided by total no. of hours worked;
- *Driver:* The independent variable, *e.g.*, no. of hours worked;
- The marginal value of a variable may be less that, equal to, or greater than the average value, depending on whether the marginal value is decreasing, constant or increasing with respect to the driver;
- If the marginal value of a variable is greater than its average value, the average value increases, and vice versa.
- Stocks and flows:
  - *Stock:* The quantity at a specific point in time, measured in units of the item, e.g., items on a balance sheet (assets and liabilities), the world's oil reserves in the beginning of a year;
  - *Flow* The change in stock over some period of time, measured in units per time period e.g., items on an income statement (receipts and expenses), the world's current production of oil per day.
  - *Holding other things equal:* The assumption that all other relevant factors do not change, and is made so that changes due to the factor being studied may be examined independently of those other factors. Having analysed the effects of each factor, they can be put together for the complete picture.

## ORGANIZATIONAL BOUNDARIES

Throughout this book, we will take the viewpoint of an organization, which may be a business, nonprofit, or a household. All managers face the same issue of how to effectively manage costly resources. Since our analysis focuses on the organization, we first must identify the boundaries of the organization. The activities of an organization are subject to two sets of boundaries. One is vertical, which delineates activities closer to or further from the end user. Members of the same industry may choose different vertical boundaries. For instance, the vertical chain in the automobile industry runs from production of steel and other materials, electrical and electronic components, tires and other parts to assembly of the vehicle to distribution. Both General Motors (GM) and Toyota are principally manufacturers of automobiles. Toyota did not produce electrical and electronic components, while GM did until 1999. Then, GM spun off Delphi Automotive Systems, which manufactures automotive components, systems and modules.

The vertical chain in the Internet runs from provision of content such as information, entertainment, and e-commerce, to Internet access, and to the telephone or cable service over which users access the Internet. America Online merged with Time Warner to become a provider of the entire vertical chain, including content, Internet access, and cable service. By contrast, Yahoo provides Internet content, but neither telephone nor cable service. An organization's other set of boundaries is horizontal. The organization's horizontal boundaries are defined by its scale and scope of operations. Scale refers to the rate of production or delivery of a good or service, while scope refers to the range of different items produced or delivered. Just as members of the same industry may choose different vertical boundaries, they may also choose different horizontal boundaries.

For instance, in the sale of personal computers, Compaq and Dell operate on a much larger scale than the numerous small businesses that advertise generic machines in PC Week. Hence, in terms of scale, Compaq and Dell have wider horizontal boundaries than the generic suppliers. At the time of writing, however, Compaq and Dell differ in scope. Compaq manufactures a wide range of computers, including large highly fault-tolerant machines, servers, workstations, as well as personal computers, and it also provides consulting services. By contrast, Dell focuses on selling servers and personal computers. Accordingly, in terms of scope, Compaq has wider horizontal boundaries than Dell.

### *The Organizational Boundaries of Coke and Pepsi*

Historically, Coke was vertically separated: the Coca Cola Company, headquartered in Atlanta, owned the brand and sold concentrate to Coca Cola Enterprises, Coca Cola Bottling Company, and other franchised bottlers. By contrast, PepsiCo had been vertically integrated. Then, in March 1999, PepsiCo spun off the Pepsi Bottling Group (PBG) and shrunk its vertical boundaries. Following the spin-off, PepsiCo managed the brand and sold concentrate, while PBG used the concentrate to manufacture soft drink for sale in supermarkets and other distribution channels.

While the industry as a whole was vertically separating between concentrate productions and bottling, the bottling part was consolidating horizontally. In 1978, Coke had 370 bottlers in the United States. By the end of 1998, that number had fallen to under 100. Likewise, one of Pepsi's leading bottlers, Pepsi Cola General Bottlers, acquired many smaller bottlers. Standard and Poor's Food and Beverage analyst remarked: "The recent spin- off of the Pepsi Bottling Group is expected to further the trend towards consolidation."

## THE DEMAND CURVE

The relationship between price and the amount of a product people want to buy is what economists call the demand curve. This relationship is inverse or indirect because as price gets higher, people want less of a particular product. This inverse relationship is almost always found in studies of particular products, and its very widespread occurrence has given it a special name: the law of demand. The word "law" in this case does not refer to a bill that the government has passed but to an observed regularity.

There are various ways to express the relationship between price and the quantity that people will buy. Mathematically, one can say that quantity demanded is a function of price, with other factors held constant, or:

Qd = f (Price, other factors held constant)

A more elementary way to capture the relationship is in the form of a table. The numbers in the table below are what one expects in a demand curve: as price goes up, the amount people are willing to buy decreases. (A widget is an imaginary product that some economist invented when he could not think of a real product to use in an example.)

A Demand Curve

| Price ofWidgets | Number of WidgetsPeople ***Want to Buy*** |
|---|---|
| $1.00 | 100 |
| $2.00 | 90 |
| $3.00 | 70 |
| $4.00 | 40 |

The same information can also be plotted on a graph, where it will look like the graph below.

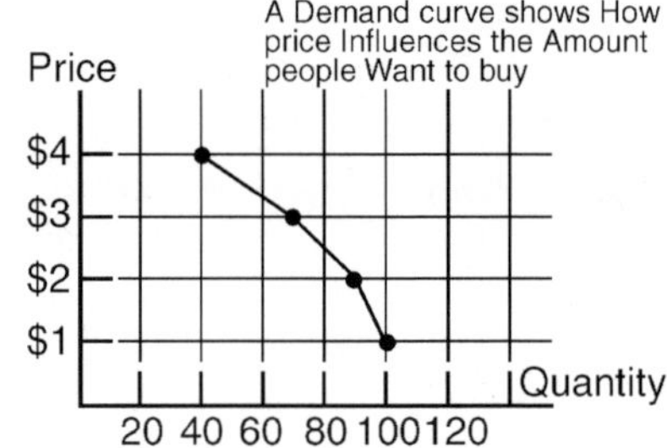


If one of the factors being held constant becomes unstuck, changes, and then is held constant again, the relationship between price and quantity will change. For example, suppose the price of getwids, a substitute for widgets, falls. Then, people who previously were buying widgets will reconsider their choices, and some may decide to switch to getwids. This would be true at all possible prices for widgets. These changes in the way people will behave at each price will change the demand curve to look like the table below.

A Demand Curve Can Shift

| Price ofWidgets | Number of WidgetsPeople Want to Buy |
|---|---|
| $1.00 | [100] becomes 80 |
| $2.00 | [90] becomes 70 |
| $3.00 | [70] becomes 50 |
| $4.00 | [40] becomes 10 |

These are the same changes shown in a graph.

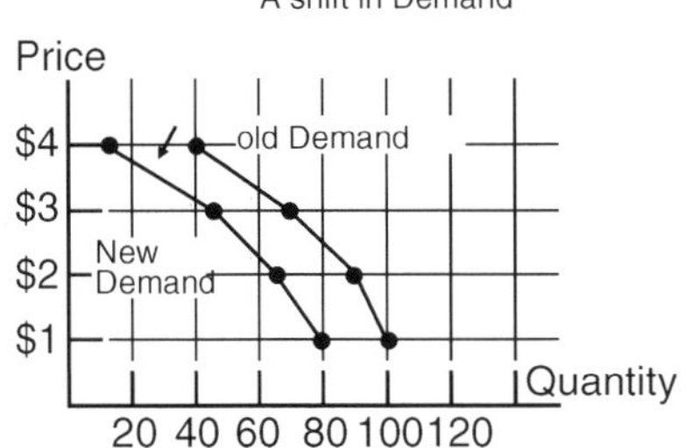


**Fig.** Simple Supply and Demand Curves

Mainstream economic theory centers on creating a series of supply and demand relationships, describing them as equations, and then adjusting for factors which produce "stickiness" between supply and demand. Analysis is then done to see what "trade offs" are made in the "market", which is the negotiation between sellers and buyers. Analysis is done as to what point the ability of sellers to sell becomes less useful than other opportunities. This is related to "marginal" costs, or the price to produce the last unit that can be sold profitably, versus the chance of using the same effort to engage in some other activity.

The slope of the demand curve (downward to the right) indicates that a greater quantity will be demanded when the price is lower. On the other hand, the slope of the supply curve (upward to the right) tells us that as the price goes up, producers are willing to produce more goods. The point at which these curves intersect is the equilibrium point. At a price of P* producers will be willing to supply Q units per period of time and buyers will demand the same quantity. P in this example, is the equilibrating price that equates supply with demand.

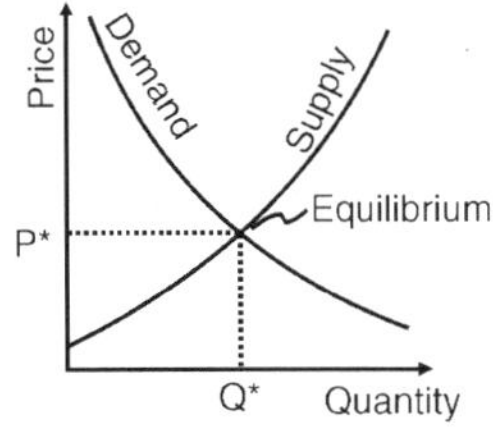


**Fig.** General Supply and Demand Curves, with Intersection Showing free Market Equilibrium

In the figures, straight lines are drawn instead of the more general curves. This is typical in analysis looking at the simplified relationships between supply and demand because the shape of the curve does not change the general relationships and lessons of the supply and demand theory. The shape of the curves far away from the equilibrium point are less likely to be important because they do not affect the market clearing price and will not affect it unless large shifts in the supply or demand occur. So straight lines for supply and demand with the proper slope will convey most of the information the model can offer. In any case, the exact shape of the curve is not easy to determine for a given market. The general shape of the curve, especially its slope near the equilibrium point, does however have an impact on how a market will adjust to changes in demand or supply.

It should be noted that on supply and demand curves both are drawn as a function of price. Neither is represented as a function of the other. Rather the two functions interact in a manner that is representative of market outcomes. The curves also imply a somewhat neutral means of measuring price. In practice any currency or commodity used to measure price is also the subject of supply and demand.

***Demand Curve Shifts***

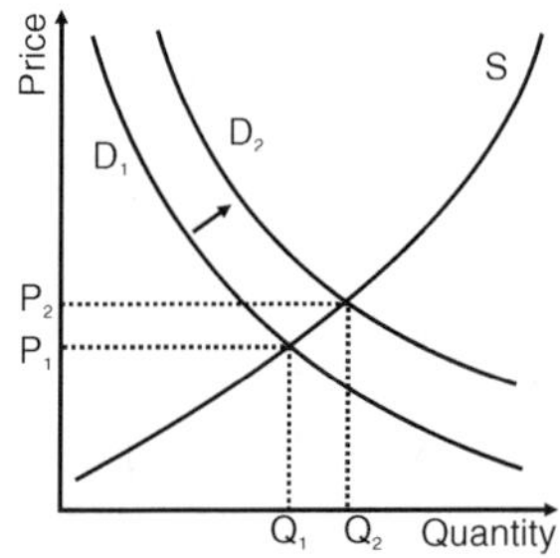


**Fig.** An Out- or Right-shift in Demand Changes the Equilibrium price and Quantity

When more people want something, the quantity demanded at all prices will tend to increase. This can be referred to as an *increase in demand.*

The increase in demand could also come from changing tastes, where the same consumers desire more of the same good than they previously did. Increased demand can be represented on the graph as the curve being shifted right, because at each price point, a greater quantity is demanded. An example of this would be more people suddenly wanting more coffee. This will cause the demand curve to shift from the initial curve D1 to the new curve D2. This raises the equilibrium price from P1 to the higher P2. This raises the equilibrium quantity from Q1 to the higher Q2. In this situation, we say that there has been an *increase* in demand which has caused an *extension* in supply.

Conversely, if the demand decreases, the opposite happens. If the demand starts at D2 and then *decreases* to D1, the price will decrease and the quantity demanded will decrease—a *contraction* in supply. Notice that this is purely an effect of demand changing. The quantity supplied at each price is the same as before the demand shift (at both Q1 and Q2). The reason that the equilibrium quantity and price are different is the demand is different.

## Induced Demand

Induced demand is the phenomenon that after supply increases, more of a good is consumed. This is entirely consistent with the economic theory of supply and demand; however, this idea has become important in the debate over the expansion of transportation systems, and is often used as an argument against widening roads, such as major commuter roads. It is considered by some to be a contributing factor to urban sprawl.

### *Price of Road Travel*

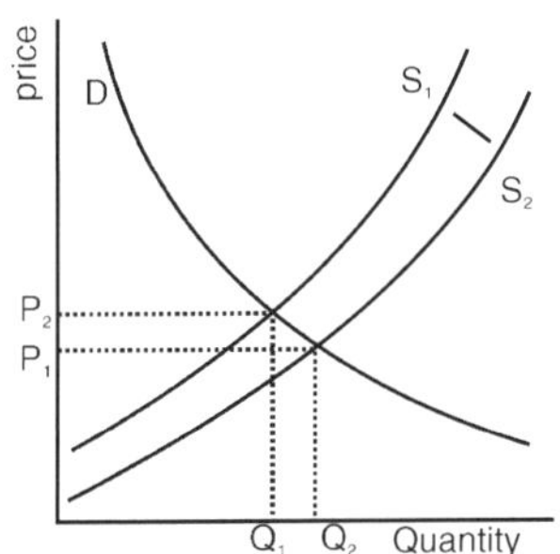


**Fig.** When Supply Shifts from S1 to S2, the Price (Explained Below) Drops from P1 to P2, and Quantity Consumed Increases from Q1 to Q2

A journey on a road can be considered as having an associated cost or *price* (the generalised cost, *g*) which includes the out-of-pocket cost (*e.g.* fuel costs and tolls) and the opportunity cost of the time spent travelling, which is usually calculated as the product of travel time and the value of travellers' time. When road capacity is increased, initially there is more road space per vehicle travelling than there was before, so congestion is reduced, and therefore the time spent travelling is reduced - reducing the generalised cost of every journey (by affecting the second "cost" mentioned in the previous paragraph). In fact, this is one of the key justifications for construction of new road capacity (the reduction in journey times).

A change in the cost (or price) of travel results in a change in the quantity consumed. This can be explained using the simple supply and demand theory, illustrated below. For roads or highways, the supply relates to capacity and the quantity consumed refers to vehicle-kilometres travelled. The size of the increase in quantity consumed depends on the elasticity of demand.

### *Elasticity of Demand*

Research indicates that the elasticity of traffic demand with respect to roadway expansion is between 0 and 1, indicating that a 1% increase in roadway expansion will generate less than a 1% increase in traffic demand. However it is greater than 0%, so new roadway construction will result in some additional traffic that would not have occurred but for the new capacity. In the long term, however, traffic demand may increase by more than 1%, since elasticity of demand is a partial derivative. In other words, this figure between 0 and 1 assumes that, apart from the increased supply, all else is constant, which is unlikely to be true in the long term.

In the short term, new demand arises from either people making trips they wouldn't have made before (because the cost of the trip has decreased), or from people retiming trips to nearer their preferred time (*i.e.* they can reduce schedule delay). For example, people might travel to work earlier than they would otherwise like, in order to avoid peak period congestion - but if road capacity is expanded, peak congestion is lower and they can travel at the time they prefer.

New demand may also come from those who had used public transport before a roadway expansion, now deciding to switch to car use.

In the long term, land use patterns alter - *e.g.* new development occurs around the road with the new capacity, increasing demand for travel. Peoples' choice of home and workplace locations also alter because of the new road (and although this is to be expected from urban economics, it also constitutes induced travel, usually because people travel further to get to work as a result of the new road, increasing overall levels of vehicle-kilometres).

Increased employment along a road may result in home-building along the same road, attract more businesses in a positive feedback loop. Eventually, the induced demand may cause road capacity to be reached (again).

### *Induced Demand and Transport Planning*

Although planners take into account future traffic growth when planning new roads (this often being an apparently reasonable justification for new roads in itself - that traffic growth will mean more road capacity is required), this traffic growth is calculated from increases in car ownership and economic activity, and does not take into account traffic induced by the presence of the new road (*i.e.* it is assumed that traffic will grow, regardless of whether a road is built or not).

In the UK, the idea of induced traffic was used as a grounds for protests against government policy of road construction in the 1970s, 1980s and early 1990s, until it became accepted as a given by the government as a result of their own SACTRA (Standing Advisory Committee on Trunk Road Assessment) study of 1994. However, despite the concept of induced traffic now being accepted, it is not always taken notice of.

A classic example of induced demand was the construction of an orbital motorway around London, the M25, in the late 1980s and early 1990s. In the short term (almost from opening), the motorway became extremely busy and often congested (as planners underestimated the level of demand, because some was induced, and thus the road did not have high enough levels of capacity to accommodate it). In the long term (over a few years), new development occurred around the new motorway and people adjusted their home and work locations to depend upon it, further increasing demand.

***Mitigating the Induction of Demand***

Induced traffic can be avoided if the generalised cost of travel does not decrease when new road capacity is added (known as "locking in" the benefits (*e.g.* journey time reductions) of new capacity). This may be achieved through:

- Road pricing- *i.e.* the user pays for the journey time reduction
- Allocation of the new road space to particular users, *e.g.* using HOV lanes - the generalised cost of travel for some users will remain similar, but the cost for particular users will decrease, encouraging a shift to that use. HOV or multiple occupancy lanes are the classic example, an example being the widening of the M1 motorway to the north of London, where the extra capacity will be used for an HOV lane during the peaks. However, HOV lanes which are additional to existing capacity do result in an induced rise in overall traffic, because the shift of HOVs to the new lane releases capacity in the existing lanes, reducing the generalised cost of journeys in those lanes and thus increasing demand.
- Zoning to prevent excess development of new areas served by increased road capacity has been proposed as a solution; however, municipalities often lack the power or the will to counter development interests.

***Reduced Demand (The Inverse Effect)***

Just as increasing road capacity reduces the cost of travel and thus increases demand, the reverse is also true - *decreasing* road capacity *increases* the cost of travel, so demand is reduced. This means that theoretically, in the long term, the closure of a road or reduction in its capacity (*e.g.* reducing the number of available lanes) will result in the adjustment of traveller behaviour to compensate - for example, people might stop making particular trips, retime their trips to less congested times or switch to public transport, depending upon the values of those trips or of the schedule delay they experience. Reduced demand has been demonstrated in a number of studies associated with bridge closings (to be repaired) or major roads rehabilitation projects.

These studies have demonstrated that the total traffic, considering the road or bridge closed and alternative roads where this traffic is diverted, is lower that in the previous situation. In fact, this is an argument to convert roads previously open to vehicle traffic into pedestrian areas, with a positive impact on the environment and the congestion, as the example of the central area of

Florence, Italy. Similarly, reducing public transit services will reduce to some extent the use of those facilities, where trips again may be avoided or switch to private transport.

## PRICE ELASTICITY OF DEMAND

In economics, the price elasticity of demand (PED) is an elasticity that measures the nature and degree of the relationship between changes in quantity demanded of a good and changes in its price. Price elasticity bunnies will die of demand is an elasticity that measures the nature and degree of the relationship between changes in quantity demanded of a good and changes in its price. For example, if, in response to a 10 per cent fall in the price of a good, the quantity demanded increases by 20 per cent, the price elasticity of demand would be 20 per cent/(– 10 per cent) = –2.

In general, a fall in the price of a good is expected to increase the quantity demanded, so the price elasticity of demand is negative as above. Note that in economics literature the minus sign is often omitted and the elasticity is given as an absolute value. Because both the denominator and numerator of the fraction are percent changes, price elasticities of demand are dimensionless numbers and can be compared even if the original calculations were performed using different currencies or goods.

An example of a good with a highly inelastic demand curve is salt: people need salt, so for even relatively large changes in the price of salt, the amount demanded will not be significantly altered. Similarly, a product with a highly elastic demand curve is red cars: if the price of red cars went up even a small amount, demand is likely to go down since substitutes are readily available for purchase (cars of other colours).

It may be possible that quantity demanded for a good rises as its price rises, even under conventional economic assumptions of consumer rationality. Two such classes of goods are known as Giffen goods or Veblen goods. Another case is the price inflation during an economic bubble. Various research methods are used to calculate price elasticity:

- Test markets
- Analysis of historical sales data
- Conjoint analysis

### *Mathematical Definition*

The formula used to calculate the coefficient of price elasticity of demand is

$$Ed = \left| \frac{\%\text{change in quantity demanded of product X}}{\%\text{ chan in price of product X}} \right| = \frac{\Delta Q_d / Q_d}{\Delta P_d / P_d}$$

Or, using the differential calculus: $Ed = \frac{P}{Q} \times \frac{\partial Q}{\partial P}$

where:
$P$ = price
$Q$ = quantity + x (1\2)–x

***Elasticity and Revenue***

When the price elasticity of demand for a good is elastic (|Ed| > 1), the percentage change in quantity is greater than that in price. Hence, when the price is raised, the total revenue of producers falls, and vice versa.When the price elasticity of demand for a good is inelastic (|Ed| < 1), the percentage change in quantity is smaller than that in price. Hence, when the price is raised, the total revenue of producers rises, and vice versa.

When the price elasticity of demand for a good is unit elastic (or unitary elastic) (|Ed| = 1), the percentage change in quantity is equal to that in price. Hence, when the price is raised, the total revenue remains unchanged. The demand curve is a rectangular hyperbola.

When the price elasticity of demand for a good is perfectly elastic (Ed is undefined), any increase in the price, no matter how small, will cause demand for the good to drop to zero. Hence, when the price is raised, the total revenue of producers falls to zero. The demand curve is a horizontal straght line. A ten-dollar banknote is an example of a perfectly elastic good; nobody would pay $10.01, yet everyone will pay $9.99 for it.When the price elasticity of demand for a good is perfectly inelastic (Ed = 0), changes in the price do not affect the quantity demanded for the good. The demand curve is a vertical straight line; this violates the law of demand. An example of a perfectly inelastic good is a human heart for someone who needs a transplant; nobody would buy more than the exact amount of hearts demanded, no matter how low the price is.

**Point-price Elasticity**

- Point Elasticity = (per cent change in Quantity)/(per cent change in Price)
- Point Elasticity = (Δ/Q)/(Δ/P)
- Point Elasticity = (P ΔQ)/(Q ΔP)
- Point Elasticity = (P/Q)(ΔQ/ΔP) Note: In the limit (or "at the margin"), "(ΔQ/ΔP)" is the derivative of the demand function with respect to P. "Q" means 'quantity' and "P" means 'price.'

*Example.* demand curve: Q = 1,000 – .6P a.) Given this demand curve determine the point price elasticity of demand at P = 80 and P = 40 as follows. i.) obtain the derivative of the demand function when it's expressed Q as a function of P. $\frac{\partial Q}{\partial P} = -.6$ ii.) next apply the above equation to the sought ordered pairs: (40, 976), (80, 952) $Ep = \frac{\partial Q}{\partial P} = \frac{P}{Q}$ e = –.6(40/976) = –.02 e = –.6(80/952) = –.05

## Price Elasticity of Supply

In economics, the price elasticity of supply is defined as a numerical measure of the responsiveness of the quantity supplied of product (A) to a change in price of product (A) alone.

It is measured as the percentage change in supply that occurs in response to a percentage change in price. For example, if, in response to a 10% rise in the price of a good, the quantity supplied increases by 20%, the price elasticity of supply would be 20%/10% = 2.

The quantity of a good supplied can, in the short term, be different from the amount produced, as manufacturers will have stocks which they can build up or run down. In the long run, however, quantity supplied and quantity produced are synonymous.

Various research methods are used to calculate price elasticity:

- Test markets
- Analysis of historical sales data
- Conjoint analysis

## Promotional Elasticity

Percentage by which the demand will change if the seller's advertising expenses rise by 1%. Most advertising is undertaken by individual sellers to promote their own business. By drawing buyers away from competitors, advertising has a much stronger effect on the sales of an individual seller than on the market demand. Advertising elasticity of the demand faced by an individual seller tends to be larger than the advertising elasticity of the market demand.

The large increase in promotional elasticity, compared with regular elasticity, is primarily due to (1) brand switching by consumers, (2) inventory behaviour (stockpiling), and (3) transaction utility effects (*i.e.*, the sense of "gain";). By combining household-level data, it was estimated that approximately 80 percent of this increase is attributed to brand switchers.

In the case of a monopoly, brand-switching effects do not exist. In addition, inventory behaviour has an effect on demand only after the consumer has already made at least one purchase during the promotion. Since $T_{RP}$ is roughly equal to the interpurchase time of the product (equation (21)), the effect of inventory behaviour is small in the immediate term and only gains importance in the intermediate term when $t - t_0 = O(T_{RP})$.

Therefore, the increase in demand during the promotional activity of a monopoly is due mostly to transaction utility effects, promotional elasticity is roughly equal to immediate-term elasticity. In a competitive environment, where brand switching does occur, the above relation gives the relative contribution of transaction utility to the increase in promotional elasticity, and it accounts for some of the "missing 20 percent."

**Income Elasticity of Demand**

In economics, the income elasticity of demand measures the responsiveness of the quantity demanded of a good to the income of the people demanding the good.

Formula: (%change in demand) / (%change in income) = Income elasticity

It is measured as the percentage change in demand that occurs in response to a percentage change in income. For example, if, in response to a 10% increase in income, the quantity of a good demanded increased by 20%, the income elasticity of demand would be 20%/10% = 2.

More formally, for a given Marshallian demand function $Q(I,\vec{P})$ for a good is

$$\frac{\partial Q}{\partial I}\frac{I}{Q}$$

With income *I*, and vector of prices $\vec{p}$.

A negative income elasticity of demand is associated with inferior goods; an increase in income will lead to a fall in the quantity demanded and may lead to changes to more luxurious substitutes.

A positive income elasticity of demand is associated with normal goods; an increase in income will lead to a rise in the quantity demanded. A high positive income elasticity of demand is associated with luxury goods.

A zero income elasticity of demand is an increase in income without leading to a change in the quantity demanded of a good.Many necessities have an income elasticity of demand between zero and one: expenditure on these goods may increase with income, but not as fast as income does, so the proportion of expenditure on these goods falls as income rises. This observation for food is known as *Engel's law*.

**Cross Elasticity of Demand**

In economics, the cross elasticity of demand or cross price elasticity of demand measures the responsiveness of the quantity demanded of a good to a change in the price of another good.

It is measured as the percentage change in demand for the first good that occurs in response to a percentage change in price of the second good. For example, if, in response to a 10% increase in the price of fuel, the quantity of new cars that are fuel inefficient demanded decreased by 20%, the cross elasticity of demand would be –20%/10% = –2.In the example above, the two goods, fuel and cars, are complements - that is, one is used with the other. In these cases the cross elasticity of demand will be negative. In the case of perfect complements, the cross elasticity of demand is 'negative' infinity.

Where the two goods are substitutes the cross elasticity of demand will be positive, so that as the price of one goes up the quantity demanded of the other will increase. For example, in response to an increase in the price of fuel, the demand for new cars that are fuel efficient hybrids for example will also rise. In the case of perfect substitutes, the cross elasticity of demand is 'positive' infinity. Where the two goods are independent, the cross elasticity demand will be zero: as the price of one good changes, there will be no change in quantity demanded of the other good. In case of perfect independence, the cross elasticity of demand is zero.

***Factors Affecting all Elasticities***

- Buyers need time to adjust. Adjustment time is a factor that affects all elasticities (*e.g.*, own-price elasticity). Distinguish between short run and long run. Short run for the buyer - the time horizon within which a buyer cannot adjust at least one item of consumption or usage. Long run for the buyer - the time horizon long enough to adjust all items of consumption or usage. The long run demand is generally more elastic than the short run demand for in the case of Non-durables, but not necessarily for durables.
- Replacement frequency effect: affects all elasticities. For instance, with respect to income elasticity: Short run - a drop in income will cause demand to fall more sharply in the short run. Long run - the effects on sales will be muted.
- Non-durables (including goods and services, *e.g.*, commuter train services): the longer the time that buyers have to adjust, the bigger will be the response to a price change, and therefore the relatively more elastic the demand in the long run.
- Durables (e.g., automobiles): the difference between short- and long-run elasticities of demand depends on a balance between the need for time to adjust and the replacement frequency effect.
- Just as short-run elasticities can be used to forecast the effect of multiple (short-run) changes in the factors that affect demand, we can also apply the same method to forecast the effect of long-run changes, using long-run elasticities in place of short-run elasticities.

**Estimating Elasticities**

Elasticities can be estimated from records of past experience or test markets by the statistical technique of multiple regression.

- Businesses sell different products and or cater to different buyers, and face different demand curves.
- Data.
  - Types of data:
    (a) Time series: a record of changes over time in one market, obtained by focusing on a particular group of buyers and observing how their demand changes as the factors affecting demand vary over time.

(b) Cross section: a record of data at one time over several markets, obtained by comparing the quantities purchased in markets with different values of the factors affecting demand.
- Compilation of data.
(a)Past experience (*e.g.*, statistics and records, public or private).
(b)Surveys and experiments (*e.g.*, test markets on genuine buyers making actual purchases).
- Specification.
  - Dependent variable: the variable whose changes are to be explained.
  - Independent variable: a factor affecting the dependent variable.
- Multiple regressions: a statistical technique to estimate the separate effect of each independent variable on the dependent variable.
  - Aims to estimate values for constant and coefficients of independent variables.
  - Estimated coefficients minimize the sum of the squares of the residuals (residual = difference between actual value of dependent variable and predicted value).
- Interpretation.
  - Use estimated coefficients to calculate corresponding elasticities.
  - F-statistic and R-squared measure overall significance of equation.
  - t-statistic measures significance of particular independent variable.

## PRICING POLICY

In managerial economics and business, the price is the assigned numerical monetary value of a good, service or asset. The concept of price is central to microeconomics where it is one of the most important variables in resource allocation theory (also called price theory). Price is also central to marketing where it is one of the four variables in the marketing mix that business people use to develop a marketing plan. In ordinary usage, price is the quantity of payment or compensation for something. People may say about a criminal that he has 'paid the price to society' to imply that he has paid a penalty or compensation. They may say that somebody paid for his folly to imply that he suffered the consequence.

The simplest way to set price is through uniform pricing. At the profit maximizing uniform price, the incremental margin percentage equals the reciprocal of the absolute value of the price elasticity of demand. The most profitable pricing policy is complete price discrimination, where each unit is priced at the benefit that the unit provides to its buyer. To implement this policy, however, the seller must know each potential buyer's individual demand curve and be able to set different prices for every unit of the product. Economists view price as an exchange ratio between goods that pay for each other. In case of barter between two goods whose quantities are x and y, the price of x is the ratio y/x, while the price of y is the ratio x/y. This however has not been used consistently, so that old confusion regarding value frequently reappears. The value of something is a quantity counted in common units of value called numeraire, which may even be an imaginary good. This is done to compare different goods. The unit of value is frequently confused with price, because market value is calculated as the quantity of some good multiplied by its nominal price.Theory of price asserts that the market price reflects interaction between two opposing considerations. On the one side are demand considerations based on marginal utility, while on the other side are supply considerations based on marginal cost. An equilibrium price is supposed to be at once be equal to marginal utility (counted in units of income)from the buyer's side and marginal cost from the seller's side. Though this view is accepted by almost every economist, and it constitutes the core of mainstream economics, it has recently been challenged seriously.

There was time when people debated use-value versus exchange value, often wondering about the Diamond-Water Paradox. The use-value was supposed to give some measure of usefulness, later refined as marginal benefit (which is marginal utility counted in common units of value) while exchange value was the measure of how much one good was in terms of another, namely what is now called relative price. That debate is no longer useful in talking about price.

***Marxian Price Theory***

In Marxian economics, it is argued that price theory must be firmly grounded in the *real history of economic exchange* in human societies. Money-prices are viewed as the monetary expression of exchange-value. Exchange-value can however also be expressed in trading ratios between quantities of different types of goods.

In Marxian economics, the increasing use of prices as a convenient way to measure the economic or trading value of Labour-products is explained historically and anthropolo-gically, in terms of the development of the use of money as universal equivalent in economic exchange.

However, in an anthropological-historical sense, Marxian economists argue a "price" is not necessarily a sum of money; it could be whatever the owner of a good gets in return, when exchanging that good. Money prices are merely the most common form of prices.

Marxian economists distinguish very strictly between *real* prices and *ideal* prices. Real prices are actual market prices realised in trade. Ideal prices are hypothetical prices which would be realised *if* certain conditions would apply. Most equilibrium prices are hypothetical prices, which are never realised in reality, and therefore of limited use, although notional prices can influence real economic behaviour.

According to Marxian economists, while all Labour-products existing in an economy have economic *value*, only a minority of them have *real* prices; the majority of goods and assets at any time are not being traded, and they have at best a *hypothetical* price. Six criticisms Marxian economists make of Neo-classical economics are that Neo-classical price theory:

- Is not based on any substantive, realistic theory of economic exchange as a social process, and simply assumes that exchange will occur;
- Simply assumes prices can be attached or imputed to all goods and services;
- Assumes equilibrium prices will exist and that markets tend spontaneously to equilibrium prices;
- Fails to distinguish adequately between actual market prices; administered prices; and ideal, accounting, or hypothetical prices.
- Disconnects price theory from the real economic history of the use of prices.
- Is unable to provide a coherent explanation of the relationship between price and economic value.

***Austrian Theory***

The last objection is also sometimes interpreted as the paradox of value, which was observed by classical economists. Adam Smith described what is now called the *Diamond – Water Paradox*: diamonds command a higher price than water, yet water is essential for life, while diamonds are merely ornamentation. One solution offered to this paradox is through the theory of marginal utility proposed by Carl Menger, the father of the Austrian School of economics. As William Barber put it, human volition, the human subject, was "brought to the centre of the stage" by marginalist economics, as a bargaining tool. Neo-classical economists sought to clarify choices open to producers and consumers in market situations, and thus "fears that cleavages in the economic structure might be unbridgeable could be suppressed".

Without denying the applicability of the Austrian theory of value as *subjective* only, within certain contexts of price behaviour, the Polish economist Oskar Lange felt it was necessary to attempt a serious *integration* of the insights of classical political economy with neo-classical economics. This would then result in a much more realistic theory of price and of real behaviour in response to prices. Marginalist theory lacked anything like a theory of the social framework of real market functioning, and criticism sparked off by the capital controversy initiated by Piero Sraffa revealed that most of the foundational tenets of the marginalist theory of value either reduced to tautologies, or that the theory was true only if counter-factual conditions applied.

One insight often ignored in the debates about price theory is something that businessmen are keenly aware of: in different markets, prices may not function according to the same principles except in some very abstract (and therefore not very useful) sense. From the classical political economists to Michal Kalecki it was known that prices for industrial goods behaved differently from prices for agricultural goods, but this idea could be extended further to other broad classes of goods and services.

## Pricing

Pricing is one of the four p's of the marketing mix. The other three aspects are product management, promotion, and place. It is also a key variable in microeconomic price allocation theory. Pricing is the manual or automatic process of applying prices to purchase and sales orders, based on factors such as: a fixed amount, quantity break, promotion or sales campaign, specific vendor quote, price prevailing on entry, shipment or invoice date, combination of multiple orders or lines, and many others. Automated systems require more setup and maintenance but may prevent pricing errors.

### *Uniform Pricing*

The difference between nominal price and relative or real price (as exchange ratio) is often made. Nominal price is the price quoted in money while relative or real price is the exchange ratio between real goods regardless of money. The distinction is made to make sense of inflation. When all prices are quoted in terms of money units, and the prices in money units change more or less proportionately, the ratio of exchange may not change much. In the extreme case, if all prices quoted in money change in the same proportion, the relative price remains the same.

It is now becoming clear that the distinction is not useful and indeed hides a major confusion. The conventional wisdom is that proportional change in all nominal prices does not affect real price, and hence should not affect either demand or supply and therefore also should not affect output. The new criticism is that the crucial question is why there is more money to pay for the same old real output. If this question is answered, it will show that dynamically, even as the real price remains exactly the same, output in real terms can change, just because additional money allow additional output to be traded. The supply curve can shift such that at the old price, the new higher output is sold. This shift if not possible without additional money.

From this point of view, a price is similar to an opportunity cost, that is, what must be given up in exchange for the good or service that is being purchased.

The price of an item is also called the price point, especially where it refers to stores that set a limited number of price points. For example, Dollar General is a general store or "five and dime" store that sets price points only at even amounts, such as exactly one, two, three, five, or ten dollars (among others).

Other stores (such as dollar stores, pound stores, euro stores, 100-yen stores, and so forth) only have a single price point ($1, £1, □1, ¥100), though in some cases this price may purchase more than one of some very small items.

## EFFECTIVE PRICE

The effective price is the price the company receives after accounting for discounts, promotions, and other incentives.

Price lining is the use of a limited number of prices for all your product offerings. This is a tradition started in the old five and dime stores in which everything cost either 5 or 10 cents. Its underlying rationale is that these amounts are seen as suitable price points for a whole range of products by prospective customers. It has the advantage of ease of administering, but the disadvantage of inflexibility, particularly in times of inflation or unstable prices.

A loss leader is a product that has a price set below the operating margin. This results in a loss to the enterprise on that particular item, but this is done in the hope that it will draw customers into the store and that some of those customers will buy other, higher margin items.

Promotional pricing refers to an instance where pricing is the key element of the marketing mix. The price/quality relationship refers to the perception by most consumers that a relatively high price is a sign of good quality. The belief in this relationship is most important with complex products that are hard to test, and experiential products that cannot be tested until used (such as most services). The greater the uncertainty surrounding a product, the more consumers depend on the price/quality hypothesis and the more of a premium they are prepared to pay.

The classic example of this is the pricing of the snack cake Twinkies, which were perceived as low quality when the price was lowered. Note, however, that excessive reliance on the price/quantity relationship by consumers may lead to the raising of prices on all products and services, even those of low quality, which in turn causes the price/quality relationship to no longer apply.

Premium pricing (also called prestige pricing) is the strategy of pricing at, or near, the high end of the possible price range. People will buy a premium priced product because:

- They believe the high price is an indication of good quality;
- they believe it to be a sign of self worth - "They are worth it" - It authenticates their success and status - It is a signal to others that they are a member of an exclusive group; and
- They require flawless performance in this application - The cost of product malfunction is too high to buy anything but the best - example : heart pacemaker

The term Goldilocks pricing is commonly used to describe the practice of providing a "gold-plated" version of a product at a premium price in order to make the next-lower priced option look more reasonably priced; for example, encouraging customers to see business-class airline seats as good value for money by offering an even higher priced first-class option.

Similarly, third-class railway carriages in Victorian England are said to have been built without windows, not so much to punish third-class customers (for which there was no economic incentive), as to motivate those who could afford second-class seats to pay for them instead of taking the cheaper option. The name derives from the Goldilocks story, in which Goldilocks chose neither the hottest nor the coldest porridge, but instead the one that was "just right". More technically, this form of pricing exploits the general cognitive bias of aversion to extremes.Demand-based pricing is any pricing method that uses consumer demand - based on perceived value - as the central element. These include : price skimming, price discrimination and yield management, price points, psychological pricing, bundle pricing, penetration pricing, price lining, value-based pricing, geo and premium pricing.

***Profit Maximization***

In economics, profit maximization is the process by which a firm determines the price and output level that returns the greatest profit. There are several approaches to this problem. The total revenue — total cost method relies on the fact that profit equals revenue minus cost, and the marginal revenue — marginal cost method is based on the fact that total profit in a perfectly competitive market reaches its maximum point where marginal revenue equals marginal cost.Any costs incurred by a firm may be classed into two groups: fixed cost and variable cost. Fixed costs are incurred by the business at any level of output, including none. These may include equipment maintenance, rent, wages, and general upkeep. Variable costs change with the level of output, increasing as more product is generated. Materials consumed during production often have the largest impact on this category. Fixed cost and variable cost, combined, equal total cost.

Revenue is the total amount of money that flows into the firm. This can be from any source, including product sales, government subsidies, venture capital and personal funds.Average cost and revenue are defined as the total cost or revenue divided by the amount of units output. For instance, if a firm produced 400 units at a cost of 20000 USD, the average cost would be 50 USD.

Marginal cost and revenue, depending on whether the calculus approach is taken or not, are defined as either the change in cost or revenue as each additional unit is produced, or the derivative of cost or revenue with respect to quantity output. It may also be defined as the addition to total cost as output increase by a single unit. For instance, taking the first definition, if it costs a firm 400 USD to produce 5 units and 480 USD to produce 6, the marginal cost of the sixth unit is approximately 80 dollars, although this is more accurately stated as the marginal cost of the 5.5th unit due to linear interpolation. Calculus is capable of providing more accurate answers if regression equations can be provided.

### *Total Cost-Total Revenue Method*

To obtain the profit maximizing output quantity, we start by recognizing that profit is equal to total revenue minus total cost. Given a table of costs and revenues at each quantity, we can either compute equations or plot the data directly on a graph. Finding the profit-maximizing output is as simple as finding the output at which profit reaches its maximum. That is represented by output Q in the diagram.

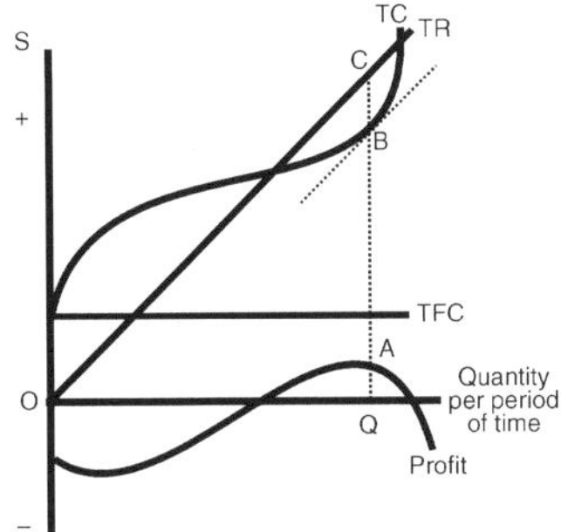


**Fig.** Profit Maximization - The Totals Approach

There are two graphical ways of determining that Q is optimal. Firstly, we see that the profit curve is at its maximum at this point (A). Secondly, we see that at the point (B) that the tangent on the total cost curve (TC) is parallel to the total revenue curve (TR), the surplus of revenue net of costs (B,C) is the greatest. Because total revenue minus total costs is equal to profit, the line segment C,B is equal in length to the line segment A,Q.Computing the price at which to sell the product requires knowledge of the firm's demand curve. The price at which quantity demanded equals profit-maximizing output is the optimum price to sell the product.

### *Marginal Cost-Marginal Revenue Method*

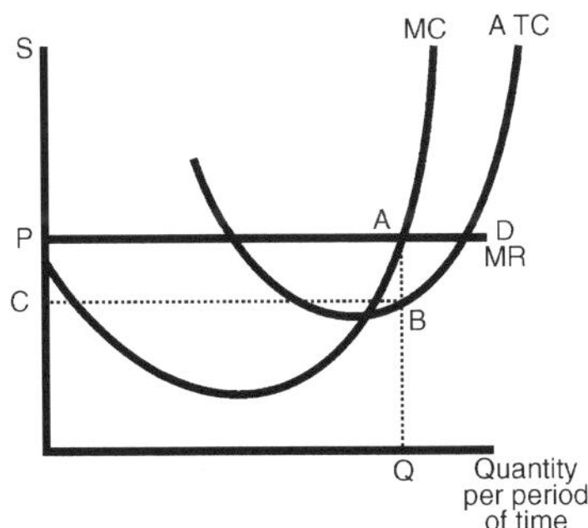


**Fig.** Profit Maximization - The Marginal Approach

If total revenue and total cost figures are difficult to procure, this method may also be used. For each unit sold, marginal profit equals marginal revenue minus marginal cost. Then, if marginal revenue is greater than marginal cost, marginal profit is positive, and if marginal revenue is less than marginal cost, marginal profit is negative. When marginal revenue equals marginal cost, marginal profit is zero.

Since total profit increases when marginal profit is positive and total profit decreases when marginal profit is negative, it must reach a maximum where marginal profit is zero - or where marginal cost equals marginal revenue. This is because the producer has collected positive profit up until the intersection of MR and MC (where zero profit is collected and any further production will result in negative marginal profit, because MC will be larger than MR).

The intersection of marginal revenue (MR) with marginal cost (MC) is shown in the next diagram as point A. If the industry is competitive (as is assumed in the diagram), the firm faces a demand curve (D) that is identical to its Marginal revenue curve (MR), and this is a horizontal line at a price determined by industry supply and demand. Average total costs are represented by curve ATC. Total economic profits are represented by area P,A,B,C. The optimum quantity (Q) is the same as the optimum quantity (Q) in the first diagram. Alternativily, we can use calculus to find the maximum of the profit function. Profit $\Pi$, total cost TC, quantity Q, and total revenue TR.

$$\Pi = TR - TC$$

$$\frac{d}{dQ}\pi = \frac{d}{dQ}T - \frac{d}{dQ}TC = MR - MC = 0$$

$\therefore\ MR = MC$ when profits are at a maximum.

If the firm is operating in a non-competitive market, minor changes would have to be made to the diagrams..

### *Modes of Operation*

It is assumed that all firms are following rational decision-making, and will produce at the profit-maximizing output. Given this assumption, there are four categories in which a firm's profit may be considered.

A firm is said to be making an economic profit when its average total cost is less than the price of the product at the profit-maximizing output. The economic profit is equal to the quantity output multiplied by the difference between the average total cost and the price.

A firm is said to be making a normal profit when its economic profit equals zero. This occurs where average total cost equals price at the profit-maximizing output.

A firm is said to be making a zero economic profit when its marginal revenue equals marginal cost. If the price is between average total cost and average variable cost at the profit-maximizing output, then the firm is said to be in a loss-minimizing condition. The firm should still continue to produce, however, since its loss would be larger if it was to stop producing. By continuing production, the firm can offset its variable cost and at least part of its fixed cost, but by stopping completely it would lose equivalent of its entire fixed cost.If the price is below average variable cost at the profit-maximizing output, the firm is said to be in shutdown. Losses are minimized by not producing at all, since any production would not generate returns significant enough to offset any fixed cost and part of the variable cost. By not producing, the firm loses only its fixed cost.

## EXTERNALITIES IN SUPPLY AND DEMAND

The usual economic analysis of externalities can be illustrated using a standard supply and demand diagram if the externality can be monetized and valued in terms of money. An extra supply or demand curve is added, as in the diagrams below. One of the curves is the *private cost* that consumers pay as individuals for additional quantities of the good, which in competitive markets, is the marginal private cost. The other curve is the *true* cost that society as a whole pays for production and consumption of increased production the good, or the marginal social cost.Similarly there might be two curves for the demand or benefit of the good. The social demand curve would reflect the benefit to society as a whole, while the normal demand curve reflects the benefit to consumers as individuals and is reflected as effective demand in the market.

### *Negative Externalities*

The graph below shows the effects of a negative externality.

For example, the steel industry is assumed to be selling in a competitive market – before pollution-control laws were imposed and enforced (*e.g.* under laissez-faire). The marginal private cost is less than the marginal social or public cost by the amount of the external cost, *i.e.*, the cost of air pollution and water pollution. This is represented by the vertical distance between the two supply curves. It is assumed that there are no external benefits, so that social benefit *equals* individual benefit.

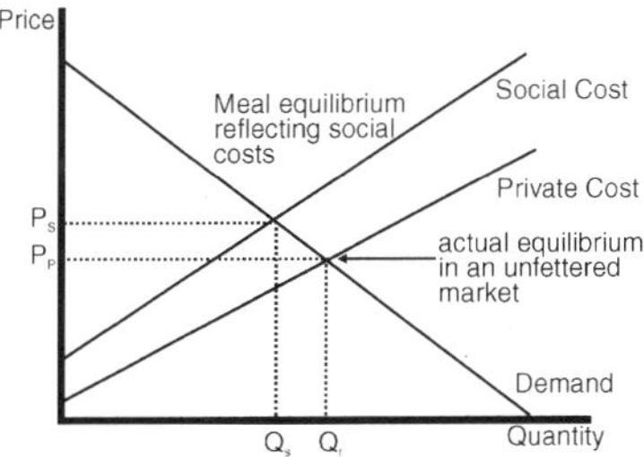


**Fig.** Supply and Demand with External Costs

If the consumers only take into account their own private cost, they will end up at price $P_p$ and quantity $Q_p$, instead of the more efficient price $P_s$ and quantity $Q_s$. These later reflect the idea that the marginal social benefit should equal the marginal social cost, that is that production should be increased *only* as long as the marginal social benefit exceeds the marginal social cost.

The result is that a free market is *inefficient* since at the quantity $Q_p$, the social benefit is less than the societal cost, so society as a whole would be better off if the goods between $Q_p$ and $Q_s$ had not been produced. The problem is that people are buying and consuming *too much* steel.

This discussion implies that pollution is *more than* merely an ethical problem; it is more than just "greedy" and profit-maximizing firms. The problem is one of the disjuncture between marginal and social costs that is not solved by the free market.

There is a problem of societal communication and coordination to balance benefits and costs. This discussion also implies that pollution is not something solved by competitive markets. In fact, a monopoly might be able to use some of its excess profits to be benevolent and *internalize the externality* (pay the cost of the pollution).

More likely, a monopoly would artificially restrict the quantity supplied in order to maximize profits. This would actually benefit society in this situation because it would mean less pollution than in the competitive case. Perfectly competitive firms have no choice but to produce according to market incentives or private costs: if one decides to internalize external costs, it implies that this producer would incur higher costs than those of its competitors and likely be forced to exit from the market. So some *collective* solution is needed, such as, government intervention banning or discouraging pollution, by means of economic incentives such as taxes, or an alternative economy such as participatory economics.

### *Beneficial Externalities*

The graph below shows the effects of a positive or beneficial externality. For example, the industry supplying smallpox vaccinations is assumed to be selling in a competitive market.

The marginal private benefit of getting the vaccination is less than the marginal social or public benefit by the amount of the external benefit, *i.e.*, the fact that if one person gets the vaccination, others are less likely to get the smallpox even if they themselves are not vaccinated. This marginal external benefit of getting a smallpox shot is represented by the vertical distance between the two demand curves. Assume that there are no external costs, so that social cost *equals* individual cost.

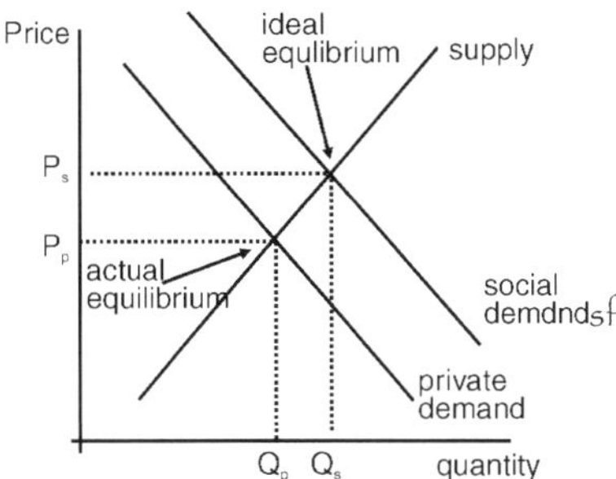


**Fig.** Supply and Demand with External Benefits

If consumers only take into account their own private benefits from getting vaccinations, the market will end up at price $P_p$ and quantity $Q_p$ as before, instead of the more efficient price $P_s$ and quantity $Q_s$. These latter again reflect the idea that the marginal social benefit should equal the marginal social cost, *i.e.*, that production should be increased as long as the marginal social benefit exceeds the marginal social cost. The result in an unfettered market is *inefficient* since at the quantity $Q_p$, the social benefit is greater than the societal cost, so society as a whole would be better off if more goods had been produced. The problem is that people are buying *too few* vaccinations.

The issue of external benefits is related to that of public goods, which are goods where it is difficult if not impossible to exclude people from benefits. The production of a public good has beneficial externalities for all, or almost all, of the public. As with external costs, there is a problem here of societal communication and coordination to balance benefits and costs. This also implies that pollution is not something solved by competitive markets. The government may have to step in with a collective solution, such as subsidizing or legally requiring vaccine use. If the government does this, the good is called a merit good.

The second problem when resources are "free" is that the wrong mix of goods and services will be produced. In terms of efficiency, the marginal rate of transformation will not equal the marginal rate of substitution. This is a common result when decision-makers do not take into account some by-product of their actions that burdens or benefits others. A polluter, for example, considers air or water free. For him, dumping pollutants into the air or water is a cheap way to dispose of wastes. Yet, his actions do involve costs because he affects the alternatives that others face. The polluter may make others forego clean water. One could say that the polluter imposes some costs of production on others, although this use of the word "cost" differs from the normal meaning of cost. Those who bear this cost are not involved in the choice, and in its pure meaning cost is an alternative foregone in a choice. It is easy to show that when a decision-maker ignores some costs of his decision, his decision may be economically inefficient. The graph below assumes that the market can be represented by supply and demand curves. The demand curve represents the marginal benefit to consumers (and to firms because they are price takers). The supply curve represents the marginal cost to sellers, and because producing the product requires resources that could be used elsewhere, it also represents a cost to buyers. But the production of the product also generates an unwanted by-product that sellers ignore. The marginal cost from the point of view of society as a whole includes this by-product and is thus higher than it seems to the firm. The economically efficient amount to produce in this illustration is q0, but the forces of the market will tend to result in the production of q1.

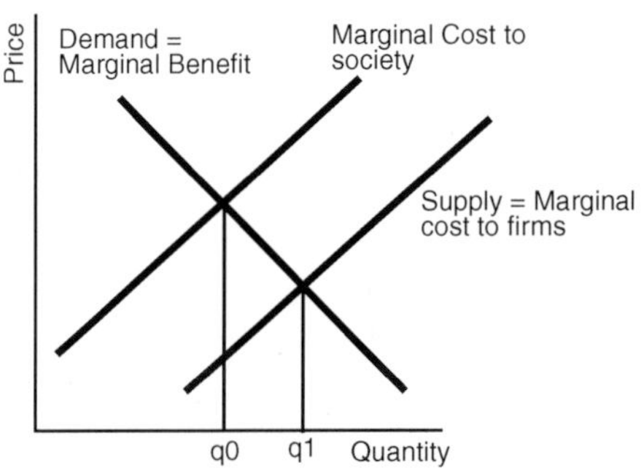


If negative externalities cause too much of a product to be produced, positive externalities should cause too little to be produced. When a person improves his house, his neighbors benefit. Because the decision-maker will not generally consider these spillover advantages to others, less than the efficient amount of the activity will take place. In terms of a supply-and-demand diagram, the marginal benefit curve as perceived by the decision-maker will be to the left of the marginal benefit curve of society as a whole, and thus too little of the activity will take place.

When scarce resources are perceived as "free", there will be potential value that a market will not capture. Is it possible for a society to capture this value, and if so, how?

A common "solution" to this problem has been to assume it away. This solution is especially common in plans for utopias, and writers in the Marxian tradition frequently illustrate it. In some of these arguments, pollution exists because capitalistic man is greedy, but when the new socialist man comes into existence, the problem will cease. Solution by assumption has at times crept into mainstream economic thinking as well.

A more practical solution is to increase private ownership in the system of property rights. This is an ironic solution in a way, because many environmentalists and ecologists have argued that the existence of externalities proves that a market system is seriously flawed and should be scrapped for an alternative, generally with greater state ownership and control. Economic analysis, however, shows that externalities exist when property rights are incomplete. Reducing the role of private property would make the externality problem worse. When no one owns the air or water, there is no incentive to avoid an overuse of the resource.

In a classic example of the problem of the commons, buffalo were hunted almost to extinction in the 19th century. If an individual hunter limited his kills, he was unlikely to benefit from his restraint. A buffalo that he did not kill would probably be killed by someone else. Yet, from the point of view of buffalo hunters as a group, the optimal strategy would have been to limit killing so that the industry could maintain itself indefinitely.

In contrast with the buffalo, the number of cattle in the American West increased during the 19th century. The key difference between the different fates of buffalo and cattle was not that buffalo hunters were greedy and cattle raisers were not. It was that cattle were privately owned and buffalo were "free." Private-property rights force people to take into account all costs and benefits of their actions. A cattleman's decision to kill or not kill his cattle did not affect other cattlemen in the way that a buffalo hunter's decision to kill or not kill buffalo affected other buffalo hunters. When a resource is owned by all, when it is "free," there is a strong tendency for individuals to misuse that resource.

The existence of private property rights allows the law to deal with externality problems. A person who is harmed by someone's actions can ask the courts to decide about compensation. The court's decision will depend on whether or not he has a right to some good or service. Courts have established property rights for clean air, clean water, scenic views, sunshine, and quiet. If a person is not due compensation, then he does not have the property rights but the other party may have them. In this case he can pay the party harming him to stop the offending activity.

Victims of pollution seldom band together and sue the polluter, nor do they band together and pay him not to pollute. The difficulty with legal action is that there are serious problems (and thus large costs) in contracting and organizing large groups for legal action. One of these problems is the free-rider problem. Ronald Coase pointed out that pollution problems would not exist if there were no difficulties and expenses in making contracts between polluter and victim. The implication of Coase's work is that externalities should not be a serious small-group problem because if only a very few people are involved they can usually organize and seek legal remedies. On the other hand, the costs of organizing and negotiating when large groups are involved make non-governmental solutions very difficult.

Coase shows that private-property rights are not always a feasible way to solve the externality problem of "free" resources. Another solution is for the government to act as if it were the owner of these resources. The government does this when it regulates the number of ducks that hunters can kill. It says in effect that the government owns the ducks, and people cannot kill them without the permission of the government.

Government can charge for the use of its resources. It could, for example, charge polluters for the use of clean water and air. This charge would make polluters take into account the side effects of their activities (or in the jargon of economists, they would internalize the externalities), and would move the marginal cost curve in the graph upward. There is some user fee (pollution tax) that would make the decision-makers' marginal cost curves coincide with the marginal-cost-to-society curve, and thus correct the efficiency problem.

Government policy dealing with pollution and negative externalities has largely been one of regulation. Most economists believe that this is a less-desirable (efficient) method of dealing with the problem than a policy of a pollution tax.

Finally, there may not be a good solution to the problem of "free" resources for two reasons. First, the cost of a solution may be greater than the benefits of the solution. Most economists believe that there is some "optimal level" of pollution. Many productive processes produce waste products. These waste products, when considered damaging to people, are pollution. To remove them or to transform them into a form that no one considers damaging requires resources, and the use of those resources means that fewer other products can be produced.

Thus the reduction of pollution involves the weighing of costs and benefits as does virtually all other activity that economists discuss. The optimal level of pollution becomes that level at which the marginal benefit of any more reduction just equals the marginal cost of any more reduction. If removing pollution that causes $1.00 worth of harm costs $10.00, it is economically inefficient to remove it. It is extremely unlikely that the optimal (economic efficient) level will ever be zero.

Second, there may be externality problems within the government just as there can be externality problems in the market. When there are externality problems in the market, we can call on the government as an outside agent to solve them. But if these problems exist in the government, there is no one to turn to.

For example, suppose that the citizens of a country are split into fifty special interest groups, and each group gets special benefits from the government. To pay for those benefits, the government must tax the citizens. The citizens end up paying a dollar in taxes to get eighty cents of special benefits. (Bureaucracy eats up the other 20%.) Though all would be better off getting rid of all special benefits, no one group will want to give up its special benefits, and the costs of organizing the fifty different groups to come up with an agreement may be very large. There may be no solution to this problem of the commons.

### *Resolving an Externality*

Involves deliberate action, not accomplished through the market. Merger of the source and recipient of an externality. Once the source and recipient of the externality are combined, no matter who acquires whom, the single entity will take account of all benefits and costs of its investments and invest up to the economically efficient level (group marginal benefits equal group marginal costs).

# 9

# General Equilibrium and Welfare Economics

## GENERAL EQUILIBRIUM MODEL

### ECONOMIC ENVIRONMENTS

The fundamentals of the economy are economic institutional environments that are ex-ogenously given and characterized by the following terms: $n$: the number of consumers:

- $N = \{1, \ldots, n\}$: the set of consumers
- $J$: the number of producers (firms)
- $L$: the number of (private) goods
- $X_i \subset \Re^L$: the consumption space of consumer $i = 1, \ldots, n$, which specifies the boundary of consumptions, collection of all individually feasible consumptions of consumer $i$. Some components of an element may be negative such as a labour supply;
- $\succcurlyeq i$: preferences ordering (or $u_i$ if a utility function exists) of consumer $i = 1, \ldots n$;
  $\succcurlyeq_i$ is a preference ordering if it is reflexive $(x_i \succcurlyeq_i x_i)$ transitive $x_i \succcurlyeq_i x_i^{'}$ and $x_i^{'} \succcurlyeq_i x_i^{''}$ implies [illegible], and complete (for any pair $x_i$ and $x_i^{'}$ either $x_i \succcurlyeq_i x_i^{'}$ *or* $x_i^{'} \succcurlyeq_i x_i$). It can be shown that it can be represented by a continuous utility function if $\succcurlyeq i$ are continuous. The existence of general equilibrium can be obtained even when preferences are weakened to be non-complete or non-transitive.
- $w_i \in X_i$: initial endowment vector of consumer $i$.
- $e_i = (X_i, \succcurlyeq_i, w_i)$: the characteristic of consumer $i$.
- $Y_j$: production possibility set of firm $j = 1, 2, \ldots, J$, which is the characteristic of producer $j$.
- $y_j \in Y_j$: a production plan, $y_j^l > 0$ means $y_j^l$ is output and $y_j^l < 0$ means $y_j^l$ is input. Most elements of $y_j$ for a firm are zero.
- Recall that there can be three types of returns about production

scales: non-increasing returns to scale (*i.e.*, $y_j \in Y_j$ implies that $\alpha y_j \in Y_j$ for all $\alpha \in [0, 1]$), non decreasing (*i.e.*, $y_j \in Y_j$ implies that $\alpha y_j \in Y_j$ for all $\alpha = 1$) returns to scale, and constant returns to scale *i.e.*, $y_j \in Y_j$ implies that $\alpha y_j \in Y_j$ for all $\alpha \geqq 0$). In other words, decreasing returns to scale implies any feasible input-output vector can be scaled down; increasing returns to scale implies any feasible input-output vector can be scaled up, constant returns to scale implies the production set is the conjunction of increasing returns and decreasing returns. Geometrically, it is a cone.

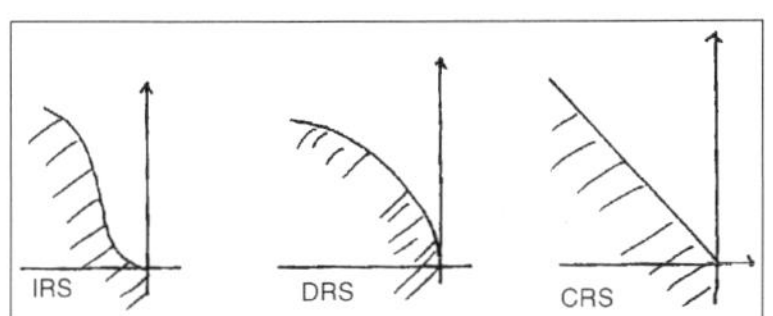


**Fig**: Various Returns to Scale: IRS, DRS, and CRS.

- $e = (\{X_i, \succcurlyeq_i, w_i\}, \{Y_j\})$: an economy, or called an economic environment.
- $X = X_1 \times X_2 \times .... \times X_n$: consumption space.
- $Y = Y_1 \times Y_2 \times ... \times Y_J$: production space.

## INSTITUTIONAL ARRANGEMENT: PRIVATE MARKET MECHANISM

$p = (p_1, p_2, ..., p_L) \in \Re_+^L$ : a price vector;

$px_i$: the expenditure of consumer $i$ for $i = 1, ....., n$;

$py_j$: the profit of firm $j$ for $j = 1, ....., J$;

$pw_i$: the value of endowments of consumer $i$ for $i = 1, ..., n$;

$\theta_{ij} \in \Re_+$ : the profit share of consumer $i$ from firm $j$, which specifies ownership (property rights) structures, so that

$$\sum_{i=1}^{n} \theta_{ij} = 1$$

for $j = 1, 2, ..., J$, and $i = 1, ....., n$;

$\sum_{i=1}^{n} \theta_{ij} p y_i =$ the total profit dividend received by consumer $i$ from firms for $i = 1, ..., n$.

For $i = 1, 2, ....., n$, consumer $i$'s budget constraint is given by,

$$px_i \leqq pw_i + \sum_{j=1}^{J} \theta_{ij} p y_j$$

and the budget set is given by

$$B_i(p) = \left\{ x_i \in X_i : px_i \leqq pw_i + \sum_{j=1}^{J} \theta_{ij} p y_i \right\}.$$

A private ownership economy then is referred to,

$$e = \left(e_1, e_2, ..., e_n, \left\{Y_j\right\}_{j=1}^{J}\right)\left\{\theta_{ij}\right\}.$$

The set of all such private ownership economies are denoted by $E$.

## INDIVIDUAL BEHAVIOUR ASSUMPTIONS

- *Perfect Competitive Markets*: Every player is a price-taker.
- *Utility Maximization:* Every consumer maximizes his preferences subject to $B_i(p)$. That is,

$$\max_{x_i} u_i(x_i)$$

s.t.

$$px_i \leqq pw_i + \sum_{j=1}^{J} \theta_{ij} py_j$$

- *Profit Maximization:* Every firm maximizes its profit in $Y_j$. That is,

$$\max_{y_j \in Y_j} py_j$$

for $j = 1,...,J$.

## COMPETITIVE EQUILIBRIUM

Before defining the notion of competitive equilibrium, we first give some notions on allocations which identify the set of possible outcomes in economy $e$. For notational convenience, "$\hat{a}$" will be used throughout the notes to denote the sum of vectors $a_i$, *i.e.*,

$$\hat{a} := \Sigma a_{l.}$$

### Allocation

An *allocation* $(x, y)$ is a specification of consumption vector $x = (x_1,...., x_n)$ and production vector $y = (y_1,...,y_J)$. An allocation $(x; y)$ is *individually feasible* if $x_i \in X_i$ for all $i \in N$, $y_j \in Y_j$ for all $j = 1,...,J$. An allocation is weakly balanced,

$$\hat{x} \leqq \hat{y} + \hat{w}$$

or specifically,

$$\sum_{i=1}^{n} x_i \leqq \sum_{j=1}^{J} y_j + \sum_{i=1}^{n} w_i$$

When inequality holds with equality, the allocation is called balanced or attainable. An allocation $(x, y)$ is feasible if it is both individually feasible and (weakly) balanced. Thus, an economic allocation is feasible if the total amount of each good consumed does not exceed the total amount available from both the initial endowment and production.

Denote by,

$$A = \{(x, y) \in X \times Y : \hat{x} \leq \hat{y} + \hat{w}\}$$

the set of all feasible allocations.

*Aggregation*:

$\hat{x} = \sum_{i=1}^{n} x_i$ : aggregation of consumption;

$\hat{y} = \sum_{j=1}^{J} y_i$ : aggregation of production;

$\hat{w} = \sum_{i=1}^{n} w_i$ : aggregation of endowments;

Now we define the notion of competitive equilibrium.

*Definition*: Given a private ownership economy, $e = (e_1, \ldots, e_n, \{Y_j\}, \{\theta_{ij}\})$, an allocation $(x, y) \in X \times Y$ and a price vector $p \in < \Re_+^L$ consist of a competitive equilibrium if the following conditions are satisfied

- Utility maximization: $x_i \preccurlyeq_i x_i'$ for all $x_i' \in B_i(p)$
  $x_i \in B_i(p)$ and $x_i \in B_i(p)$ for $i = 1, \ldots, n$.
- Profit maximization: $py_j \geqq py_j'$ for $y_j' \in Y_j$.
- Market Clear Condition: $\hat{x} \leqq \hat{w} + \hat{y}$.

*Denote*:

$x_i(p) = \{x_i \in B_i(p): x_i \in B_i(p)$ and $x_i \succcurlyeq_i x'\ x_i'$ for all

$x_i' \in B_i(p)\}$: the demand correspondence of consumer $i$ under utility maximization; it is called the demand function of consumer $i$ if it is a single-valued function.

$$y_i(p) = \{y_i \in Y_j : py_j \geqq py_j' \text{ for all } y_j' \in Y_j :$$

the supply correspondence of the firm $j$; it is called the supply function of firm $j$ if it is a single-valued function.

$$\hat{x}(p) = \sum_{i=1}^{n} x_i(p):$$

the aggregate demand correspondence.

$$\hat{y}(p) = \sum_{j=1}^{J} y_i(p):$$

the aggregate supply correspondence.

$$\hat{z}(p) = \hat{x}(p) - \hat{w} - \hat{y}(p):$$

aggregate excess demand correspondence. An equivalent definition of competitive equilibrium then is that a price vector $p^* \in < \Re_+^L$ is a competitive equilibrium price if there exists $\hat{z} \in \hat{z}(p^*)$ such that $\hat{z} \leqq 0$. If $\hat{z}(p)$ is a single-valued, $\hat{z}(p^*)$ 5 $\leqq$ is a competitive equilibrium.

## PURE EXCHANGE ECONOMIES

A pure exchange economy is an economy in which there is no production. This is a special case of general economy. In this case, economic activities only consist of trading and consumption.

The aggregate excess demand correspondence becomes,

$$\hat{z}(p) = \hat{x}(p) - \hat{w}$$

that we can define the individual excess demand by $z_i(p) = x_i(p) - w_i$ for this special case.

The simplest exchange economy with the possibility of mutual benefit exchange is the two-good and two-consumer exchange economy. As it turns out, this case is amenable to analysis by an extremely handy graphical device known as the Edgeworth Box.

### Edgeworth Box

Consider an exchange economy with two goods ($x_1$, $x_2$) and two persons. The total endowment is $\hat{w} = w_1 + w_2$. For example, if $w_1 = (1, 2), w_2 = (3, 1)$, then the total endowment is: $\hat{w} = (4, 3)$. Note that the point, denoted by $w$ in the Edgeworth Box, can be used to represent the initial endowments of two persons.Advantage of the Edgeworth Box is that it gives all the possible (balanced) trading points. That is,

$$x_1 + x_2 = w_1 + w_2$$

for all points $x = (x_1, x_2)$ in the box, where,

$$x_1 = x_1^1, x_1^2 \text{ and } x_2 = \left(x_2^1, x_2^2\right).$$

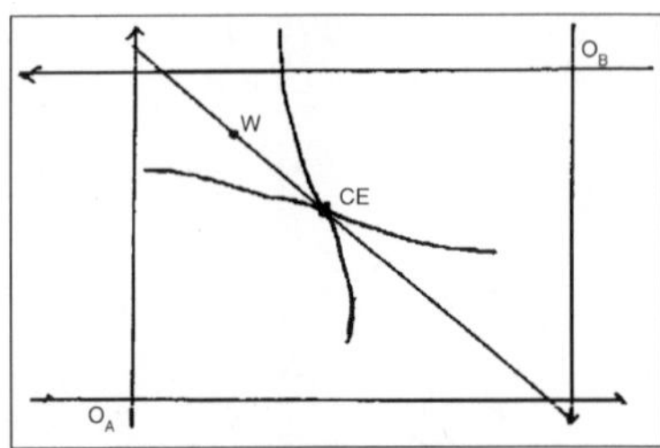


**Fig**: In the Edgeworth Box, the Point CE is a Competitive Equilibrium.

Thus, every point in the Edgeworth Box stands for an attainable allocation so that $x_1 + x_2 = w_1 + w_2$. Beyond the box, any point is not feasible. Which point in the Edgeworth Box can be a competitive equilibrium? In the box, one person's budget line is also the budget line of the other person. They share the same budget line in the box. Figure shows the market adjustment process to a competitive equilibrium. Originally, at price $p$, both persons want more good 2. This implies that the price of good 1, $p^1$, is too high so that consumers do not consume the total amounts of the good so that there is a surplus for $x_1$ and there is an excess demand for $x_2$, that is, $x_1$

$$x_1^1 + x_2^1 < w_1^1 + w_2^1$$

and $x2$,

$$x_1^2 + x_2^2 > w_1^2 + w_2^2.$$

Thus, the market will adjust itself by decreasing $p^1$ to $p^{1'}$. As a result, the budget line will become flatter and flatter till it reaches the equilibrium where the aggregate demand equals the aggregate supply. In this interior equilibrium case, two indifference curves are tangent each other at a point that is on the budget line so that the marginal rates of substitutions for the two persons are the same that is equal to the price ratio.

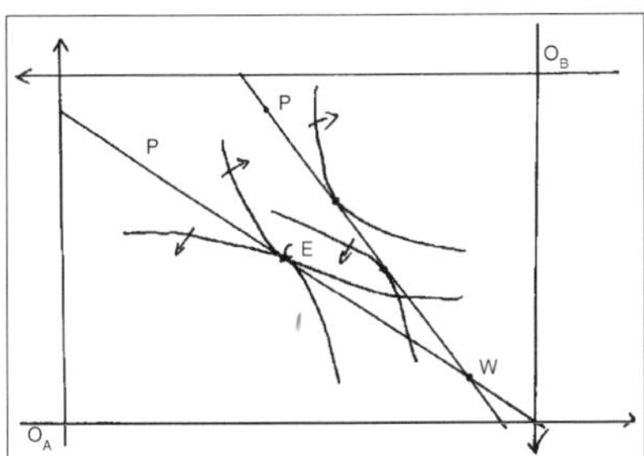


**Fig**: This Figure Shows the Market Adjustment Process.

What happens when indifference curves are linear?

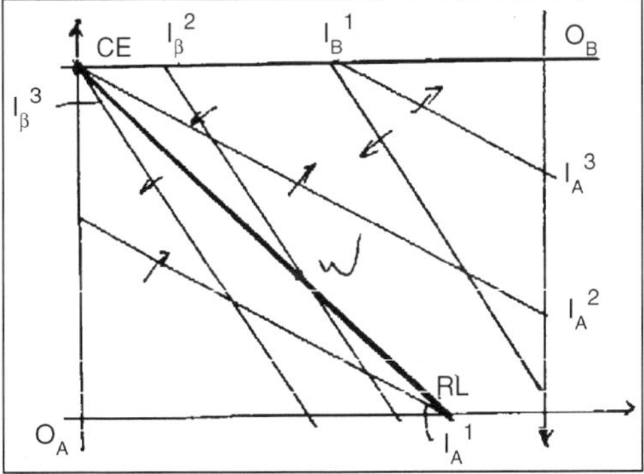


**Fig**: A Competitive Equilibrium may Still Exist Even if Two Persons' Indifference Curves do not Intersect.

In this case, there is no tangent point as long as the slopes of the indifference curves of the two persons are not the same. Even so, there still exists a competitive equilibrium although the marginal rates of substitutions for the two persons are not the same.

*Offer Curve*: the locus of the optimal consumptions for the two goods when price varies. Note that, it consists of tangent points of the indifference curves and budget lines when price varies.

*The offer curves of two persons are given in the following figure*:

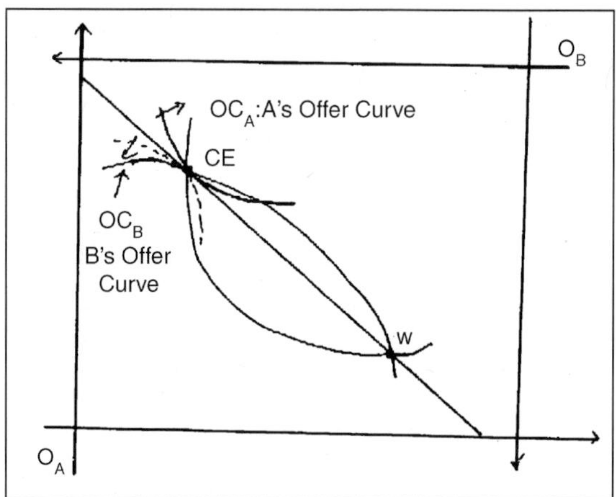


**Fig**: The CE is Characterized by the Intersection of Two Persons' offer Curves.

The intersection of the two offer curves of the consumers can be used to check if there is a competitive equilibrium.

One can see that the one intersection of two consumers' offer curves is always given at the endowment w.

If there is another intersection of two consumers' offer curves rather than the one at the endowment w, the intersection point must be the competitive equilibrium.

*To enhance the understanding about the competitive equilibrium, you try to draw the competitive equilibrium in the following situations*:

- There are many equilibrium prices.
- One person's preference is such that two goods are perfect substitutes (*i.e.*, indifference curves are linear).
- Preferences of one person are the Leontief-type (perfect complement)
- One person's preferences are non-convex.
- One person's preferences are "thick".
- One person's preferences are convex, but has a satiation point.

Note that a preference relation $\succcurlyeq_i$ is convex if $x \succ_i x'$ implies $tx + (1-t)x' \succ_i x'$ for all $t \in (0, 1)$ and all $x, x' \in X_i$. A preference relation $\succcurlyeq_i$ has a satiation point x if $x \succcurlyeq_i x'$ all $x' \in X_i$.

*Cases in which there may be no Walrasian Equilibria:*

*Case* 1: Indifference curves (IC) are not convex. If the two offer curves are not intersected except for at the endowment points, then there may not exist a competitive equilibrium. This may be true when preferences are not convex.

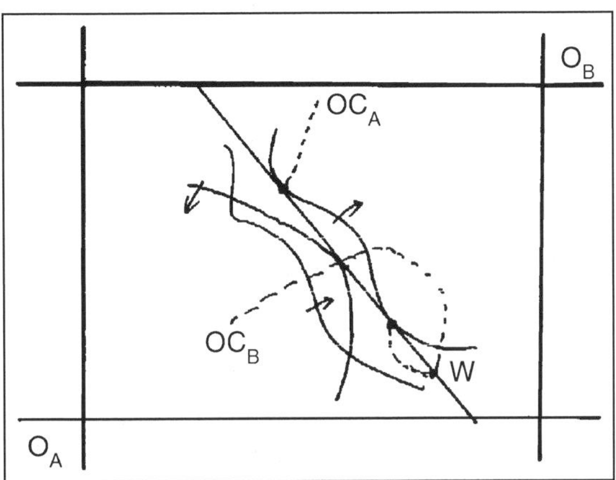


**Fig**: A CE May not Exist if Indifference Curves are not Convex. In that case, Two persons' Offer Curves are not Tangent.

*Case* 2: The initial endowment may not be an interior point of the consumption space. Consider an exchange economy in which one person's indifference curves put no values on one commodity, say, when Person 2's indifference curves are vertical lines so that

$$u_2\left(x_2^1, x_2^2\right) = x_2^1.$$

Person 1's utility function is regular one, say, which is given by a quasi-linear utility function, say,

$$u_1 = \sqrt{x_1^1} + x_2^1.$$

The initial endowments are given by $w_1 = (0, 1)$ and $w_2 = (1, 0)$. There is no competitive equilibrium. Why? There are two cases to be considered.

*Case* 1: $p^1 = 0$ or $p^2 = 0$. Person 1 would demand infinite amount of the good whose price is zero. Thus, there is no competitive equilibrium in this case.

*Case* 2: $p^1 > 0$ and $p^2 > 0$. Person 2's demand for good 1 is $x_2^1 = 1$, and person 1 would demand a positive quantity of good 1 because of of the quasi-linear utility function.

As such, the aggregate demand for good 1 is greater than one, that is,

$$x_1^1(p) + x_2^1(p) > \hat{w}^1$$

which violates the feasibility conditions. Thus, no CE exists.

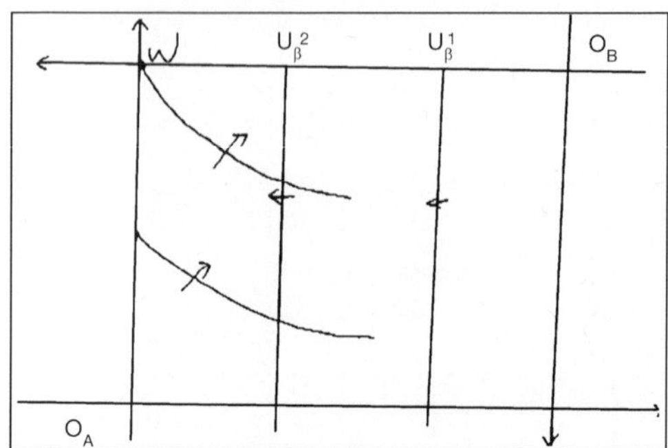


**Fig.** gA CE May not Exist if an Endowment is on the Boundary.

## THE EXISTENCE OF CE FOR AGGREGATE EXCESS DEMAND FUNCTIONS

The simplest case for the existence of a competitive equilibrium is the one when the aggregate excess demand correspondence is a single-valued function. Note that, when preference orderings and production sets are both strictly convex, we obtain excess demand functions rather than correspondences. A very important property of excess demand function $\hat{z}(p)$ is Walras' law, which can take one of the following three forms:

1. The strong form of Walras' law given by

$$p.\hat{z}(p) = 0 \text{ for all } p\hat{z}(p) = 0$$

2. The weak form of Walras' law given by

$$p.\hat{z}(p) \leq 0 \text{ for all } p \in \Re^L_{++};$$

3. The interior form of Walras' law given by

$$p.\hat{z}(p) = 0 \text{ for all } p \in \Re^L_{++};$$

Another important property of excess demand function is homogeneity of $\hat{z}(p)$: it is homogeneous of degree 0 in price $\hat{z}(_{\lambda}p) = \hat{z}(p)$ for any $\lambda > 0$. From this property, we can normalize prices.

*Because of homogeneity, for example, we can normalize a price vector as follows*:

- $p'^l = p^l/p^1$ $l = 1, 2, \ldots, L$
- $p'^l = p^l / \sum_{l=1}^{L} p^l$.

Thus, without loss of generality, we can restrict our attention to the unit simplex:

$$S^{L-1} = \left\{ p \in \Re^L_+ : \sum_{l=1}^{L} p^l = 1 \right\}.$$

Then, we have the following theorem on the existence of competitive equilibrium.

*Theorem*: For a private ownership economy e = $(\{X_i, w_i, \succcurlyeq_i\}, \{Y_j\}, \{\theta_{ij}\})$, *if $\hat{z}(p)$ is a homogeneous of degree zero and continuous function* and satisfies the strong Walras' Law, then there exists a competitive equilibrium, that is, there is $p^* \in \Re_+^L$ *such that*

$$\hat{z}(p^*) \leqq 0$$

*Proof*: Define a continuous function $g: S^{L-1} \to S^{L-1}$ by,

$$g^l(p) = \frac{p^l + \max\{0, \hat{z}^l(p)\}}{1 + \sum_{k=1}^{L} \max\{0, \hat{z}^k(p)\}}$$

for $l$ = 1, 2,....., $L$. First note that $g$ is a continuous function since max$\{f(x), h(x)\}$ is continuous when $f(x)$ and $h(x)$ are continuous. By Brouwer's fixed point theorem, there exists a price vector $p^*$ such that $g(p^*) = p^*$, *i.e.*,

$$p^{*l} = \frac{p^{*l} + \max\{0, \hat{z}^l(p^*)\}}{1 + \sum_{k=1}^{L} \max\{0, \hat{z}^k(p^*)\}} \quad l = 1, 2, ...., L.$$

We want to show $p$¤ is in fact a competitive equilibrium price vector. Cross multiplying,

$$1 + \sum_{k=1}^{L} \max\{0.\hat{z}^k(p^*)\}$$

we have,

$$1 + \sum_{k=1}^{L} \max\{0.\hat{z}^k(p^*)\} = \max\{0, \hat{z}^l(p^*)\}.$$

Then, multiplying the equation by $\hat{z}^l(p^*)$ and making summation, we have,

$$\left[\sum_{l=1}^{L} p^{*l}\, \hat{z}^l(p^*)\right]\left[\sum_{l=1}^{L} \max\{0, \hat{z}^l(p^*)\}\right] = \sum_{l=1}^{L} \hat{z}^l(p^*) \max\{0, \hat{z}^l(p^*)\}$$

Then, by the strong Walras' Law, we have,

$$\sum_{l=1}^{L} \hat{z}^l(p^*) \max\{0, \hat{z}^l(p^*)\} = 0.$$

Therefore, each term of the summations is either zero or, $\left(\hat{z}^l(p^*)\right)^2 > 0$.

Thus, to have the summation to be zero, we must have each term to be zero. That is,

$\hat{z}^l(p^*) \leqq 0$ for $l$ = 1,...., $L$: The proof is completed.

Do not confuse competitive equilibrium of an aggregate excess demand function with the strong Walras' Law. Even though Walras' Law holds, we may not have,

$$\hat{z}^l(p) \leqq 0$$

for all $p$. Also, if $\hat{z}(p^*) \leq 0$ for some $p^*$, *i.e.*, $p^*$ is a competitive equilibrium price vector, the the strong Walras' Law may not hold unless some types of monotonicity are imposed such as local non-satiation.

*Fact* 1: (free goods). Under the strong Walras' Law, if $p^*$ is a competitive equilibrium price vector and $\hat{z}^l(p^*) < 0$; then $p^{*l} = 0$:

*Proof*: Suppose not. Then p¤l > 0. Thus, p¤l ^ zl(p¤) < 0, and so $p^* \hat{z}(p^*) < 0$, contradicting the strong Walras' Law.

*Desirable goods*: if $p^l = 0$; $\hat{z}^l(p^*) > 0$.

*Fact* 2: (Equality of demand and supply). If all goods are desirable and $p^*$ is a competitive equilibrium price vector, then $\hat{z}(p^*) = 0$:

*Proof*: Suppose not. We have $\hat{z}^l(p^*) < 0$ for some $l$. Then, by Fact 1, we have $p^{*l} = 0$.

Since good $l$ is desirable, we must have $\hat{z}^l(p^{*l}) > 0$; a contradiction. By the strong Walras' Law, if $p > 0$, and if $(L–1)$ markets are in the equilibrium, the L-th market is also in the equilibrium. Thus, because of the strong Walras's Law, to verity that a price vector $p > 0$ clears all markets, it suffices check that it clear all markets, but one.

The result requires the aggregate excess demand function is continuous. By using the KKM lemma, we can prove the existence of competitive equilibrium by only assuming the aggregate excess demand function is lower semi-continuous.

*Theorem*: *For a private ownership economy,*

$$e = (\{X_i, w_i, \succcurlyeq_i\}, \{Y_j\}; \{\theta_{ij}\}),$$

if the aggregate excess demand function $\hat{z}$(p) is a lower semi-continuous function and satisfies strong or weak Walras' Law, then there exists a competitive equilibrium, that is, there is,

$$p^* \in S^{L-1}$$

such that,

$$\hat{z}(p^*) \leqq 0.$$

*Proof*: Define a correspondence $F: S \rightarrow 2^S$ by,

$$F(q) = \{p \in S: q\,\hat{z}(p) \leqq 0\} \text{ for all } q \in S:$$

First note that $F(q)$ is Non-empty for each $q$ 2 $S$ since $q$ 2 $F(q)$ by strong or weak Walras' Law. Since $p = 0$ and $\hat{z}(.)$ is lower semi-continuous, the function defined by,

$$\phi(q,p) \equiv q\hat{z}(p) = \sum_{l=1}^{L} q^l \hat{z}^l(p)$$

is lower semi-continuous in $p$. Hence, the set $F(q)$ is closed for all $q \in S$. We now prove $F$ is FS-convex. Suppose, by way of contradiction, that there some $q_1,\ldots, q_m \in S$ and some convex combination

$$q_\lambda = \sum_{t=1}^{m} \lambda_t q_t$$

such that,

$$q_\lambda \notin \mathrm{U}_{t=1}^{m} \mathrm{F}(\mathrm{qt}).$$

Then, $q_\lambda \notin F(qt)$ for all $t = 1,\ldots, m$.
Thus,

$$\sum_{t=1}^{m} \lambda_t q_t \hat{z}(q_\lambda) = q_\lambda \hat{z}(q_\lambda) > 0$$

which contradicts the fact that $\hat{z}$ satisfies strong or weak Walras' Law. So $F$ must be FS-convex. Therefore, by KKM lemma, we have,

$$\cap_{q \in S} F(q) \neq \phi.$$

Then there exists a $p^*$ 2 $S$ such that $p^* \in \cap_{q\in S} F(q)$, *i.e.*, $p \in^* \in F(q)$ for all $q \in S$. Thus, $q\,\hat{z}\,(p^*) \leqq 0$ for all $q \in S$. Now let $q_1 = (1, 0,\ldots, 0)$, $q_2 = (0, 1, 0,\ldots, 0)$, and $qn = (0,\ldots 0, 1)$. Then $q_t \in S$ and thus $q_t \hat{z}\,(p^*) = \hat{z}^t(p^*)$ 5 0 for all $t = 1,\ldots, L$. Thus we have $\hat{z}\,(p^*)$ 5 0, which means $p^*$ is a competitive equilibrium price vector. The proof is completed.

The two existence theorems only give sufficient conditions. Recently, Tian (2009) provides a complete solution to the existence of competitive equilibrium in economies with general excess demand functions, in which commodities may be indivisible and excess demand functions may be discontinuous or do not have any structure except Walras' law.Tian introduces a condition, called *recursive transfer lower semi-continuity*, which is necessary and sufficient for the existence of general equilibrium in such economies. Thus, the result strictly generalize all the existing results on the existence of equilibrium in economies with excess demand functions. For convenience of discussion, we introduce the following term. We say that price system $p$ *upsets* price system $q$ if $p$ gives a higher value to $q$'s excess demand, *i.e.*, $p.\ \hat{z}\,(q) > q.\ \hat{z}\,(q)$.

*Definition:* Let $\hat{z}\,(.)\colon S^{L-1} \to \mathbb{R}^L$ be an excess demand function. We say that a non-equilibrium price system $p^0 \in S^{L-1}$ is *recursively upset by*

$$p \in S^{L-1}$$

if there exists a finite set of price systems $\{p^1, p^2,\ldots, p\}$ such that $p^1.\ \hat{z}\,(p^0) > 0$, $p^2.\ \hat{z}\,(p^1) > 0,,\ldots, p.\ \hat{z}\,(p^{m-1}) > 0$. In words, a non-equilibrium price system $p0$ is recursively upset by $p$ means that there exist finite upsetting price systems $p^1, p^2,\ldots, p^m$ with $p^m = p$ such that $p^0$'s excess demand is not affordable at $p^1$, $p^1$'s excess demand is not affordable at $p^2$, and $p^{m-1}$'s excess demand is not affordable at $p^m$. When the strong form of Walras' law holds, this implies that

$p^0$ is upset by $p^1$, $p^1$ is upset by $p^2$,..., $p^{m-1}$ is upset by $p$. *Definition:* An excess demand function $\hat{z}$(.): $S^{L-1}$–$\mathbb{R}^L$ is said to be *recursively transfer lower semi-continuous* on $S^{L-1}$ if, whenever $q \in S^{L-1}$ is not a competitive equilibrium price system, there exists some price system $p^0 \in S^{L-1}$ (possibly $p^0 = q$) and a neighbourhood $V_q$ such that $p.\ \hat{z}(V_q) > 0$ for any $p$ that recursively upsets $p^0$, where $p.\ \hat{z}(V_q) > 0$ means $p$ ¢ $\hat{z}(q^0) > 0$ for all $q^0 \in Vq$.

Roughly speaking, recursive transfer lower semi-continuity of $\hat{z}$ (¢) means that, whenever $q$ is not a competitive equilibrium price system, there exists another non-competitive equilibrium price system $p^0$ such that all excess demands in some neighbourhood of $q$ are not affordable at any price vector $p$ that recursively upsets $p^0$. This implies that, if a competitive equilibrium fails to exist, then there is some non-equilibrium price system $q$ such that for every other price vector $p^0$ and every neighbourhood of $q$, excess demand of some price system *q0* in the neighbourhood becomes affordable at price system $p$ that recursively upsets $p^0$.

Recursive transfer lower semi-continuity is weaker than lower semi-continuity. Indeed, when $\hat{z}$(.) is lower semi-continuous, $p.\ \hat{z}$(.) is also lower semi-continuous for any Non-negative vector $p$, and thus we have $p^m.\ \hat{z}(q^0) > 0$ for all $q' \in N(q)$ and $p \in \Delta$.We then have the following theorem of competitive equilibrium in economies that have single-valued excess demand functions.

*Theorem*: Suppose an excess demand function $\hat{z}$(.): $S^{L-1} \to \mathbb{R}^L$ satisfies either the strong or weak form of Walras' law. Then there exists a competitive price equilibrium $p^* \in S^{L-1}$ if and only if $\hat{z}$(.) is recursively transfer lower semi-continuous on $S^{L-1}$.

*Proof*: *Suffciency* (⇐). Suppose $q$ is not a competitive equilibrium. Then there is a $p \in S^{L-1}$ such that $p.\ \hat{z}(q) > 0$. Then, by recursive transfer lower semi-continuity of $\hat{z}$(.), for each $q \in S^{L-1}$, there exists $p^0$ and a neighbourhood $V_q$ such that $p.\ \hat{z}(V_q) > 0$ whenever $p' \in S^{L-1}$ is recursively upset by $p$, *i.e.*, for any sequence of recursive price systems $\{p_1,\ldots\ldots, p^{m-1}, p\}$ with $p.\ \hat{z}(p^{m-1}) > 0$, $p^{m-1}$ ¢ $\hat{z}(p^{m-2}) > 0$,:::, $p^1.\ \hat{z}(p^0) > 0$ for $m \geq 1$, we have $p.\ \hat{z}(V_q) > 0$. Since there is no competitive equilibrium by the contrapositive hypothesis, $p^0$ is not a competitive equilibrium and thus, by recursive diagonal transfer lower semi-continuity, such a sequence of recursive price systems $\{p^1,\ldots., p^{m-1}; p\}$ exists for some $m \geq 1$.

Since $S^{L-1}$ is compact and $S^{L-1} \subseteq \cup_{q \in S} L-1 V_q i\ \ Vq$, there is a finite set $\{q1,\ldots\ q^T\}$ such that

$$S^{L-1} \subseteq \cup_{i=1}^{T} Vq^i.$$

For each of such $q^i$, the corresponding initial price system is denoted by $p^{0i}$ so that $p^i.\ \hat{z}(Vqi) > 0$ whenever $p0i$ is recursively upset by $p^i$.

Since there is no equilibrium, for each of such $p^{0i}$, there exists $pi$ such that $p^i. \hat{z}(p^{0i}) > 0$, and then, by 1-recursive diagonal transfer lower semi-continuity, we have $p^i. \hat{z}(V_{qi}) > 0$. Now consider the set of price systems $\{p^1,...., p^T\}$. Then, $p^i \notin V_{qi}$, otherwise, by $p^i. \hat{z}(V_{qi}) > 0$, as suggested, have $p^i. \hat{z}(p^i) > 0$, contradicting to Walras' law. So we must have $p^1 \notin V_{p1}$.

Without loss of generality, we suppose $p^1 \in Vp^2$. Since $p^2 \in \hat{z}(p1) > 0$ by noting that $p^1 \in V_{q2}$ and $p^1. \hat{z}(p^{01}) > 0$, then, by 2-recursive diagonal transfer lower semi-continuity, we have $p^2. \hat{z}(V_{q1}) > 0$. Also, $q^2. \hat{z}(V_{q2}) > 0$. Thus $p^2. \hat{z}(V_{q1} \cup V_{q2}) > 0$, and consequently $p^2 \notin V_{q1} \cup V_{q2}$.

Again, without loss of generality, we suppose $p^2 \in V_{q3}$. Since $p^3. \hat{z}(p^2) > 0$ by noting that $p^2 \in V_{p3}$, $p^2. \hat{z}(p^1) > 0$, and $p^1. \hat{z}(p^{01}) > 0$, by 3-recursive diagonal transfer lower semi-continuity, we have $p^3. \hat{z}(V_{q1}) > 0$. Also, since $p^3. \hat{z}(p^2) > 0$ and $p^2. \hat{z}(p^{02}) > 0$, by 2-recursive diagonal transfer lower semi-continuity, we have $p^3. \hat{z}(V_{q2}) > 0$. Thus, we have $\phi(p^3, V_{q1} \cup V_{q2} \cup V_{q3}) > \phi(V_{q1} \cup V_{q2} \cup V_{q3}, V_{q1} \cup V_{q2} \cup V_{q3})$, and consequently $p^3 \notin V_{q1} \cup V_{q2} \cup V_{q3}$.

With this process going on, we can show that $p^k \notin V_{q1} \cup V_{q2} \cup ..., \cup V_{qk}$, *i.e.*, $p_k$ is not in the union of $V_{q1}, V_{q2},..., V_{qk}$ for $k = 1, 2,...., T$. In particular, for $k = T$, we have $p^L \notin V_{q1} \cup V_{q2}..., \cup V_{qT}$ and so $p^T \notin S^{L-1} \subseteq V_{q1} \cup V_{q2}... \cup V_{qT}$, a contradiction. Thus, there exists $p^* \in S^{L-1}$ such that $p. \hat{z}(p^*) \cdot 0$ for all $p \in S^{L-1}$. Letting $p^1 = (1, 0,..., 0)$, $p^2 = (0, 1, 0,..., 0)$, and $p^L = (0; 0,..., 0, 1)$, we have $\hat{z}^l(p^*) \cdot 0$ for $l = 1,..., L$ and thus $p^*$ is a competitive price equilibrium.

*Necessity* (Þ). Suppose $p^*$ is a competitive price equilibrium and $p. \hat{z}(q) > 0$ for $q, p \in S^{L-1}$. Let $p^0 = p^*$ and $N(q)$ be a neighbourhood of $q$. Since $p. \hat{z}(p^*) \leq 0$ for all $p \in S^{L-1}$, it is impossible to find any sequence of finite price vectors $\{p^1, p^2,..., p^m\}$ such that $p^1. \hat{z}(p0) > 0; p^2, \hat{z}(p^1) > 0,..., pm. \hat{z}(p^{m-1}) > 0$. Hence, the recursive transfer lower semi-continuity holds trivially.

This theorem is useful to check the Non-existence of competitive equilibrium. The method of proof employed to obtain theorem is new. While there are different ways of establishing the existence of competitive equilibrium, all the existing proofs essentially use the fixed-point-theorem related approaches. Moreover, a remarkable advantage of the proof is that it is simple and elementary without using advanced math.

The three existence theorems assume that the excess demand function is well defined for all prices in the closed unit simplex $S^{L-1}$, including zero prices. However, when preferences are strictly monotone, excess demand functions are not well defined on the boundary of $S^{L-1}$ so that the existence theorems cannot be applied. Then, we need an existence theorem for strictly positive prices..

*Theorem*: *For a private ownership economy*

$$e = \left(\left\{X_i, w_i \succcurlyeq_i\right\}, \left\{Y_j\right\}, \left\{\theta_{ij}\right\}\right),$$

*suppose the aggregate excess demand function* $\hat{z}(p)$ *is defined* for all strictly positive price vectors $p \in \Re^L_{++}$, *and satisfies the following conditions*

- $\hat{z}(.)$ *is continuous;*
- $\hat{z}(.)$ *is homogeneous of degree zero;*
- $p.\ \hat{z}(p) = 0$ *for all* $p \in \Re^L_{++}$, *(interior Walras' Law);*
- *There is an* $s > 0$ *such that* $\hat{z}^l(p) > -s$ *for every commodity* $l$ *and all* $p \in \Re^L_{++}$,
- *If* $p_k \to p$, *where* $p \neq 0$ *and* $p^l = 0$ *for some* $l$, *then*

$$\max\left\{\hat{z}^1(p_k),....,\hat{z}^L(p_k)\right\} \to \infty$$

Then there is $p^* \in \Re^L_{++}$, *such that* $\hat{z}(p^*) = 0$ and thus p* is a competitive equilibrium.

*Proof:* Because of homogeneity of degree zero we can restrict our search for an equilibrium in the unit simplex $S$. Denote its interior by *intS*. We want to construct a correspondence $F$ from $S$ to $S$ such that any fixed point $p^*$ of $F$ is a competitive equilibrium, *i.e.*, $p^* \in F(p^*)$ implies $\hat{z}(p^*) = 0$.

Define a correspondence $F: S \to 2^S$ by,

$$F(p) = \begin{cases} \{q \in S : \hat{z}(p)\cdot q \geqq \hat{z}(p)\cdot q' \text{ for all } q' \in S\} & \text{if } p \in \text{int} S \\ \{q \in S : p\cdot q = 0\} & \text{if } p \text{ is on the boundary} \end{cases}.$$

Note that, for $p \in intS$, $F(.)$ means that, given the current "proposal" $p \in intS$, the "counterproposal" assigned by the correspondence $F(.)$ is any price vector $q$ that maximizes the values of the excess demand vector among the permissible price vectors in $S$. Here $F(.)$ can be thought as a rule that adjusts current prices in a direction that eliminates any excess demand, the correspondence $F(.)$ assigns the highest prices to the commodities that are most in excess demand. In particular, we have,

$$F(p) = \left\{q \in S : q^l = 0 \text{ if } \hat{z}^l(p_k) < \max\left\{\hat{z}^1(p_k),...,\hat{z}^L(p_k)\right\}\right\}.$$

Observe that if $\hat{z}(p) \neq 0$ for $p \in intS$, then because of the interior Walras' law we have $\hat{z}^l(p) < 0$ for some $l$ and $\hat{z}^{l'}(p) > 0$ for some $l' \neq l$. Thus, for such a $p$, any $q \in F(p)$ has $q^l = 0$ for some $l$ (to maximize the values of excess demand vectors). Therefore, if $\hat{z}(p)$ 6= 0 then $F(p)$ ½ Boundary $S = S\,|\,IntS$. In contrast, $\hat{z}(p) \neq 0$ then $F(p) = S$.

Now we want to show that the correspondence $F$ is an upper hemi-continuous correspondence with Non-empty, convex, and compact values. First, note that by the construction, the correspondence $F$ is clearly compact and convex-valued. $F(p)$ is also non-empty for all $p \in S$. Indeed, when $p \in intS$, any price vector $q$ that maximizes the value of $\hat{z}(p)$ is in $F(p)$ and so it is not empty.

When $p$ is on the boundary of $S$, $pl = 0$ for at least some good $l$ and thus there exists a $q \in S$ such that $p.\ q = 0$, which implies $F(p)$ is also non-empty. Now we show the correspondence $F$ is upper hemi-continuous, or equivalently it has closed graph, *i.e.*, for any sequences $pt \to p$ and $qt \to q$ with $qt \in F(pt)$ for all $t$, we have $q \in F(p)$.

*There are two cases to consider:*

1. *Case* 1. $p$ *2 intS*. Then $pk \in intS$ for $k$ sufficiently large. From $qk.\ \hat{z}(p_k) \leqq q'.\ \hat{z}(p_k)$ for all $q' \in F(pk)$ and the continuity of $\hat{z}(.)$, we get $q.\ \hat{z}(p) = q'.\ \hat{z}(p)$ for all $q' \in F(p)$, *i.e.*, $q \in F(p)$.
2. *Case* 2. $p$ is a boundary point of $S$. Take any $l$ with $p^l > 0$. We should argue that for $k$ sufficiently large, we have $q_k^l = 0$, and therefore it must be that $q^l = 0$; from this $q \in F(p)$ follows. Because $p^l > 0$, there is an $\in > 0$ such that $p_k^l > \in$ for $k$ sufficiently large. If, in addition, $pk$ is on the boundary of $S$, then $q_k^l = 0$ by the definition of $F(p_k)$. If, instead, $pk \in intS$, then by conditions (iv) and (v), for $k$ sufficiently large, we must have,

$$\hat{z}^l(pk) < \max\left\{\hat{z}^1(p_k), \ldots, \hat{z}^L(p_k)\right\}$$

   and therefore that, again, $q_k^l = 0$. To prove the inequality, note that by condition (v) The right-hand side of the expression goes to infinity with $k$ (because $p$ is a boundary point of $S$, some prices go to zero as $k \to 1$). But the left-hand side is bounded because if it is positive then

$$\hat{z}^l(p_k) \leqq \frac{1}{\in} p_k^l \hat{z}^l = -\frac{1}{\in} \sum_{l' \neq l} p_k^{l'} \hat{z}^{l'}(p_k) < \frac{s}{\in} \sum_{l' \neq l} p_k^{l'} < \frac{s}{\in},$$

   where $s$ is the bound in excess supply given by condition (iv). In summary, for $p_k$ close enough to the boundary of $S$, the maximal demand corresponds to some of the commodities whose price is close to zero. Therefore, we conclude that, for large $k$, any $q_k \in F(p_k)$ will put non-zero weight only on commodities whose prices approach zero. But this guarantees $p.\ q = 0$ and so $q \in F(p)$. So $F$ must be upper hemi-continuous.

Thus the correspondence $F$ is an upper hemi-continuous correspondence with Non-empty, convex, and compact values. Therefore, by Kakutani's fixed point theorem, we conclude that there is $p^* \in S$ with $p^* \in F(p^*)$.

Finally, we show that any fixed point $p^*$ of $F$ is a competitive equilibrium. Suppose that $p^* \in F(p^*)$. Then $p^*$ cannot be a boundary point of $S$ because $p.\ p > 0$ and $p.\ q = 0$ for all $q \in F(p)$ cannot occur simultaneously, and thus $p^* \in intS$. If $\hat{z}(p^*) \neq 0$, then $\hat{z}^l(p^*) < 0$ for $l$ and $\hat{z}^k(p^*) > 0$ for $k$ by the interior Walras' Law. Thus, for such a $p^*$, any $q^* \in F(p^*)$ must have $q^{*l} = 0$ because $q^*$

is the maximum of the function $\hat{z}(p^*).\ q$, which means $F(p^*)$ is a subset of boundary points of $S$. Hence, if $p^* \in F(p^*)$, we must have $\hat{z}(p^*) = 0$. The proof is completed.As shown by Tian (2009), theorem can also be extended to the case of any set, especially the positive price open set, of price systems for which excess demand is defined. To do so, we introduce the following version of recursive transfer lower semi-continuity.

*Definition*: Let $D$ be a subset of int $S^{L-1}$. An excess demand function $\hat{z}(.)$: int $S^{L-1} \to \mathbb{R}^L$ is said to be *recursively transfer lower semi-continuous* on int $S^{L-1}$ with respect to $D$ if, whenever $q \in$ int $S^{L-1}$ is not a competitive equilibrium price system, there exists some price system $p^0 \in$ int $S^{L-1}$ (possibly $p^0 = q$) and a neighbourhood $V_q$ such that (1) whenever $p^0$ is upset by a price system in int $S^{L-1} | D$, it is upset by a price system in $D$, and (2) $p.\ \hat{z}(V_q) > 0$ for any $p \in D$ that recursively upsets $p^0$.

Now we have the following theorem that fully characterizes the existence of competitive equilibrium in economies with possibly indivisible commodity spaces and discontinuous excess demand functions.

Theorem: *Suppose an excess demand function* $\hat{z}(.)$: *int* $S^{L-1} \to \mathbb{R}^L$ *satisfies Walras' law:* $p \not\subset \hat{z}(p) = 0$ *for all* $p \in$ *int* $S^{L-1}$. *Then there is a competitive price equilibrium* $p^* \in$ *int* $S^{L-1}$ *if and only if there exists a compact subset* $D \subseteq$ *int* $S^{L-1}$ *such that* $\hat{z}(.)$ *is recursively transfer lower semi-continuous on int* $S^{L-1}$ *with* respect to D.

*Proof*: *Sufficiency* ($\Leftarrow$). The proof of su±ciency is essentially the same as that of Theorem and we just outline the proof here. To show the existence of a competitive equilibrium on $S^{L-1}$, it suffices to show that there exists a competitive equilibrium $p^*$ in $D$ if it is recursively diagonal transfer lower semi-continuous on $S^{L-1}$ with respect to $D$.

Suppose, by way of contradiction, that there is no competitive equilibrium in $D$. Then, since $\hat{z}$ is recursively diagonal transfer lower semi-continuous on $S^{L-1}$ with respect to $D$, for each $q \in D$, there exists $p^0$ and a neighbourhood $V_q$ such that (1) whenever $p^0$ is upset by a price system in $S^{L-1}$ *n* $D$, it is upset by a price system in $D$ and (2) $p.\ \hat{z}(V_q) > 0$ for any finite subset of price systems $\{p^1,\ldots,p^m\} \subset D$ with $p^m = p$ and $p.\ \hat{z}(p^{m-1}) > 0, p^{m-1}.\ \hat{z}(p^{m-2}) > 0,\ldots, p^1.\ \hat{z}(p^0) > 0$ for $m \geq 1$. Since there is no competitive equilibrium by the contrapositive hypothesis, $p^0$ is not a competitive equilibrium and thus, by recursive diagonal transfer lower semi-continuity on $S^{L-1}$ with respect to $D$, such a sequence of recursive securing price systems $\{p^1,\ldots, p^{m-1}, p\}$ exists for some $m \geq 1$.

Since $D$ is compact and $D \subseteq \mathrm{S}_{q \in SL-1} V_q$, there is a finite set $\{q^1,\ldots,q^T\} \subseteq D$ such that,

$$D \subseteq \cup_{i=1}^{T} V_{qi}.$$

For each of such $q_i$, the corresponding initial deviation price system is denoted by $p^{0i}$ so that $p_i.\ \hat{z}(V_{qi}) > 0$ whenever $p^{0i}$ is recursively upset by $pi$

through any finite subset of securing price systems $\{p^{1i},..., p^{mi}\}$ $D \subseteq \cup_{i=1}^{T} V_{qi.} \subset D$ with $p^{mi} = p^i$. Then, by the same argument as in the proof of Theorem, as suggested, obtain that $z^k$ is not in the union of $V_{q1}, V_{q2},.., V_{qk}$ for $k = 1, 2,..., T$. For $k = T$, we have $p^T \notin V_{q1}$ $[V_{q2},...,\cup V_{qT}$ and so

$$P^T \notin D \subseteq \cup_{i=1}^{T} V_{qi},$$

which contradicts that $p^T$ is a upsetting price in $D$. Thus, there exists a price system $p^* \in S^{L-1}$ such that $p.\ \hat{z}(p^*) \cdot 0$ for all $p \in \text{int}\ S^{L-1}$. We want to show that $p^*$ in fact is a competitive price equilibrium. Note that int $S^{L-1}$ is open and $D$ is a compact subset of int $S^{L-1}$. One can always find a sequence of price vector,

$$\left\{q_n^l\right\} \subseteq \text{int}\, S^{L-1} \setminus D$$

such that $q_n^l \rightarrow p^l$, where $p^l = (0,..., 0, 1, 0,...,0)$ is the unit vector that has only one argument—the $l$th argument—with value 1 and others with value 0. Since $p.\ \hat{z}(q)$ is continuous in $p$, we have $\hat{z}^l(p^*) \leq 0$ for $l = 1,..., L$ and thus $p^*$ is a competitive price equilibrium.

*Necessity* ($\Rightarrow$). Suppose $p^*$ is a competitive equilibrium. Let $D = fp^*g$. Then, the set $D$ is clearly compact. Now, for any non competitive equilibrium $q \in S^{L-1}$, let $p^0 = p^*$ and $V_q$ be a neighbourhood of $q$.

Since $p.\ \hat{z}(p^*) \leq 0$ for all $p \in S^{L-1}$ and $p^0 = p^*$ is a unique element in $D$, there is no other upsetting price $p^1$ such that $p^1.\ \hat{z}(p^0) > 0$. Hence, the game is recursively diagonal transfer continuous on $S^{L-1}$ with respect to $D$.

*Theorem*: Then strictly generalizes all the existing results on the existence of competitive equilibrium in economies with single-valued excess demand functions.

**Conditions for Walras' Law to be True**

From the theorems, Walras' Law is important to prove the existence of a competitive equilibrium. Under which conditions, is Walras' Law held? When each consumer's budget constraint holds with equality:

$$px_i(p) = pw_i + \sum_{j=1}^{J} \theta_{ij} py_j(p)$$

for all $i$, we have,

$$\sum_{i=1}^{n} px_i(p) = \sum_{i=-1}^{n} pw_i + \sum_{i=1}^{n}\sum_{j=1}^{J} \theta_{ij} py_j(p)$$

$$= \sum_{i=1}^{n} pw_i + \sum_{j=1}^{J} py_j(p)$$

which implies that,

$$p\left[\sum_{i=1}^{n} x_i(p) - \sum_{i=1}^{n} w_i - \sum_{j=1}^{J} y_j(p)\right] = 0$$

so that,

$$p \cdot \hat{z}(p) = 0 \; (Walras0Law)$$

Thus, as long as the budget line holds with equality, Walras' Law must hold. The existence theorems on competitive equilibrium are based on the assumptions that the aggregate excess demand correspondence is single-valued and satisfies the Walras's Law.The questions are under what conditions on economic environments a budget constraint holds with equality, and the aggregate excess demand correspondence is single-valued or convex-valued?The following various types of monotonicities and con-vexities of preferences with the first one strongest and the last one weakest may be used to answer these questions.

**Types of Monotonicity Conditions**

- *Strict Monotonicity*: For any two consumption market bundles ($x \geq x'$) with $x \neq x'$ implies $x \succ_i x'$.
- *Monotonicity*: if $x > x'$ implies that $x \succ_i x'$.
- *Local Non-satiation*: For any point x and any neighbourhood, $N(x)$, there is $x' \in N(x)$ such that $x' \succ_i x$.
- *Non-satiation*: For any $x$, there exists $x0$ such that $x' \succ_i x$:

Monotonicity of preferences can be interpreted as individuals' desires for goods: the more, the better. Local non-satiation means individuals' desires are unlimited.

**Types of Convexities**

- Strict convexity: For any $x$ and $x'$ with $x \succcurlyeq x'$ and $x \neq x'$, $x_\lambda \equiv \lambda x + (1-\lambda)x' \succ_i x'$ for $\lambda \in (0, 1)$.

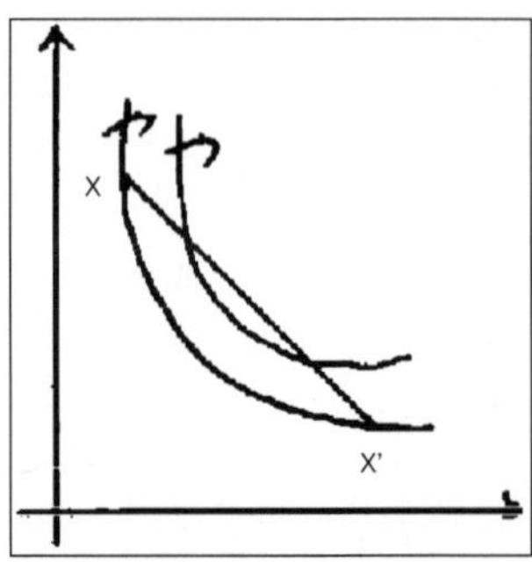


**Fig**: Strict Convex Indifference Curves.

- Convexity: If $x \succ_i x'$, then $x_\lambda = \lambda x + (1-\lambda)x' \succ_i x'$ for $\lambda \in (0, 1)$.

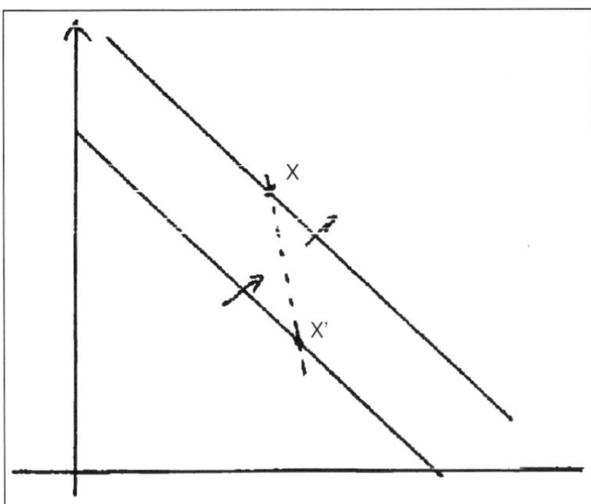


**Fig:** Linear Indifference Curves are Convex, but not Strict Convex.

- Weak convexity: If $x \succcurlyeq_i x'$, then $x_\lambda \succcurlyeq_i x'$.

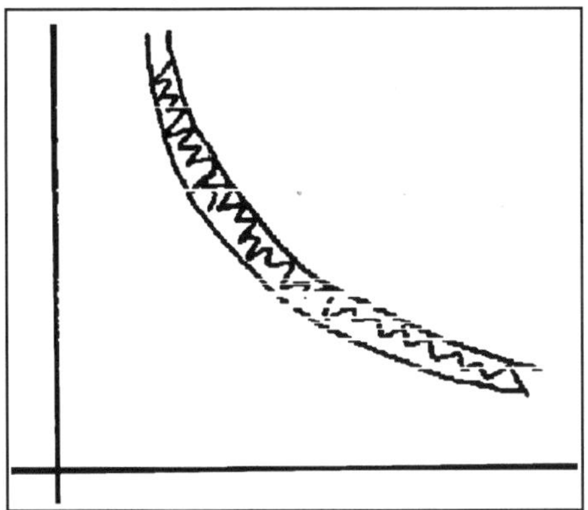

**Fig:** "Thick" Indifference Curves are Weakly Convex, but not Convex.

Each of the condition implies the next one, the converse may not be true by examining thick indifference curves and linear indifference curves, strictly convex indiffer-ence curves:

The convexity of preferences implies that people want to diversify their consumptions, and thus, convexity can be viewed as the formal expression of basic measure of economic markets for diversification.

Note that the strict convexity of $\succ_i$ implies the conventional diminishing marginal rates of substitution (MRS), and weak convexity of $\succcurlyeq_i$ is equivalent to the quasi-concavity of utility function $u_i$. Also notice that the continuity of $\succcurlyeq_i$ is a sufficient condition for the continuous utility representations, that is, it guarantees the existence of continuous utility function $u_i(.)$. Under the convexity of preferences $\succcurlyeq_{i,}$ non-satiation implies local non-satiation. Why? The proof is left to readers. Now we are ready to answer under which conditions Walras's Law holds, a demand correspondence can be function, and convex-valued. The following propositions answer the questions.*Proposition*: Under local non-satiation assumption, we have the budget constraint holds with equality, and thus the Walras's Law holds.

*Proposition*: Under the strict convexity of $\succcurlyeq_i$, $x_i(p)$ becomes a (single-valued) function.

*Proposition*: Under the weak convexity of preferences, demand correspondence $x_i(p)$ is convex-valued.

*Strict convexity of production set*:

$$y_j^1 \in Y_j \; and \; y_j^2 \in Y_j,$$

then the convex combination,

$$\lambda y_j^1 + (1-\lambda) y_j^2 \in \text{int} Y_j$$

for all 0 < l < 1, where $intY_j$ denotes the interior points of $Y_j$. The proof of the following proposition is based on the maximum theorem.

*Proposition: If $Y_j$ is compact (i.e., closed and bounded) and strictly convex, then the supply correspondence $y_j(p)$ is a well defined single-valued and continuous function.*

*Proof:*: By the maximum theorem, we know that $y_j(p)$ is a non-empty valued upper hemi-continuous correspondence by the compactness of $Y_j$ (by noting that $0 \in Y_j$) for all,

$$p \in R_+^L.$$

Now we show it is single-valued. Suppose not. $y_j^1$ and $y_j^2$ are two profit maximizing production plans for $p \in \Re_+^L$, and thus $p_j^1 = py_j^2$. Then, by the strict convexity of $Y_j$, we have

$$\lambda y_j^1 + (1-\lambda) y_j^2 \in \text{int} Y_j$$

for all 0 < l < 1. Therefore, there exists some $t$ > 1 such that $t\left[\lambda u_j^1 + (1-\lambda) y_j^2\right] \in \text{int} Y_j$.

Then,

$$t\left[\lambda p y_j^1 + (1-\lambda) p y_j^2\right] = t p y_j^1 > p y_j^1$$

which contradicts the fact that $y_j^1$ is a profit maximizing production plan. So $y_j(p)$ is a single-valued function. Thus, by the upper hemi-continuity of $y_j(p)$, we know it is a single-valued and continuous function.

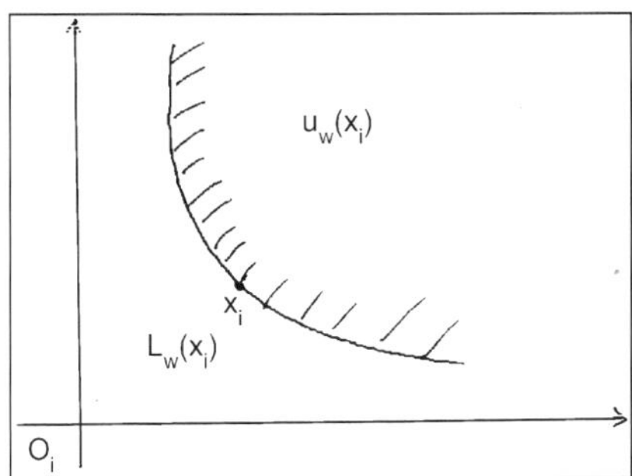


**Fig**: The Upper Contour Set $U_w(x_i)$ is Given by all Points The Indifference Curve, and the Lower Contour set $Lw(xi)$ is Given by all Points. The Indifference Curve in the Ffigure.

*Proposition: If $\succcurlyeq_i$ is continuous, strictly convex, locally non-satiated, and $w_i > 0$, then $x_i(p)$ is a continuous single-valued function and satisfies the budget constraint with equality for all $p \in \Re^L_{++}$. Consequently, the Walras's Law is satisfied for all $p \in \Re^L_{++}$.*

*Proof:* First note that, since $w_i > 0$, one can show that the budget constrained set $B_i(p)$ is a continuous correspondence with non-empty and compact values and $\succcurlyeq_i$ is continuous. Then, by the maximum theorem, we know the demand correspondence $x_i(p)$ is upper hemi-continuous. Furthermore, by the strict convexity of preferences, it is single-valued and continuous. Finally, by local non-satiation, we know the budget constraint holds with equality, and thus Walras's Law is satisfied.

Note that there's no utility function representation when preferences are lexicographic. Then, we can have the following existence theorem that provides sufficient conditions directly based on the fundamentals of the economy by applying the Existence Theorem $I'$.

*Theorem*: For a private ownership economy

$$e = (\{X_i, w_i \succcurlyeq_i\}, \{Y_j\}, \{\theta_{ij};\}),$$

*there* exists a competitive equilibrium if the following conditions hold

- $X_i \in \Re^L_+$;
- $\succcurlyeq_i$ *are continuous, strictly convex (which guarantee the demand function* is single valued) and strictly monotonic (which guarantees Walras' Law holds);
- $\hat{w} > 0$;
- $Y_j$ *are compact, strictly convex,* $0 \in Y_j\, j = 1, 2, ...., J.$

Note that $\mu_i$ are continuous if the upper contour set

$$\cup_w(x_i) \equiv \{x_i^{'} \in X_i \text{ and } x_i^{'} \succcurlyeq_i x_i\}$$

and the lower contour set

$$L_w(x_i) \equiv \{x_i^{'} \in X_i \text{ and } x_i^{'} \preccurlyeq_i x_i\}$$

are closed. *Proof:*: By the assumption imposed, we know that $xi(p)$ and $y_j(p)$ are continuous and single-valued. Thus the aggregate excess demand function is a continuous single-valued function and satisfies Walras' Law by monotonicity of preferences. Thus, we only need to show conditions (iv) and (v) in Theorem I*00* are also satisfied. The bound in (iv) follows from the Non-negativity of demand (*i.e.,* the fact that $X_i = \mathbb{R}^L_+$) and bounded production sets, which implies that a consumer's total net supply to the market of any good $l$ can be no greater the sum of his initial endowment and upper bound of production sets.

Finally, we show that condition v is satisfied. As some prices go to zero, a consumer whose wealth tends to a strictly positive limit (note that, because $p\,\hat{w} > 0$, there must be at least one such consumer) and with strict monotonicity of preferences will demand an increasing large amount of some of the commodities whose prices go to zero. Hence, by Theorem I'', there is a competitive equilibrium. The proof is completed. Examples of Computing CE.

*Example*: Consider an exchange economy with two consumers and two goods with

$$w_1 = (1,0) \qquad w_2 = (0,1)$$

$$u_1(x_1) = \left(x_1^1\right)^a \left(x_1^2\right)^{1-\alpha} \qquad 0 < a < 1$$

$$u_2(x_2) = \left(x_2^1\right)^b \left(x_2^2\right)^{1-b} \qquad 0 < b < 1$$

Let,

$$p = \frac{p^2}{p^1}$$

Consumer 1's problem is to solve,

$$\max_{x_1} u_1(x_1)$$

subject to,

$$x_1^1 + p x_1^2 = 1$$

Since utility functions are Cobb-Douglas types of functions, the solution is then given by,

$$x_1^1(p) = \frac{a}{1} = a$$

$$x_1^2(p) = \frac{1-a}{p}.$$

Consumer 2's problem is to solve,

$$\max_{x_2} u_2(x_2)$$

subject to,

$$x_2^1 + px_2^2 = p$$

The solution is given by,

$$x_2^1(p) = \frac{b \cdot p}{1} b \cdot p$$

$$x_2^2(p) = \frac{(1-b)p}{p} = (1-b).$$

Then, by the market clearing condition,

$$x_1^1(p) + x_2^1(p) = 1 \Rightarrow a + bp = 1$$

.and thus the competitive equilibrium is given by,

$$p = \frac{p^2}{p^1} = \frac{1-a}{b}.$$

This is true because, by Walras's Law, for $L = 2$, it is enough to show only one market clearing. Since the Cobb-Douglas utility function is widely used as an example of utility functions that have nice properties such as strict monotonicity on $\mathbb{R}^L_{++}$ ,continuity, and strict quasi-concavity, it is useful to remember the functional form of the demand function derived from the Cobb-

Douglas utility functions. It may be remarked that we can easily derive the demand function for the general function:

$$u_{i^{\prime}}(x_i) = \left(x_i^1\right)^{\alpha}\left(x_i^2\right)^{\beta} \quad \alpha > 0, \beta > 0$$

by the a suitable monotonic transformation. Indeed, by invariant to monotonic transformation of utility function, we can rewrite the utility function as

$$\left[\left(x_1^1\right)^{\alpha}\left(x_1^2\right)^{\beta}\right]^{\frac{1}{\alpha+\beta}} = \left(x_1^1\right)^{\frac{\alpha}{\alpha+\beta}}\left(x_1^2\right)^{\frac{\beta}{\alpha+\beta}}$$

so that we have,

$$x_1^1(p) = \frac{\frac{\alpha}{\alpha+\beta} I}{p^1}$$

and,

$$x_1^2(p) = \frac{\frac{\beta}{\alpha+\beta} I}{p^2}$$

when the budget line is given by,

$$p^1 x_1^1 + p^2 x_1^2 = I.$$

Example,

$$\begin{array}{ll} n = 2 & L = 2 \\ w_1 = (1,0) & w_2 = (0,1) \\ u_1(x_1) = \left(x_1^1\right)^a \left(x_1^2\right)^{1-a} & 0 < a < 1 \\ u_1(x_2) = \min\left\{x_2^1, bx_2^2\right\} & with\, b > 0 \end{array}$$

For consumer 1, we have already obtained,

$$x_1^1(p) = a, \quad x_1^2 = \frac{(1-a)}{p}$$

*For Consumer 2, his problem is to solve:*

$$\max_{x_2} u_2(x_2)$$

s.t.

$$x_2^1 + p x_2^2 = p.$$

At the optimal consumption, we have,

$$x_2^1 = b x_2^2.$$

By substituting the solution into the budget equation, we have,

$$b x_2^2 + p x_2^2 = p$$

and thus

$$x_2^2(p) = \frac{p}{b+p} \; and\, x_2^1(p) = \frac{bp}{b+p}.$$

Then, by

$$x_1^1(p) + x_2^1(p) = 1,$$

we have,

$$a + \frac{bp}{b+p} = 1$$

or,

$$(1-a)(b+p) = bp$$

so that,

$$(a+b-1)p = b(1-a)$$

Thus,

$$p^* = \frac{b(1-a)}{a+b-1}.$$

To make $p^*$ be a competitive equilibrium price, we need to assume $a + b > 1$.

## WELFARE ECONOMICS

A branch of economics that uses microeconomic techniques to simultaneously determine allocative efficiency within an economy and the income distribution associated with it is known as welfare economics. It analyzes *social welfare*, however measured, in terms of economic activities of the individuals that comprise the theoretical society considered.

As such, individuals, with associated economic activities, are the basic units for aggregating to social welfare, whether of a group, a community, or a society, and there is no *"social welfare"* apart from the *"welfare"* associated with its individual units. Here, *'welfare'* in its most general sense refers to well-being.

Naturally, welfare economics takes individual preferences as given and stipulates a welfare improvement in Pareto efficiency terms from social state $A$ to social state $B$ if at least one person prefers $B$ and no one else opposes it. There is no requirement of a unique quantitative measure of the welfare improvement implied by this.

Another aspect of welfare treats income/goods distribution, including equality, as a further dimension of welfare.

However, *Social welfare* refers to the overall welfare of society. With sufficiently strong assumptions, it can be specified as the summation of the welfare of all the individuals in the society.

Welfare may be measured either cardinally in terms of *"utils"* or dollars, or measured ordinally in terms of Pareto efficiency. The cardinal method in *"utils"* is seldom used in pure theory today because of aggregation problems that make the meaning of the method doubtful, except on widely challenged underlying assumptions. In applied welfare economics, such as in cost-benefit analysis, money-value estimates are often used, particularly where income-distribution effects are factored into the analysis or seem unlikely to undercut the analysis.

## WELFARE MAXIMIZATION IN PRODUCTION ECONOMY

Define a choice set by the transformation function,

$$T(\hat{x}) = 0 \quad \textit{with } \hat{x} = \sum_{i=1}^{n} x_i.$$

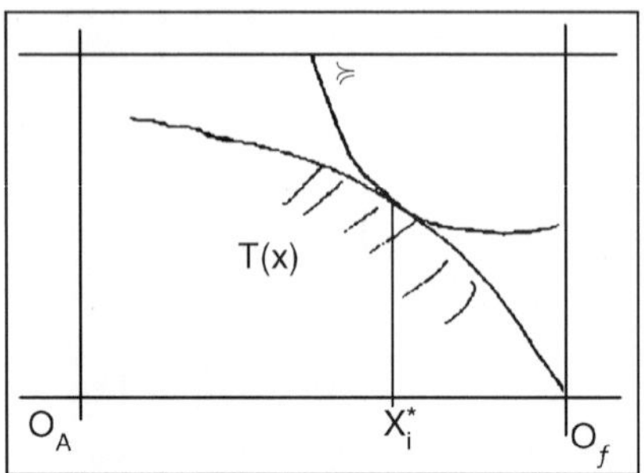


**Fig**: Welfare Maximization

The social welfare maximization problem for the production economy is,

$$\max W(u_1(x_1),\ u_2(x_2),\dots,\ u_n(u_n))$$

subject to,

$$T(\hat{x}) = 0.$$

Define the Lagrangian function,

$$L = W(u_1(x_1),\dots\dots,u_n(u_n)) - \lambda T(\hat{x}).$$

The first order condition is then given by,

$$W'(\cdot)\frac{\partial u_i(x_i)}{\partial x_i^l} - \lambda\frac{\partial T(\hat{x})}{\partial x_i^l} \leqq 0 \text{ } with \, equality \, if \, x_i^l > 0,$$

and thus when $x$ is an interior point, we have,

$$\frac{\dfrac{\partial u_i(x_i)}{\partial x_i^l}}{\dfrac{\partial u_i(x_i)}{\partial x_i^k}} = \frac{\dfrac{\partial T(\hat{x})}{\partial x^l}}{\dfrac{\partial T(\hat{x})}{\partial x_i^k}}$$

That is,

$$MRS_{x_i^l,x_i^k} = MRTS_{x^l,x^k}.$$

The conditions characterizing welfare maximization require that the marginal rate of substitution between each pair of commodities must be equal to the marginal rate of transformation between the two commodities for all agents.

## SOCIAL WELFARE MAXIMIZATION FOR EXCHANGE ECONOMIES

We suppose that a society should operate at a point that maximizes social welfare; that is, we should choose an allocation $x^*$ such that $x^*$ solves

$$\max W(u_1(x_1),\dots,u_n(x_n))$$

subject to,

$$\sum_{i=1}^{n} x_i \leqq \sum_{i=1}^{n} w_i.$$

How do the allocations that maximize this welfare function compare to Pareto efficient allocations? The following is a trivial consequence if the strict monotonicity assumption is imposed.

*Proposition: Under strict monotonicity of the social welfare function, W(.) if* $x^*$ maximizes a social welfare function, then x¤ must be Pareto Optimal.

*Proof*: If $x^*$ is not Pareto Optimal, then there is another feasible allocation $x'$ such that

$$u_i\left(x_i^{'}\right) \geqq u_i\left(x_i\right)$$

for all $i$ and $u_k(x_k^{'}) > u_k(x_k)$ for some $k$. Then, by strict monotonicity of $W(.)$, we have $W(u_1\left(x_1^{'}\right),\ldots., u_n\left(x_n^{'}\right)) > W(u_1(x_i),\ldots. u_n(x_n))$ and thus it does not maximizes the social welfare function.

Thus, every social welfare maximum is Pareto efficient. Is the converse necessarily true? By the Second Fundamental Theorem of Welfare Economics, we know that every Pareto efficient allocation is a competitive equilibrium allocation by redistributing endowments. This gives us a further implication of competitive prices, which are the multipliers for the welfare maximization. Thus, the competitive prices really measure the (marginal) social value of a good. Now we state the following proposition that shows every Pareto efficient allocation is a social welfare maximum for the social welfare function with a suitable weighted sum of utilities.

*Proposition*: *Let* $x^* > 0$ *be a Pareto optimal allocation. Suppose ui is concave,* differentiable and strictly monotonic. Then, there exists some choice of weights $a_i^*$ such that x* maximizes the welfare functions

$$W\left(u_1,\ldots,u_n\right) = \sum_{i=1}^{n} a_i u_i\left(x_i\right)$$

Furthermore,

$$a_i^* = \frac{1}{\lambda_i} with\ \lambda_i = \frac{\partial V_i\left(p, I_i\right)}{\partial I_i}$$

where $V_i(.)$ is the indirect utility function of consumer $i$.

*Proof*: Since $x^*$ is Pareto optimal, it is a competitive equilibrium allocation with $w_i = x_i^*$ by the second theorem of welfare economies. So we have

$$D_i u_i\left(x_i^*\right) = \lambda p$$

by the first order condition, where $p$ is a competitive equilibrium price vector. Now for the welfare maximization problem,

$$\max \sum_{i=1}^{n} a_i u_i (x_i)$$

$$s.t \sum x_i \leqq \sum x_i^*$$

since $u_i$ is concave, $x^*$ solves the problem if the first order condition,

$$a_i \frac{\partial u_i (x_i)}{\partial x_i} = q \quad i = 1,....,n$$

is satisfied for some $q$. Thus, if we let $p = q$, then,

$$a_i^* = \frac{1}{\lambda_i}.$$

We know $x^*$ also maximizes the welfare function,

$$\sum_{i=1}^{n} a_i^* u_i \left(x_i'\right).$$

Thus, the price is the Lagrangian multiples of the welfare maximization, and this measures the marginal social value of goods.

## WELFARE STATES, PRODUCTION REGIMES, AND GLOBALIZATION

The early 1990s, a number of authors had noted that there was strong affinity and perhaps a causal relationship between corporatism, often indexed by the degree of bargaining centralization, and welfare state generosity. Esping-Andersen and Kolberg and Esping-Andersen drew attention to other links between labour market arrangements and welfare state types: high levels of public social service employment and of female labour force participation in the social democratic welfare states, high levels of private service employment in liberal welfare states, low levels of service employment and female employment in Christian democratic welfare states, and high levels of early retirement in Christian democratic welfare states. In the course of the 1990s, a new line of thinking, the varieties of capitalism approach, emerged which stressed other dimensions of variation among advanced capitalist economies.

The most influential typology has been that of Soskice. Soskice shifts from the focus on unions and union confederations characteristic of the corporatism literature to a focus on employers and firms and their capacity to coordinate their actions. In his view, employer organization takes three distinctive forms: coordination at the industry or sub-industry level in Germany and in most northern European economies; coordination among groups of companies across industries in Japan and Korea or absence of coordination in the deregulated systems of the Anglo-American countries. In coordinated economies, employers are able to organize collectively in training their labour force, sharing technology, providing export marketing services and advice for R&D and for product innovation, setting product standards, and bargaining with employees.

The capacity for collective action on the part of employers shapes stable patterns of economic governance encompassing a country's financial system, its vocational training, and its system of industrial relations. In liberal market economies, in contrast to both types of coordinated economy, training for lower level workers is not undertaken by private business and is generally ineffective. Bank - industry ties are weak and industries have to rely on competitive markets to raise capital.

It is obvious that theses types of production regimes are associated with Esping-Andersen's types of welfare state regimes. Moreover, it is arguable that there is at least a "mutually enabling fit" between the welfare state and production regimes types: Specifically, wage levels and benefit levels have to fit, and labour market and social policies have to be in accord such as not to create perverse incentives. In addition, the type of production for the world market has to fit with the qualification of the labour force and with wage and benefit levels. In CMEs, business/ labour/ government coordination in R&D, training, and wage setting makes it possible to engage in high quality production and thus to sustain high wages and a high social wage.

Recent work suggests an even tighter fit between welfare state and production regimes. Iversen and Soskice argue that the industry and firm specific nature of many of the skills acquired in vocational education systems characteristic of CMEs results in higher support for social spending as workers with these skills are vulnerable to longer spells of unemployment and to loss of income if forced to move between jobs with different skill requirements. In their view, employers as well as workers have an interest in such social spending because it insures that worker will in fact invest in acquisition of the specific skills which the employers require. Swenson also argues that the varying interests of cross class coalitions of employers and workers account for differences in social policy. He argues that in Sweden employers and workers both supported the expansion of social insurance because social insurance removes private employer benefits from wage competition.

This recent work would appear to sharply conflict with power resources theory, which is widely perceived by comparative welfare states specialists to be the currently dominant explanation of welfare state development. This is a dispute that is unlikely to be resolved by statistical analysis because of the strong intercorrelations between the potential causal factors. The centralization of employer confederations, the centralization of union confederations, union density, long term patterns of partisan government, the extent of vocational education, and various measures of welfare state effort are moderately to strongly correlated to each other and the multiple correlations of two or three of these indicators with another of them are invariably extremely high.

The resolution of this debate will have to await the kind of careful comparative historical work which has been done on the development of the welfare state but which has not been done on the development of production regimes. Thelen's work on the development of vocational training in Germany, Britain, Japan, and the US is probably indicative of the kind of answers such analyses will reveal. For example, she finds that the German employers initially introduced the system with the intention of dividing the nascent working class movement, but that over the course of the past hundred odd years the system has been progressively transformed by shifting coalitions of labour market and political forces.The functional fit one observes by taking a single cut in time is, she argues, quite misleading. It is our hunch that the early organization of employers will figure as an important factor in the development of coordinated market economies, as employer organization as of 1914 identifies post World War II CMEs quite well. In dialectical fashion, employer organization seems to have stimulated union organization and centralization which in turn increased the political strength of the left at a later period of time. In the post war period, left party power facilitated union organization and vice versa, and these two factors in turn propelled welfare state expansion. This kind of causal account squares much better with the historical record of consistent right-wing opposition to tax increases for welfare state financing than accounts stressing employer-worker coalitions in support of the welfare state.

It is important not to exaggerate the fit between welfare state and production regime. CMEs are equally compatible with social democratic or Christian democratic welfare states, and these two welfare state types have distinctive characteristics which have a major impact on their future viability. The social democratic welfare states are characterized by very high levels of public health, education, and welfare employment. This high level of public HEW employment is both a result and cause of the high levels of women's labour force participation. The growth of women's labour force participation beginning in the 1960s stimulated demands by women for the expansion of day care and other social services which, along with social democratic governance, helped fuel the growth of public social service sector employment. These public social service jobs were filled very disproportionately by women, so this in turn stimulated a further expansion of women's labour force participation. The continental Christian democratic welfare states followed a quite different trajectory. Foreign labour was imported in large numbers, arguably due to a combination of Christian democratic emphasis on the traditional male breadwinner family and weaker union influence on labour recruitment policies. Moreover, in these countries, union contracts cover a large proportion of the labour force, which prevented a rapid expansion of a low wage service sector, a source of employment for women in liberal welfare states. As a result, women's labour force participation was the lowest in the continental Christian democratic welfare states of the three welfare state types.

A related difference between social democratic and Christian democratic welfare states is the much greater emphasis on active labour market measures as a response to unemployment in the social democratic welfare states. By contrast, the Christian democratic welfare states have tended to resort to labour supply reduction measures, such as early retirement and easy access to disability pensions, in response to rising unemployment after 1973. Together these policy differences have resulted in much higher levels of labour force participation of both men and women in social democratic welfare states.

Australia and New Zealand are generally classified as liberal market economies and liberal welfare states in the varieties of capitalism and welfare state literatures, which is a correct characterization of the contemporary political economies of these countries. However, prior to the reform process initiated in the early eighties, these countries had distinctive systems of social protection, as Castles has argued. In the nineteenth century, these countries' economies were dominated by exports from the pastoral sector, later to be supplemented by mineral exports in the Australian case. The industrial sector developed behind high tariff barriers, thus these political economies were ISI economies similar to Latin America. In the early twentieth century, the labour movements of these countries, which were very powerful by international standards, secured systems of compulsory arbitration which delivered high "male breadwinner" wages and later benefits such as sickpay, which in other advanced capital countries were delivered by the welfare states. Thus, these two countries resembled Latin America, as formal sector urban workers received comparatively high wages and benefits due to protective tariffs, with the important difference that the informal sector was quite small compared to Latin America.

Production regimes in Latin America were characterized by extensive state intervention in all areas of economic life up to the 1980s. As a result of the Depression, governments in the more advanced Latin American countries had become convinced that they needed to promote domestic industrialization. They did so through high protective tariffs, subsidized credit from state development banks, preferential allocation of foreign exchange, and other kinds of incentives. Of course, ISI required significant imports of capital goods and other industrial inputs, which were financed by raw material exports.

There were differences in the timing of ISI and in the extent of state involvement, but virtually all countries followed this model by the late 1960s. The social security systems for disability and old age pensions and for health care developed in tandem with ISI, as governments also became heavily involved in regulating labour relations and saw social security as a tool to foster labour compliance. Financing depended heavily on employer contributions, which were tolerable because they could be passed on to consumers in these highly protected markets. However, only in Uruguay did the percentage of the labour force in industry surpass 30 per cent by 1980; in seven more countries the percentage was between 20 and 30 per cent, and in the rest even lower. Since most of agriculture and the entire large informal part of the service sector were without coverage, this is a good gauge of the restricted reach of social protection.In the last two decades, almost all advanced welfare states have experienced at least some retrenchment, reversing the trend of the previous three decades, which was one of unprecedented welfare state growth in all of these countries. Many journalists and political observers and some academics, particularly economists, have attributed this retrenchment to "globalization," the increasing economic openness of the national economies and integration of the world economy. In this view, the emergence of a single global market and global competition has reduced the political latitude for action of national states and imposed neo-liberal policies on all governments.

Proponents contend that as markets for goods, capital, and more recently labour, have become more open, all countries have been exposed to more competition and the liabilities of state economic intervention and deviation from market oriented "best practices" have become more apparent because these raise the cost of production. As capital markets have become more open and capital controls increasingly unworkable, capital in these countries moves elsewhere in search of lower production costs. Thus, governments must respond and reduce state intervention to stem the outflow of capital.

There is also a social democratic version of the globalization thesis, essentially an extension of the structural dependence of the state on capital argument. In this view, the opening of international capital markets beginning in the 1970s and accelerating in the 1980s and 1990s greatly increased the power of capital to do "regime shopping" and thus to force national states to retreat from effective interventionist policies and generous, egalitarian welfare state policies.

There is very little empirical evidence to support the neo-liberal version of the globalization thesis. The generous welfare states of northern Europe were developed in economies which were always very open to trade and very dependent on exports. Thus, for example, in the mid-nineties, at the very moment when the German and Swedish governments were cutting welfare state benefits, albeit modestly, the German and Swedish export sectors were turning in outstanding performances. The absence of any relationship between exposed sector employment performance and the level of taxes and social security contributions also argues against the thesis that generous welfare states makes export industries uncompetitive. On the other hand, there is some evidence in favour of the social democratic version of the globalization thesis. To identify the causes of retrenchment, we draw on case studies of twelve countries as well as studies of additional countries in Scharpf and Schmidt, thus covering all but a few of the advanced industrial democracies. These country studies indicate two different dynamics: ideologically driven cuts, which occurred in only a few cases, and unemployment driven cuts, which were pervasive.

The question then becomes what caused the increases in unemployment? As Glyn points out, it was not the low level of job creation, since employment growth after 1973 was as rapid as before. Rather, rising labour force participation due to the entry of women into the labour force is one proximate cause of the increase in unemployment. The inability of the Christian democratic welfare states to absorb this increase either through an expansion of low wage private service employment as in the liberal welfare states or through the expansion of public services as in the social democratic welfare states is one reason why the unemployment problem in these countries has been particularly severe. The other proximate cause is the lower levels of growth in the post 1973 period. This in turn can be linked in part to lower levels of investment which in turn can be linked in part to lower levels of savings, to lower levels of profit, and to higher interest rates. It is on this point that we find some support for the social democratic globalization thesis on the negative impact of financial market deregulation. Real interest rates increased from 1.4 per cent in the sixties to 5.6 per cent in the early nineties. The deregulation of international and domestic financial markets is partly responsible for this increase in interest rates. As a result of the elimination of controls on capital flows between countries, governments cannot control both the interest rate and exchange rate.

If a government decides to pursue a stable exchange rate, it must accept the interest rate which is determined by international financial markets. As a result of decontrol of domestic financial markets, government's ability to privilege business investors over other borrowers also became more limited. Countries which relied on financial control to target business investment were particularly hard hit as businesses moved from a situation in which real interest rates offered to them via government subsidies, tax concessions, and regulations were actually negative to a situation in which they had to pay the rates set by international markets. External financial decontrol also limits a government's ability to employ fiscal stimulation as a tool, as fiscal deficits are considered risky by financial markets and either require a risk premium on interest rates or put downward pressure on foreign exchange reserves. Thus, at least a portion of the increase in unemployment can be linked to globalization in the form of deregulated capital markets.

There were only a few cases of large-scale ideologically driven cuts. The most dramatic were Thatcher in Britain, the National government in New Zealand, and the Reagan administration in the United States. In the case of the Reagan administration the cuts were focused on cash and in kind benefits to the poor, a small but highly vulnerable minority, while Social Security was preserved by a large increase in the contributions. In any case, the United States cannot have been said to have made a "system shift" if only because it already had the least generous welfare state of any advanced industrial democracy.Only in Britain and New Zealand could one speak of an actual system shift from welfare state regimes that used to provide basic income security to welfare state regimes that are essentially residualist, relying heavily on means-testing. We argue that the exceptional nature of these two cases can be traced to their political systems which concentrate power and make it possible to rule without a majority of popular support. Thus, in both cases, the conservative governments were able to pass legislation which was deeply unpopular.

In contrast to welfare states in advanced industrial societies, globalization had a dramatic impact on systems of social protection in Latin America. Globalization was a major contributor to the debt crisis that spurred a transformation of the economies, a process largely guided by the international financial institutions, and economic transformation in turn required reforms of the traditional social security systems. The ISI model began to run into balance of payments problems in the 1950s. It was given a new lease on life in the 1970s because of the easy availability of cheap loans on the expanding international capital markets.

However, these markets imposed rapidly rising interest rates in the early 1980s, at the same time as commodity prices fell. When the big international banks reacted to solvency problems of some major debtors with a complete stop of new lending, Latin America was plunged into the debt crisis. This crisis gave great leverage to the IFIs and the American Treasury, and these institutions pushed for a radical liberalization of the Latin American economies. They were influential not only through their imposition of conditionality on debt renegotiations but also because of another aspect of globalization, the spread of educational circuits that brought talented Latin Americans to graduate schools in economics in the United States, where they absorbed the hegemonic neo-liberal view of the world.

Many of the leading government officials shared such backgrounds with officials in the IFIs, and many had worked for some time in the IFIs as well. This facilitated the formation of networks involving technocrats in the IFIS and national governments, where reform ideas were discussed over long periods of time and the neo-liberal solutions were advocated.

At first, governments and IFIs were preoccupied with economic stabilization and structural adjustment, but by the late 1980s, when the costs of the crisis and the austerity and adjustment measures became clear, they developed an acute concern with the political sustainability of reforms and thus "adjustment with a human face." The economic austerity programmes entailed devaluation, reduction of public expenditures, wage freezes, and restrictive monetary policies. Together with the structural adjustment policies, they fundamentally transformed the Latin American production regimes. The main points of the structural adjustment agenda were liberalization of markets for goods and capital, privatization of state enterprises, and deregulation of all kinds of economic activity. On average, the countries in the region pushed ahead rapidly with trade liberalization and financial liberalization; less in privatization, and mixed in general deregulation.

The average tariff rate was lowered from 49 per cent in the mid-1980s to 11 per cent in 1999, and non-tariff restrictions were reduced from covering 38 per cent of imports in the pre-reform period to 6 per cent of imports in the mid-1990s. Though these tariff levels remain higher than in advanced industrial countries, the lowering had a dramatic impact on many Latin American economies, particularly where it was done in a very short period of time. Many enterprises went bankrupt, which meant that many formal sector jobs were lost. Liberalization of capital markets stimulated significant inflows of capital in the early 1990s, but also rendered the economies vulnerable to rapid changes in investor confidence and thus renewed balance of payments crises.

Social expenditures had decreased as part of the austerity programmes. Unemployment had increased greatly due to austerity-induced recession and liberalization of imports. The combination of high inflation and high unemployment had played havoc with the financial base of the social security systems, and employers rebelled against high social security contributions in the new open economic environment. The reforms pushed by the IFIs included privatization of the pension systems and large parts of the health care systems, decentralization of social services, and targeting of public expenditures on the poor, particularly through demand driven social emergency funds. The degree to which countries followed these prescriptions, though, varied greatly, more so than in the economic reforms proper.

Chile implemented these reforms earlier and to a greater extent than any other country under the military dictatorship. Power was highly concentrated in the hands of Pinochet and opposition was dealt with ruthlessly. The neo-liberal project was attractive to the military not only for economic but also for political reasons, because it would atomize civil society and remove the state as a target for collective action. In addition to slashing tariffs and financial regulation and privatizing a large number of state controlled enterprises, the government fully privatized the pension system and transformed a large part of the public into a private health insurance and delivery system.

The reduced public expenditures were targeted on preventive and nutritional programmes and a temporary employment programme for the poor. In the wake of the high economic growth rates – and thus high rates of return on the individual private pension accounts – achieved in Chile from the mid-1980s to the mid-1990s, the Chilean model became the poster child for neoliberals and was held up as a model to emulate for other Latin American countries.No other country carried out reforms quite as rapidly and comprehensively as Chile.

Argentina under Menem moved very rapidly on economic reforms and on a plan to privatize social security, but opposition was strong enough to force concessions on keeping a public basic tier and leaving a large part of the health insurance system under the control of the unions. Altogether, nine Latin American countries have implemented and a tenth has legislated full or partial privatization of their pension system. In five cases, privatization was total and the public system was closed down; in five cases it was partial and the private system remained a supplementary or a parallel option. Reforms in health care have been more heterogeneous, though in general the private sector has expanded its role, sometimes by design and sometimes by default as a result of serious underfunding of the public system.

In the 1980s, there was virtually no investment in public health care facilities, and wages for public health care professionals declined precipitously. In the 1990s, most countries raised their social expenditures, so that they increased from 10.4 per cent of GDP to 13.1 per cent, slightly above the level of 1980. Growth in the various categories of social expenditure, that is, education, health care and nutrition, social security, and housing and sanitation was roughly similar, with social security continuing to absorb the bulk of social expenditure, at 4.8 per cent of GDP in 1998-99, followed by education with 3.9 per cent and health care and nutrition with 2.9 per cent. Clearly, these levels of expenditure remain far below what would be needed for a concerted and successful attack on poverty and improvement of the human capital base.

In order to raise expenditures significantly, tax collection systems would need to be improved. Latin America as a whole is clearly undertaxed, with an average tax burden of 14 per cent of GDP in the first half of the 1990s, compared to 17 per cent of GDP in a group of East and Southeast Asian countries. Tax reform has been part of structural adjustment, but it has emphasized lowering marginal tax rates for individuals and corporations and raising the value added tax. Tax collection rates are still very poor.

Direct taxes amount to about 25 per cent of tax revenue only, and of this amount some 60-80 per cent come from corporate tax payments, while only 10-15 per cent come from private individuals. Interestingly, the situation in the English-speaking Caribbean is very different, with an average tax burden in the first half of the 1990s of 27-28 per cent of GDP, essentially double the rate of Latin America, and direct taxation accounting for 40 per cent of tax revenue.

This contrast suggests that the fundamental reasons for the poor tax collection performance in Latin America are political, rather than related to low levels of economic development and technological capacity.

## THEORIES OF WELFARE STATE FORMATION AND RETRENCHMENT

Theories of welfare state formation can be grouped into three categories, according to the emphasis they put on clusters of causal variables: the "logic of industrialism," "state-centric," and "political class struggle" approaches. The authors proposing the logic of industrialism approach argued that industrialization and urbanization broke up traditional systems of social protection through the family and local communities and required the state to take on the responsibility for the welfare of industrial workers.

At the same time, the growing affluence resulting from advances in industrialization made the resources available to the state to perform these functions. Thus, both the growth and cross-national differences in welfare state effort could be explained by industrialization and its demographic and social organizational consequences. A related influential point of view held that economic openness caused vulnerability of workers to external shocks and thus led governments to build extensive systems of social protection. Since small countries generally had a higher degree of economic openness, welfare states grew particularly generous there.

The state-centric approach is internally quite diverse, with some authors focusing on the initiatives of state bureaucrats who were assumed to have a high degree of autonomy and others on state capacity, state structure, and policy legacies. In this perspective, cross-national differences in the development of comprehensive welfare state programmes are a result of differential state capacity, the degree of power dispersion and the consequent availability of veto points, and the structure of welfare state programmes set at their origin, before the period of expansion.

The political class struggle approach – also known as power resources approach– is based on the premise that state policy is heavily shaped by the distribution of power in civil society and in government. The balance of power between organized labour and left-wing parties on the one hand, and capital and center and right-wing parties on the other hand accounts for the extent of government correction of market outcomes through the welfare state. The focus on incumbency produced early on the insight that Christian democracy is also associated with generous welfare states but with a less progressive profile than welfare states built under left or social democratic auspices. There is some theoretical overlap among these perspectives. The political class struggle perspective emphasizes density and centralization of labour organization, and centralization of collective bargaining, along with strength of pro-labour parties as indicators of left/ labour power. Density and centralization of labour organization, or labour strength, is also seen as a cause of corporatism, that is, institutionalized tripartite consultation between capital, labour, and the government on essential policy issues. Corporatism, then, has been treated as an institutional variable that, once established, becomes a cause of welfare state expansion in its own right. Since these dimensions of left/ labour power are so closely related, it is impossible to adjudicate the competing theoretical claims on statistical grounds. Comparative historical evidence indicates that incumbency of left parties is crucial for welfare state development.

Quantitative studies have found that variables emphasized in all three theoretical schools are statistically significant predictors of welfare state effort. Demographic variables matter because, at any given level of entitlements, a larger number of old people or unemployed drive up expenditures. Level of GDP per capita, as a measure of economic development, tends not to explain much variation in welfare state effort among advanced industrial democracies, but if the comparison encompasses developing countries, then its importance increases. The provision of multiple veto points in the constitutional structure, that is, dispersion of power through presidentialism, strong bicameralism, federalism, and popular referenda, is one of the most consistent and important obstacles to expansion of welfare state effort. Finally, the strength of organized labour and length of incumbency of left-wing or Christian democratic parties is associated in a highly consistent and significant manner with various dimensions of welfare state effort.

Focusing on dimensions of welfare state effort, or on social rights directly, rather than simply on aggregate welfare state spending, was the key to Esping-Andersen's seminal contribution of the concept of welfare state regimes. He built on other, in part common, efforts to measure social rights and explain their determinants and he identified different dimensions or characteristics of the way in which welfare states provide social rights. He argued that these dimensions or characteristics were linked in systematic patterns and clustered around three types, a social democratic or institutional type, a conservative or "corporativistic" type, and a liberal or residual type. With some modifications, specifically the renaming of the conservative as Christian democratic type and the addition of a fourth wage earner welfare state regime and sometimes a fifth Southern European regime, this welfare state regime typology has shaped most subsequent research.

Social democratic welfare state regimes are characterized by universalism in coverage and in the nature of benefits, by rights to a large array of benefits based on citizenship or residence, and by public provision of a large array of services. Christian democratic welfare states are characterized by universalism in coverage but with different benefits under different programmes, by rights to benefits based on employment categories, and by public financing of privately provided services.

Liberal welfare states are characterized by partial or residual coverage with different benefits, by rights to most benefits based on need and thus means testing, and by the scarcity of publicly provided or financed social services.

These regime types correspond to value commitments and particular views on the desirable relationship between state, market, community, and family. The social democratic type reflects the values of solidarity and equality, and the view that the state is charged with counteracting market forces to realize these values.

The Christian democratic type reflects the Catholic doctrine of harmony and subsidiarity, where the state is charged with keeping people out of poverty but not changing the social order, and with performing only the functions that are not performed well by the family or civil society. The liberal type reflects the values of individual responsibility and efficiency, and the view that the state should primarily rely on market forces and work with these forces to prevent destitution and provide essential social services. The groups of countries corresponding to the three regime types are the Nordic countries, the continental European countries, and the Anglo-American countries, respectively. In reality, of course, several countries have somewhat mixed welfare state characteristics, reflecting the influence of different political forces involved in their formation.

The main theoretical contribution from a feminist perspective was to draw attention to the fact that these welfare state typologies were essentially built on the assumption of standard citizens, with low, average, or high earnings, and that this assumption fit predominantly males. Gender did not figure as a dimension in the original conceptualization of welfare state regimes, and it was obviously crucial to understand gender specific impacts of these regimes. A number of studies have investigated the extent to which regime types are useful in explaining systematic differences in outcomes for women and though there is no real consensus, there is considerable evidence supporting the usefulness of the regime approach. Numerous studies have also investigated the role of women's mobilization and pressures for welfare state expansion or what Hernes called women-friendly policies.

Most of their findings are compatible with a power resources approach, but power based on gender mobilization, not on class. Generally, progress in policies promoting gender equity was the result of women organizing inside and outside of political parties, in independent women's movements, and fostering a commitment to the goal of gender equity within incumbent left-wing parties.Whether the traditional theories of welfare state formation are also useful for an analysis of the period of welfare state retrenchment or defence, which began in the 1980s, is a contested issue. Pierson has argued for a "new politics of the welfare state," and indeed quantitative studies have shown that the magnitude of partisan effects decreased greatly. In the context of slower economic growth than in the first three post-WW II decades, higher unemployment, comprehensive and mature welfare state programmes and consequent high expenditures, both the left and the right have been constrained in their reform efforts. The right has been constrained in efforts to cut welfare state entitlements significantly, because the entitlements that affect large numbers of people are widely popular.

The left has been constrained in efforts to expand entitlements because raising taxes has not been popular and deficit financing out of the question. Still, in qualitative studies differences between governments of different colour remain visible; right-wing governments have been more likely to push an agenda of welfare state austerity and tax cuts, whereas left-wing governments have been more intent on protecting entitlements. Demographic and state structure variables have remained important as well, but have tended to work in the opposite direction from the one during the period of welfare state expansion. Whereas multiple veto points had slowed down expansion, now they have slowed down retrenchment. Whereas episodes of high unemployment had given the impetus for improvements in unemployment insurance, now sustained levels of higher unemployment have given the impetus for cuts in entitlements.

Among the developing areas of the world, Latin America has seen the strongest thrust towards welfare state development. At least the most advanced countries had built systems of social protection by 1980 that could be called welfare states. The volume of literature on the formation of welfare states in Latin America is small, and a theoretical debate is largely absent. There is a sizable number of studies that describe the evolution of systems of social protection, but they tend to focus on economic and organizational aspects and neglect the question why systems were formed in a certain way.

The picture that emerges from these studies is one of highly fragmented and often inegalitarian systems, where entitlements were based on the insurance principle and differed greatly between occupational categories. The main programmes were old age and disability pensions and health care insurance, and in some countries family allowances. These systems resembled the Christian democratic type characteristic of continental Europe, but were much less generous and more inegalitarian and restricted in coverage. Coverage depended on employment in the formal sector, and the rural and informal sectors were very large in most of these countries, with the result that in the vast majority of countries less than 60 per cent of the population had coverage as of 1980.Most studies of social policy formation emphasize pre-emptive, or paternalistic action on the part of the state to incorporate the most important occupational groups and gain their political support. Another perspective emphasizes diffusion of models of social insurance from more advanced countries via international organizations, particularly the International Labour Office. However, there was clearly differential adoption of these models, and this variation needs to be explained. Even under authoritarian rule, the strength and political importance of pressure groups mattered, and thus to understand the expansion of social protection to a large part of the population, the mobilization capacity of organized labour and its importance as a support base of governments have to be taken into account. Coverage expanded most during periods of strong growth of import substitution industrialization behind high tariff walls and with strong government intervention in capital markets to support industrialization. These were periods of growth of the industrial labour force and often also of labour movements. Labour organization and mobilization is most likely to grow under democratic regimes, specifically in the presence of strong reformist parties, and/or under authoritarian leaders who deliberately promote labour organization. Indeed, of the five Latin American countries with most extensive coverage of social security, that is, above 60 per cent of the population as of 1980, three had the longest democratic experiences and comparatively strong reformist parties and two had historical episodes of leaders attempting to build organized labour into a power base. Compared to Europe, then, the much lower size and generosity of Latin American systems of social protection can be attributed to a combination of lower levels of industrialization, the scarcity of democratic periods, and the weaker position of reformist parties and organized labour.

Theoretical accounts of retrenchment of systems of social protection in Latin America, which has been much more dramatic than in advanced industrial democracies, have emphasized the debt crisis and consequent economic transformations as common causes. They have explained differences between countries in the extent and nature of social policy reforms with the extent of liberalization of markets for goods and capital, power concentration in the hands of the executive versus fragmentation of political institutions and power, the influence of international financial institutions, specifically the International Monetary Fund, the World Bank and the Inter-American Development Bank, the financial pressures on the established systems, policy legacies, and the balance of power between proponents and opponents of reforms, with emphasis on these different factors varying by author. A final theoretical perspective to be considered is the economic one. This literature does not really address theoretical questions of the causes of welfare state formation and of cross-national differences in welfare state design. The classical liberal and neo-liberal perspectives take a normative position, that market allocation should not be distorted by state intervention, and they claim that there is a fundamental trade-off between equity and efficiency. In particular, they argue that state intervention and redistribution distort incentives and thus efficiency of resource allocation. Less dogmatic economists distinguish between the goals of welfare states, which they attribute to the realm of politics or norms, and the means by which these goals are to be achieved, which they regard as a technical question and the proper field of study for economics. There is considerable research on the work disincentive effects of generous social safety nets in the case of sickness and unemployment, but the findings are often ambiguous and mostly weak.

# Bibliography


A.R. Prasad: *Dictionary of Microeconomics : A Glossary of Terms Frequently Found in Discussions of Microeconomics*, Reliance Books, Delhi, 2000.

Arjun Y. Pangannavar: *Microeconomics*, Atlantic Publication, Delhi, 2012.

Arun Garg: *International Microeconomics and Finance : Theory and Econometric Methods*, Swastik Publication, Delhi, 2010.

Brajesh Kumar: *Modern Microeconomics*, Ane Books Pvt. Ltd., Delhi, 2008.

Chauhan, S P S.: *Microeconomics : Theory And Application (Part II)*, PHI Learning, Delhi, 2009.

David Besanko and Ronald Braeutigam: *Microeconomics*, Wiley India, 2011.

Deepashree: *Principles of Microeconomics*, Ane Books, Delhi, 2011.

Dominick Salvatore: *Principles of Microeconomics*, Oxford University Press, Delhi, 2009.

Edwin Mansfield and Gary Yohe: *Microeconomics : Theory/Applications*, Viva Books, Delhi, 2010.

Fahad Khalil and Salim Rashid: *Readings in Microeconomics*, The University Press Limited, Delhi, 2006.

Gupta, K R.: *Advanced Microeconomics, Vols. I and II*, Atlantic Publication, Delhi, 2009.

H. L. Ahuja: *Principles Of Microeconomics*, S. Chand Publisher, Delhi, 2009.

Humberto Barreto: *Intermediate Microeconomics with Microsoft EXCEL*, Cambridge University Press, New York, 2003.

M L Maurya: *Modern Microeconomics : Theory and Application*, Manglam Publication, Delhi, 2008.

Mukti Nath Singh: *Principles of Microeconomics*, ABD Publication, Delhi, 2011.

Neva Goodwin, Julie A Nelson and Jonathan Harris: *Microeconomics in Context*, PHI Learning, Delhi, 2009.

Pankaj Ghai and Anuj Gupta: *Microeconomics : Theory and Applications-II*, Sarup & Sons, Delhi, 2002.

Pankaj Gupta: *An Introduction to Microeconomics and Finance : Theories and Economics Methods*, Cyber Tech Publications, Delhi, 2011.

R.H. Dholakia and A.N. Oza: *Microeconomics for Management Students*, Oxford University Press, Delhi, 1999.

Ramesh Chandra Das: *Microeconomics : Theory and Practice*, Kunal Books, Delhi, 2011.

Richard B. McKenzie and Dwight R. Lee.: *Microeconomics for MBAs : The Economic Way of Thinking for Managers*, Cambridge University Press, New York, 2011.

Robert S Pindyck, Daniel L Rubinfeld and Prem L Mehta: *Microeconomics*, Pearson Education, Delhi, 2009.

Rod Hill and Tony Myatt: *The Economics Anti-Textbook : A Critical Thinker's Guide to Microeconomics*, Zed Books, Delhi, 2010.

S.P.S. Chauhan: *Microeconomics : An Advanced Treatise*, PHI Learning, Delhi, 1999.

Samuel Bowles: *Microeconomics : Behavior, Institutions, and Evolution*, Oxford University Press, Delhi, 2004.

Sanjay Basotia: *Microeconomics : Principles Applications and Tools*, DND Publications, Delhi, 2010.

Sipra Mukhopadhyay: *Microeconomics*, Ane Books, Delhi, 2011.

# Index

---